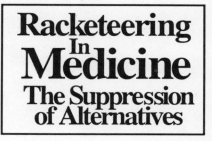

Racketeering
In
Medicine
The Suppression
of Alternatives

Racketeering In Medicine

The Suppression of Alternatives

James P. Carter, M.D., Dr. P.H.

HAMPTON ROADS
PUBLISHING COMPANY, INC.

For information write:

Hampton Roads Publishing Company, Inc.
134 Burgess Lane
Charlottesville, VA 22902

Or call: (804) 296-2772
FAX: (804) 296-5096
e-mail: hrpc@hrpub.com
Website: www.hrpub.com

If you are unable to order this book from your local
bookseller, you may order directly from the publisher.
Quantity discounts for organizations are available.
Call 1-800-766-8009, toll-free.

ISBN 1-878901-32-X

12 11 10 9 8 7 6 5 4

Printed on acid-free paper in the United States of America

DEDICATION

To my wife, Carolyn, who tolerated my writing this book and who demonstrated patience in seeing this project through to the end.

To my peers world-wide, who enhanced my knowledge and inspired me to learn and to document scientifically the safety and efficacy of alternative therapies and convinced me of the miscarriages of justice and the harassment of alternative medical practitioners.

To my mentors, the late Amos Christie, M.D., Cecily Williams, M.D., William Darby, M.D., Ph.D., and Nevin Scrimshaw, M.D., Ph.D., who have been leaders in medicine, maternal and child health, nutrition and public health, and who have been exemplary in their commitment and dedication to scientific truth and its applications to help people.

To all those medical comrades persecuted by the past and recent medical inquisitions for making unpopular discoveries in medicine and for daring to be creative in their medical practices in the interests of their patients.

To my colleagues in ACAM, GLACM and the Loon Society and to numerous others who shared their insight and recommendations. We are truly comrades in this struggle of what Ghandi would call "Right Against Might."

ACKNOWLEDGEMENTS

The author would like to acknowledge the invaluable assistance of his agent, Arle Hagberg, in obtaining a publisher, Hampton Roads Publishing Company, and her assistance in editing and reorganizing parts of the manuscript to make it more readable to the public. Hers is a strong commitment to holistic medicine, with a sense of mission, as is the commitment of advocates nationwide, who are striving with much sacrifice to educate the public about their medical alternatives.

The author would also like to acknowledge the research support provided to him and his graduate student, Carmen Garcia, by the Efamol Research Institute of Nova Scotia, Canada, which is under the direction of Dr. David Horrobin.

The author would also like to acknowledge Le Trombetta of the Burzinski Research Institute, who is representative of the many individuals, health professionals and consumers who constituted a chain of information sources not unlike those utilized by a good investigative reporter. We even had our own version of Deep Throat, whom we called Sore Throat. These individuals constituted an "underground" working against an unjust system. In this regard, it was not unlike the underground which worked against the Nazis during WWII and some communist regimes during the Cold War and counter-revolutionary and counter-racketeering activities against subversive, criminal and special interest groupsd in this country. They secretly conspire to influence events and outcomes, i.e. have things go their way, usually for profit, in an otherwise democratic society. Also, in a professional sense, assassination was employed, just as it was in a literal sense during WWII. Thanks to each and every one of the individuals in the network.

There is no difficulty for any person of integrity in telling the "good guys" from the "bad guys" in the saga of events recounted in this book. So, once again, thanks to the "good guys" who came forward to help me every step of the way.

James P. Carter
July, 1992

TABLE OF CONTENTS

PART 1
ORGANIZED MEDICINE:
THE MOST POWERFUL AMERICAN LOBBY

INTRODUCTION

The American public has no idea how politics secretly control the practice of medicine. If a doctor dares to introduce a natural, less costly method, no matter how safe or effective, Organized American Medicine can target this doctor for license revocation using fear tactics and legal maneuverings. Why do holistic therapies threaten medicine?

—They involve a major change in scientific thought,

—They imply that current methods are inadequate, and

—They threaten huge profits of a powerful branch of medicine or a drug company.

Quite the opposite occurred with the immediate embrace of heart bypass surgery and balloon angioplasty. These money-makers quickly brought wealth and fame to heart specialists and surgeons, large teams of health care professionals, and the hospital industry. The fact that they save lives and improve the quality of life for many is not disputed. Such high-tech breakthroughs, however, were never "proven" by double-blind, placebo-controlled studies.

But far less risky and cheaper alternative therapies with astonishing healing results are frequently blocked. Why? Their safety and effectiveness have not been "proven" through FDA-required studies that now cost over $200 million to complete. American medicine either doesn't know or doesn't care about naturally-based medical practices, indigenous to cultures all over the world, that have promoted healing at a fraction of the cost.

American medicine has also isolated and quarantined new ideas and treatments which have arisen in this country, especially when they have been contrary to the prevailing point of view or when the discoverer was unpopular or did not have the right credentials. American medicine has been incapable of taking a world point of view and of overcoming professional classism, which prevents them from accepting the innovations of "outsiders."

"DO DOCTORS PRESCRIBE WHAT'S GOOD
FOR YOU OR WHAT'S LUCRATIVE FOR THEM?"

This article, which appeared in the *Chicago Sun Times,* revealed how the drug industry is a doctor's main source of information about drugs. Drug companies provide lavish incentives for the prescription of those drugs, and sales incentives border on bribes.

It is "business as usual" for drug companies to introduce themselves early in the doctor's career. Often, companies will buy a medical student's first stethoscope or black bag. During a doctor's internship and residency, it is a good investment for a drug company to offer, say, a free weekend at a ski resort to interns who agree to attend a seminar on one of the company's currently-featured drugs.

As a doctor begins to build his or her practice, drug companies provide free business cards and free samples of medicine. Sales reps leave prescription pads and pens emblazoned with their companies' logos for the drugs they just advised the doctor to prescribe.

To promote their products (which carry an average 800% price mark-up), drug companies spent more than $5,000 on every single doctor in the U.S. in 1988—all 479,000 of them. Drug industry critics note that patients must pay this $5,000 per-doctor ad campaign through the sky-high cost of their prescriptions.

When the patent on the beta-blocker drug Inderal expired, the competition from other drug manufacturers heated up. To thwart the expected drop in sales, the manufacturer of Inderal, Wyeth-Ayerst, developed a promotional package that went like this: Frequent flyer points for American Airlines were awarded to doctors who prescribed Inderal. Doctors who wrote fifty prescriptions for the heart drug could claim a free round-trip ticket to anywhere in the continental United States. This tactic backfired in Massachusetts, however. Inderal is on the Medicaid formulary in that state; the state, therefore, will pick up the tab. The Attorney General's office got wind of this unethical promotion and investigated. The Attorney General ruled that the frequent flyer incentive amounted to fraud and threatened the company with criminal charges. Wyeth-Ayerst settled out of court with Massachusetts for $195,000 and withdrew its offer—in that state.

There are many money incentives in modern medicine, and often medical research can result in corporate crimes—a type of "white collar" crime. The apparent criminal behavior addressed in this book involves mostly fraud and anti-trust violations. At the root of all of these transgressions is undoubtedly a dogmatic pursuit of profit.

Throughout this book, reference is often made to Organized Medicine. This term is *not* meant to be synonymous with the American Medical Association to the exclusion of other entities.

Rather, it is a term used to refer to a broad range of established medical interests, which include the American Medical Association, state medical associations, medical specialty organizations, state boards of medical examiners, medical schools and teaching hospitals, the American Hospital Association, the National Health Insurance Association (representing some 1,500 companies) and the entire drug, pharmaceutical, and medical equipment industry. They have also been lumped together as the medico-pharmaceutical-industrial complex, and this book uses the two terms interchangeably. The reader should understand that references to an individual's connections to or representation of Organized Medicine refers to that person's relationship with any segment of the wide-ranging mosaic of special-interest groups who wield undue influence for maximizing profit and perpetuating the status quo in medical fields.

This book will tell you the true story about the frightening power-mongers who have orchestrated financially-motivated cover-ups for the purpose of:

—controlling the treatment of heart disease and the related conditions of stroke and peripheral vascular disease,

—controlling the treatment of cancer,

—promoting the use of drugs in the treatment of psychosomatic disorders which respond better to stress management,

—promoting drugs instead of acupuncture to relieve chronic pain,

—discounting natural remedies and nutritional therapies as being useless, and

—controlling the treatment of advanced cases of AIDS, which have remained incurable, in part, because of the failure to consider alternatives.

In the appendix of this book the reader will find medical and advocacy services to further your introduction into 21st-century medicine.

James P. Carter, M.D., Dr.P.H.
Head, Nutrition Section
Department of Applied Health Sciences
School of Public Health & Tropical Medicine
Tulane University
March, 1993

PREFACE:
WHY DO DOCTORS THINK THE WAY WE DO?

Medicine is a discipline firmly rooted in science. The day-to-day practice of medicine by most physicians, however, is an art. The best physicians are those who thoroughly understand science; but, when caring for patients, they practice the art of medicine, always administered with appropriate compassion. The general decline, or at least the perceived decline, in compassion for the patient over the past fifty years due to increasing specialization and fragmentation has become a major contributing factor to malpractice litigation.

A recent administrative visitor, Patrick E. Shields from the Children's Foundation of the University of Minnesota, inspired me to recall my role models of the physician-scientist that I had, when I first began my career in the clinical practice of medicine twenty-four years ago. Shields left a brochure entitled *Children and the University of Minnesota Health Sciences: a Local, Regional and National Resource for Research and Education to Solve the "Mysteries of Childhood Disease."*

I served as a pediatric intern in 1958 to the most outstanding physician-scientist on the faculty of the University of Minnesota, Dr. Robert A. Good, considered a genius by those who knew him. I recall that he was the youngest professor ever appointed to the Department of Pediatrics and the Department of Microbiology and was later appointed Chief Pathologist at the Children's Medical Center.

Dr. Good talked about how he was influenced by the late Professor John McQuarrie. It was Dr. McQuarrie who, according to Dr. Good, first coined the term "experiments of nature" in reference to the "mysteries of childhood disease." He believed that these diseases provide us with opportunities to unravel these mysteries and to develop new treatments and prevention procedures, using the methods of science. Dr. Good, without a doubt, was the major physician-scientist role model for those of us in training at the university at the time. His Saturday morning rounds, when all of the difficult cases in the hospital were brought and presented to him, are indelibly imprinted in my mind.

So it was particularly interesting to meet, over dinner, Dr. Nick

Gonzalez, who was also influenced by Dr. Good forty years later, when the latter was president of the Sloan Kettering Memorial Institute in New York City. While a medical student at Cornell, Dr. Nick Gonzalez, a physician now practicing on Park Avenue in New York City, became interested in the Gerson therapy for the treatment of cancer, as adapted by Dr. William Kelley, an orthodontist practicing in Texas in the 1960s. Dr. Kelley was diagnosed with a hopeless case of pancreatic cancer which had spread to the liver. This patient-doctor sought medical help in misery for more than two years before his doctors told him, "It's all in your head." Within a few weeks, the ill Dr. Kelley passed blood and was told that he had only a few months to live. Dr. Kelley fortunately accessed the Gerson therapy and developed his own innovations. Dr. Gonzalez was introduced to Dr. Kelley's self-care and his subsequent work with other cancer patients. A conservative doctor, Dr. Gonzalez was greatly impressed by the excellent medical records of this cranial orthodontist/maverick physician. Dr. Gonzalez then approached Dr. Good at Memorial Sloan Kettering in New York, which had a teaching arrangement with Cornell. Using Dr. Kelley's records, Dr. Gonzalez was able to document the fact that many of Dr. Kelley's cases had actually gone into remission.

At that time, Dr. Good had been described by science writer Ralph Moss, Ph.D., author of *The Cancer Industry* (Paragon Press), as a "very complex person who in his heart of hearts is really interested in alternatives; he is fascinated with them and repelled at the same time, frustrated by the inability to treat cancer the conventional way and at the same time worried about the inevitable damage to his reputation that would follow if he ever publicly supported any of the methods that he was privately interested in investigating." Perhaps the expression "learning about a person's character from his enemies" fits this astute observation by Dr. Moss, who had recently been fired by Dr. Good. Dr. Moss's description of Dr. Good coincides with my recollection of him and his approach to experiments of nature back in 1958. He believed that these experiments of nature could lead a physician-scientist in many different directions. No area was taboo or forbidden territory because of vested commercial interests.

Dr. Gonzalez, during five years of working with Dr. Good at Sloan Kettering, the University of Oklahoma, and Children's Hospital in St. Petersburg, Florida, investigated Dr. Kelley's pancreatic enzyme treatment and nutritional detoxification of cancer patients. He eventually compiled a book of fifty documented cases, all biopsy-proven cases from the Mayo Clinic, the Sloan Kettering Memorial Institute, and other cancer treatment centers around the country. His book documents the fact that Kelley's patients went into remission from cancers which were many times metastasized and given up on by orthodox doctors. At Dr. Good's urging, Gonzalez did a special study on pancreatic cancer. In the cases that he studied, the patients who failed to follow Kelley's regimen all died within a couple of months; those who followed it partially lived double the time; and those who complied with the regimen completely (there were five patients in this category) lived on the average of approximately nine years. One of them died from Alzheimer's disease with no signs of cancer. The significance of the cases in Dr. Gonzalez's book becomes apparent when we contrast them with patients treated by conventional methods, who usually survive for less than six months.

These results concur with Dr. Moss's observation: "If we were really interested in finding and developing new treatments for cancer, then what is going on with Kelley's cases and in Dr. Gonzalez's current Park Avenue practice needs to be investigated further, unless we can prove that Nick Gonzalez is a total charlatan or that Dr. Robert Good is totally inept in evaluating cases, which is hardly the case since he was the Chief Pathologist at the Children's Medical Center in Minneapolis, before he ever went to Sloan Kettering in New York."

Despite appearances, we must not look at Dr. Good's professional demotion from Sloan Kettering as evidence of incompetence; he may, in fact, have been victimized by an organized effort to "cut him off at the knees." According to newspaper accounts, Dr. Good left the Sloan Kettering Institute almost ten years after a widely publicized scandal involving scientific fraud which had occurred while he was at the helm. In a study of the allergic response, a junior investigator had deliberately falsified his results by the direct application of paint and/or chemicals to the experimental laboratory animals. (The investigator is now in the clinical practice of allergy and immunology in Louisiana.) There is no evidence that Dr. Good's leaving is related to this instance of scientific fraud despite the media's attempt to connect the two. The turnover in the position of President of Sloan Kettering is traditionally about every ten years, because that person is charged with finding a cure for cancer. Given the Institute's commitment to surgery, radiation, and chemotherapy, it is likely that Dr. Good's private support for Dr. Gonzalez's efforts did not help him at the Institute.

The average physician who graduates from medical school and who trains in one of the medical specialties is not a scientist. I am always suspicious when one of them proclaims himself to be a scientist, especially if it is in the context of criticizing one of his colleagues whose practice may differ from the norm. These doctor "scientists" are quick to label as "unscientific" a treatment or practice whose success they have never evaluated. A treatment or practice not being "usual and customary" cannot be equated with being "wrong."

A landmark law recently passed by the Alaska state legislature states that "A physician cannot be disciplined or his license revoked, purely on the basis that his practice differs from the norm, *i.e.*, that it is not usual and customary, particularly in the light of the absence of any demonstrable harm to his patients." This important legislation can help to promote the development of new treatments, prevention procedures, and freedom of choice in the practice of medicine.

A great deal of good can come of the philanthropic support of medical education. As a recipient of a five-year faculty fellowship from the Milbank Memorial Fund, I recognize the benefits of this kind of general support to the furtherance of one's career. At the time of my fellowship in 1968, the Milbank Memorial Fund was interested in improving the quality of teaching of the social and preventive aspects of medicine in medical schools and schools of public health throughout the western hemisphere. The $40,000 grant, combined with my association with the foundation's consultants and the interaction with the other forty-five or so recipients of Milbank faculty fellowships all invaluably stimulated my interest in the social and preventive aspects of medicine and furthered my development as a teacher and researcher.

According to Gerald Donas, who wrote *The Circuit Riders, Rockefeller Money and the Rise of Modern Science*, the practice of giving fellowships in the sciences to graduate students began in 1925 with the creation of the Guggenheim Foundation. The post-WWI boom in fellowships, granted with the intention of giving research experience to scholars still undecided about a scientific career, raised the status of scientific research in the academic community.

In the manner of the Nobel Prize for scientific achievement, this fellowship trend provided direct support to scientific researchers rather than indirect support through their institutions. Among the first candidates to receive a Guggenheim Fellowship was the 24-year-old Linus C. Pauling, who had just received his doctorate from the California Institute of Technology. There is another side to the philanthropic patronage of science research of individuals. Business motives often confuse the issue. Fleming, for example, is generally recognized as the discover of penicillin; few know that a Dr. Florey, supported by the British Medical Research Council (MRC) was a full-fledged partner and collaborator in this research. Fleming and Florey had collaborated to save the life of one of Fleming's friends by administering penicillin. The Rockefeller Foundation, however, made tremendous efforts afterwards to publicize its role as being pivotal in the penicillin story, pointing to its $1,280 grant in 1936 to Fleming and Florey's laboratory at Oxford. In 1944, Rockefeller Foundation President Fosdick commented that "seldom has so small a contribution led to such momentous results."

This comment had repercussions both in England and in the United States. The editorial page of a Republican newspaper in Massachusetts lauded the success of this investment by a privately-endowed institution and lambasted a Democratic administration in Washington for its leaning toward government control of scientific research.

In the *London Evening News,* however, a columnist commented on the original 1936 Rockefeller grant of $1,280 by saying, "Now I cannot help thinking that research in this country must be shamefully starved if an Oxford professor, for a paltry sum of less than five hundred pounds for sensational research, has to go to the United States with a request for aid." Mellanby, head of the British Medical Research Council, furiously labeled the Rockefeller Foundation's attempt to hog the credit for the support of penicillin as "simply grotesque." The controversy even reached the floor of the House of Commons, where a government spokesman offered figures showing that the MRC had contributed in excess of £7000 to Florey's research since 1927.

Meanwhile, in the United States, while the controversy raged over who should get the credit for funding Fleming and Florey's research, American companies (whose interest in penicillin had been aroused by Florey's visit to the United States) went on to reap handsome profits from the manufacture of penicillin. Part of these profits came from license fees paid by British firms which discovered to their embarrassment that a number of the processes indispensable to the large-scale production of penicillin had been patented by American drug and chemical companies.

Because of World War II, there was a certain amount of secrecy involved in releasing information about the development of penicillin. Fosdick did not make his announcement about the role of the

Rockefeller Foundation until 1944, when there was no longer a need for strict secrecy. Florey, on the advice of both Mellanby of the Medical Research Council and Sir Henry Dale, had refused to speak to the press because of the fear that publicity could spur the Germans to develop their own penicillin.

Dr. Fleming and his friends, however, did not feel such constraints. The impression therefore left by the resulting stories was that penicillin had been given to the world solely through the efforts of Fleming, a keen observer of bacterial cultures at St. Mary's Hospital. So widespread was this impression that the Nobel Committee, according to one rumor, almost awarded the 1945 prize to Fleming alone.

What is important here, however, is not who first discovered penicillin, but how the facts about the discovery were leaked with the help of the Rockefeller Foundation to American drug and chemical companies, giving them a competitive advantage over even the British companies who presumably should have been closer to the source.

Another example of the down-side of philanthropic support for the sciences is the Abraham Flexner Report. In 1909 Flexner was commissioned by the Carnegie Foundation for the Advancement of Teaching to visit medical schools and to write a report on the status of medical education in the United States and Canada. There were many proprietary medical schools in existence at the time, where the education and training offered were substandard. Many of these medical schools were operated solely for profit. Flexner published a report entitled "Medical Education in the United States and Canada in 1910."

This report established a common interest shared by the basic sciences, organized medicine, and university education. It ushered in a program for medical education reform and placed a heavy emphasis on linking medical schools to universities. It also stressed the importance of scientific research and the application of the fruits of this research to medical practice. It proclaimed the biological sciences as the knowledge base for the practice of medicine. It even emphasized the ideal of the pursuit of knowledge for its own sake.

The Flexner Report's recommendations were so attractively presented that the Rockefeller Foundation was encouraged to help bring about their implementation through additional grants.

Noted conservative journalist G. Howard Griffin, drawing from his 1974 book, *World Without Cancer—Part II*, has made this observation: "Efficiency in philanthropy was John D. Rockefeller's motto—never give it away unless it comes back with another dollar attached!" As long as Rockefeller was a (but not the only) contributor, he saw to it that he got all the credit and had all of the control.

This strategic approach to philanthropy originated with a not-so-very-Reverend Fred Gates, who abandoned the ministry after using his ministerial title with considerable success in fund-raising. He attracted the attention of the Minnesota flour baron George Pillsbury, who had a problem similar to Mr. Rockefeller's—a bad reputation. Gates had first attracted Pillsbury's attention by advocating, "Why give away $1 million when you can give only half that amount and call for matching funds? Let the hospital or school raise the other half; get the community involved; your name will still be attached to the fund drive; you can still be the hero and the populace with identify with you, Mr. Pillsbury. Everyone, businessmen and housewives will dig into their pockets and Mr. Pillsbury's name will still appear on the stoned archways—at half the price!"

Pillsbury's success with this approach intrigued Mr. Rockefeller. He invited Gates to his office and quickly hired him to head the Rockefeller philanthropy operation. Rockefeller said, "I realized I had met a commercial genius in Mr. Gates and persuaded him to become a man of business."

The first tax-exempt organization created by the Rockefellers was the General Education Board. Under the tutelage of the Reverend Fred Gates, three basic goals were mapped out regarding foundation assistance to education—not to raise the level of education, but to use education to accomplish the following:

1. To preserve the wealthy donors' vast family fortune from inheritance and other taxation,

2. To use education to change society and mold the attitude of the unsuspecting public to accept foundation leadership and direction, and

3. To use foundation money under the guise of public good to fund lucrative commercial and ideological ventures with their own tax-exempt dollars under the guise of philanthropy.

The General Education Board of the Rockefeller Foundation retained Flexner and engaged in funding efforts to implement his report and also to elucidate its meaning. The Rockefeller and Carnegie corporations could "rescue" the schools with the right amount of financial investment. The schools that accepted the proposed curriculum and approach were granted lucrative grants. The more amenable the school, the more money it received.

Those schools who accepted the money were naturally influenced by the donors, who in turn asked to be named members of the board of directors or trustees in order to have a voice in how their money would be spent. The representatives of the Rockefellers and the Carnegies were highly respected gentlemen, and the medical schools were honored to have their presence in positions of authority.

For the most part, the medical schools that survived the reforms in the years following 1910 were those which accepted formal inclusion into universities. Most of them managed to become incorporated into universities, but many have also managed to remain somewhat autonomous, specifically for fund-raising purposes. Curiously enough, however, Flexner did support lesser standards of admission to the Southern medical schools, because of the region's retarded economic and cultural conditions, which were aggravated by the scarcity of physicians there.

The Flexner Report helped to establish the Association of American Medical Colleges, presently a public/private group of 127 medical schools. The impetus for implementing the Flexner Report, however, came from the medical educational group within the American Medical Association and the Association of American Medical Colleges (AAMC), which is involved in the health and medical fields throughout the United States and Canada. The combination of money from the Rockefeller Foundation and influence from the AMA and the AAMC has created the strongest professional monopoly in the United States—Organized Medicine. There was no effective opposition to the implementation of the reforms recommended in the Flexner Report, and, to this day, Organized Medicine is a very powerful lobbying influence and PAC contributor.

Over the next seventy-eight years, the Flexner blueprint of what a medical school should look like (the qualifications of its incoming students, what they should be taught and by whom, the characteristics of the faculty and the amounts of time that they should spend in teaching, service, and research, the emphasis given to the basic sciences, the emphasis and amount of time devoted to practical experience in the clinical years, etc.) was implemented in every single American school that wished to survive. If these changes were not made, a school would not be approved by the Association of American Medical Colleges, and its graduates would not be licensed by the medical boards of any of the states.

Organized Medicine, citing as their authority the Flexner Report and aided by the influence of the Rockefeller Foundation, gradually eliminated all of the other schools of the healing arts, sparing only allopathic medical schools affiliated with universities which had incorporated the teaching of the basic sciences during the first two years and which were committed to the applications of scientific research to the clinical practice of medicine. This movement gradually resulted in the closing of schools where homeopathy was taught, including Hahnemann Medical College of Philadelphia, which was named after the father of homeopathic medicine; it also resulted in the closing of schools which taught herbal medicine (phyto-pharmacy) and schools which taught manipulative medicine. (These latter healing techniques were subsequently salvaged with the development of osteopathic schools of medicine and schools of chiropractic, both of which came on the scene twenty to thirty years after the Flexner Report had been released.) In this manner, all healing arts other than allopathic medicine, underpinned by the basic sciences, were effectively eliminated.

Because of the importance of the biological sciences and of the scientific method, the major drug companies at the time (spear-headed by the move by Standard Oil of New Jersey into the development and manufacture of oil-based, synthetic drugs) were able to exert a great deal of influence on the medical schools by supporting research in pharmacology and by supporting clinical drug trials. These trials were initially controlled, and later the double-blind technique was introduced in order to eliminate investigator bias. The drug trials constituted a significant portion of the research conducted by medical schools. To many physicians, they became synonymous with science in medicine. It was not until the revolution in molecular biology took place in the '60s and '70s that many physicians began to realize that there was more to science than the evaluation of drugs, the development of new diagnostic technology, and the development of new surgical techniques.

Flexner died in 1959. At a dinner in New York in his honor three years earlier, many laudatory things were said about him. For example, an AMA spokesman said that he had "made the greatest single contribution in history to medical teaching." For more than a decade following his death, the praise continued about his influence in shaping American medical schools. Gradually, however, this legacy is adapting to more modern awareness. As Dr. Thomas N. Bonner pointed out in an editorial in *Academic Medicine*, "since that time new research and new perspectives have eroded the Flexner legacy." Robert Hudson has written that reform was already well underway when Flexner wrote his famous report in 1910, and that his contribution was not so much revolutionary as it was catalytic to an already-evolving process. Hudson said that Flexner should be remembered not so much for the "fire he set to the medical schools of the day, as for his blueprint of the new structure which was to rise from the ashes." On the other hand, other critics, including this author, have challenged Flexner's blueprint as well.

Flexner is responsible for the heavy emphasis in American medical education on scientific research and high technology. The Flexner model of learning has all but destroyed the holistic approach of the clinically-effective physician to his patients. It has valued scientific research at the expense of teaching. It has helped to ensure an exclusive and extremely expensive brand of medicine.

What has emerged in medical education and clinical practice in the seventy-eight years since the Flexner Report in some ways is a tribute to the growth of medical technology. In other ways it is a travesty of the humanistic, compassionate approach to caring for the sick. Some of our modern medical institutions have reached a point where they are no longer capable of "putting Humpty Dumpty together again." Flexner himself insisted on incorporating courses in the social and behavioral sciences as part of the curriculum in medical school; either the curriculum has not been effective in these areas, or philosophies and interpersonal skills are so entrenched in students before they enter medical school that they are unteachable in these areas. No one in medicine today can deny that the process of making a physician is largely de-humanizing. Professor Lowell Levin of Yale has put it best: the end-product, the licensed physician, is more like "some kind of a bug with antennae than a fellow human being."

PART 1
ORGANIZED MEDICINE:
THE MOST POWERFUL AMERICAN LOBBY

CHAPTER 1
IF ALTERNATIVES WORK,
WHY ARE THEY REPRESSED?

In the last ninety days, at least three chelation doctors have been hauled before the board—one lost his license, the other two were threatened and told, they're going to get us all, one at a time!

—from a 1986 letter to the author from chelation doctor John Trowbridge, Humble, Texas

By the 21st century, chelation therapy will be warmly praised by Organized Med with no admission of past attempts to destroy the doctors who pioneered its use.

As you read this book, chelation is still under attack. Just what is this life-saving, life-enhancing procedure that is causing much commotion behind the scenes? Chelation therapy is a slow-drip IV injection of the synthetic amino acid EDTA. It was first used by doctors in the late 1940s to remove lead poisoning from workers who had been poisoned in battery factories and ship painters who used lead-based paint.

By chance, doctors discovered that it also helped remove the deadly plaque from clogged arteries and veins and the calcium that accumulated in their walls from the aging process and from pollutants such as lead, mercury, cadmium, and excessive iron and copper in the environment. Chelation not only prevented many heart-circulatory diseases, but reversed these conditions.

But there was a drawback to this wonderful discovery by medical doctors who achieved this breakthrough in their humble clinics. They had not first obtained permission from those who control the practice of medicine. Sounds unreasonable, and it is.

Organized Medicine refuses to acknowledge chelation's 30+ year track record in the prevention and healing of heart disease, stroke, senility, diabetic gangrene and many other vascular-related conditions.

There are documented cases of patients who were scheduled for leg amputation within a few days but saved their legs by switching to a chelation doctor for chelation therapy. Perhaps Organized Med should worry more about the wrath of chelated patients who learn their options too late than about the financial loss chelation will eventually cost them.

But until the truth comes out, chelation specialists must endure frightening injustice at the hands of their superiors. Their colleagues who are not using this alternative procedure offer no sympathy, as they are not aware of its benefits; quite the contrary, they have been repeatedly told that it is a dangerous therapy and that it does not work. Medical skeptics fear that their own methods might become obsolete if an alternative emerges. Traditional doctors must realize that if established treatments were more effective, had fewer side effects and were cheaper, patients would never switch.

Behind closed doors, Organized Med inflicts severe pressure on alternative practitioners to halt their methods. They are ostracized from their peers and endure frightening attacks alleging lack of ethics, fraud and other fabrications; even mental competence can be questioned. Alternative practitioners are falsely accused of exploiting their patients for money. (If insurance companies would only pay for these procedures, the patient would not have to be "exploited.") Libeled and slandered as quacks/charlatans, they endure unwarranted attacks and trumped-up charges—not objective investigation.

Sadly, my profession is guilty of a bad attitude and even worse behavior toward colleagues who adopt drug-sparing therapies which are indigenous to many different cultures. Some of these remedies were discovered right here in the United States and ignored because of arrogance and closed-mindedness. Worse, many alternative doctors have been persecuted, forced to halt their practices because they threaten the medical "bottom line." Natural techniques have helped to heal chronic illness throughout the 19th and 20th centuries, with a degree of success about which sometimes the finest of medical specialists can only dream.

THERE'S A HISTORY OF REPRESSION IN MEDICINE

Western medicine is full of "heretics" now credited with major advances by organized medicine—a safe century or more later.

The 16th-century Swiss alchemist-physician Paracelsus was the first to be labeled a quack. When he used toxic mercury to treat syphilis, he was viciously attacked by medical peers and called "quack"—short for the German word for mercury, *quacksalber*. Many medical treatments use potentially lethal substances at a low, therapeutic dose.

English doctor Joseph Lister was attacked for proposing that deadly infections would not result from surgery if aseptic techniques were used. Organized Medicine ignored his findings for many decades.

Austrian doctor Ignaz Semmelweis was persecuted for urging doctors in 1859 to wash their hands before delivering babies to prevent maternal death from childbirth fever. His colleagues persecuted him into insanity and to an early death. Organized Med was incensed by the notion that they themselves transmitted disease from morgue to maternity ward on their dirty hands. Mothers needlessly suffered and died throughout Europe.

Has the medical ego changed enough in the last century to permit objective evaluation of new discoveries? Unfortunately, this is not the case.

May we assume that objectivity goes hand in hand with scientific inquiry? No! Despite the unprecedented advances from modern research, there exists a strong inertia, a resistance to change, in science and medicine. Corporations now control the practice of medicine with the weight of their wallets. Driven by the stock market, medicine is embroiled in an economic turf war.

Stock investments in stable moneymakers (such as the currently-used chemicals for cancer and heart diseases) favor the status quo. If stock shares produce this kind of money, why make changes? Why relinquish profits for mostly unpatentable, much cheaper alternative medicines? In the case of chelation therapy, a number of medical specialists and industries would undergo economic upheavals if chelation were widely available to heart- diseased patients.

Corporate interests determine which medical procedures will be researched and developed. Behind-the-scenes dealings in corporate and medical board rooms, government agencies and even on Capitol Hill determine the course of research at major university medical centers. Such research centers depend on these cash grants from corporate, philanthropic and tax sources.

The financial giants of business and industry and their corporate-sponsored philanthropies, such as the American Cancer Society, spend and lobby mightily for laws representing their investments. These forces are intended to maintain the strong financial return on medical investments and to suppress the competition from alternative treatments which might have prevented medicine's financial mess we are faced with today.

Big money's resistance to alternative medicine is compounded by a tradition of arrogance in medicine. Doctors' egos are preened and propped up by their social standing and people's dependence on them. Doctors can believe that their education gives them a strange sort of infallibility to lend their expertise in areas of medicine for which they have received no training. This arrogance, conceit if you will, conveys to the public an expertise to discount alternatives which traditional doctors neither research nor try, or do so incompetently.

Negative peer review (judgment of colleagues through published criticism) is usually authored by doctors and researchers who know little, sometimes nothing at all, about the alternative methods they have been asked or directed to criticize. Sloppy or contrived research has, at times, been used to debunk an alternative therapy. This inaccurate peer review blocks alternatives from gaining approval as accepted medical practice.

It doesn't seem to matter that nearly all great medical advances have started with courageous individuals or small groups who were ambushed by those in control and their followers—after all, those in power say, "I'm an expert—I don't use this therapy—neither do my colleagues and they're experts—we've gotta be right and that loner/small bunch over there—they have to be wrong because, well, we're the experts." And so it goes in medicine.

MEDICAL JOURNALS—MYTH AND MYSTIQUE

The major medical journals which keep doctors current have refused to publish the effective results of chelation research in the treatment of heart disease; but they do find the hard-to-get editorial space to bash chelation and print frivolous letters to the editors doing the same. This false information and censorship have poisoned the attitudes of doctors who inquire about chelation.

Most literature searches begin and end with the *Index Medicus* or its electronic counterpart, the Medline computer database. Research studies of chelation must be published in medical journals with a limited circulation, many of which are excluded in the *Index Medicus*.

Few physicians and medical students know that only 10% of the world's total biomedical literature is located in those databases. If a doctor attempts a computer search of chelation for the treatment of vascular diseases, he will find all sorts of negative editorial propaganda but no negative data to support the criticism.

Clinical data supporting chelation is found only in medical journals not politically or financially dependent on the pharmaceuticals for advertising revenue. Since they are not that well-heeled, they have a narrow circulation. Some years ago the advertising revenue of the AMA's *Journal of the American Medical Association* (*JAMA*) accounted for over 40% of their income.

THE DARK SIDE OF CAPITALISM

Medicine's special interest groups exert a major influence on continuing education for the practicing physician and the public through print and broadcast media. Medical journals, newspapers, magazines, TV, radio—all survive on advertising revenue provided by interlocked corporations. The fear to bite the hand that feeds is understandable. Without media cooperation, it would be difficult to guide the public and educate the doctors-in-the-trenches according to Organized Medicine's goals.

Even medical schools dare not offend their corporate sources (grants, foundations) by encouraging discovery not sanctioned by those power groups that dispense the research money and determine what will be discovered.

Who loses? Not the power brokers, but the American people. The middle-income patients pick up the tab, but the best interests of all patients—rich, poor or in the middle—are pushed aside in this intricate, covert and dogmatic pursuit to suppress the competition. Hippocrates, your oath is forsaken for profit!

DO AS WE SAY. . .NOT AS WE DO!

Drugless or drug-sparing techniques for treating chronic disease are not new by European standards. Sometimes referred to as complementary, alternative, or non-toxic, they are usually adaptations of original methods used for many years throughout Europe by a small number of doctors. They include a multifaceted protocol: body detoxification, fresh-juice fasting, enemas, colonics, spinal manipulation, reflexology massage, herbal and homeopathic remedies, to name only a few.

In Europe, medical facilities which use these drug-sparing techniques are referred to as biologic clinics or sanatoriums. They have quietly operated throughout the 20th century. Other European doctors who adopt these therapies are finding resistance—a backlash if you will. In the United States, practitioners of these methods are actively harassed. The European facilities are not to be confused with the loosely-termed health spa, which can refer to anything from a horse-back riding resort to a weight-loss center.

But drug-driven American medicine is not interested in the many years' case documentation of holistic protocols. In the U.S. such approaches are dismissed as quackery. The current buzz word used by Organized Medicine to describe these holistic approaches is "pseudo-science." Their reasoning? They argue that new treatments are "unproven" because double-blind controlled studies have not been performed to prove efficacy beyond a doubt. However, about 80% of all medical procedures now used in the daily practice of medicine have never been "proven" through such research studies. Organized Medicine never complains about that.

The Office of Technology Assessment, OTA, is the respected research branch department for the U.S. Congress. Assisted by an advisory board of eminent university faculty, the OTA recently published a report on this matter with the conclusion that "only 10-20% of all medical procedures currently used in medical practice have been shown to be efficacious by controlled trial." Therefore, 80-90% of medical procedures routinely performed are unproven. Does that mean that 80-90% of all procedures are ineffective? Certainly not. It does signify that a procedure can be effective without dancing through $200+ million worth of testing as required by the FDA.

The OTA report further notes that the remaining 10-20% of medical procedures which purport to having been proven effective are in some cases based on flawed research.

So, the main excuse for the rejection of chelation therapy by Organized Medicine—that no controlled studies have been performed—shows a flagrant double standard. It's a cop-out; and besides, controlled studies showing good success for chelation have actually been published.

The double-blind study was developed to prevent bias in agricultural research up in Canada. To test the effects of fertilizer on crop yields, Canadian agriculturists planted two patches. The experiment was "double-blind" because neither the harvester who measured the crop nor the researchers knew which patch was fertilized and which one was not, eliminating the element of subjective bias. Double-blind studies were never meant to be used as the sole criterion for determining scientific truth, however.

WHY ORGANIZED MEDICINE DOESN'T LIKE CHELATION

The fundamental reasons are ignorance about its benefits and misinformation about its complications. Behind this veil of ignorance and cloud of disinformation, however, there is also a definite manipulation of the marketplace by "medical wise guys" who are aware of what chelation can do.

A complete program of chelation includes lifestyle restructuring: quitting smoking, taking up regular aerobic exercise, and making certain dietary modifications. None of these are patentable. The patent of EDTA expired years ago. It is now a generic drug—any company can manufacture and sell EDTA. The program also includes supplementation with various nutrients (also not patentable). Such doctor's orders sharply contrast with expensive, highly profitable, patentable drugs with their typical 800% markup for heart disease.

To obtain the FDA seal of approval for the treatment of blockage of arteries and veins, over $200 million would be needed for double-blind studies to "prove" effectiveness. The American public hardly knows that chelation exists, so there is no pressure coming from the public to fund such research. Ironically, about 600 certified chelation specialists are bravely and quietly practicing in over forty-six states and in other countries.

Chelation, therefore, until recently remained an unprofitable medical orphan with no daddy drug-bucks to adopt it. It is humbly performed in doctors' offices, without need for hospitals, heart surgeons, cardiologists and large teams of health-care professionals who continue to profit handsomely in dollars and reputation from the annual $10 billion high-tech heart industry.

Recent reports conclude that 44-85% of bypass surgery is performed on patients who do not meet the criteria for benefit, even using standards derived from non-blinded studies. The AMA admitted in its official journal, *JAMA*, that 44% of all coronary bypass surgery is performed for inappropriate reasons.

Medicare regulations do not require scientific "proof" for treatments which are used by a majority of physicians. In this manner the federal government adds support to this double standard.

When a new therapy is sanctioned by the medical profession, therefore, scientific proof of effectiveness is not always required—anecdotal evidence has been accepted as valid criteria. But alternative therapies, with thousands of proven case studies that put prestigious hospitals to shame, are told to undergo $200+ million studies.

FDA law allows a licensed doctor to use a drug sanctioned for one purpose for any other as is deemed fit by the attending physician, with the patient's consent. There is one restriction that applies to the use of EDTA: pharmaceuticals which manufacture EDTA cannot make advertising and marketing claims of effectiveness in the treatment of atherosclerosis, in the absence of FDA approval for that purpose.

With EDTA's patent expiration, there is no patent (monopoly) protection to allow financial recovery of research, development and licensing costs. A very recent deal has been negotiated between Wyeth-Ayerst and the FDA and this will be shared with you in another chapter.

Chelation has survived, despite the behavior of Organized Medicine and the drug companies directing their "gophers" in government to destroy this profit-threatener. Demanding professional standards must be met for a licensed M.D. or doctor of osteopathy, a D.O., to meet certification requirements by the American College for the Advancement of Medicine (ACAM), the professional organization of chelation physicians.

Also on the bright side, research funds have been obtained from private foundations, patients and doctors. By 1990, patients had completed double-blind studies with the expected good results. It is estimated that over 80% of patients undergoing chelation therapy are significantly helped. Many have avoided expensive and potentially dangerous bypass and angioplasty surgery, even leg amputation. There are numerous cases in which patients who were severely impaired are years later leading normal lives, thanks to chelation therapy.

Because of chelation's medical value, patients reach deeply into their pockets, sometimes into their life's savings, to pay several thousand dollars, because medical insurance will rarely pay. Friends and relatives are known to have sacrificed their hard-earned money to save a loved one. Simultaneously, they may be paying out of their other pockets for soaring insurance premiums on health insurance plans (that may or may not pay for a bypass).

Medicare will not pay for chelation. When Medicare refuses to pay for a therapy, most insurance companies follow suit. It costs far more for the poor patient to fight the injustice in court than to pay for the life-saving treatment.

The controversy over chelation is not the only battle fought between traditional and progressive medicine. Many talented doctors in this century have been quietly targeted for license revocation when they refused to stop using alternative treatments that have helped their patients.

CANCER COVERUP—NOT THE FIRST TIME!

There is astounding documentation that throughout the 20th century there have been American doctors who have successfully treated cancer patients, even in terminal stages of that supposedly incurable disease. Many of them were pre-/post-examined by leading cancer centers in America. But, shockingly, these doctors have suffered literal persecution, mostly in secret, known only to their patients who were struggling or had struggled so hard with their condition that they did not have the resources to effectively advocate for their doctors. Space permits the mention of only a few in this book, such as Dr. Max Gerson and Dr. William Koch. Gerson's therapy had to be brought out of the country after his death, and Dr. Koch had to leave the U.S. to continue his research in Brazil.

One instance where this behavior was brought to the attention of Congress occurred in August, 1953. Senator Charles Tobey, Jr., entered into the Congressional Record an investigative report by Special Counsel Benedict Fitzgerald. Fitzgerald's investigation revealed evidence of a conspiracy to suppress medical advances in the treatment of cancer in the 1950s. Throughout the 20th century, a small group of American doctors have successfully employed some drug-sparing methods to treat malignant tumors using a protocol of body detoxification, immune system stimulation, juice fasting, etc., approaches used mostly in Europe but also in Tibetan, Indian, and Chinese medical systems.

Fitzgerald strongly criticized those who supported the party line of the AMA, and he presented evidence that the latter was directly involved with the suppression and harassment of doctors who were successful in treating their cancer patients.

Their successes were evident in pre- and post-clinical records such as case histories, pathology and other lab reports and x-rays. Former cancer patients testified that years before they had been told that there was no hope, that they should go home, make out their wills and accept their fate of an early death. Case studies document that many such patients were alive decades after such pronouncement of doom from prestigious cancer centers.

Fitzgerald concluded that a conspiracy did indeed exist and that public and private funds had been "thrown like confetti at a country fair" to shut down clinics, hospitals and research labs which had not conformed to the AMA's dictates. Murder of a sort? You be the judge.

Unlike the chelation doctors, these alternative cancer doctors have not been able to establish a permanent presence in the U.S. Some were forced to leave the U.S. to continue their work "off-shore"; others have left the field of medicine, some financially ruined. There is now "off-shore" a growing number of medical facilities, some considered to be on a par with their European counterparts. The best of the time-honored biological approaches, when merged with modern medical technology, show better results than conventional surgery, radiation, and chemotherapy. In this country of the biggest and the best of everything else, why can't the chronically-ill patients have the best treatment?

ENDING THE MYTH OF SCIENTIFIC MEDICINE

Dr. Eveleen Richards, a member of the Department of Science and Technology Studies at the University of Wollongong in New South Wales, Australia, wrote an article in *Social Studies of Cancer* entitled "The Politics of Therapeutic Evaluation: the Vitamin C and Cancer Controversy" (SAGE, London, 1988). Because of the importance of her views, a lengthy excerpt from her writing follows:

> It will not be easy to come to grips with the problems posed by this revised view of medical knowledge, but the urgency of the task is manifest in the current widespread dissatisfaction with modern scientific medicine.
>
> As a necessary preliminary, defenders, critics and reformers of medicine will have to move forward to a better understanding of its inherent limitations. The randomized controlled clinical trial, no matter how tightly organized and evaluated, can neither guarantee objectivity nor definitively resolve disputes over contentious therapies or technologies.
>
> According to the revised view, these conflicts must be treated as essentially political issues where there are no impartial experts. The medical expert must be seen as a necessarily "partisan participant" in a political debate, not as an apolitical arbiter of medical truth, and this implies a radical review of the expert's role in therapeutic evaluation.
>
> It also opens the way to an active and acknowledged evaluative role for non-experts, for patients and the public at large, in the processes of assessment and decision making; such a development would not only undercut medicine's self-interested hegemony over the determination and evaluation of medical knowledge, but also permit the explicit expression and introjection of social values and needs into the evaluation and choice of available treatments.
>
> The difficulties of the enterprise, however, are not to be underestimated. The institution of medicine has a great deal invested in the perpetuation of the myth of objective evaluation.

It underpins the cognitive and social authority of its practitioners and legitimate powerful vested interests, not only in medicine, but in society at large. As David Edge has recently reminded us:

Ideas about the nature of science are but one aspect of modern political rhetoric, and changes in the structure and exercise of power and authority in society—in other words, political changes—are a necessary condition for their effective reform.

THE NATURE OF THE BEAST

Investigations against alternative practitioners follow a pattern of arrogance, dogmatism, deprivation of constitutional rights and a might-makes-right attitude. To suppress alternative medicine, Organized Med resorts to bad behaviors: disinformation, smear campaigns of libel and slander, harassment, unwarranted IRS audits, enticement of patients and family members to sue doctors when there is no reason (even offering financial payment to do so), entrapment by undercover agents posing as sick patients who may persistently beg for alternative treatments, illegal wiretaps, and break-ins and records theft.

It's difficult to believe that these tactics are used against chelation doctors even though chelation is legal, safe and effective in competent hands. Once Organized Medicine targets an alternative practitioner, the following sequence of events occurs:

1.Negative, sometimes fabricated, evidence is presented to the state board of medical examiners with a request for an official investigation.

2.This process results in prosecution.

3.Intimidating pressures are exerted on the doctor to cease his alternative approach or lose his license to practice medicine.

4.The licensing boards engage in investigations and proceedings which are often confidential and kept secret even from the doctor.

If only the American public knew! It has been difficult to learn the specifics of such covert operations, but a good approximation has emerged over the years.

The power structure of Organized Medicine may be described in terms of a pyramid structure. The wide base represents the broad, general membership with no voice about how medicine will operate. Specialists and their administrators are a step higher, with fewer members and somewhat more of a say in how things will be run. At the apex of the pyramid are the governing boards and officers from key specialty groups. Each level delegates its power to the level above, so that the relatively few at the top basically run the whole show.

Although the composite organization draws its authority from the individual members on the bottom, these people are basically unaware of the larger picture within which power brokers and medical politicians operate. By representing most of the practicing doctors and specialty groups in the country, those in control wield enormous influence in national affairs as they cooperate with institutions in business and government for mutual benefit.

Organized Medicine, drug companies and food processing corporations work together. For example, a food industry can profit handsomely from medically-endorsed margarines, unsaturated (but free-radicalized) fats, fake eggs and other refined, denatured foods.

The AMA and other segments of Organized Medicine are second only to the National Rifle Association in PAC contributions to lawmakers on the national level. These two groups invest more lobbying money than any other special interest groups in the country. Their political influence, bought and paid for, can determine policies of public institutions and federal and state regulatory agencies. Medical lobbyists' influence affects all medical schools, universities, government agencies, state medical licensing boards, even the agencies with quasi-police powers such as the anti-fraud division of Medicare.

I know many alternative practitioner doctors who, because they provided chelation therapy and other safe alternatives for their patients, were attacked by the very parts of government designed to protect what is good and right in our society. Could patient protection really be the concern in cases where patients died or suffered serious relapse when cut off from their treatment when their doctor was forced to close his office? Not until the public learns what is happening and protests will such deplorable behavior cease.

A case related by Dr. Oscar Rasmussen, Ph.D., provides one chilling example of what goes on, unknown to the public. Dr. Rasmussen is the former Nutrition Consultant of the acclaimed and controversial American International Hospital, north of Chicago in Zion, Illinois. He spoke at the semi-annual meeting of the Great

Lakes Association of Clinical Medicine in February, 1990, in Toronto, Ontario. He described a doctor in private practice, who was affiliated with the hospital and who was participating in the promising experimental research in the use of magnets to treat such conditions as peripheral neuropathy, non-union fractures, bed sores, psoriasis and other chronic, difficult-to-heal skin rashes.

Shortly thereafter, American International officially adopted this modality of treatment, making it known to referring physicians and to the public at large. They were visited by an FDA official who, after his tour, was quoted as saying to this research physician, "You've got a nice office and a nice home. If you want to keep them, quit promoting and advertising the therapeutic use of electromagnetic fields."

LICENSING BOARDS: "THE GOOD, THE BAD AND THE UGLY"

About 60% of state medical licensing board efforts are devoted to confronting, rehabilitating or removing the licenses of impaired or incompetent doctors. Most of these doctors are chemically dependent on alcohol and drugs. Some 15% of all doctors suffer from chemical dependency, and these addicted physicians are finally getting help from medical societies and recovered physicians. That focus of medical boards is in everyone's interest. The dangerous denial and enabling among colleagues is coming to an end.

The very worst doctors, however, are seldom disciplined in a manner known to the public; thus the image of physicians is protected, and malpractice lawsuits are discouraged. One extreme example, but certainly not the only one of its kind, involved the delayed handling of a perverted anesthesiologist in Massachusetts who engaged in oral sex with sedated female patients. His state board finally just rapped him on the knuckles, and he resumed practice in New Hampshire.

In another case, a physician-murderer in Ohio continued to practice because of his board's inaction on reports of his killing patients by lethal injection, until he was finally arrested by the police, arraigned and prosecuted—by the DA, not the AMA.

On the other hand, an M.D. in North Carolina had his license revoked because he incorporated homeopathic medicine (a natural European method based on principle of "like cures like") into his practice after a year of study in Greece with the world-renowned Dr. George Vithoulkas, M.D. This behavior on the part of medical examining boards raises serious questions of medical ethics.

Medical leaders drag their feet in disciplining the truly bad doctors or just quietly ease them out of the profession secretly. Often, with a rap on the knuckles, bad doctors are allowed to slip over into another state to practice there.

But within the remaining 40% of state medical board efforts, "doctor-hunting" goes on to control the practice of medicine. The specific purpose is to force conformity in the practice of medicine as protection from financial competition from innovative doctors who dare to use alternative treatments that can frequently cancel the need for surgery and drugs. The goal is restraint of trade in order to maintain a monopoly with the support of government.

Academic physicians on medical school faculties and research scientists are also influenced by propaganda and disinformation instead of relying on their own analytical ability and scientific methodology to determine scientific truths. Few doctors in practice are even aware of these behind-the-scenes operations to thwart competition and keep their financial monopoly of the health care industry in the U.S.

In 1964, the AMA formed the CCHI (Coordinating Conference on Health Information) as an offshoot of their Committee on Quackery. The CCHI was a secretive, covert organization which operated with other similar groups, intertwining itself throughout a network with no public scrutiny.

Working toward the same end is the National Council Against Health Fraud (NCAHF) which has regional chapters in many states. An oath of secrecy was requested of one applicant who sought to start a regional chapter. Chapters of the NCAHF stay in touch with members of each state's Board of Medical Examiners.

While the CCHI claimed and NCAHF now claims to be "scientific and authoritative" sources of information, much of their behavior has had nothing to do with confronting real quackery, but has served as a means to coerce and intimidate alternative practitioners to toe the line drawn by medical politicians. Again the purpose: to preserve the trade monopolies enjoyed by Organized Medicine.

Clinical research on the treatment of heart disease with chelation practically ceased from the early '60s to the mid-'80s due to a vicious campaign of libel/slander and intimidating harassment. Even scientists researching chelation were targeted.

Unknown to the American public, chelation doctors are summoned before their state examining boards to answer charges that are often contrived and rarely documented with careful investigation. Remember, the state boards are connected with the secretive

NCAHF (and former CCHI) network. The boards are legally-constituted bodies with ultimate authority to revoke a doctor's license to practice medicine. In at least six states, they have attempted to ban chelation therapy. Fortunately, the courts or the governors have quickly nullified most of these unjust rulings.

GOOD INTENTIONS CAN MISLEAD

In June, 1990, the Public Citizen Health Research Group (founded by Ralph Nader) published a listing of medical professionals throughout the U.S. who had been disciplined by local, state, and federal agencies. Although this is a well-intentioned public service, those who understand the misuse of regulatory agencies are concerned that among the bad apples listed in the publication are some good "chelation apples" and other reputable practitioners who got caught using alternative or drug-sparing procedures. Their names, of course, were released by the state examining boards right along with those truly guilty of misconduct or incompetency.

PATIENTS' NEEDS ARE NOT MEDICINE'S NEEDS

The 30+ year harassment of chelation doctors started as scientific arrogance, but persecution now stems from chelation's threat to the enormously profitable surgical breakthroughs of coronary bypass, angioplasty, peripheral and carotid artery surgery and the accompanying business for hospital staff.

Organized Med intends to restrain trade, which is illegal, in order to make as much money as possible. If about 70% of bypass patients can benefit from chelation as well as or better than from surgery, Organized Med faces a potential profit loss of way over one-half of the annual $10 billion heart-disease industry. Just observe the difference in cost between bypass surgery and chelation:

Cost of a coronary bypass: $30,000-50,000
Cost of chelation: $3,000
Patient savings: $29,000-47,000.

Serving as an expert witness on behalf of chelation doctor Warren Levin of New York, I found the charges against this doctor fabricated on nearly all medical points. The fabrication of wrong-doing by Dr. Levin appeared to be the work of a creative con artist. Dr. Levin has recorded this bizarre, hilarious kangaroo court on audiotape to let those interested know what's really going on in "quack hunting."

Looming on the horizon for Organized Med is the inevitable public awareness about what has been wrongfully denied them. While 800,000 Americans die every year from heart disease, a cheap, effective medical remedy continues to be suppressed. The self-appointed guardians cannot forever keep this treatment from the public.

Let us now explore medicine's shadowy past to understand how such injustice could continue to the present time. Only by learning the truth can people in a democratic society demand what is rightfully theirs—the best medicine money can buy.

CHAPTER 2
DOES MEDICINE HAVE A BAD ATTITUDE?

"...And besides, looking through those spectacles gives me a headache."

—Prof. Cesare Cremonini in 1610, explaining why he would not look through Galileo's telescope at the moons of Jupiter.

ARROGANT IGNORANCE

The sort of excuse above has delayed medical discoveries for decades, even half-centuries. Canadian nutritionist Dr. David Rowland describes this repression of medical innovation as a bad attitude which he termed "arrogant ignorance." This negative attitude toward many great discoveries represents a tremendous ego threat. Today such negativity is compounded with the industrialization of medicine, which has brought on that "greed is good (for me)" philosophy expressed in the recent movie *Wall Street*. Segments of the medical profession take what they want when they can get it.

Arrogant ignorance has followed science and medicine throughout history. Beginning with the learned colleagues of Galileo who refused to even look through the glass of his new invention, the telescope, because they believed they already knew all about the laws of physics, that not-invented-here attitude is alive and well at the dawn of the 21st century. Is it only a coincidence that "not invented here" shares initials with our government's National Institutes of Health?

Past suppressions—at least those safely back in past centuries—are readily admitted by contemporary medicine. French explorer Jacques Cartier, for example, in 1535 learned from the American Indians that pine-needle tea prevented and cured scurvy, a vitamin C deficiency disease. Upon his return to France, Cartier excitedly shared his discovery with French doctors, who turned a cold shoulder—such a primitive therapy was witchcraft. If we pass this off as Eurocentrism, we miss the similarities to present-day rejections of alternative healing methods that are getting the cold shoulder. The case of Dr. Charles Peres, M.D., of Ft. Meyers,

Florida, provides an excellent example.

Dr. Peres was diagnosed with a stage D2 prostate cancer spread throughout his body. In lay terms, you can't have a gloomier prognosis. After he adopted a natural regimen based on a low-fat vegetarian macrobiotic diet, his cancer went into complete remission. Naturally overjoyed, upon his return to functional living he noticed that many of his medical colleagues actually appeared angry that he had survived. Would they rather he die than heal himself with this unorthodox treatment? This very same disdain has been noted by cancer patients who have sought out alternative cancer doctors and have gone into permanent remission, only to be told by their first doctor that they never had cancer to begin with (despite the complete diagnostic work-up that he had witnessed). Negative reactions range from obvious anger to feigned indifference. It must also be told that there are doctors who secretly recommend alternative treatments but warn their patients to never tell the wrong party lest the doctor get in trouble.

In 1747, James Lind, a surgeon's mate in the British Navy, conducted dietary experiments on board ship. He concluded that citrus fruits prevented and cured the killer disease scurvy which ravaged sailors. Captain Cook was one of the first ship commanders to supplement his sailors with rations of lime. The captain sailed throughout the world for over three years without a single death from scurvy—unprecedented for that time.

But it took forty-eight years before the British Admiralty made it official policy to distribute one ounce of lime juice daily for each sailor. This simple nutritional supplement of vitamin C was a factor in Britain's ascent to being the world's greatest sea power. It was as though they doubled their forces. Britain sailed farther than any other navy into uncharted territory, easily defeating weakened enemies who had lost many sailors to scurvy.

Now, neither the British nor the American Indian performed any double-blind, cross-over studies to arrive at their discovery. In their respective ways, they learned that it worked very well for their needs. James Lind had conducted empirical studies (based on observation) to determine that a citrus fruit could save naval forces from certain death. Ridiculed by their rivals for this use of lime juice, the British were derisively referred to as "limeys." Had they never conducted their simple experiment, or had another sea power done so, world history could have been altered.

Dr. Jenner, a British doctor, discovered in the early 1800s that milkmaids who had previously contracted cowpox were protected against smallpox. Jenner scientifically developed a vaccine from the crusty lesions of smallpox patients to inoculate others against smallpox. It took more than fifty years for the medical power structure to endorse his simple remedy for a killer disease.

In 1848, Dr. Semmelweis, a graduate of the prestigious University of Vienna Medical School, introduced a revolutionary idea while assisting in the Vienna Obstetrical Clinic: he required medical students to wash their hands in chlorine water before entering the clinic. There was an immediate and dramatic decrease in the high death rate from puerperal (childbirth) fever. The good doctor became an outspoken advocate, pleading with obstetricians to tend maternity patients only after proper hand washing. After a vicious attack on his personal and professional integrity, he was fired from the hospital where he had just eradicated a cause of death.

This courageous, principled doctor then spent ten years gathering evidence to prove that hand washing would prevent terrible misery and death from childbirth fever. He published his research in 1861 and distributed the medical text to the major medical societies throughout Europe. It was completely ignored. In one of those years, 40% of the maternity patients in Stockholm, Sweden, contracted the fever; 16% of those new mothers died.

The deadly fever continued to ravage women while the handwashing prevention/cure was "put on hold" by Organized Medicine. The poor doctor could no longer cope with the preventable death and misery of so many women. In 1865 he died after a mental breakdown; such tragedies still occur among gifted researchers whose great discoveries are ignored. So, from the safety of the next century, Dr. Semmelweis can be credited by the medical profession with his lifesaving discovery—hand washing.

In 1867, Dr. Joseph Lister introduced sanitation in surgery, but not without a big fight with the leading surgeons of 19th-century England. His paper, "On the Antiseptic Principle in the Practice of Surgery," was read before the British Medical Association in Dublin, Ireland. His noteworthy summary concluded:

> Since the antiseptic treatment has been brought into full operation, my wards though in other respects under precisely the same circumstance as before, have completely changed their character; so that during the last 9 months not a single instance of pyemia, hospital gangrene or erysipelas has occurred in them.

Dr. Lister's contribution outraged the leading surgeons of the day.

An 1869 conference of the BMA devoted the surgery address to a scathing attack on the antiseptic theory. What presumptuous London surgeon would believe a lowly provincial from Scotland who was telling them how to improve surgical protocol?

As evidence of similar incredible intolerance in the United States, U.S. Senator Paul Douglas related the following story, which was recorded in the Congressional Record in 1963:

> I spent a part of 1923 with Dr. W.W. Keen. In the Civil War he was a surgeon and had seen many men die from the suppuration of wounds after he had operated.
>
> He went to Scotland and studied under Lister. Dr. Keen came back from Scotland. He was referred to as a crazy Listerite. He was denied an opportunity to practice in every hospital in Philadelphia.
>
> Finally there was one open-minded surgeon in the great Pennsylvania General Hospital. He said, "Let us give this young fellow a chance!" So they let him operate.
>
> No one died from infection under Keen. Keen began to chronicle the results in statistical articles. He was threatened with expulsion from the Pennsylvania Medical Society.
>
> This was in the 1890s. Finally he was accepted as the greatest surgeon in the U.S.

Next came Dr. Louis Pasteur, a chemist. His germ theory for infectious diseases provoked violent opposition from the medical community of the late 1800s. How could a mere chemist poach upon their scientific turf?

Dr. Harvey's monumental work on the theory of blood circulation was forbidden to be taught at the University of Paris Medical School twenty-one years after Harvey published his findings. And it doesn't end there. . .

Austrian botanist Gregory Mendel's theory of genetic composition was generally ignored for thirty-five years. His pioneering work was dismissed as that of an idle, rich dilettante by the leading scientists of his day.

Dr. Fleming's mid-twentieth-century discovery of the antibiotic penicillin was ridiculed and ignored for twelve years before this life-saver was admitted into the medical circle. Once scorned, Dr. Fleming was eventually knighted and received the Nobel Prize in Medicine for what had once been denounced.

As a final example, Dr. Joseph Goldberger unravelled the mystery of pellagra, a disease which ravaged especially the poor in the American South. Pellagra was at first thought to be an infectious disease causing the three D's of dermatitis, diarrhea and dementia. Goldberger discovered that, like scurvy, pellagra was a vitamin-deficiency disease. The milling or refining process of corn removed important vitamins and minerals from the husk. Those people dependent on corn-based foods such as grits, corn bread, etc., became deficient in vitamins and minerals.Goldberger's recommendation—to re-fortify corn flour—is now a routine practice in refining most flours. But the foot-dragging over this minor business expense by the greedy flour barons of the time dragged on for fifty years.

These examples are just a handful of so very many courageous doctors and scientists who braved a battle with Organized Medicine on behalf of what could help patients. They have the honor and distinction of representing "The Enemy of the People" that was portrayed in Ibsen's drama of that name.

The role of deficiency in causing disease is carried a step further by Dr. Max Gerson in his text for doctors, *A Cancer Therapy—50 cases*. He exposes the depletion of farm soil from chemical fertilization as early as the 1930s and concludes that the depletion subsequently affects nutritional levels in the plants growing in depleted soil.

IT'S THE SAME IN SCIENCE

Throughout the course of Western Civilization, there has been a strong resistance to new information in the other scientific fields. There is so much evidence of this bigotry that only a few brief examples are offered here.

Thomas Kuhn's book *The Structure of Scientific Revolution* (2nd Edition, University of Chicago Press, 1970) relates the typically bitter conflict between an independent science researcher who discovers something important and the current power structure which fights to maintain the status quo.

German biologist Hans Zimmer wrote, "Academies and learned societies are slow to react to new ideas, this is in the nature of things...The dignitaries who hold high honors for past accomplishments do not like to see the current of progress rush too rapidly out of their reach!"

In his 1966 book, DeGrazia recounted the mistreatment of scientist Immanuel Velikovsky for his theories in astronomy. Velikovsky had proposed that the catastrophic events recorded in the Old Testament and in Hindu vedas and Roman and Greek mythology were due to the earth repeatedly passing through the tail of a comet during the 15th to the 7th centuries, B.C.

DeGrazia wrote,

> What must be called the scientific establishment rose in arms, not only against the new Velikovsky theories but against the man himself. Efforts were made to block dissemination of Dr. Velikovsky's ideas, and even to punish supporters of his investigations. Universities, scientific societies, publishing houses, and the popular press were approached and threatened; social pressures and professional sanctions were invoked to control public opinion.
>
> The issues are clear; Who determines scientific truth? Who are its high priests, and what is their warrant? How do they establish their canons? What effect do they have on the freedom of inquiry and on public interest? In the end, some judgment must be passed upon the behavior of the scientific world, and if adverse, some remedies must be proposed.

Philosopher and professor of physical chemistry Michael Polanyi commented in 1969, referring to the persecution of Velikovsky, that new ideas in science are not accepted in a rational manner, based on factual evidence, but instead are determined by random chance, the ruling economic/political powers or the ruling ideology.

A recent paper by sociologist Marcell Truzzi, "On the Reception of Unscientific Claims," delivered at the annual American Academy for the Advancement of Science, proposed that it is even harder today for new discoveries and ideas to break through, due to the escalating economics of research. Truzzi wrote, "Unconventional ideas in science are seldom positively greeted by those benefitting from conformity." Truzzi predicted that new forms of vested interest will emerge from today's programs that must compete for massive funding. He warned, "This has become a growing and recognized problem in some areas of modern science."

There is another reason for resistance to scientific discoveries. Many of the major advances have come either from a scientist in another scientific discipline or from researchers who just don't qualify for membership in the scientific elite (as in high school "in crowds"). No wonder advances so often come not from the "in crowd" who are blinded or corrupted by prevailing dogma.

ORGANIZED MED IGNORES SUCCESS

Currently there exists impressive statistical and clinical (case study) data on alternative approaches to reversing or controlling some cancers without the use of chemotherapy, radiation and surgery. But covert politicking and overly rigid systems of testing and approval suppress these biological approaches that Americans are increasingly accessing. Desperate cancer patients rarely learn about all their medical options; in fact, a full 80% of those who travel outside the U.S. for alternative cancer therapies are so terribly advanced in their diseases that it is too late, even for alternative approaches. This fact alone obscures the value of these therapies when they are promptly applied under competent medical supervision and not tried as a last resort, following, for example, chemotherapy. Chemotherapy alone can destroy a patient's immune system, and biological methods usually require a functioning immune system.

Sadly, in this supposed age of enlightenment, the ridicule of the medical orthodoxy and a rigid system of testing and approval (calcified by the same suspicions of alternative therapies that plagued discoveries for centuries) keeps these treatments from ill patients who might benefit from them, as De Felice, Director of the Foundation for Innovation in Medicine, in 1987 lamented:

> One of the tragedies of our times is that over the past 20 years, a pervasive and aggressive regulating system has evolved that has effectively blocked the caring clinical innovator at nearly every step. Let there be no doubt that we have quietly, but effectively, eliminated the Louis Pasteurs of our great country.

DR. HORROBIN'S CALL FOR AN END TO THE SUPPRESSION OF INNOVATION

JAMA, in March, 1990, published selections from the first International Congress on Peer Review in Biomedical Publications. Dr. David Horrobin presented "The Philosophical Basis of Peer Review and The Suppression of Innovation," a classic presentation. Dr. Horrobin stressed that the ultimate aim of peer review in biomedical science cannot differ from the ultimate aim of medicine—"to cure sometimes, to relieve often, to comfort always." (Believed to be a French folk saying of medieval origin, this beautifully simplistic description of medicine's intent is inscribed on the statue of Edward Trudeau at Saranac Lake, New York.)

Dr. Horrobin stated that the purpose of peer review should be nothing less than to facilitate the introduction of improvements in curing, relieving and comforting. Even in the fields of biomedical research that are remote from clinical practice, the peer reviewer should always ask whether the proposed innovation could realistically lead to improvements in the treatment of patients.

He notes the necessity for a creative tension between innovation on the one hand and quality control on the other. The innovators who generate the future are often impatient with the precision and systematic approach of the quality controllers. On the other hand, the quality controllers are often exasperated by the seeming lack of discipline and predictability of the innovators. If either side dominates, research progress falters.

The public is the ultimate source of money for medical research. They agree to this use of their money for the sole purpose of improving their medical care. When improvement does not progress satisfactorily, support for medical research (and medical journals) will dwindle. The public wants satisfactory progress; if such progress is not forthcoming, the present medical research enterprise will crumble. For satisfactory results, quality control must comprise only one side of the editorial equation. There must also be an encouragement of innovation. Presently, quality control is overwhelmingly dominant, and encouragement of innovation receives very little attention. Without appropriate balance, peer review fails its purpose.

Dr. Horrobin notes that, in the last six decades, the accuracy of medical articles has improved substantially but so has a failure to acknowledge innovation. Between 1930 and 1960, patient care improved dramatically. Many infectious diseases were controlled by drugs and immunization. Prototypes of drugs used today were discovered during that time. However, by 1960 (despite major developments, especially in the field of diagnosis), patients increasingly felt dissatisfied, and we must accept the fact that their dissatisfaction stems from our trading innovation for quality control.

Dr. Horrobin presents many situations in which, through peer review, Organized Medicine has tried to suppress an innovative concept but failed. He shows how the use of peer review influences journals, conference choices and grant awards.

Pathologist Charles Harris has written editorials about the "Cult of Medical Science" in which he says pseudo-science in medicine is currently a cult which inhibits innovation and considers participation in clinical drug trials (which have been designed by statisticians) as the work of scientists because these trials reject so-called anecdotal evidence based on clinical observations alone. But this narrow attitude is not real science which leads to discovery. It is merely indoctrination and a pledge of allegiance to the flag of pseudoscience.

Harris also asserts that diagnosis, which is supposed to be the determination of the nature of disease either by examination or by exclusion, is not being practiced as it should be. Diagnosis today too often does not consist of examination, exclusion, clinical or therapeutic trials; rather, it often consists only of a rushed referral to a medical specialist under the guise of a diagnosis. The specialist may accept and act on the initial diagnosis which was not valid in the first place. The initial diagnosis serves to justify referral and satisfy the CPT code in order for the doctor to get reimbursed.

The *New York Times,* on March 26, 1991, carried an article by Philip J. Hilts entitled "How Investigation of Lab Fraud Grew Into a Cause Celebre" recounting how scientists turned a tangled dispute into a defense of science. This article is about a draft report which had been recently released by the newly-established Office of Scientific Integrity at the National Institute of Health. This office had been investigating the case of Dr. Thereza Imanishi-Kari and a paper she published with Dr. David Baltimore in the April, 1986, issue of the scientific journal *Cell* about the basis of an immune reaction. Questions about the paper arose when Dr. Margot O'Toole, a post-doctoral fellow in Dr. Imanishi-Kari's laboratory, went to Dr. Baltimore (who was then at the Massachusetts Institute of Technology) and told him her reasons for doubting the authenticity of the data in the article. She alleged that the paper made false statements, a conclusion she reached after seeing seventeen pages of data that supposedly, but did not, support claims in the paper. She persisted in her accusations, and, as a result, two scientific reviews of the paper were conducted in 1986—one at MIT, where the work was done, and the other at Tufts University, where Imanishi-Kari was seeking employment. Both of these reviews found problems with the work but found no reason to believe misconduct was involved. Dr. O'Toole, who was eventually fired from her job at MIT, had been told by Dr. Baltimore that she could publish her objections to the paper, but that if she did he would also publish his views of it.

The matter lay dormant for two years after the initial scientific reviews conducted at MIT and Tufts, until Representative John D. Dingell, who heads the House Subcommittee on Oversight and Investigations, asked the Secret Service to examine Dr. Imanishi-Kari's notebooks for their authenticity. This action raised the hackles of the scientific community. Supporters of Dr. Baltimore criticized Rep. Dingell for prying into the notebooks of science and described his panel as the "science police." Dingell revealed that his committee was soon buried in letters from scientists concerned with the subcommittee's actions, but he also said that in perhaps 50% or more of the letters the scientists included disclaimers, saying that they did not know the facts of the case. What had begun as a small dispute within Dr. Imanishi-Kari's laboratory had become a national debate, pitting Dr. Baltimore and his many supporters in the scientific community against Dingell's House Subcommittee and generating bitter controversy over a period of five years.

The controversy was eventually addressed by the National Institute of Health's Office of Scientific Integrity and put to rest by its draft report. In that report, the OSI concluded that Dr. O'Toole's actions were heroic and that Dr. Baltimore's response was troubling because he, instead of ending the matter within weeks of its beginning, allowed it to mushroom into a national debate. Dr. O'Toole's allegations were vindicated, and most of Dr. Baltimore's supporters have withdrawn their objections to the Congressional action after confronting the evidence uncovered by the OSI and presented in their draft report.

This case of scientific fraud illustrates the need for an office such as the Office of Scientific Integrity. Dr. David Goodstein, Vice-Provost of the California Institute of Technology, helped to write the rules for dealing with misconduct. He stated in regard to the Imanishi-Kari/Baltimore case, "The scientific community until recently was disposed to believe that fraud didn't exist. So, in the rare cases that it did come up, the community was not prepared for it."

Having established that fraud can exist in the scientific community and having acknowledged the need for an agency to investigate such fraud, we now need to address a disturbing question: What about fraud and deceit that is conducted by individuals who work for organizations such as the AMA and the FDA? Why doesn't the Office of Scientific Investigation inquire about what happened with the Koch reagents and how an injunction was issued by the FDA prohibiting interstate shipment and the making of any medical claims, without the FDA even investigating them? What about the recall by the FDA of all contaminated tryptophan products sold in health food stores while allowing the continued use of the contaminated product in infant formulas and in intravenous pharmaceutical preparations?

The statute of limitations has expired in the case of the Koch reagents, but it is arguable that there should be no statute of limitations in science, particularly regarding a therapeutically useful drug. In any case, the statute of limitations has not expired in the recent contaminated-tryptophan case. Why is this case not investigated by the OSI? If their mandate is not to investigate cases like this, then what is it? Surely their mandate goes beyond an occasional nabbing of a cheating researcher. It appears that the Office of Scientific Integrity is prepared to investigate individual instances of fraud but not collusion and conspiracy within the ranks of government itself.

The story of vitamin C and cancer was thoroughly researched by Dr. Evelleen Richards and published in "Social Studies of Science" in 1988. Her paper received much publicity. Dr. Richards documented in great detail the failure of two Mayo Clinic studies to test vitamin C in the correct manner proposed by Nobel winner Linus Pauling and his associate, E. Cameron.

Richards noted the repeated refusal of the *New England Journal of Medicine* to publish letters and articles by Pauling and Cameron that demonstrated why the second Mayo trial was not a test of their hypotheses. Cameron showed that highly toxic treatments for cancer, including 5-fluorouracil for colon cancer, continued to be used despite their failure to demonstrate efficacy in placebo-controlled trials. Richards posed a valid question: Why does the full weight of disapproval fall on vitamin C (which has low toxicity), when toxic drugs with no demonstrated efficacy are widely used?

Dr. Horrobin contends that the peer-review process harbors antagonism toward innovation. While this is not the norm, it certainly is not the exception. Editors must encourage innovation as much as they now ensure quality control, and that will require a conscious effort of will. He points out that the hypercritical reviews and behaviors of many distinguished scientists are unwarranted and pathological. Such professionals are gate-keepers against innovation unless the new thought or discovery is their own.

Dr. Horrobin concludes with a call for editors to muster the courage to select reviewers of the highest caliber without vested interest, or at least to note when vested interest is present. Editors must stop rejecting innovative articles for minor details which never keep establishment-approved articles out of the journals. An editor must never lose sight of the ultimate aim of biomedical science—to improve quality of patient care. Only after scrupulous study of both the article's contents and the peer review should the editor make an objective decision.

WE MUST STOP PERSECUTING ALTERNATIVE PRACTITIONERS

To refuse to learn from history is to repeat it. The medical profession continues to libel and slander innovative doctors. The term "quack" has no legal definition. It is too often misused to libel a doctor who is bright, full of initiative and well-loved by patients and who has made an original discovery or happened to acquire the non-toxic methods that in the U.S. are referred to as alternative. Real chariatans should certainly be stopped. But should there be these pogroms aimed at American doctors such as the chelation doctors or those who employ alternative methods for treating cancerous tumors or other chronic diseases such as arthritis, multiple sclerosis, etc?

This moral injustice should be halted. The involved branches of business, government and the medical profession will in the near future have to answer the well-documented evidence spanning the 20th century, that, hidden from the trusting public, a horrible orchestration of doctor-bashing has occurred to destroy the competition.

And what does Organized Medicine say for itself? Why, they believe in an overly-rigid definition of what constitutes scientific proof. The Canadian agriculturalist who developed the double-blind study never intended for it to be used in such a rigid manner. It was intended to eliminate the subjective bias of scientific investigators and their research assistants, not to become the gold-standard bearer for scientific proof in clinical medicine. Most genuine scientists (the term excludes the majority of the medical profession) do realize this fact. Real scientists understand that all science starts with careful observation and the recording of events.

This point can be best illustrated with a story. In the time of Julius Caesar, there was a legendary bandit by the name of Procrustes. Now, a Procrustean bed which bears his name is an adjustable hospital bed. Legend had it that Procrustes would kidnap people, bring them to his home and force them to lie down on his bed. If they were too tall to fit his bed, he just cut off their legs and they bled to death. Too short? He put them on a rack and stretched them until they died screaming. The highly regarded Dr. Edward Whitmont, homeopathic physician of New York City, likens the rigidity of the cruel Procrustes to the rigid adherence to a methodology that blinds one to an obvious truth in medicine—that an alternative treatment works. The obsession with a rigidly narrow definition of what constitutes scientific proof is more slavishly believed by physician scientists than by modern physicists. Recognizing only this rigid, narrow definition of proof, orthodox medicine holds a sword of Damocles over their competition.

Do they really believe that they can keep alternatives out of medicine? Or do they know that the exclusion will end in the near future and so "make hay while the sun still shines"?

CHAPTER 3
IS THERE A SECRET TEAM?

"I was sick to my stomach; I knew I'd been had and somebody cheated!"

—Dr. Spain-Ward, having learned that her research on Dr. Gerson's cancer therapy was omitted from a government report.

DR. MAX GERSON

Several years ago, Dr. Patricia Spain-Ward, a respected professor of medical history at the University of Illinois in Chicago, was commissioned by the Office of Technology Assessment to research the medical evidence for alternative cancer therapies.

In response to growing pressure from alternative practitioners and patient advocates, the Office of Technology Assessment (OTA), the research branch of Congress, was assigned by Congress to investigate claims that there already existed successful methods of combatting cancer. The advocates maintained that these methods were withheld from the public because they were not included in medical school curricula, that alternative doctors were denied research grants, and that any alternative research submitted was ignored.

Dr. Spain-Ward reviewed several alternative cancer therapies. She researched their history and examined the conflict that arose between the proponents of the therapy and the opponents, the AMA and the FDA. Her examination of the Hoxsey treatments for cancer is covered in a later chapter.

Dr. Spain-Ward readily acknowledges her initial skepticism of alternatives, but her research changed her prejudice entirely.

Dr. Max Gerson, a German doctor who entered the U.S. in 1933 to escape Nazi Germany, was one of the alternative practitioners that Dr. Spain-Ward investigated. Dr. Gerson had developed a clinical dietary approach to the treatment of a number of chronic diseases including tuberculosis, asthma, arthritis, diabetes, heart conditions, multiple sclerosis and, in particular, many types of cancer.

Originally he developed the therapy to cure his own severe migraines which left him bedridden. His application of his dietary regimen to tuberculosis attracted the attention of the internationally acclaimed surgeon Ferdinand Sauerbruch who, in his autobiography *Master Surgeon,* described his own research with Gerson's therapy for treating a form of skin TB. Dr. Sauerbruch achieved a 99% cure rate on 450 patients.

Before his immigration to the U.S., Dr. Gerson successfully treated the wife of Dr. Albert Schweitzer for lung TB and Schweitzer's daughter for a rare skin ailment. Dr. Gerson also administered a dietary protocol for Dr. Schweitzer's advanced adult-onset diabetes which had forced him to retire. With the dietary regimen, Dr. Gerson had his famous patient off of all insulin within a month. Dr. Schweitzer fully credits Dr. Gerson for restoring his health so that he could resume his humanitarian medical work at Lambarene Hospital in Gabon, Africa, into his eighties.

Although Dr. Gerson's theory and methods threatened the European medical establishment of the time, he was able to publish and to present his findings at professional meetings of his colleagues interested in cancer research. Upon his arrival in the U.S., Dr. Gerson found an even more hostile climate for new medical ideas, particularly those not involving drugs or surgery.

The Gerson dietary protocol consisted of detoxification with raw vegetable and fruit juices, raw calf liver juice (now discontinued because of the toxic chemical residue now found in calves), a vegetarian diet and caffeine implants in the form of coffee enemas to provoke the liver and open the bile ducts. This technique, a German therapy, was supposed to expel toxins accumulated from the manifestations of illness as well as "dissolved tumor masses," which, once caught in the liver, would be released in the bile and exit the kidneys.

After the initial period of juice fasting and enemas, he placed the patients on a long-term dietary program involving low- sodium/high-potassium foods to put right the imbalance of the sodium potassium pump.

The Gerson diet was actually very similar to one that is used today by the famous Mexican cardiologist Sodi Pallares. Dr. Pallares has reasoned that sodium causes entropy, a resistance or a negative energy force which prevents the heart, for example, from doing maximal work. His reasoning is based on the theories of Albert Einstein. A roller coaster, for example, expends energy when it goes down. When it comes back up, it never reaches the original height at which it started, because of negative resistance. This resistance is an energy force which is called entropy. Sodium increases entropy in human organs—not only the heart, but also other organs such as the kidneys, musculoskeletal system, etc.

THE PEPPER COMMISSION, 1946

In 1946 Dr. Gerson proudly demonstrated medical proof of complete remissions of cancer in over one-third of his patients before the Pepper-Neeley Congressional Sub-committee for Hearings on S. 1875. This was the first bill to authorize the president to "wage war on cancer." For three days, Dr. Gerson demonstrated evidence of cured cancer patients who had been given no hope of recovery by leading cancer centers in the U.S. Dr. Gerson envisioned receiving the Nobel Prize for Medicine for his findings. Instead, lobbying forces for surgery, radiation and chemotherapy defeated his dietary protocol through intensive lobbying efforts. By only four votes a Senate bill that could have supported research of dietary means of preventing and reversing cancer was thwarted in 1946.

Dr. Spain-Ward's research uncovered systematic harassment on the part of the New York State Medical Society and the New York State Licensing Board. Dr. Gerson's publications were blacklisted, and none of the reputable journals would accept them. His hospital privileges at Gotham Hospital in New York City were revoked after his impressive demonstration of success before the Pepper Sub-committee in 1946. He ultimately lost his license to practice medicine in the State of New York. The campaign to discredit him was likely coordinated by individuals in the AMA.

In 1949, the AMA Council of Pharmacy and Chemistry went on record stating that diet could in no way have anything to do with the prevention or the treatment of cancer. Its conclusions were supposedly based on a review of the literature. However, no real research had ever been done by the committee as a whole or by any of its members. The conclusions stated in their report were issued as though an edict from on high, as is the present case with EDTA chelation therapy. To review the literature and render an opinion is not the same as doing actual research.

The case of Max Gerson was a medical tragedy. Deeply hurt and concerned for his patients, he published *A Cancer Therapy—Results of Fifty Cases* in 1959 before his death. The AMA, on the pretext of protecting the public and the FDA, and in violation of their legislative mandate, succeeded in destroying the professional career of this prominent clinical researcher who proved many times that he could reverse cancer with diet and without drugs and surgery. They proudly displayed their arrogant ignorance of the role of nutrition and diet in the development of cancer. Certainly Dr. Gerson's public denunciation in *JAMA* of smoking as a health hazard (at a time when physicians openly served as advertisement models for major cigarette brands) did not help his situation.

The third alternative cancer treatment that Dr. Patricia Spain-Ward reviewed was that of BCG. BCG stands for the bacillus of Drs. Calmette and Guerin, the French researchers who cultivated this avirulent (non-disease-causing) strain of tuberculosis. BCG has been used to vaccinate children against tuberculosis, because the microorganism has many of the same proteins that are found in the microorganism which causes tuberculosis. It therefore can be used as a vaccine, similar to the way in which the virus that causes cowpox can be used as a vaccine against smallpox.

In France, BCG is still used to treat cancer. Professor Georges Mathe, a world-renowned French cancer specialist, has said that BCG, when it is injected intravenously, causes the patient to develop a high fever. This generalized febrile response is accompanied by a stimulation and augmentation of "all aspects of the immune system." All of the various cells, antibodies, and chemicals involved in the immune response are stimulated in various amounts, and their activities are increased.

This stimulation provides a boost to the patient's immune system and appears to help fight off the cancer. The treatment has never caught on in the United States, presumably because it causes fever and, at least initially, appears to make the patient worse. What you cannot see, however, is what is going on internally, with the subsequent stimulation of all immune defenses, and this is where research will ultimately focus in unlocking this 20th-century medical mystery of cancer.

Dr. Spain-Ward's historical review was not exactly what OTA had expected. In the first draft of their report on alternative cancer therapies, her research on Dr. Gerson and Dr. Hoxsey was excluded, causing an uproar among the members of the advisory committee to OTA for this project. Those sympathetic to an objective examination of existing alternative therapies roundly protested the exclusion of Dr. Spain-Ward's findings. In the words of one emergency medicine doctor from Pennsylvania, confronting the committee about this omission: "What kind of scientists are you?"

IS THERE REALLY A SECRET TEAM?

David Corn, writing in the July, 1988, issue of *The Nation,* posed this question regarding a lawsuit filed by the Christic Institute against a number of Contra supporters. "Secret team" was the term used in that lawsuit to describe the complex workings of an inter-agency governmental operation. The secret team theory alleges that crimes can be attributed not to a small gang of rogue operatives or government officials, acting on their own, but to a secret agency policy—therefore a U.S. government policy. The secret team theory had, at that time, gained credibility in left-of-center circles. "Stop the Secret Team" bumper stickers proliferated; mass mailings introduced the secret team to hundreds of thousands. The lawsuit was even mentioned on the TV show "Cagney and Lacey."

THE STRIKE FORCE—A MEDICAL SECRET TEAM

Although the concept of a secret team operating behind the scenes in medicine originated in the AMA during 1973 and 1974, it came into its own and acquired the name Strike Force in 1984, when it was implemented and coordinated after legislation proposed by the late Congressman Claude Pepper to establish such a "force" failed to pass. The purpose of the Pepper legislation was allegedly to combat health fraud, and it included provisions for setting up a national clearing house for information on quackery and also a Strike Force to go after persons or groups accused of health fraud. Congressman Pepper's bill, however, died in committee following an avalanche of opposing mail from the growing force of pro-choice advocates in health care groups, such as the National Health Federation, who feared such a group would limit the public's choices. When the bill died, it was generally assumed that the concept of a national clearinghouse and the idea for a Strike Force died with it. But we have since learned that this was not the case.

The Strike Force which the Pepper bill (HR6051) had proposed to establish covertly came into existence. Without the approval of Congress and without the knowledge or the consent of the public, it was established and put into operation. From sources who attended clandestine meetings, we know that the Strike Force included representatives of the Food and Drug Branch of the California State Department of Health, the USFDA, the California State Board of Medical Quality Assurance, the U.S. Postal Service, and the Federal Trade Commission. It is a reasonable assumption that policy decisions were made by senior government officials in various agencies, and those policies were carried out through the covert actions of the Strike Force, as outlined in the Pepper legislation, in the absence of Congressional approval.

An example of this covert action by the Strike Force is the disinformation inserted into Virginia Knauer's speech by Dr. Cort,

Deputy Director of the National Cancer Institute, alleging that Dr. Burton's vaccine used in his immune-system augmentation therapy (IAT) had been contaminated with the AIDS virus. This single statement of disinformation released to the press resulted in disastrous complications for Dr. Burton's patients and forced the temporary closure of his clinic in Freeport, Bahamas.

Another example can be found in the $500,000 grant awarded to attorney Grace Monaco and her company, Emprise, by the National Cancer Institute, to establish a data base on unproven cancer therapies, as was originally proposed in the Pepper legislation, and the subsequent misuse of the information contained therein to eliminate alternative practitioners and alternative cancer treatments.

A third example involves former FDA head Stuart Nightingale, who, at a House of Delegates meeting in Honolulu in 1984, put his foot into his mouth, saying, "We, [the FDA] cannot put these doctors using chelation therapy out of business by ourselves; we need the active assistance, participation, and cooperation of you, the American Medical Association, in order to do this."

Not only can government agencies be involved, but private voluntary organizations, such as the American Cancer Society, can also participate, at least in the spreading of disinformation. *USA Today* published on August 1, 1990, a "scoop" on the impending release of the OTA Unconventional Cancer Therapies Study:

> Unconventional cancer therapies are taken to task. Desperate cancer patients are paying up to $28 billion a year for untested and unproven treatments, says a new study being considered by a congressional panel. The report questions the scientific basis of such remedies, ranging from strict diets of fruits and vegetables and herbal mixtures, to human urine extracts, and coffee bean enemas.

USA Today then referred to a "500-page study by Congress's Office of Technology Assessment." Frank Wiewel, a leading alternative advocate and president of People Against Cancer, Inc., immediately knew something was fishy with the grossly-exaggerated estimate of $28 billion spent annually on "quack" remedies. He asked OTA Assistant Director Roger Herdman, M.D., if the final OTA report had any such figure and, if so, the source of the figure. Herdman replied,

> In a phone conversation today (Aug. 2) you asked whether the dollar figure (apparently ascribed to us) of $28 billion for

the cost of unconventional cancer treatments annually to U.S. cancer patients originated in any OTA work. It did not; it does not appear in our final review draft (of February 1990) or the final Technology Assessment Board copy of our report (of July 1990)—you yourself know that there is no dollar figure for annual U.S. unconventional cancer treatment costs.

We would be reluctant to give a figure as data are not available on which we could ground such an estimate. Thus we cannot support any figure, including $28 billion.

Wiewel then contacted *USA Today* reporter Sherry Jacobson, writer of the article, to find out where she had gotten the figure. Ms. Jacobson revealed that the figure came from the American Cancer Society, the sacred cow of all charities.

During the Christic Institute lawsuit attempting to tie a multitude of covert Central American activities into a single conspiracy, the term "secret team" was replaced in the Declaration of Plaintiffs Counsel by the term "Enterprise." Enterprise was the name given by the late CIA Director William Casey to describe an off-the-shelf organization, separate from the CIA but capable of carrying out all of the covert activities and functions of the CIA. By having operatives such as Gen. Secord and LTC Oliver North carry out covert activities under the banner of such an officially-independent organization, the government eludes responsibility for them. As the need arises, operations take on new names, which are merely the same organization in a different permutation. In much the same way, the Coordinating Conference on Health Information of the AMA became the National Council Against Health Fraud, another free-standing, off-the-shelf, independent operation providing lots of plausible deniability to the mother-organization, the AMA, which gave birth to it.

The Christic Institute's effort to tie all of the covert activities in Central America to a single conspiracy inevitably led to some internal inconsistencies and inaccuracies. The task, however, is made much easier in the case of our medical Strike Force, because all of their nefarious activities were laid out beforehand in the last meeting of the CCHI of the AMA, and, to a certain extent, in the legislation proposed by the late Congressman Pepper. They told us what they were going to do, and they did it.

Just as Enterprise's covert actions are abhorrent to a democratic society, so too are the existence of the Strike Force and its activities. Covert operations of this type are incompatible with an open and democratic society. There exists plenty of evidence that racketeers and thugs have engaged in illegal activities for purposes of obtaining power and money; but it is often hard to differentiate between random, independent activities and coordinated conspiracies. The British film *Hidden Agenda: Every Government Has One,* which won a 1990 Cannes Film Festival Jury Prize and whose plot involves crimes committed by government officials but blamed on rogue police officers and the IRA, is a good revelation of how government officials at the highest level can cross the line and engage in crimes on the pretext of doing "the greatest good for the greatest number." The film demonstrates the difficulty in distinguishing officially-sanctioned government activities from individual criminal actions, how they are not mutually exclusive, and how the border between them can be obscure.

Whenever a secret team emerges, such as the medical Strike Force, we must not overlook the system that spawned it. Confronting the system is a formidable, complex task, but one which must be tackled by first exposing the problem. We must search out the "root of all evil" which spawns the lies, deceit, and subterfuge. Our right to good health and fully productive lives is at risk, and we must find a way to secure it.

CHAPTER 4
DOCTOR HUNTING

"The highly trained medical professional is like an accessory to the vast pharmaceutical and health-care industries, as a stewardess is to a jet airliner and the aviation industry."
Ross Scholes
New Zealand health writer

A Canadian advocate for preventive medicine, Ron Dugas, asserts that citizens are prisoners of the pharmaceutical industry, and many suspect that the drug companies hold tremendous power over the medical profession, governments, and even citizens. Alternative-medicine advocates sense that conventional medicine has a monopoly in health care, a monopoly which is closely guarded by professional associations and regulatory bodies. While a profession, like a trade union, has a right to protect itself and its professional interests, the regulatory bodies are supposed to act in the interest of the public. There is a growing public awareness, however, that these bodies are safeguarding the monopoly interests of the profession under the guise of protecting the public.

Does the conventional medical profession have a closed shop in health practices? In the 19th century, Organized Med exerted strong political pressure to acquire more power for self-regulation. The federal government caved in and allowed medical practitioners to regulate themselves because politicians and bureaucrats lack expertise in the medical field and had difficulty understanding the complex technical questions involved. However, the present Canadian dilemma is described by H.L. LaFramboise, former Assistant Deputy Minister in the Health and Welfare Department:

> Figuratively speaking, each expert group has a mysterious "black bag" in which it carries the body of knowledge, peculiar to it. Society does not have access to the esoteric knowledge and language in that black bag, and relies on the elite experts to tell them, in words they can understand, what its content means. What they are told, of course, is that things are just dandy the way they are, and that reform will only work

to society's disadvantage.

The public and the government now realize that important public health questions can no longer be left to the conventional medical elite for at least three reasons:

1. Health care is now accepted as an essential public *service* for certain segments of the population.

2. Billions of tax dollars are invested in the health *sector,* so there should be public supervision over *spending.*

3. The medical profession faces a conflict of interest *when* it must create policy which could benefit society but hurt the profession.

In his book *The High Price of Health,* Jeffrey York boldly states the issue:

> The rhetoric about professional rights and freedom has obscured the fact that doctors are private businessmen who hold a monopoly over the provision of medical services.
>
> They wield extraordinary powers over the market for their services, and they enjoy the right to use hospitals which are paid for, in part, at public expense. Other monopolies such as AT&T and the Bell Telephone companies are carefully regulated by government, to ensure that the public is protected.
>
> The medical profession which provides essential public service and is funded, at least in part, by the taxpayer, cannot expect to be free from public regulation. Indeed, it is remarkable that the profession has escaped without public regulation for so long.
>
> Medicine has traditionally been a self-governing profession and doctors have assumed that this gives them an inherent right to be exempted from outside regulations. In fact, the power of self-government was delegated to the medical profession. It is a delegated privilege, not a divine right.

Ron Dugas describes the health industry in Canada in words that could just as easily describe our situation in the United States, saying, "They appear to be on a treadmill of still more drugs, surgery, and hospitals that create escalating health care costs." He goes on to describe the goals of the Canadian Holistic Medical Association:

We seek an alternative which is more effective and less expensive. We see that alternative in the development of preventive health care, and improved diet and nutrition, in exercise, and in medical and health practices which are less invasive, less toxic, and which give us access to a whole range of health promotion and restoration services. These are the services which deal with the whole person; body, mind, and spirit. These are the services provided by practitioners associated with the Canadian Holistic Medical Association.

THE STRIKE FORCE

Federal laws require public accountability for organizations to which federal government representatives belong as members in an official capacity. The Strike Force that Organized Medicine established in 1984 is able to get around this law by calling its meetings "conferences," which government representatives may attend as participants rather than as members.

In addition to covertly establishing a Strike Force, this group of organizations and their representatives openly established the proposed Information Network, which was also a major part of the defeated Pepper bill. This Information Network was taken over by the National Council Against Health Fraud (NCAHF), formerly known as the California Council Against Health Fraud.

There was, of course, no need to conceal the setting up of a central health-fraud information network at both the federal and state levels. This network was to include a computer hook-up between government computers used in criminal investigations and the computers used by the NCAHF in which they had inserted the names of individuals they had accused and judged guilty of health fraud, without any regard for due process.

This group began to meet on a regular basis beginning in May, 1984. The group has also managed to obtain free rent and free labor from Loma Linda University, a Seventh Day Adventist Institution, and continues to use its facilities to assist its intelligence network to gather information and to target practitioners who are using alternative or so-called unproven methods all across the nation.

The group met again, early in 1985, in Los Angeles. This meeting was also attended by representatives of the FDA, the Federal Trade Commission, and the Postal Service, among others. The fact that representatives of federal agencies have been involved in these covert activities is illegal.

TARGET: THE CHIROPRACTIC PROFESSION

The AMA Committee on Quackery was established by the AMA Board of Trustees in November, 1963. The purpose of this Committee was "to direct its attention to a study of the chiropractic problem." The AMA considered chiropractic a problem because chiropractors were taking business away from physicians. Dr. Joseph Sabatier of Louisiana played an important role in the establishment of the AMA Committee on Quackery.

Mr. H. Doyl Taylor was appointed Secretary of the Committee on Quackery. In January, 1971, Taylor sent a memo to the AMA Board stating, "Your Committee has considered its prime mission to be first the containment of chiropractic and ultimately the elimination of chiropractic."

Mr. Taylor was not a physician. He had been employed for ten years as the head of the AMA Headquarters Department of Investigation (DOI), during which time he accumulated massive files on various groups and individuals the AMA considered to be its enemies. Files were kept on Dr. Andrew Ivy, Dr. Wilhelm Reich, the National Health Federation, the International Association of Cancer Victims and Friends (recovered cancer patients of alternative physicians), Dr. Carlton Fredericks, and the Palmer Chiropractic College, among others. This department of the AMA also kept files on such subjects as health foods, vitamins, acupuncture, faith healing, and scientology.

Mr. Taylor's Department of Investigation conducted itself in the manner of a private CIA for the AMA. The staff of the Department of Investigation also became the staff of the Committee on Quackery when the Committee was established in November, 1963.

In the 1970s, Americans were treated to "dirty tricks" when the Nixon campaign planted false and misleading stories in the media to smear its opponents. But the Nixon campaign certainly did not invent this tactic. In fact, Nixon's defenders tried to deflect blame by pointing out that such procedures were commonplace in the political arena. Dirty tricks are by no means exclusive to politicians, however. Throughout the 20th century, elements in Organized Medicine have employed dirty tricks against practitioners of alternative health care, including medical doctors. Deceit was used to create a climate of public opinion regarding quackery which justified discrediting those practitioners. The AMA campaign to smear chiropractic during the '60s and '70s is an example of a well-organized dirty tricks campaign.

First the CCHI sent fictitious letters of inquiry to chiropractic colleges, attempting to entice these colleges into making medical claims which could then be turned over to postal inspectors as evidence of false and misleading advertising and mail fraud. They also sent undercover observers to chiropractic conventions to try to gather evidence of quackery. When the Department of Labor proposed a "Health Careers Guide Book" which included a chapter on chiropractic as a career, the AMA Committee on Quackery managed to get this chapter deleted. They also managed to falsify a study of chiropractic being conducted by Stanford Research Institute so that the results were negative. The scenario is ludicrous: The AMA paid for a study of chiropractic efficacy that was conducted by Stanford Research Institute and then it falsified the data to achieve negative results; and, although the AMA had paid for the study, it managed to get the Department of Health, Education, and Welfare of the federal government to accept it as independent research.

The libel and slander campaign of dirty tricks against the chiropractic profession continued well into the 1980s. The AMA was aware that it was engaging in a conspiracy to restrict free trade, which is totally illegal. The chiropractors obtained evidence of this conspiracy and sued the AMA. The Federal Trade Commission agreed with the chiropractors and ruled that the AMA was in violation of monopoly laws, in their attempts to eliminate the chiropractic profession. After a lengthy court battle, *Wilk v. AMA,* in 1987, Federal District Judge Susan Getzendanner ruled that the AMA had indeed led an effort to destroy the chiropractic profession by engaging in "systematic, long-term wrong-doing with the long-term intent to destroy a licensed profession." This was also the ruling in an anti-trust lawsuit filed in 1976.

Certainly the chiropractic doctors represent a departure from allopathic medicine (localized, disease treatment by drugs and surgery) because it is primarily manipulative medicine. The chiropractic approach—through diagnosis and procedures of spinal manipulation to alleviate vertebral subluxation and the resulting health benefits of restoring balance within the two branches of the autonomic nervous system, the sympathetic and the parasympathetic—is something of which opened-minded research scientists should take notice.

Shortly after the founding of the Committee on Quackery, another covert group was formed, also under the leadership of Mr. Taylor. This group was called the Coordinating Conference on Health Information, created in 1964. In contrast to the Committee on Quackery, this group operated in total secrecy. Just as the present

National Network or Clearinghouse for Information on Health Fraud, an open and official organization, is paired with the covert Strike Force, so the earlier group, the Committee on Quackery, operating openly, formed a subgroup of itself, the CCHI, to conduct covert activities.

The CCHI was made up of representatives of the AMA, the American Cancer Society, the American Pharmaceutical Association, the Arthritis Foundation, the Council of Better Business Bureaus, and government agencies such as the FDA, the U.S. Postal Service, and the Federal Trade Commission. In fact, in documents obtained from the AMA, one of the objectives of the CCHI was stated as "the establishment of a national clearinghouse of information on unproven methods of disease management." They preferred to do this under the aegis of the federal government, since a collection of data and derogatory information compiled by themselves and using funds from the AMA would clearly taint this information by the AMA's special interests. One goal of the CCHI was to remove that perception of bias. CCHI also had discussions about initiating criminal prosecution of those who have committed fraud and who practice quackery. The CCHI formally existed for ten years, all that time under the leadership of Mr. Taylor. It seemingly disbanded in 1974, about the same time that the Committee of Quackery was also formally disbanded.

Evidence, however, gathered by investigator P.J. Lisa indicates that the conspirators simply went underground. Lisa wrote in his book *Are you a Target for Elimination?*:

> In late 1974, in the last recorded minutes of any CCHI meeting, a memo was written by Taylor which said that at the May 1974 meeting, it was decided to compile a list of items for CCHI members, including the goals and objectives of CCHI, as well as its operating procedures. The entire document was written as the group was disbanding and turning over its functions to some other entity to carry on. At this particular meeting, it was also stated that the proceedings of the CCHI were for information of members only, and that the minutes should not formally be recorded.

It is Lisa's contention that the activities of the CCHI were turned over to the National and Regional Councils Against Health Fraud, in particular the California Council Against Health Fraud and the Lehigh Valley Committee Against Health Fraud in Pennsylvania. These Councils then became the lead organizers of the Network or

Clearinghouse for Information and the covert Strike Force. They had a number of secret meetings, according to documents discovered in Sacramento.

Also, an entire underground medical network, along with members of the U.S. Postal Service, the FDA, FTC and others, met in an effort to launch attacks against alternative practitioners. The chilling parallels between these underground networks and the CCHI are so close that this network was referred to by Lisa as the "shadow CCHI." The first official meeting of this group, under the rubric of Clearinghouse for Health Information Against Fraud, was held in May, 1984.

The National Council Against Health Fraud, which was the 1984 offspring of The California Council Against Health Fraud, and the Lehigh Valley Committee Against Health Fraud in Pennsylvania are unique organizations. They sound as if they are consumer organizations or advocates of consumers such as Ralph Nader and others. But when you analyze their make-up and how they came into existence, you soon realize that they don't represent consumers at all.

They represent the interests of a select group of health-care providers—physicians in the private practice of medicine—and they represent the interests of pharmaceutical manufacturers. In addition, they include representatives of federal agencies charged with regulatory responsibilities to protect the public. But even these latter representatives do not constitute the core or founding group of the organization. They are cooperating or collaborating members at best. Why does such an organization need to conduct many of these activities in secrecy? This raises suspicion that the organization is involved with activities other than what its name implies, protecting the consumer against health fraud.

Recently, investigative reporter Sharon Bloyd-Peshkin described the large spectrum of quackbusters. She detailed how what emerged in 1977 as a successor to the AMA's Coordinating Conference on Health Information (CCHI, which served as the AMA's "CIA") was the California Committee Against Health Fraud, which was founded by William Jarvis, Ph.D. This organization later became the National Council Against Health Fraud. According to George P. McAndrews, who was counsel for the chiropractors in their case against the AMA, "When the lawsuits started popping out, the AMA and the medical societies needed a spokesperson to talk on quackery." What has emerged, however, since 1977, when the CCHI was disbanded, is the development of a network of propaganda organizations which not only engage in spreading disinformation, but also send their members into court as so-called expert witnesses and engage in overt and covert activities to protect the economic interests of the medico-pharmaceutical and hospital-health insurance industrial complexes. The AMA in the past, for example, has opposed all non-traditional treatments, including chiropractic, optometry, midwifery, acupuncture, chelation therapy, and self-care. In 1977, therefore, the NCAHF began to speak for, or become a mouthpiece for, the medical establishment.

Investigative reporter Peshkin published her article in the August, 1991, issue of *Vegetarian Times* entitled "The Health-Fraud Cops—Are the Quackbusters Consumer Advocates or Medical Mc-Carthyites?" In this excellent article, she describes the Network, which consists of these groups:

—The National Council Against Health Fraud (NCAHF)

—The American Council on Science and Health (ACSH)

—The Committee for the Scientific Investigation of Claims of the Paranormal (CSICOP)

—The Consumer Health Information Research Institute (CHIRI)

Peshkin wrote, "They each have their own quack-busting agenda . . . leaders of each organization are on the boards of nearly every other affiliate group."

The NCAHF has chapters in thirteen states and receives funds from pharmaceutical manufacturers. It is discussed in more detail elsewhere in this book.

The ACSH receives most of its funds from industry, *e.g.* Dow Chemical, the National Agricultural Chemicals Association, E.I. duPont de Nemours and Co., Montsanto Co., and the Procter and Gamble Fund. It has received grants from the National Dairy Council and the American Meat Institute, Burger King, Oscar Meyer Foods, Hershey Foods Fund, Frito-Lay and Land O'Lakes. Not surprisingly, it questions all claims that pesticides and food additives are harmful, praises fast foods, and defends the use of hormones in cattle.

Because ACSH's sources of funds are easily discernible, and they don't deny them, it is a fair assumption that they are probably not involved in covert activities and/or racketeering. They simply take industry's side in certain disputes and twist the results of scientific studies to suit their own purposes, with the possible exception of defending cigarette manufacturers.

Such is not the case with NCAHF and with the newcomer on the block, the CHIRI. It is nearly impossible to determine where their money comes from; it is even more difficult to determine the financial support for individual quackbusters, such as Victor Herbert, Stephen Barrett, and John Renner. The *Vegetarian Times* exposé is conspicuous for its absence of information on the funding sources for these organizations and individuals, in marked contrast to the openly-acknowledged business and industrial supporters for the ACSH.

The CSICOP organization is targeted against faith healers and other proponents of spiritual healing. It also discredits extra-sensory perception and paranormal experiences.

The CHIRI has for its constituency the health insurance industry. It purports to serve that industry in an advisory capacity, by approving or disapproving a particular treatment provided by a health-care provider. It plans to serve as a health-insurance consultant regarding the legitimacy of certain disabilities and health practitioners. An example of an "illegal" disability would be chronic fatigue syndrome. CHIRI is also said to have a computerized list of more than 40,000 American physicians and other medical practitioners who are suspected of using "questionable medical practices." Dr. John Renner of Kansas City, who is the head of CHIRI, recently gave a deposition under oath, during which he admitted having a list of physicians and other health care providers who practice medicine using alternative, or what he calls "unproven," therapies. He allegedly reports those practitioners to state medical boards; he also admitted that he advises the insurance companies not to pay for their treatments.

There has been one improvement, however slight. When the 1990 National Health Fraud Conference was again held in Kansas City, as it was two years prior, it was not co-sponsored by the FDA. There had been complaints from the health-freedoms organizations, after the last conference, that by serving as a co-sponsor, the FDA, at taxpayer expense, was taking sides and promoting one side of what should have been a debate. The FDA was accused of siding with the medical-drug industrial complex. Now, they do it on the QT.

John Renner, M.D., also head of the Midwest Council Against Health Fraud in Kansas City and the contact person for the scheduled meeting, stated, "there will be plenty of FDA there." The AIDS Coalition to Unleash Power (ACT UP) was also there and disrupted the meetings and protested the actions of the Councils and the Strike Force. Unfortunately, on TV and in other media, these demonstrators came off simply as rabble-rousers.

There are two sides or two arms of this power group. Already mentioned is the dominant arm: Organized Med. But there is another, a left arm to this conspiracy.

This left arm is made up of organizations such as Emprise (pronounced ahm prise), which was founded in the 1980s and operated until 1991. *Emprise* is a French word for "control or consolidation of power," and "influence." Attorney Grace Powers Monaco, who also represented the American Cancer Society in their litigation against the proponents of Laetrile, headed Emprise. She apparently recognized early on the monetary rewards from engaging in so-called quackbusting in the early 1980s, and she went out on her own and organized Emprise. This company evolved into one which related more to the health-insurance industry than to the Councils Against Health Fraud and the State Boards of Medical Examiners. Although this left arm of the conspiracy, Emprise, was not as strong as the right arm, it actively sought out government grants, collaborated with the insurance companies, and waged some successful litigation, as in the case of the maligned Laetrile.

Emprise received a $500,000 grant from the National Cancer Institute, officially to establish a data bank on unproven cancer and AIDS therapies and unofficially to facilitate a legal war against the proponents, manufacturers, and distributors of substances which they consider unproven remedies or treatments for cancer, AIDS, and other diseases. Emprise did not follow through on data about AIDS, presumably because the threat of demonstrations on the part of the organization known as ACT UP caused Ms. Monaco to reconsider, withdraw her application for a heftier grant and put this campaign on the back burner. After all, previous demonstrations had forced the FDA to back away from their original plans to seize substances not approved for clinical use in the United States, imported from other countries by AIDS patients. The demonstrations had forced the FDA to acknowledge that it is difficult to prohibit a U.S. citizen who is suffering from an incurable disease from using a substance which is licensed and approved in another country, in an effort to save his own life. According to R.H. Rogers of Vancouver, such a prohibition would be denying patients "the right to try, before they die."

Data collection and information gathering is one thing, not necessarily offensive in and of itself; but using that data for harassment, persecution, and disinformation purposes is something else and should not be tolerated. Today, society needs to be aware of the ever-greater potential for such offenses; in the health field, the use of modern computers facilitates the persecution of alternative practitioners.

Following is a data-collection form used by the National Council Against Health Fraud for "Suspected Nutritional Mismanagement." It is self-explanatory.

REPORT OF SUSPECTED
NUTRITIONAL MISMANAGEMENT

Code# or Patient's Name: Date:
Age: Sex: M F   City   State

How did the patient hear about this practitioner?

Does the patient now believe (s)he was victimized? Yes No Unsure

Does the patient appear to have suffered any physical or psychological harm as a result of this therapy? Yes No
Too soon to tell If yes, describe briefly:

Practitioner's name: Phone:
Address:

Is this practitioner a licensed health professional? No   OD DC RD Psychologist DDS RN PT Other

Did the practitioner appear to the patient to be diagnosing and/or prescribing for a specific symptom of complaint? Yes No Uncertain

What was the approximate cost of this practitioner's services?

What was the approximate cost of this practitioner's products?

Did the patient's health insurance company reimburse the

patient or this provider for questionable tests, therapies or
nutrition counseling? Yes No Uncertain If yes, approximately what amount?

Were any of the following questionable methods of nutri-
tional assessment utilized?
Hair Mineral Analysis Cytotoxic Test Psychic Powers
Applied Kinesiology/Muscle Testing Dark Field live Cell
Analysis Computerized Nutrient Deficiency Test
Other:

Was a questionable nutritional therapy prescribed or
recommended?
Megadoses of vitamins Fasting Inappropriate Diet
HCL Unbalanced diet Laetrile (B-17) Pangamate (B-15)
Enzymes Excessive Minerals Chelated Minerals Oral
Chelation Product Unproven Weight Loss Aid Glandular
Product(s) Amino Acid(s) Protein Pollen Detoxification
Spirulina Herbs Other, Describe briefly

Did the practitioner claim to be a nutrition expert? Yes No,
if yes, where were they trained?

Report taken by:

May we contact you for more information? No Yes,
Phone:

Similar data was gathered by Monaco's company, Emprise, with
the $500,000 grant she was awarded by the National Cancer Institute
to establish a Data Bank on Unproven Cancer Treatments.

At the same time that Monaco was engaging in such supposedly
objective data gathering, she was, through Emprise, serving as a
consultant to members of the insurance industry in cases where they
refused to pay for alternatives, often called "experimental therapies"
by insurance companies. Aetna, one of its biggest clients, has a
reputation for taking health-insurance policy holders to court over
any kind of disputed claim, not just experimental or unproven
therapies. Disputes over managed care, such as in-patient versus
outpatient treatment of alcoholism, for example, are often settled by
lawyers; the insured parties often cannot afford litigation and therefore lose by default.

AETNA "SLAP SUITS" DOCTOR BURZYNSKI

A "slap suit" is filed by a big corporation which wants to get an agitator or activist, who is opposing it in some way, off its back, so to speak. It stops the activist in his tracks and usually prevents him from demonstrating, even though the suit is frivolous in nature and substance. Aetna filed such a suit, a RICO suit, against Dr. Burzynski and the Burzynski Research Institute, Inc., in Houston, Texas. Dr. Burzynski, for some years, has offered an effective, non-toxic alternative cancer therapy which is based on the administration of "antineoplastons," which are substances found in the urine of cancer patients. Grace Powers Monaco and Emprise widely publicized Aetna's position in the alert they distributed. The alert was widely circulated to individuals who do either scientific research or business with Burzynski Research Institute and to government agencies, for the purpose of discrediting the Burzynski Research Institute. How can Monaco serve as a consulting attorney for Aetna in this instance and be fair and objective about the alternative cancer therapies for which Aetna does not want to pay? It is unconscionable that Monaco and Emprise be awarded a $500,000 grant from the National Cancer Institute to set up a data base on unproven cancer therapies, while simultaneously lobbying against the successful Dr. Burzynksi and antineoplastons, one of the unproven methods on which they are "objectively" collecting information. Dr. Burzynski confronted NCI officials about Monaco's activities, but NCI did nothing to alter her funding or to curtail her activities. Both Dr. Wu and Dr. Browder of NCI seemed either unable or unwilling to call a halt to these questionable activities, despite gross conflict of interest. Dr. Wu and Dr. Browder of NCI are hardly unethical government officials. They appear to be controlled by official NCI and NIH policy, set by other higher-ups and predecessors. A federal court recently dismissed Aetna's RICO suit against Burzynski Research Institute, Inc., and Burzynski Research Institute has brought suit against Aetna, their attorneys, Emprise, and Grace Monaco under the same RICO statute. Peter Mantius, staff writer for *The Atlanta Journal and Constitution*, wrote an article which appeared on September 18, 1989, entitled "Aetna Accused of Conspiring to Cut Payments on Claims." In the article, Mantius stated:

> Two routine lawsuits charging Aetna Casualty and Surety Co. with failure to pay small medical claims have mushroomed into a full-scale legal crisis for the company...The cases could have been averted if Aetna hadn't refused to pay

medical claims totaling less than $3,000...Now Aetna stands accused in the suits of a conspiracy to cut payments arbitrarily on legitimate claims and of hiding court-ordered documents.

HAS IT COME TO THIS—A DING-DONG INDEX?

The National Council Against Health Fraud has taken its data gathering one step further. In cooperation with other groups, such as the National Health Insurance Association of America, and Emprise, it has developed two indices to classify alternative practitioners. The first is called the Notoriety Index for visibility or profile; the second is called the Ding Dong Index for deviation from orthodox medical practice. On a scale from 1 to 20, for example, New York alternative practitioner Warren Levin might have a Notoriety Index (N.I.) of 17; and on a scale of from 1 to 10, his Ding Dong Index (D.D.) might be, say, a 7. We are tempted to find this situation laughable until we remember the purpose of these non-science (nonsense) indices—the destruction of doctors who hold "the keys to the kingdom" for safe, successful treatments of chronic degenerative diseases.

CHAPTER 5
DOCTOR BASHING

THE CASES OF HOXSEY AND IVY

Perhaps the most colorful battle between Organized Med and the alternative medicine medical movement was the riotous drama played out between Dr. Fishbein of the AMA (who had never practiced medicine a day in his life) and a determined son of a country veterinarian. This conflict over alternative methods, which did not even involve a licensed physician, is brought to the reader's attention to point out how a simple remedy can have a strong effect on certain cancers. Moreover, it is significant that the AMA was determined to confiscate the formula and resorted to great extremes to try to get it.

Neither the veterinarian, Dr. John Hoxsey, nor his son Harry ever pretended that they were licensed physicians. In fact, the remarkable Harry Hoxsey fit the image of the proverbial quack with a snake-oil remedy that duped desperate cancer patients. He also looked the part of the stereotypical red-neck with only a high-school education. But reality was quite different. The herbal formulas developed by his father John were so effective in remissing certain forms of officially diagnosed cancer that the AMA allegedly went all out to get hold of them.

Dr. John Hoxsey discovered these herbal formulas and developed them with his expertise in veterinary medicine. Dr. Hoxsey noticed that his favorite horse had developed a cancerous lesion on his foreleg. Unable to shoot the beast, he turned the beloved animal out into a separate pasture, to live out his last days out of his master's sight. Several weeks later, Hoxsey went to retrieve the animal's body, only to find him perfectly healthy and in high spirits. Joyful and stunned, the vet began a critical study of the animal's craving for certain herbs and grassy plants in the unused pasture. Scientifically, he investigated their ingredients.

Using his observations, he developed two tonics, one taken by mouth and the other topically applied to skin malignancies. In time, he began administering series of applications to local people with medically-diagnosed cases of cancer. After a certain number of applications, the malignancies decreased in size, and some of them disappeared. Word spread, and to accommodate the vast patient load,

Hoxsey and his licensed medical staff opened several clinics, the most famous in Dallas. Hoxsey advertised on the radio, and people came to Dallas from all over the U.S. and other Western countries. Numerous patients attained long-term remissions, even cures. The younger Hoxsey eventually wrote a book, aptly entitled *You Don't Have to Die!*

On his death bed, John Hoxsey passed on the herbal formulas, having his son promise to provide the remedies to all who needed and asked for them, even if they could not afford to pay. So commissioned by his father, the bold-mannered son faced the onslaught of Organized Med and the challenge that lasted to his death by prostrate cancer (which could not be cured with the formulas that worked so well for other types of cancer).

Dr. Morris Fishbein held a powerful public relations position within AMA as editor of all their publications. The system, in the manner of tyrannical political governments, was simple and straightforward. If anyone within the AMA hierarchy disagreed with the unscrupulous Fishbein—if he crossed Fishbein—he was banished. So many good doctors within the organization who saw Fishbein's vices kept silent or were booted out.

Among his many duties, Dr. Fishbein served as a spokesman on quackery and as a broker between the drug industry, the AMA and the researchers who discovered drug remedies. If blessed by the AMA, a new drug could reap tremendous profit for all interested parties. Collaborators in the FDA could expect lucrative post-retirement jobs, while collaborators within the universities could expect substantial research grants.

Shrewd Fishbein set the agenda within the federal government for the FDA to identify individuals and their treatments which were quackery or health fraud. Through its legislative authority, liberally interpreted, the FDA could be "sicced," like a well-trained dog, on any alternative practitioner or manufacturer. The FDA used a number of techniques, including threats, intimidation, confiscation, libel, slander and other forms of harassment.

Had Dr. Fishbein or others from the scientific community interviewed Hoxsey's patients and observed pre- and post-treatment photographs of their lesions, they would have suspected that the mixtures contained ingredients which had anti-tumor or anti-cancer activity, and that the identification of these compounds or chemical ingredients could be the basis of a scientific inquiry. Since there was little or no damage to normal tissues, they might have suspected the ingredients were stimulating the body's natural defenses or the immune system. These investigations would have focused cancer research on the immune system, where we have circuitously arrived sixty years later.

Many of the specific plants, some of which had been used in medical systems indigenous to American Indian and other cultures, in both of the Hoxsey mixtures were in fact subsequently shown to possess anti-tumor or anti-cancer activity, by researchers at none other than the National Cancer Institute.

But the record indicates that it was more than medical arrogance or ignorance of the value of the formulas that led Fishbein to lead a campaign against Harry Hoxsey. Most likely it was a deliberate vendetta. Hoxsey allegedly had rejected an offer from Fishbein and the pharmaceutical industry to take over and commercialize his herbal remedies on a large scale. Fishbein and his associates, therefore, apparently actually investigated the Hoxsey remedies and concluded that they had clinical value.

The AMA met with Hoxsey and proposed that he turn over the formulas to the AMA and an unnamed pharmaceutical company, for which they would then pay him a royalty that would begin in ten years. He was to have no say in the price of the mixtures to patients, nor in how they were to be further processed or prepared for use in treating patients. Nor was he to have any input in their clinical application. As a final injustice, there would be no provisions made to provide the remedies to those who could not afford to pay.

Hoxsey refused, and Fishbein and FDA officials waged a propaganda war against Hoxsey, his clinic in Dallas, and the licensed health professionals who staffed the clinic because they saw the efficacy of this cancer treatment. It has been observed that Morris Fishbein, clever and unscrupulous, was as effective at propaganda as was Adolf Hitler's Goebbels. The libel and slander rained down, eventually forcing the clinic in Dallas to close and to subsequently move to Tijuana, Mexico. To this day, the clinic operates under the administration of Hoxsey's registered nurse, Mildred Nelson, with a staff of physicians who continue to dispense the original formulas as well as other non-toxic procedures with impressive results for a number of types of cancers. Mildred Nelson has remained steadfast in her commitment to the Hoxsey methods because, before she joined Mr. Hoxsey's clinic in Dallas, she had been strong skeptic of the success stories and had bet him that if the Hoxsey formulas could reverse her mother's terminal cancer she would work as an R.N. for him. Hoxsey won the bet upon her mother's cancer remission, and the loyal nurse continues her professional calling for American cancer patients, ironically not in their own country. An interesting footnote to the Hoxsey story: before his death, Dr. Fishbein admitted that he had lied to destroy the work of the Hoxsey family, who had worked so valiantly to treat many terminally ill cancer patients with herbal formulas that the AMA had tried so hard to obtain.

Illich says that "professional classism" is even worse than racism, and that it is a major impediment to education. Discounting Hoxsey's claim that Fishbein tried to buy him out, had Fishbein visited Hoxsey's clinic and talked to some of his patients, he might have been convinced that there was something to what we now know as immune system augmentation therapy. An example of this successful therapy is the six-year survivor of a malignant tumor. After treatment at NIH by incomplete surgical removal, the patient underwent direct injection into the brain of his own immune cells, which had been activated in the test tube in the laboratory. Clinical observation by Fishbein and others might have opened up new avenues for research, in addition to the well-traveled road which has led to the current overemphasis on chemotherapy. Chemotherapy has not worked on most of the cancers which develop later in life, after the age of 40. The pharmaceutical industry, of course, has favored and poured money into the development of new drugs for chemotherapy.

The Hoxsey-Fishbein conflict repeated itself in the 1950s when the AMA fought Dr. Ivy over the anti-cancer drug Krebeiozen. Once again, an offer of a buy-out, which was rejected by Dr. Ivy, was followed by a vicious attack by the AMA on Dr. Ivy and Krebeiozen.

The rejection of alternative modalities is based on emotionalism, fueled by professional classism and backed up with money and dirty tricks. Not the least bit scientific, the wise guys are unwilling to make observations of their own. Even Sir Isaac Newton had to see the apple fall, first, before he formulated his theories about the laws of gravity. He could not have just imagined that it happened. Nor could he have said that it did not fall, if he had not seen it. Logic in medicine, however, is often displaced by prejudice. Is this because of the God-like attributes assigned by society to doctors, or which doctors assign to themselves? "They may not think they are God; they just think they ought to be!"

DESTROY A TOP SCIENTIST—NO PROBLEM

The same confrontational strategies were used against Dr. Andrew Ivy, developer of Krebiozen, another non-toxic, apparently effective cancer remedy. The AMA officials and representatives from the drug companies tried to cut a deal with this inventor, just as they had with Mr. Hoxsey. Dr. Ivy stood his ground as well. When he refused, and only after he had refused, the AMA and FDA started their attack. It was the malicious ruination of Dr. Ivy to which Mr. Fitzgerald, first quoted in Chapter 1, referred when he spoke of money being "thrown around like confetti at a state fair." The campaign succeeded in destroying Dr. Ivy, a first-rate scientist who had better success at cancer therapy than orthodox doctors. Instead of receiving deserved accolades, Dr. Ivy was branded for the public to see as just another clever quack.

Of course the underlying reason for destroying or hiding innovative methods of cancer therapy is the brutal, economic turf war for profit. And, once again, the FDA cooperated with the unscrupulous Dr. Fishbein and his AMA, to control and monopolize new, safe, and effective patentable treatments in collaboration with the drug companies.

Whether or not the involved thugs would have actually put those non-toxic therapies out on the market will never be known. They certainly tried to get the formulas, and, when they could not obtain them, they tried to made sure no one else would ever use them. So, whether or not they would have overcharged for the therapies or simply eliminated them, these men acted with no conscience; as individuals holding medical licenses, they betrayed their Hippocratic Oath.

THE ATTACKS CONTINUE

Today, some sixty years later, these "wise-guys" and thugs are still at it behind the scenes. They involve licensed doctors as well as Ph.D.'s with the same goals as Dr. Fishbein's—to keep drug sales and profits up. Their work was facilitated by the AMA helping to establish the National and Regional Councils Against Health Fraud. These councils, similar in concept to what the late William Casey referred to as a Free-Standing Enterprise to take over some of the CIA's covert activities, help to coordinate the Strike Force of the medical field.

The actual "hit-squads" in the cases of targeted physicians are orchestrated through the Federation of State Boards of Medical Examiners. Wise Guy members from each of the state boards are contacted. Then, a letter of complaint against the targeted physician is usually written by one of the members of the regional or national councils. One member of the Oregon State Board was quoted as saying, "You'd be surprised how easy it is to get an alternative practitioner!"

Next, insurance companies and Medicare are contacted, usually by officials of the FDA or the Health Care Financing Administration, or even higher up in Health and Human Services, at the request of members of the national or regional councils (NCAHF) and the involved state board of medical examiners. Insurance companies and Medicare are directed to deny claim from the targeted doctor who is allegedly doing wrong by using experimental or unproven therapies.

If that doctor is using certain equipment or procedures not yet approved by FDA, such as intravenous administration of ozone, the FDA may intervene directly. Also, at the request of the FDA, the IRS, a remarkable example of unbridled government power, is directed to audit the finances of the targeted doctor.

And the IRS has its share of integrity slips. Chris Wallace of CBS News has said, "There is evidence that arrogance, corruption, abuse of power are now widespread" in the IRS.

Georgia Congressman Gus Barnard investigated the IRS for two years and reported, "After we finally got into it, we found evidence of wrong-doing in San Francisco, Chicago, Cincinnati, Atlanta, the nation's capital, Dallas, all across the country." Barnard's sub-committee heard testimony that in Los Angeles the chief criminal investigator for the IRS had harassed one company at the urging of a rival firm that had offered him a job. In Chicago, IRS employees turned in a top official for accepting gratuities from a taxpayer; the IRS employee informants were demoted for turning him in. Citizens who heard of the investigation offered their horror stories to Barnard's committee. "We must have received at least 4,000-5,000 letters from citizens with complaints about the IRS," Barnard observed.

IRS wrong-doing should not be too surprising. With 20,000 employees, it is the largest and possibly the most powerful law enforcement agency in the country. The IRS can acquire sensitive information from banks or employers without a warrant. It can seize assets without a court order. If a citizen challenges the IRS, the burden of proof is on the citizen, not the IRS.

Even senators and congressmen have come under the power of the IRS. In the 1960s, Missouri Senator Edward Long investigated the agency's use of wiretaps and bugs. Information on Long's finances was leaked to *Life Magazine,* and the Senator was defeated for re-election.

In the 1970s, it was New Mexico Senator Joseph Montoya's turn to announce his investigation of the IRS. The agency promptly looked into his tax records, which were later reported in *The Washington Post.* He too was defeated for re-election.

Certainly the IRS needs special powers to collect nearly a trillion dollars annually in taxes. But what happens when certain IRS employees or administrators lose sight of their professional mission and abuse power? To whom do they answer?

Undercover agents are sent into the physician's offices, posing as patients, to gather data and information which may be used against the physician in a formal hearing before the State Board. In some cases these agent "patients" are encouraged to initiate malpractice suits which are paid for, in part, by the State Board. So, we have a legally-constituted body, a State Board of Medical Examiners (a major complainer about the rising costs of malpractice-insurance premiums), instigating malpractice suits against other physicians, who represent the competition and whose alternative therapies they would like to destroy.

It is common knowledge that when a Regional Council on Health Fraud is formed, the chairperson who is recruited is asked to swear to an oath of secrecy. This requirement indicates that the Council's business may be more than eliminating health fraud—perhaps eliminating health-promoting medicine.

To be against health fraud is to be for motherhood and apple pie. Who could support health fraud? This universal disdain for health fraud provides an ideal "cover" for implementing strategies to control medical practice by maintaining the status quo, thus eliminating competition to maintain high profit levels for both the medical profession and the drug companies. In effect:

1. Prescription drugs are preferred to less toxic, equally effective, natural remedies,and

2. Narcotics and tranquilizers are advocated for pain relief, instead of the use of acupuncture, acupressure, the injection of trigger points with local anesthetic, massage therapy, stress reduction, and relaxation techniques.

In various combinations, the alternative methods are superior solutions for controlling and living with pain.

"SORE THROAT" IN THE FDA

Much of our recent information about the involvement of the FDA comes from the public record in openly-stated campaigns jointly undertaken by the FDA, the AMA, and the Councils on Health Fraud. They have held a number of conferences around the country. In March, 1990, the rascals put together a list of ten most common health frauds, with EDTA chelation therapy ranking number seven on that list. But at the same time, another branch of the

FDA had approved an IND (Investigative New Drug) for clinical studies to evaluate the effectiveness and the proper dosage of EDTA to be used in the treatment of peripheral vascular disease. This branch of the FDA, Cardio-Renal, had agreed to call a halt to negative information campaigns, as long as the IND was in force and clinical research was in progress. It doesn't matter that the right hand of this agency doesn't coordinate with the left hand, since all four of their paws are firmly planted in the pharmaceutical industry trough.

Our need for an in-depth source of information about the FDA has been met by an informant. Dr. Sterling M. Planters of Michigan has been in touch with an unnamed informant, an official of the FDA. Let us dub this informant Sore Throat, our counterpart to the mysterious Deep Throat in the Nixon Administration Watergate Scandal.

The Watergate informant Deep Throat advised "follow the money" to determine who is behind a conspiracy." So advises our Sore Throat. It is widely believed that the Councils Against Health Fraud are funded at least indirectly by the pharmaceutical industry; various food companies are also involved. Some honestly believe they are contributing to a worthwhile cause to eliminate health fraud. There are those among them, however, who know exactly what they are contributing to. It is their intent to eliminate the competition, just as it was the intent of the auto industry to eliminate public transportation when the American auto industry was in its heyday.

But in medicine we are dealing with a life and death matter— human health. Dr. Fishbein and company stymied a logical course for cancer research for sixty years. The anti-chelation forces—the NCAHF, the American Heart Association—-all claimed that they already knew the answers, that they had reviewed enough literature to determine that chelation did not work. Of course, they conducted no controlled clinical trials themselves. A careful review of their statements indicate that they never actually investigated whether chelation therapy worked or not. They simply reviewed the literature and formulated a position statement.

The records show an ongoing strategy of harassment by certain members of the medical establishment, and of misleading the public, saying that chelation is dangerous and a fraud. Their unscrupulous conduct may be illegal with regard to Federal Trade Commission regulations, and people are dying as a result.

Why so? Profit!

For whom? For certain health care providers; for pharmaceutical manufacturers of the newer cardiac drugs such as the beta-blockers and calcium channel blockers; and those who perform surgical procedures such as coronary artery bypass graft and procedures performed during cardiac catheterization, such as balloon angioplasty. A scandal indeed.

Meanwhile, these same State Boards of Medical Examiners have been pressuring state legislators to give them more power and more immunity from lawsuits. The Boards claim they need this immunity in order to more efficiently bring before them and prosecute those physicians who are repeatedly sued for malpractice and, presumably, are responsible in large part for the increasing rates of malpractice insurance.

In reality, these doctors are rarely brought before the Boards; recall from Chapter I that 60% of the Boards' efforts are focused on dealing with impaired physicians (usually from chemicals). The remaining 40% of their time involves "doctor hunting" for physicians using alternative therapies, usually for chronic conditions (80% of our industrial society's illnesses), that deviate from traditional drug-prescription medical practice.

Most legislators have legal backgrounds and are attorneys. They have little or no knowledge of clinical medicine and tend to leave regulatory agencies such as the State Boards of Medical Examiners to regulate themselves; afterwards, they tend to accept or rubber-stamp the Boards' decisions.

Because of this, most physicians who are falsely accused and brought before Boards have little or no chance of winning their cases at the Board level. The pattern around the country has been that they have to lose first at the Board hearing level, in order to get into a real court of law, where they might have a chance of winning their case and achieving some sort of justice.

AN OREGON DOCTOR SUES HIS SUPERIORS AND WINS

Recently, the U.S. Supreme Court decided a landmark case in which an Oregon physician sued the credentialing board of a local hospital, claiming that his hospital privileges were revoked because of the influence of other physicians on the staff, with whom he was competing for patients. The Court's decision stated that the physician had a right to sue the members of the Board, because they had gone beyond their authority as a credentialing body and had been using their authority as a means of eliminating competition.

This decision, hopefully, may set a precedent for other state boards and legislators. As long as the state legislators take it for granted that the board members are honorable men with no "wise guys" among them, they will allow this abuse of power to continue.

PART 2
ORGANIZED MEDICINE:
THE MOST POWERFUL AMERICAN LOBBY

CHAPTER 6
GOING FOR THE KILL

A GOOD DENTIST LOSES HIS LICENSE

The field of dentistry can also discriminate against doctors whose practices may deviate from the norm, regardless of how advantageous or effective the alternative therapy may be.

It is a well-known fact that the mercury used in dental fillings is a highly toxic substance. It is not known exactly how toxic it is, but it is known that it is more toxic than lead, cadmium, or arsenic and can penetrate all living cells of the human body. The use of mercury in fillings increases the health risk to patients, dentists, and dental personnel. So why was a dentist in New York charged with professional misconduct (he was accused of practicing medicine) for replacing a patient's mercury fillings with less harmful composite materials? And why was his license to practice dentistry revoked?

A 1990 issue of the American Dental Association's *ADA News* carried an article written by Daniel McCann entitled "Dentist Accused of Practicing Medicine: Dental License Revoked for Removing an Amalgam." The New York Dental Board revoked the license of a dentist charged with practicing medicine by removing a patient's dental amalgam in order to cure the patient of arthritis-like arm and leg pain. The Board's March 9, 1990, decision cited nine counts of professional misconduct against Dr. Joel M. Berger of Bayside, New York, for the treatment he provided a patient in 1984. In its investigation, the state found that in April, 1984, Dr. Berger reviewed the patient's medical history and concluded that her amalgam fillings were the source of her symptoms of rheumatoid arthritis. Dr. Berger then conducted tests for mercury vapor and electric current in the patient's mouth and told her that, as she chewed food, mercury was released from the amalgam and was poisoning her. With the patient's consent, Dr. Berger removed her ten amalgam fillings, replaced them with composite materials, and assured her that in six months her arm and leg pain would be greatly reduced.

The Dental Board's fact-finding committee stated in July of 1989 that "[t]he evidence and testimony overwhelmingly proved that Dr. Berger's testing was beyond the scope of dental practice and his treatment had no basis in scientific fact."

In addition, in 1986 the ADA House of Delegates adopted a resolution which said in part:

> Based on current documented scientific research, the conclusions of conferences and symposiums on the biocompatibility of metallic restorative material, and upon the joint reports of the Council on Dental Materials, Instruments and Equipment and the Council on Dental Therapeutics of the Association, the continued use of dental amalgam as a restorative material does not pose a health hazard to the non-allergic patient.

Moreover, the ADA Council on Ethics, Bylaws, and Judicial Affairs stated in an advisory opinion:

> Based on available scientific data, the ADA has determined through the adoption of resolution 42 H 1986, that the removal of amalgam restorations from the non-allergic patient for the alleged purpose of removing toxic substances from the body, when such treatment is performed solely at the recommendation or suggestion of the dentist, is improper and unethical.

Dr. Joel Berger lost his license to practice dentistry in New York State. His legal fees were so high that Dr. Berger elected to go to law school for three years and is now representing himself in a lawsuit against the board to regain his license.

Now let me tell you about a friend of mine. Sandra Denton, M.D., is a board-certified specialist in emergency medicine. I first met her when we were both on the program for the spring meeting of the American College for the Advancement of Medicine (ACAM) held in New Orleans in May, 1988. I will always remember her remarks in a conversation which included Dr. Warren Levin of New York City. Dr. Denton stated that her attendance at academy meetings had changed her entire professional approach, and if she had to return to practicing medicine the way she used to (listening to a patient's history and recording his/her symptoms, examining the patient and then writing a prescription for a drug), she would quit medicine all together. Sandy has not only achieved proficiency in alternative medicine, but has also specialized in mercury toxicity.

In the June, 1989, issue of *Health Consciousness* magazine, Dr. Denton wrote:

> In 1988, scrap dental amalgam was declared a hazardous

waste material by the Environmental Protection Agency. Once a doctor removes an amalgam filling from your mouth and places it in a tray, it once again becomes a hazardous material. I ask the reader—What is it about the mouth that makes the same item non-toxic?

Mercury comprises over 50% of the "silver" dental filling. Researchers from all over the world have measured mercury vapor coming off the filling, particularly after stimulation through chewing, bruxism (grinding of the teeth), hot and/or acidic food, and tooth brushing.

Every scientist knows that mercury is a poison. It is in fact, as Sharma and Oversteiner have stated, "a strong protoplasmic poison that penetrates all living cells of the human body. mercury is a powerful biological poison with no necessary biological function." Mercury is even more toxic than lead, cadmium, and arsenic!

How then can we be so certain that the amount coming out of our dental filling is insignificant? Drs. Thomas Clarkson and John Hursh of the University of Rochester, School of Medicine, Department of Toxicology, and Drs. Magnus Nylander and Lars Friberg of the Karolinska Institute of Stockholm, Sweden, concluded from their research, "The release of mercury from dental amalgam makes the predominant contribution to human exposure to inorganic mercury, including mercury vapor in the general population."

Based on the known toxic potential of mercury and its documented release from dental amalgams, usage of mercury-containing amalgam increases the health risk of patients, dentists, and dental personnel.

Autopsy studies have shown a positive correlation between the number of occlusal surfaces of dental amalgam and mercury levels in the brain and kidney cortex. Research has also shown mercury dental amalgam to have an adverse effect on the T-lymphocyte count (a vital part of our immune system). With all the concern about the immune system diseases of today, does it make sense to continue using a dental material that may have a drastic effect on one's defense system?

Multiple sclerosis patients have been found to have eight times higher levels of mercury in the cerebral spinal fluid compared to neurologically healthy controls. Inorganic mercury is capable of producing symptoms which are indistinguishable from those of multiple sclerosis. Is it possible that the mouths of some 80% of

Americans with amalgam fillings are "toxic waste dumps"?

Dentists have the highest suicide and divorce rate of all professionals. Neuro-psychological dysfunction was present in 90% of dentists tested by Joel Butler, Ph.D., a professor of psychology at the University of North Texas.

Another alarm: Female dental hygienists have a higher spontaneous abortion rate, an increased incidence of premature labor, and an elevated perinatal mortality. The neonatal blood of these women who were exposed to mercury while working in dental offices were found to contain significantly higher mercury levels than in control women with no occupational exposure to mercury.

Another concern: Why do dentists, according to the insurance industry, have one of the highest utilization rates of medical insurance? Dr. Magnus Nylander published a report in *The Lancet* describing an increased uptake of mercury in the pituitary glands of dentists. Just because over 100 million people have mercury fillings in their mouths, we must not assume that this is medically safe. Powerful decision-makers are not always right.

A report which appeared in a Swedish newspaper in May, 1987, stated, "The Swedish Health Board declares amalgam toxic and unsuitable as a dental filling material." It was quickly disregarded. Headlines in the ADA literature read "Amalgam ban reports are bogus." Significant public hearings on the report were held in Sweden a year later, and the original ruling that amalgam was dangerous was upheld.

There exists a great discrepancy in the pronouncements quoted in Mr. Daniel McCann's article and the conclusions of the Swedish Government Health Board. Are ego and economics at work here? Is there a "mercury cover-up," as Dr. Sandra Denton has suggested?

The CBS program *60 Minutes*, produced by Don Hewitt, who has an appreciation for alternative medicine, did an excellent piece of investigative reporting on the mercury-amalgam toxicity issue, on December 16, 1990. By just presenting the facts and allowing the ADA representative to speak in front of the camera and to make a fool out of himself, the program went a long way in making the public aware of the issue and in getting the ADA to modify its rigid position.

The National Institute for Dental Research subsequently issued a position paper calling for a gradual phase-out of the use of mercury-amalgams, in favor of less toxic composite materials to be developed—a gradual phase out, so as not to create panic in the 100 or so million people who have mercury fillings in their mouths and who are still apparently in good health. This seems to be a prudent course of action, more favorable to investigation than the obfuscation or previous denial of mercury toxicity on the part of the ADA, who seem to be motivated, more than anything else, by a desire not to admit that they may have harmed some of their patients, for obvious dento-legal reasons.

THE AGONY OF ALLERGY
GETTING THE DOCTOR TO UNDERSTAND

There is presently a dispute among allergists and immunologists against a new discipline called clinical ecology. It is a discipline which specializes in environmental medicine and how environmental factors can interplay with one's health. But many traditional physicians do not recognize this area of medicine, simply because it does not abide by the strict definitions of scientific medicine, which confine diagnoses to that which can be scientifically explained. Environmental factors such as chemicals in foods are not always explainable in traditional scientific terms. Traditional doctors stubbornly refuse to change their thinking, despite the increase of chemical pesticides and other toxic compounds in the environment, with a corresponding increase in adverse allergic reactions.

For our purposes, food allergies are adverse reactions to chemicals. These chemicals may occur naturally in the food or may be ingredients added through food processing, e.g. additives, preservatives, fillers, etc. People without abnormal sensitivities can tolerate these chemicals.

But, increasingly, people are experiencing adverse reactions to certain food intake:

—1/3 of the women surveyed reported food allergies

—22% of the women avoided particular foods to prevent adverse reaction

—20% of the women's family members are on food allergy diets, in contrast to
9% on ulcer diets
9% on low salt diets
7% on diabetic diets

Despite the widespread occurrence of food allergy, the traditional (conservative) allergists and immunologists do not recognize adverse reactions to chemicals or common foods as true allergic reactions because they cannot be explained in terms of classical immunologic reactions (cellular immunity, chemical messengers or antibodies produced by cells). Therefore tradition-bound allergists do not accept the adverse reaction as an allergic one. In their ultra-conservative view, such reactions do not exist, and the people who suffer from these chemical sensitivities are hypochondriacs—it's all in their heads.

These conservative allergists and immunologists have bitterly disputed their liberal colleagues who have established a discipline called clinical ecology. This discipline is a specialty in environmental medicine. Their ever-increasing patient load has severe problems with chemical sensitivities from foods and the environment. The clinical ecologists have their own medical society, the American Academy of Environmental Medicine. They have responsibly created their own specialty boards and certification procedures. But many doctors are not even aware of this valuable sub-specialty in environmental medicine.

The dispute between the traditionalists and the new clinical ecologists has escalated from a philosophical difference to an angry professional war on the part of the traditionalists. In 1990 a number of State Boards of Medical Examiners or their Offices of Quality Medical Assurance targeted for destruction certain prominent clinical ecologists. First they called them in for informal hearings or physician conferences. Then they were hauled up on charges before state attorneys general in attempts to revoke their licenses to practice medicine, just as the Boards have done to doctors in the past who use chelation therapy.

What Organized Med should be doing is targeting doctors who are repeatedly sued for malpractice. How about confronting the illegal monopolistic behaviors of the medical-pharmaceutical-industrial complex? But no, they continue their attack on good doctors who dare to use alternative methods to heal the patients they care about.

Interest groups such as the American Academy of Allergy and Immunology and the Chemical Industry also joined in the fight. It is also interesting how both the *New England Journal of Medicine* and the *Journal of the American Medical Association* over the past months have attacked clinical ecologists in articles and editorials. These attacks are indicative of more than just a desire to jump on the current bandwagon of skeptics. They coincide with the carefully-orchestrated attacks by State Boards of Medical Examiners and their Offices of Medical Quality Assurance. On the one hand, the attack is from a blow by the regulatory arm, and on the other, the attack is legitimized by articles and editorials in professional journals.

The clinical ecologists, however, are beginning to fight back. They have issued a statement of purpose; they have hired a public-relations consultant to advise them on how to offset the negative propaganda being spread about them. The Model of Environmental Medicine for 1990 as stated by the American Academy of Environmental Medicine is as follows:

THE MODEL OF ENVIRONMENTAL MEDICINE (1990)

OPTIMAL HEALTH requires that all of the body's biologic systems must be in homeostasis with all environmental stressors.

ENVIRONMENTALLY TRIGGERED ILLNESSES (EI) result from a disruption of homeostasis by environmental stressors. This disruption may result from a wide range of possible exposures, ranging from a severe acute exposure to a single stressor, to cumulative relatively low-grade exposures to many stressors over time. The disruption can affect any part of the body via the dysfunction of any number of the body's many biologic mechanisms and systems. The ongoing manifestations of Environmentally Triggered Illnesses are shaped by the nature of stressors and the timing of exposures to them, by the biochemical individuality of the patient, and by the dynamic interactions over time resulting from various governing principles such as the total load, the level of adaptation, the bipolarity of responses, the spreading phenomenon, the switch phenomenon, and individual susceptibility (biochemical individuality).

ENVIRONMENTAL MEDICINE is that discipline dedicated to the recognition, management, and prevention of the adverse reactions resulting from Environmentally Triggered Illnesses.

RECOGNITION of Environmentally Triggered Illnesses is accomplished by use of a chronologic, sufficiently detailed, environmentally-focused history designed to accurately detect the various clinical patterns generated by the involvement of specific stressors and by the dynamic interactions resulting from the above governing principles. A positive history is then confirmed as indicated by appropriate physical examination, laboratory testing, medical imaging techniques, diagnostic surgical techniques, and endorsed diagnostic testing techniques.

MANAGEMENT of appropriately identified Environmentally Triggered Illnesses is by use of the endorsed treatment techniques of patient education, correction of abnormal nutritional and metabolic dysfunctions, reasonable avoidance of identified stressors, immunotherapy, and symptomatic drugs and surgery where appropriate.

PREVENTION is by skillful prophylactic application of the principles of Environmental Medicine, resulting in the adoption of appropriate lifestyles that specifically minimize exposures to identified stressors as much as emphasizing practical measures that generally ensure less contaminated air, food, and water, and ongoing optimal nutrition and metabolic function.

THE ULTIMATE LONG-TERM GOAL of an appropriate diagnosis and treatment plan is the cost-effective return to optimal physical and psychological health, with significant reduction or elimination of acute and chronic symptoms, improvement in measured functions of involved organs or systems, return to vigorous activities of daily living, improvement in psychological well-being, improvement in the ability to sustain gainful employment, reasonably feasible elimination of incriminated environmental stressors, improved tolerance to stressors that previously caused adverse reactions, and through education, the adoption of appropriate lifestyles to prevent the recurrence and development of new illnesses.

This goal will be best achieved by an ongoing and dynamic partnership between a well-educated patient and a physician and staff who are well-trained and experienced in the discipline of Environmental Medicine.

Dr. Zane Gard is one of the progressive clinical ecologists. He discovered this field while in family practice in Missouri, in a town called Sturgeon. The reader may recall that some years ago there was a railway accident in Sturgeon which resulted in a serious dioxin spill (a total of 3-4 ounces in two tank cars of herbicides, on January 10, 1979, probably the largest spill in the world). As a result of this spill, Dr. Gard observed first hand the effects of exposure to dioxin on the residents of Sturgeon, including some members of his own family. There was also destruction of the grass and other vegetation, including trees. Many people within a short time developed various cancers.

The following account of the spill is taken from Dr. Zane Gard's report of it:

Sturgeon, Missouri, railroad accident, January 10, 1979. Two tank cars containing herbicides (Orthochlorophenol containing 3-4 oz dioxin) spilled in this small town. Accident site was across from the elementary school and high school.

Dr. Gard, his wife (a PHN) and their two teenaged children moved to Sturgeon in the spring, unaware of the town's toxic exposure. The Public Health Department was contacted questioning the danger; however, the Health Department as well as Monsanto Chemical Co. assured the townspeople that there was no danger to their health.

All small ground life died within 2-3 miles of the spill. Cattle on a farm 7-8 miles downstream from the spill died. The farmer who owned the cattle died within the first 6 months, another within a year and a half. A young Amish boy died of bi-lateral retinoblastoma, and a young Amish man died of a malignant lymphoma that same year. There was a 10-15 times increase in flu-like symptoms, allergies, and kidney infections (many were in young boys). The urinary infections always followed a rain. There was an increased number of cases of infectious mono diagnosed.

Dr. Gard's daughter developed infectious mono shortly after arriving in Sturgeon. The symptoms never cleared. The weakness and lethargy became so great that at times she would be unable to attend school. When she did attend school she would return in the afternoon and go to bed, refusing to eat or even to talk on the phone. Dr. Gard developed sensory-motor peripheral neuropathy in his right arm and hand, muscle weakness, and severe headaches, as well as other flu-like symptoms. Zane Jr. and Mrs. Gard also developed similar problems, including kidney infections similar to those of the residents of the area. After 18 months, they decided to leave and return to California, where they were acquainted with the researchers that could help them with their extensive search regarding the effects of toxic exposure on humans and find some form of treatment.

After extensive research for methods of treating exposed victims, it was noted that most chlorinated hydrocarbons have a half-life in man of up to fifty years and that these compounds are fat-stored, accounting for these patients not doing well in hot weather or when exerting enough energy to raise a sweat. A treatment program consisting of many physical therapy modalities (which contained 2 1/2 to 3 hours in a dry thermal chamber) was started which has been consistent in helping these victims improve, some completely recover. The entire Gard family recovered. They are more chemically-sensitive now and attempt to avoid the usual chemical exposures in their everyday life. Headaches accompany stress and tension. But this is a great improvement over what could have been.

A visit to the area ten years following the accident was revealing. The damage to this small town was evidenced by visiting with some of the residents. The funeral home admitted a marked increase in deaths from cancer. One of the secretaries that worked for Dr. Gard was anxious to report what has happened to her family. Their home is in the Amish community, near where the top soil was dumped during the original clean-up. The trees along the bank of the stream near their home are all dead. Her husband died six years ago of cancer of the brain. A son has some type of cancer, another son died in an accident, and her friend has an inoperable tumor in the neck. She also has cancer and has aged considerably.

Many who witnessed the Sturgeon spill have died. The longest court battle in history may have been won by the people, but few will live to benefit or begin to gain back what was lost.

The children still play in the playground, within a few yards from the track and the actual site where the accident occurred. But there is a hush in the town that was not there ten years ago.

The people are genuine and friendly. They are hard-working and honest. The sun shines warm, and the rain falls gently upon their fields. With knowledge of how to survive following a toxic accident, and with a little help to regain some of what was lost, this does not have to become another "ghost town," such as Times Beach, or Love Canal. Their children deserve the right to live today, and grow up to enjoy tomorrow.

After moving to California, Dr. Gard became the Medical Director of the Bio-Tox Reduction Program. This is a program which used diet, exercise, sauna baths, massage, niacin supplementation and chelation therapy to detoxify (remove) chemicals from individuals who had been exposed to them in the environment and/or who were allergic to constituents in foods. The Bio-Tox Reduction Program's detoxification strategies were taught to health care providers around the world, and franchises were opened in many locations.

Dr. Gard has commented on our use of, and exposure to, toxic chemicals:

We are feeding the insects and poisoning the people. We used to say eat, drink and be merry for tomorrow you may die. We now say eat, drink and be worried because today is the tomorrow you worried about yesterday.

There has been a ten-fold increase in the use of chemical pesticides on farmland over the past thirty years. In spite of this increased use, the average annual crop losses have remained constant, and the specific losses due to insects have actually doubled. Furthermore, 99% of the pesticides applied to gardens and crops never hit their intended pest targets. After all the spraying, the crop losses due to all pests, ie. micro-organisms, fungi, insects, rodents, etc., are about the same as they were fifty years ago.

There is almost no toxicity data for 80% of the 49,000 commercially-used chemicals; data is inadequate or non-existent for 64% of 3,400 pesticides and inert ingredients; they are also inadequate or non-existent for 74% of 3,400 cosmetic ingredients, for 61% of 1,800 drugs, and for 80% of 8,600 food additives. In the work-force, 20%-35% of workers are affected by chemicals in building materials, chemicals which cause illness, absenteeism, and low productivity.

Dr. Gard recently came under fire from the California Board of Medical Quality Assurance, because of alleged complaints about the Bio-Tox Reduction Program—complaints that vary from the "unscientific nature" of the treatments to accusations of fraud. The Board depicted saunas as "new and unproven" therapy, even though saunas have a proven utility going back to the time of Hippocrates. They are one aspect of detoxification, a cornerstone of Chinese and ayurvedic medical systems as well as the medically-run European biologic clinics and hospitals. The Board dismissed them as useless quackery.

Dr. Gard says that he didn't get into trouble with the Board until he started to testify as an expert witness on behalf of some of his patients in their lawsuits against such chemical giants as Dow Chemical, Monsanto, and Union Carbide. All of a sudden, his medical practice was an issue for Quality Assurance, and they alleged that the Bio-Tox Reduction therapy did not work.

A disturbing development in Dr. Gard's case is the unusual length to which the California Board of Medical Quality Assurance went to destroy an alternative practitioner who was targeted for elimination and the degree of unethical activity and deceitful entrapment they engaged in—activities which amount to racketeering.

Get this: The expert witness for the Board, who was to testify against Dr. Gard for using unproven methods in clinical ecology, approached several of Dr. Gard's patients and offered each one of them $5,000, if they would file a malpractice suit against Dr. Gard. This same technique was used, unsuccessfully, by the expert witness and cardiovascular surgeon who testified against his peer, Dr. Ralph Lev of Amboy of New Jersey, an advocate of chelation therapy.

Dr. Zane Gard in California, Dr. William Rhea in Dallas, and other successful clinical ecologists around the country are being hauled into kangaroo courts and are being charged with medical heresy now, in the 1990s. Dr. Gard, a most competent expert witness and an experienced medical consultant and seminar leader for other health professionals, decided not to retain legal counsel that would cost hundreds of thousands of dollars. He knew he was up against an orchestrated effort by the medical establishment to destroy a branch of medicine by professionally assassinating all physicians who ascribe to this new, promising and effective sub-specialty known as clinical ecology.

Dr. John Salvaggio, past president of the American Academy of Allergy and Immunology at Tulane University in New Orleans, published a recent article in the *Journal of Allergy and Immunology*. This informative article addresses the impact of allergy and immunology in determining the present industrial environment. He begins with a history of environmental illness: how the Egyptians and Greeks were aware of industrial chemicals causing harm, even designing masks to protect themselves. He explains indoor pollution and the importance of healthy indoor air, relates episodes of asthma in England, and documents the growth of our knowledge during the 1950s and 1960s.

The article highlights the importance of chemicals in the induction of disease. Dr. Salvaggio summarizes the effects of low-dose and high-dose immuno-toxicants and their routes of entry and states that the primary target is the immune system, with secondary targets being other organ systems. The effects include altered immune function, increased infection, neoplasia and hypersensitivity.

After documenting the importance of chemicals in the induction of disease, however, Dr. Salvaggio draws a confusing conclusion:

> More recently, in the 1980s, we have been faced with the spectre of so-called environmental illness or immune system dysregulation in which individuals exhibit multi-system protein symptoms, allegedly because of or exacerbated by exposure to a wide range of industrial chemicals and atmospheric pollutants. The signs and symptoms are usually reported in the absence of abnormal physical signs and tissue pathology. They lack specificity and often include mental status changes, fatigue, muscle pain, headache, depression, irritability, and a sense of fear of the environment. Although

cellular and immune system abnormalities have been reported in this alleged syndrome, there is no proof of immune system dysregulation.

Dr. Salvaggio goes on to recommend that physicians who are confronted with such patients should use only "approved tests of immune parameters" and they should also conduct psychological and psychiatric evaluations when appropriate. He concludes, "There is considerable doubt that such a syndrome or environmental illness, as described above, really exists."

Dr. Salvaggio's article leaves us with a question: What is the difference between immune system "abnormalities" and immune system "dysregulation"? Immunologists would have a difficult time answering. Most cases of environmental illness have associated immune system abnormalities. Is this not the same as immune system dysregulation? The difference is hair-splitting, a question of semantics. This difference is also hardly justification for a full-scale assault on the clinical ecologists by medical licensing boards.

I know Dr. Salvaggio, as we both work for the same institution and his daughter was one of our graduate students. I know him as an internationally-respected investigator and a man of integrity. Others are responsible for the brutal treatment of clinical ecologists. His article, however, has been used by the Academy of Immunology/Allergy to justify their unwarranted position. I question that the difference between immune system abnormalities and immune system dysregulation is the real reason for calling a physician before the California Board of Medical Quality Assurance, and for subsequent prosecution by the Attorney General's Office.

I concur with Dr. Gard that clinical ecologists' troubles stem from the fact that their patients have sued for damages against chemical companies and have used their clinical ecology doctors as expert witnesses that the chemicals did harm them. As a result, the State Boards and Medical Quality Assurance Offices may be acting at the behest of industrial chemical manufacturers who lose many millions of dollars in product liability and wrongful injury/death lawsuits. Their best way to win (and not to pay) is to destroy the medical specialist who could point the finger in their direction.

DISTORT AND DESTROY—A PROFESSIONAL COUPLE'S ORDEAL

Sharon Barclay Kime is a nurse with a master's degree in Public Health, also a practicing attorney with a law degree from the University of California-Davis. Sharon Kime, R.N., M.P.H., J.D., grew up in a medical family; her father was a practicing dentist. Her husband, a fellow of the American Academy of Family Practice and an affiliated member of the American Academy of Otolaryngologic Allergy with a Master's of Science in biochemistry, was completing his doctorate in biochemistry at University of California-Davis. But his doctoral studies were interrupted when he was hauled up on charges before the California Board of Medical Quality Assurance for using "unproven methods," although there was no evidence of any harm to his patients.

Mrs. Kime described their unwarranted ordeal at the May, 1991, conference of ACAM. Her law firm specializes in administrative law and cases of physician discipline, primarily before medical boards and hospital peer-review committees. These cases differ from malpractice actions, which are in the civil courts. Attorney Kime told the chelation conference that most attorneys and judges find it difficult to understand complex debates in science. Hence the court room is not the proper forum in which to resolve scientific disputes.

In 1981, her husband was charged by the California Board of Medical Quality Assurance with using experimental and unscientific techniques in treating his allergy patients. The "unscientific and experimental techniques" were, in fact, endorsed by the sixty-year-old, 8,000-member American Academy of Otolaryngology—Head and Neck Surgery. Curiously, in twenty-five years of practice Dr. Kime had not had a single malpractice action brought against him. A legal battle ensued, and this high-level professional couple have lost nearly $225,000 in legal fees. By May, 1991, some estimate that the state of California may have spent nearly $500,000 of California taxpayer's money to pay for this legal quarrel with a doctor who had done no harm. The unharmed patient has been forgotten, and the tax-backed California medical establishment is pushing science through the mouthpieces of lawyers and judges who don't understand what they are talking about.

This particular battle is being waged in the field of allergy. It reflects the stubbornness and intellectual dishonesty involved in the battle between traditional allergists, ENT's and clinical ecologists. This is a classic battle of turf-fighting. For years, the traditional allergists were regarded as quacks by the rest of medicine. With the growth of immunology, the specialty acquired scientific respectability. Now they, the traditional allergists, assault any "deviants" or "breakaway groups" who have made new observations about the allergic response and how to measure, treat or prevent it. Do they have a "do it to them because someone did it to you" attitude?

Physician discipline by peers is far more serious than any malpractice action. According to Attorney Kime:

> The physician is up against larger entities or organizations. The state agency brings the action against the physician and the state Attorney General's office represents the state as its attorney. The courts give great deference to the state agency's positions.
>
> There is also no requirement of patient harm in medical board actions; this is in contrast to civil malpractice actions, where you have to demonstrate some physical injury or harm to the patient. There is also no statute of limitations in medical board actions.
>
> The medical board also has unlimited tax resources to pay legal fees. They also have the well-established, well-equipped Attorney General's office who (paid with your taxes) is your opposing attorney! All of the presumptions are against you.

What is the reason for this power of expanded litigation without a statute of limitations, even in the absence of demonstrable harm to a patient? It was given to the medical boards by the state legislatures as a trade-off for a solution to the malpractice crisis. In an effort to cap malpractice awards and damages, the physicians agreed to increase their efforts to police themselves.

Ironically, the original intent has been misused to thwart alternative practices by competent physicians. Legislation intended to identify doctors ripe for malpractice, who are going to do harm to the public, has been aimed at doctors using alternative therapies not usual and customary, even if they are superior and do no harm.

INCREASING COMPLEXITY IN MEDICINE—DECREASING COMMUNICATION

There will always be conflicts in science and differences of opinion when it comes to standards of care, despite the public perception that a doctor is a doctor, and that there is a simple, black-and-white standard of care. It is important for the betterment of the profession to allow legitimate conflicts in medicine to exist. With increasing degrees of specialization and sub-specialization, it is becoming more difficult for physicians to communicate with one another. The quality of the medical evidence for all of medicine is very poor. The clear line that the establishment would like to draw between "proven" and "unproven" medical procedures is simply not there. The fact is, most medical procedures are "unproven," if one defines "proven" as being supported by a double-blind study or even clinically-controlled trials.

And, because of the explosion of knowledge in medicine, it is virtually impossible for medical board members to keep up with the latest advances in all of the various specialties and sub-specialties. The medical boards are forced to rely more and more on the state medical associations and also on the medical schools for the expertise that they need in the various fields.

Case law in many states supports the legal principle that a physician should be held to the standard of practice which prevails in the specialty he practices and not to the standard of a competing specialty or sub-specialty. There are many cases in which charges are filed against a physician by other physicians who practice in a competing specialty, to eliminate the competition.

For this reason California Assemblywoman Jackie Spier, attorney Kime and others have introduced legislation (not yet passed) in California which would state that, when he is called up on charges, a physician should be judged by his or her true peers, and not by other physicians who know little or nothing about the specialty. For example, only clinical ecologists should judge other clinical ecologists; traditional allergists should review other traditional allergists.

Because of their dependence on state medical associations and on academia, medical boards can simply become tools of the state medical associations. In addition, the court room is an inappropriate forum in which to resolve widespread scientific debate. Furthermore, the law usually lags behind what is occurring in society; law cannot be a leader of what is occurring in society. In addition, the law is still functioning under the illusion that physicians operate under a code of silence. In some cases that is true. However, the court is only beginning to understand that the medical marketplace has changed, and that the increasing competition among physicians has brought out hostility and concerted efforts to eliminate competition. In some cases, physicians operate on "search and destroy" missions. The courts should begin to depend less on the medical peer review and look more into conflict of interest.

The opposing groups in Dr. Kime's case are ear, nose and throat (ENT) allergists versus general allergists. Both are well-recognized specialists in medicine. The ENT allergists use a technique called serial endpoint titration, a refinement of the scratch and prick skin test that the traditional allergists use. The ENT allergists also use a technique called provocative neutralization.

The ENT allergists say that their techniques are simpler to use and that it takes only a few months for the patients to show signs of symptom relief. The usual time for immunological therapy is two years. The general allergists, on the other hand, state that they frequently treat their patients with immunological therapy for five years. The ENT techniques are considered by their proponents to be much safer; there has never been a death attributed to these techniques. The Federal Registry, on the other hand, reports regular deaths from the use of general allergy techniques. It would appear that the ENT techniques are safer and more cost-effective, bring about quicker symptom relief, and are more drug-sparing.

These are the techniques for which a physician is disciplined, supposedly in the public's interest. The AMA and the Council of Medical Specialties Society have both taken positions of neutrality in this uneven, unfair war between the ENT allergists and the general allergists. This is a case, then, of sub-specialty in-fighting, which has resulted in the misuse of the legal system to literally persecute a physician in order to eliminate the competition.

The legislation introduced by Jackie Spier attempts to define what is appropriate peer review. The legislation defines specialty boards, specialty academies, and peer review. Hopefully it will not be vetoed by the California governor, out of ignorance or pressure, a second time.

DIETITIANS SEEK TO ESTABLISH THEIR OWN MONOPOLY

In the field of nutrition, new restrictive laws are being established in various states which declare candidates eligible to teach or practice dietetics only if they fit the stringent requirements as established by the states' Boards of Dietetics. For instance, the Dietitian's Law in Ohio states that only licensed and certified dietitians can offer nutritional counseling; no other degree, training, or education is adequate. This restriction excludes many competent and learned people from practicing nutrition, such as Dr. George Kindness, Ph.D., a biochemist and internationally-renowned writer in the fields of nutrition and food technology who was cited in violation of Ohio's law because he is not registered with the state's Dietetics Board.

These newly-created rules and regulations are an effort by dietitians to monopolize the field, excluding other health professionals who compete by practicing clinical nutrition.

In contrast to Ohio's Dietitian's Law, the Dietitian's Law in the state of Florida allows for a parallel recognition of nutrition counselors who are separate from registered dietitians and require less training to be certified as such. It is reported that the state of Michigan is about to pass a dietitian's bill into law that is even more restrictive than Ohio's, eliminating multi-level sales of nutritional supplements and also restricting health food store sales.

Dietitians' bills in other states have added phrases that are even more restrictive. Some have used language that indicates that it is acceptable for physicians to use nutrition in their office practices, as long as it is "incidental" to their practices and not the major focus of what they do. Insiders speculate that the dietitians would like to restrict the practice of nutrition to only themselves, *i.e.,* registered dietitians.

Established in 1987, the Ohio Board of Dietetics, on December 4, 1989, issued subpoenas for all of the medical records of one Anne Coble (Voss), a dietitian who had posed as a patient in Dr. William Schmelzer's office. The Board cited Mr. William Strandwitz, who worked as a nutritionist for Dr. Schmelzer, on two counts of violation of the new law.

Count one cited Mr. Strandwitz for representing himself as a nutritionist by way of business cards, television, newspapers and publications. It should be noted here that, prior to the law's enactment, the lobbyist for the dietitians recommended that the word "nutritionist" be removed from the bill because it would be difficult to pass. All such references to the term "nutritionist" were thereafter deleted. In spite of this, the dietitians in Ohio or at least the Ohio Board of Dietetics have now, after the fact, decided to consider the term "nutritionist" and "dietitian" as synonymous. They have decided that they want to control nutritionists as well. They have also decided to ignore the fact that those who work under the direction of medical doctors and dentists were exempt from the law as it was written.

Count two cited Mr. Strandwitz for performing a "nutritional assessment" based on the results of a hair analysis. He was also cited for using vitamins, minerals and nutritional counseling in preventive, curative, and restorative health care. Although dietitians do not believe hair analysis is useful in dietary nutritional assessment and most dietitians do not believe in the therapeutic use of vitamins and minerals, they nevertheless want to control the use of these practices.

Dr. George Kindness, a biochemist and director of a medical laboratory in Ohio who holds a Ph.D. from the University of Edinburgh, Scotland, was also cited by the Ohio Board of Dietetics. Dr. Kindness is internationally recognized and has published widely in the fields of nutrition and food technology.

Both Dr. Kindness and William Strandwitz were called before the Ohio Board of Dietetics for formal hearings on March 30, 1990. The hearings were held before four members of the Ohio Board of Dietetics. The Board permitted their attorney to go on a "fishing expedition," questioning far afield from the alleged offenses. The attorneys for the defendants were consistently overruled when they pursued questions in a like manner. On May 3, 1990, both Dr. Kindness and Mr. Strandwitz were notified that they were judged by the full Ohio Board of Dietetics to be in violation of the law. A court action is now pending.

By June, 1990, there was a request for a preliminary injunction hearing against the Ohio Board of Dietetics in the Franklin County courts. This injunction was sponsored on behalf of Mr. Strandwitz and Dr. Kindness by the Great Lakes Association of Clinical Medicine, a large group of preventive medicine physicians who recognized the danger of this law and its threat to freedom of choice in health care.

SUFFERING FROM THE CANDIDA SYNDROME

Most candidiasis patients have a long history of antibiotic use for acne, chronic bronchial infections, bladder infections, etc. The prolonged use of antibiotics is well-documented in literature to set the stage for an overgrowth of candida in the gastro-intestinal and reproductive tracts. This fact alone discounts the prevailing negative attitude physicians hold toward the existence of chronic illness stemming from the presence of candida organisms.

This story begins some fifteen years ago, when Dr. Orion Truss published his concerns about candidiasis in the *Journal of Orthomolecular Medicine*. He described a chronic candida problem, infection and/or sensitivity.

Dr. William Crook of Jackson, Tennessee, an associate of Dr. Truss, subsequently revealed the full spectrum of this disease. Crook's writings have stimulated discussions, debates, symposia, and, in 1990, a paper in the *New England Journal of Medicine* entitled "A Randomized Double Blind Trial of Nystatin in the Treatment of the Chronic candidiasis Hypersensitivity Syndrome." This study was conducted at the University of Alabama in Birmingham. The paper was accompanied by an editorial by Dr. John Bennett of NIH, which states:

Few illnesses have sparked as much hostility between the medical profession and a certain segment of the public as the

Chronic Candidiasis Hypersensitivity Syndrome has. Those who argue for this complex of symptoms have leveled a serious charge against the medical community, claiming that it is not fulfilling one of its most important obligations to its patients. Namely, that they are not listening to their patients, and they have failed to hear and believe their patients when they say they are unwell, and that they pay more attention to the patients' normal laboratory results than they do to what they say.

They are also seen to be unwilling to learn from their patients when they claim to have been helped by therapeutic regimens not considered acceptable by the medical community.

Bennett's editorial on the National Institute of Allergy and Infectious Diseases concludes by raising a question:

How will the existence of this particular syndrome be proved or disproved? The American Academy of Allergy and Immunology has published a position paper and the Infectious Diseases Society of America is also preparing a position statement, both of which are critical of the existence of the syndrome. Yet more than 3/4 of a million copies of Dr. Crook's book, *The Yeast Connection,* have been sold to lay readers, and support groups have been formed in various parts of the U.S. for those thought to be afflicted. Therefore the proposed study by the University of Alabama is a reasonable way to sort out this problem, but it is only a beginning. Additional studies will be required to determine if this syndrome does or does not exist, and if it does, to further determine what constitutes optimum treatment.

It is generally agreed that chronic candidiasis syndrome is a multifactorial disease state, meaning it has multiple causes. The particular study published in the *New England Journal of Medicine* used only one modality in the treatment of these patients, the administration of the drug Nystatin. No attention was paid to diet, which is generally regarded by yeast-treating doctors to be the first line of treatment for patients with this condition; patients are usually put on a diet before they are treated with Nystatin.

Many of the patients with chronic candidiasis syndrome also have environmental sensitivities. This means they may be sensitive to tobacco smoke, formaldehyde, and other chemical substances which pollute the home environment. If these pollutants are not reduced or eliminated, these patients will not get better. Dr. William Crook usually demonstrates this with a picture of an overloaded camel with so many bundles of straw on his back that he can't get up; when you remove one bundle, the animal still cannot get up. The *New England Journal* article proved that one bundle (Nystatin alone) does not seem to help these chronically-ill patients.

There have also been numerous studies which suggest that women with recurrent vaginal yeast infections who have been treated with long-term antibiotics often have an overgrowth of yeast or candida infection, which then causes a defect in cellular immunity. These immune-system defects may also be related to endocrine dysfunction. The antibiotics, therefore, knock out the normal gut bacterial flora; there is then an overgrowth of candida, and the candida exerts its effects on the immune system. This immune-system disturbance then causes an endocrine imbalance.

Iwata in Japan discovered nearly twenty years ago that candida species produce toxins. Iwata, injecting candida toxin into mice, showed that it caused immuno-suppression, among other abnormalities. Stress, sugar, and alcohol have also long been recognized as precipitating factors in recurrent vaginal candidiasis. In 1977, *JAMA* published the results of a study done at Michigan State University on college students who had recurrent vaginal candidiasis. The authors pointed out that it was insufficient to treat only the vaginal infection. They also recommended changes in diet and lifestyle and suggested back then (1977) that the infection may have some effects on the immune system.

Also, although candida infection may not be the primary cause of the chronic fatigue syndrome (CFS), Carol Jessop, from the University of California at San Francisco, treated 1,100 CFS patients with the anti-fungal drug ketoconazole, and 84% of these patients showed significant improvement. All of her patients met the Centers for Disease Control's definition of CFS. Of the therapies that work, anti-fungal treatment and diet are generally regarded by chronic fatigue sufferers as the most efficacious. In addition, Crook and others believe that all of these candida patients have food sensitivities to such common foods as wheat, milk, corn, yeast, eggs, and legumes, and other foods.

The American Academy of Allergy and Immunology has for some years taken a very dim view of the specialty of clinical ecology. The academy associates the candida story with clinical ecology although Dr. Truss was not a clinical ecologist, nor are many other physicians who support the Truss hypothesis. It would appear that candida in the gut is elaborating some sort of soluble toxin; Dr. Truss feels that it may be acetaldehyde; this toxin circulates to various parts of the body affecting the immune system, the endocrine system, and the nervous system. Dr. Crook, therefore, prefers the term "candida related complex," to include all of the varied manifestations of the syndrome.

Dr. Crook also tells the story of a young woman physician on the faculty of a major medical school who, having read his book, felt that she had the problem and asked for his help. He referred her to an internist who put her on Nystatin, Nizoral, and a controlled diet, and she improved remarkably. She called Dr. Crook back and said that she wanted to organize a conference. She obtained a grant of $30,000 from the Lederle Pharmaceutical Company. Her chief was not enthusiastic, but he did not oppose the holding of the conference. She invited sixteen board-certified physicians, including Dr. Truss; her chief also insisted on inviting the president of the American Academy of Allergy and Immunology, who would definitely be opposed to the existence of the syndrome.

Six days before the Conference was to take place, however, the money was withdrawn. The American Academy of Allergy and Immunology speaks with a "forked tongue." On the one hand, they call for additional studies; on the other hand, they call this "fringe medicine," acting as if the proponents of the candidiasis related complex don't know what they are talking about.

It is still unclear whether the symptoms seen with candida are the cause of the problems or the effects from other problems. Immune-system depression, for example, sets the stage for an organism present in the gastrointestinal tract, on the skin, and on the mucous membranes to proliferate and to undergo a transformation from a yeast state to a more invasive fungal state. It is not at all clear which is the cause and which is the effect.

Whether it's the patient with AIDS or the patient who has received an organ transplant and is receiving immuno-suppressive drugs, candida is not particular; it will invade either and can even get into the bloodstream. Many patients subsequently die from this infection. Numerous factors wear down the immune system—high-sugar diets, environmental pollutants, toxic insecticides, and viral infections can all weaken the immune system, creating an environment in which candida can become invasive.

DR. KOCH FLEES THE U.S.

William Frederick Koch, Ph.D., M.D., a professor at the University of Michigan Detroit College of Medicine from 1910 to 1919, a giant in American medicine, fled to Brazil for his life because his theories and treatments had been quarantined by American medicine and the FDA. According to the doctor himself, a middle-aged patient of his, Janet Worsley, was nearly strangled to death by an undercover FBI agent who tried unsuccessfully to choke her to death. Whether out of compassion or incompetency we'll never know, but he didn't finish the job. She positively identified her attacker in a court of law for the charge, but because of his governmental immunity from prosecution, he got off. And what had this poor middle-aged cancer patient done to deserve such an attempted murder? Why, she had achieved an unprecedented remission from her cancerous condition which no one else had been able to accomplish.

And what had her "bad" doctor discovered to warrant this attack on his patient? An accomplished researcher, clinical professor and medical author, Dr. Koch is credited with developing glyoxilide, a non-toxic, oxidative catalyst which has the capacity to reverse neoplasms and viral parasitisms—in plain English, this means cancers and other degenerative diseases, infections such as the viral scourges of rabies and distemper, and allergies due to the presence of foreign protein polymers in the tissues.

To further his research, Koch could no longer work in the U.S. Assassination was not out of the question, in his mind, so he fled to Brazil and published his findings from the safety of another country. With the promise of a vicious district attorney—"I'm gonna get you yet, Koch"— ringing in his ears, he left behind numerous patients whose lives he had saved with a simple, safe chemical discovery that threatened someone else's financial turf.

Dr. Koch's oxidative catalyst triggers the cells' oxidative mechanisms to regenerate the impaired (anaerobic) respiration of cancer cells to a more normal (aerobic or mixed) respiration, thereby helping to reverse the course of the disease. This ability to restore oxygen to non-oxygenating cells was confirmed by the Nobel Laureate Professor Otto Warburg, a renowned German physician and researcher.

Koch's text, *The Survival Factor,* shows a picture of an unusual protrusion of the abdomen of an infant with inoperable liver cancer. Progressive pictures show a progressive reduction in the swelling, until she is pictured as a healthy young girl. This child recovered through the use of glyoxilide.

Spontaneous remissions from cancer occur in only one out of 10,000 cases. In Dr. Koch's cases, there are far too many documented remissions to simply attribute the patients' recoveries to chance remission. When presented with documentation, traditional doctors generally state in vague terms that a particular patient "didn't have cancer at all," or they just get a little red in the face and pronounce, "pseudo-science!"

Word of Dr. Koch's successes reached the Detroit public, and the Strike Force took aim and fired. Dr. Koch was put on trial by the FDA and competing drug company interests, both in 1942 and 1946. The FDA was unable to prove Koch a charlatan and glyoxilide a quack remedy. The outpouring of valid testimonials and case histories backed by the referring medical doctors and their patients in remission saved Dr. Koch.

Yet the FDA continued to persecute this fine medical scholar and practitioner. To thwart his use of glyoxilide, in 1950 the FDA obtained a permanent injunction against interstate shipments and claims of efficacy of glyoxilide.

Dr. Koch felt compelled to flee to Brazil to continue his research. There he developed enviable case studies of patients whose diseases he was able to reverse. Through the efforts of a Michigan businessman whose relative was saved by Dr. Koch, his non-toxic substances of glyoxilide and parabenzoquinone survived. Mr. Laurence Thatcher's sister-in-law had been given one month to live by her orthodox doctors; she was then cured of her lymphosarcoma by Dr. Koch's regimen, which included glyoxilide. Thatcher introduced and distributed glyoxilide and parabenzoquinone under the name of Christian Medical Research, Inc., which he and others operated for eleven years until the FDA and AMA forced their license to be returned to the Koch family.

Thatcher also organized Koch's Cattle-Shots, Inc., which produced and distributed the products for veterinary use, primarily in the treatment of bovine mastitis and dairy cow infertility. Thousands of doses were administered to cattle, with 100% recovery.

Dr. Koch named this type of remedy the synthetic survival reagent (SSR). In 1961, he published a book entitled *The Survival Factor in Neoplastic and Viral Diseases.*

There are two forms of this reagent—the quinone form and the carbonyl group chain form with free radical terminals. trichinoyl D is produced by the Germans under license by the Koch family.

Koch had used SSR successfully in the treatment of cancer, allergies, polio and infectious disease agents, because it initiates a process of oxidation of the pathogens causing these conditions. Koch postulated that these pathogens had become integrated into the host cell and polymerized or built-up into larger protein molecules, which were fixed in the tissues and responsible for disease. As long as these pathogens were there, the disease process would continue. By the process of oxidation, initiated by the administration of the SSR, these integrated pathogen host-cell protein complexes could be unraveled and the patient would recover—and recover they did.

FLV/23,A: HEIR-APPARENT TO GLYOXILIDE

The ubiquinones, such as co-enzyme Q10, discovered by Professor Karl Volkers of the University of Texas at Austin, can be thought of as oxidative catalysts. They provide singlet oxygen in the form of the functional carbonyl group, which can serve as a "spark-plug" for the oxidation of molecules containing the C=C double bond with carbon groups on either side. This process is accomplished through a series of free-radical reactions which produce energy and result in the oxidation and destruction of the pathogens causing cancer, infection, and allergy. This extra boost in oxidation can be likened, therefore, to jump-starting a battery, and sometimes it is all that is needed to fight off a viral infection, to eliminate cancer cells, or to depolymerize an allergen.

Dr. David Hughes of London has such an oxidative catalyst, an oxide of hexylene containing five or six functional carbonyl groups, which he discovered while doing research in diving medicine and seeking a cure for the "bends." The oxidant that he discovered, FLV/23,A, has been used clinically in patients with AIDS, with cancer or with allergies, with some success. To get maximum benefit, the drug should be given when there is no hypoxia or when the patient's tissues are as fully oxygenated as possible. The patient should not be smoking or consuming alcohol, coffee, or other caffeinated beverages, all of which generate free radicals. He should not be taking anti-oxidants of any kind and should restrict oxidative stresses such as foods high in fat, anaerobic fermentation in the colon, and vigorous exercise before and immediately after administration of the catalyst. The object is to give the catalyst at a time when the oxidation stimulated can go solely for the purpose for which it was intended i.e. to "burn-up" viruses, allergy-causing proteins, and cancer cells.

Dr. Hughes says he has also treated mothers and babies infected with HIV, but who had not yet developed AIDS, in the country of Malawi in southern Africa. Mother and infant pairs were given the oxidative catalyst FLV/23,A intramuscularly on several occasions. Many of the mothers and infants allegedly converted from being HIV positive to HIV negative.

More recently, Dr. Dahlia Kirkpatrick, of Tulane University Medical School, on behalf of the International Medical Research Foundation, which supports Dr. David Hughes' research, went to Romania as a consultant to a project to treat some of the babies who had contracted AIDS from the therapeutic administration of blood. She suggested that they treat only the sickest babies who were diagnosed as having AIDS and who were not expected to survive. She suggested that both orphaned babies as well as some babies whose parents were alive (fewer than 80% were orphans) be treated. The same time that Dr. Kirkpatrick was in Romania, the wife of ex-Beatle George Harrison arrived on behalf of a foundation which supplies nurses called "angels" to look after some of the orphans in Romania. Ms. Harrison, however, had been told, possibly by representatives of Burroughs-Wellcome, manufacturers of AZT, not to place any nurses in hospitals that were conducting clinical trials using "unauthorized agents," e.g., FLV/23,A. Wellcome PLC had refused to provide AZT free of charge to the Romanians for fear of establishing a precedent which might cost them a great deal of money in the long run. The head "angel" threatened a boycott if the clinical trial with FLV/23,A continued as planned.

In addition, several hand-picked newspaper reporters arrived to do a story on the clinical trial. A Burroughs-Wellcome consultant, Dr. Dunbar, also arrived. They were not allowed access to the hospital, nor to any of the doctors and nurses participating in the trial. Nevertheless, they wrote newspaper articles and press releases condemning the trial and insinuating that Dr. Hughes and FLV/23,A were frauds. They even convinced the Romanian government to request WHO to send a delegation to review the experiment. The WHO group recommended that the Romanian authorities call a halt to the trial.

Press releases were issued before a report on the experiment could be prepared. The press releases reached New Orleans and Tulane University, prompting an investigation of Dr. Kirkpatrick's involvement in the project. The Tulane University investigating committee concluded that Dr. Kirkpatrick had not acted improperly; she had gone to Romania on her own time, when she was on vacation, not to conduct university business. The Romanian authorities who had originally approved the trial changed their minds at the instigation of Dr. Baldescu, Director of Preventive Medicine and Secretary of the National AIDS Committee. The authorities were forced to recant their decision and to call a halt to the trial in view of the adverse publicity. The trial was stopped before the fourth dose of FLV/23,A could be given and was therefore never completed. According to articles in the Romanian press, Dr. Baldescu, earlier in 1990, was responsible for a £1.57 million purchase of medical supplies from Wellcome PLC., the makers of AZT. At no time, however, did anyone ever ask if the compound FLV/23,A was safe or if the infants with AIDS who were treated with it were getting better. Part of the blame for this fiasco lies with Dr. Hughes and his co-workers. They were not forthcoming with complete specifications on FLV/23,A reagent for proprietary reasons. All that is known is that it is in the ubiquinone family and provides five or six singlet functional carbonyl groups. Its exact structure has not been made public; it is not a new compound, and therefore its patent status is unclear. For all these reasons, Dr. Hughes has not made available to anyone who asks all of the data he has accumulated on the reagent. In addition, a similar but not identical reagent, trichinoyl D, which contains six carbonyl groups on a benzene ring, is already being marketed by the German company Heel, which is based in Baden-Baden.

The official WHO team's report concluded that "[t]he study in Bucharest is scientific fraud." Is it really fraud, or lack of proof of efficacy? The only way left to restore the credibility of FLV/23,A is to continue to follow the babies treated with this compound to see how they do.

Diane Sawyer of ABC also did some investigative reporting on Dr. Hughes, FLV/23,A, and its trial in babies with AIDS in Romania. The ABC documentary, which aired on March 7, 1991, barely left open the possibility that the reagent FLV/23,A could work at all. It made no connection between the Hughes Reagent FLV/23,A and the Koch synthetic survival reagent or any of its successors produced by Heel, including trichinoyl D. There was no attempt made by the producer or by ABC "Prime Time" staff members to do any serious in-depth research on oxidative catalysts and how their discovery in the 1940s came into sharply-focused conflict with the newly-discovered antibiotic penicillin and with the somewhat older sulfa drugs.

The volunteer British nurses or "angels" came across in the TV report as biased and incompetent, one of them criticizing the taking of blood from the jugular vein of an infant who was being restrained (standard procedure on most hospital pediatric wards). Their other anecdotal comments contributed little or nothing to an objective evaluation of the research methodology being employed. Despite ABC's fine reputation for investigative reporting, the network must have been put up to this irresponsible "hatchet job." Why, and by whom? There are few explanations for such a piece of biased and targeted (with intent to kill) journalism.

In this regard, ABC's report is similar to the purposefully-targeted piece of TV journalism done four or more years ago which brought down the newly-established nutritional company, United Sciences of America (USA). Connie Chung exposed dissent among the members of the Scientific Advisory Committee, and this public airing of "dirty linen," plus some very real problems with some of the company's products, such as allergic reactions to a fiber supplement made from cottonseed protein, contributed to a lack of public confidence and to the eventual demise of the company. These are both examples of media support for monopolistic practices of the medical and pharmaceutical industries.

The latest correspondence indicates that the Romanian government is interested in completing the clinical trial with Dr. Hughes and in licensing and producing the reagent. They are even interested in entering into an agreement with the foundation to define the conditions under which Romanian and foreign AIDS patients may be treated on a compassionate basis in a local hospital. The government recommended that the "foundation should return to Romania in order to re-examine and test all of the babies who participated in the clinical trial. Dr. Strauss, the principal Romanian pediatrician who participated in the joint clinical trial, confirms that those treated compassionate patients who returned to the Colentina Hospital for examination are doing well and continuing to show clinical improvement." To date, the foundation has not been able to raise enough funds to do this.

The most recent (January, 1991) evidence from the clinical trial of FLV/23,A in Romania was that the group of some 82 infants who were treated with the reagent have done far better, as measured by clinical improvement and increase in T-helper immune cells, than the group of infants who were not treated. The treated group has maintained their weight, and many have gained weight. Few of them have died; many of them have been discharged from the hospital. The results for the most part were statistically significant or showed well-established trends which would have been significant had the sample size been larger.

Despite numerous case reports, some of America's greatest

biochemists and clinical experts refused to accept Koch's work and claimed, "The oxidation mechanism has no significant action or position in the maintenance of health or in the combat of disease."

Quietly, behind the scenes, competitive drug interests misused their power to "sic" the U.S. government in a full-scale attack against Dr. Koch, castigating his clinical observations and experimental research which had borne remarkable results. The war against Dr. Koch raged most intensely from 1943 to 1946. As it is done today, the battle lines were drawn and fought out in federal court. For Koch it was in his city of Detroit.

This case was one of the important early attempts to resolve scientific controversy through the legal process. Dr. Koch prevailed in the legal system, due substantially to the support of two leaders in American science and industry, Dr. Willard H. Dow and Dr. William J. Hale. These gentlemen built the powerful Dow Chemical Company. They took an interest in humanitarian efforts such as the clinical research and practice of Dr. Koch, whom they had investigated fully and evaluated very carefully and then supported successfully in his court battle. This was long before the Dow Chemical Company got into the drug business.

To reiterate Koch's hypothesis: There is a far more efficient process of energy production than the Krebs cycle. This process is a decarboxylation process, which has not been previously recognized because no intermediaries have been trapped, isolated and identified. The process results in the oxidation of the pathogen-host cell complex. It is this process which is initiated by the synthetic survival reagent (SSR) in its two different forms: the quinone form and the carbonyl group chain form with free radical terminals.

Both of these forms lose these catalytic properties when they are exposed to heat, light, x-rays, etc. This might explain why some samples have been found to be inactive when tested by outside laboratories. They also do not work well in patients who are consuming high-fat and high-protein diets and in those who consume coffee, tea, and alcohol; they also do not work as well in those who smoke cigarettes or who are constipated and colonized by anaerobic bacteria which cause fermentation and putrefaction of undigested food constituents in the colon. To attain maximum benefit, the drug should be given when there is no hypoxia and when the patients' tissues are as fully oxygenated as possible.

CHAPTER 7
THE "CASE" AGAINST EDTA CHELATION THERAPY

We can't put these chelation doctors out of business without your help.
—FDA administrator Dr. Stuart Nightingale in a speech
to the AMA House of Delegates, Honolulu, Hawaii, 1984

SITTING ON THE DATA

By 1990, five controlled and blinded scientific studies had been started to evaluate the safety and efficacy of EDTA in the treatment of peripheral vascular disease. Only three have been completed, and only one has been published, in the *Journal of the National Medical Association,* in April, 1990. Studies are in progress, one under the auspices of the U.S. Army. Another one has been completed, and the data from Denmark is being analyzed in Denmark. Also, the New Zealand Heart Association has recently made funds available to Prof. A.M. van Rij for clinical research on chelation therapy and has now sanctioned its use.

One of the completed studies was the controlled study of Dr. Gerhard Schettler of Heidelberg, West Germany. This study compared EDTA to Thiemann Pharmaceuticals' drug, bencyclan, which they market under the brand name Fludilat (R). The data, which was never released, showed that EDTA was at least as effective as Fludilat (R); it would have been shown to be substantially more effective if cases with "exceptional improvement" had not been eliminated. Since the data was the exclusive private property of Thiemann Pharmaceuticals, the results favoring EDTA over Fludilat could be suppressed.

It is unknown why a pharmaceutical company would fund a study of a generic drug for which the patent had expired. It is possible that Thiemann believed AMA propaganda stating that EDTA was ineffective. Why else would Thiemann put EDTA up against their own Fludilat (R)?

Thiemann did take precautions, however. When the grant was awarded, Thiemann reserved the right, in its written contract with Schettler, to edit any published reports of the study, to interpret the final data for publication and to do the statistical analysis themselves. All recorded data from the study were to be the property of Thiemann, and it was agreed that all data would be given to Thiemann at the end of the study. Such a contract seems to eliminate the guarantee of an unbiased report, and it eliminates free access to the original data by other investigators.

A total of approximately 48 patients were treated, 24 in the Fludilat (R) group and 24 in the EDTA group. Disodium EDTA was administered in a dose of 2.5 gms in 500 ml 1/2N saline. Treatments were given five days each week for a total of four weeks. Each patient received 20 infusions. Only patients with peripheral vascular disease were included in the study. Pain-free walking distance was measured before, during and after therapy on a treadmill, at 3.5 km/hr with a 10% gradient.

The measured results showed a 250% increase in distance walked before onset of claudication pain in the EDTA-treated group after four weeks of therapy. By comparison, there was only a 60% increase in the bencyclan group. Bencyclan, however, is a drug proven to be of benefit in this disease and is widely prescribed in Europe for that indication.

There were four patients in the EDTA group who experienced more than a 1,000-meter increase in their pain-free walking distance at the end of only 30 days of treatment. Highly favorable data from those four patients mysteriously disappeared when the final results were made public. Thiemann, of course, had a legal right under terms of the contract to edit the final results and to interpret the data in any way that suited the company. Their final report contained data which reduced observed benefit from EDTA by 72%, from 250% increase to only 70%. The fact that data from the best EDTA responders were altered would not have been known if scientists from Heidelberg with intimate knowledge of the study had not been shocked by what they considered unethical and dishonest scientific conduct. Raw data from the study was personally delivered to an official of ACAM for an independent interpretation.

The fact that a highly-placed representative of American organized medicine went to Heidelberg and met with Dr. Schettler while the study was in progress may or may not be significant.

The study was reported at the Seventh Atherosclerosis Congress in Melbourne, Australia, in 1985. An attachment to the abstract of that presentation, available at the meeting, contained a graphic plot of pain-free walking distance extending out to three months after the end of therapy. By that time, even using the modified data made public, the increase in pain-free walking distance in the EDTA-treated patients had increased to 130% of the baseline, while bencyclan-treated patients averaged less than half that much, increasing 60% above baseline, with no further improvement after therapy was stopped at 30 days. Nothing in the text of the abstract described that graphically-depicted observation, despite its great clinical significance in proving the effectiveness of EDTA chelation therapy. The report analyzed data only to the end of 30 days, when the bencyclan and EDTA groups had responded equally. It is well known that full benefit from EDTA is often delayed for up to three months after therapy.

The data reported in Australia shows only a 70% average increase in pain-free walking distance in the EDTA-treated group (instead of the 250% increase at 30 days indicated by the raw data) and was compared with a 76% average increase in the group treated with bencyclan. Even that amount of improvement is significant, since it is rare for placebo effect alone to exceed 33%.

The only patient death was in the bencyclan group. No serious side effects were observed from EDTA. The reportedly negative results of this study received widespread coverage in the news media, but the data was never published in a peer-reviewed journal. Furthermore, the press release stated that "EDTA was no better than a placebo," without mentioning that the "placebo" in this case was Thiemann Pharmaceutical's very own Fludilat (R), a drug proven to be effective.

Another study was started in Saskatchewan, Canada, by the Vancouver Island Chelation Therapy Research Society, a group of physicians who used chelation therapy in their practices. The purpose of the Society was to conduct a study of EDTA in peripheral vascular disease. Naturally, the College of Physicians and Surgeons in Saskatchewan was opposed to the chelation study. They generated a great deal of adverse publicity about the study, especially about the method of payment, which required that the patients pay an additional fee. The press coverage was especially negative on this point, because Canadian citizens are not accustomed to paying directly for health care. The Vancouver Island Chelation Therapy Research Society, therefore, was forced to call a halt to its study.

One of the completed but non-published studies was conducted by the Department of Medicine at Baylor College of Medicine in Houston, Texas, between approximately 1984 and 1990, using private funds donated by an interested party. This particular study had a unique origin; it was undertaken when a medical student,

Kimberly Dunn, confronted Dr. Anthony Gotto, Chairman of the Department of Medicine, and demanded why he and his research team had not investigated chelation therapy. Her grandmother had been treated for macular degeneration due to cerebrovascular disease by Dr. Ronald Davis, and the patient got a good response. A double-blind study of EDTA in peripheral vascular disease was subsequently designed, and this same medical student became one of the physician-investigators. The study was under the direction of Dr. Phillip Henry, in Dr. Gotto's department.

Little wonder that a respected scientist such as Dr. Anthony Gotto of Baylor University and Methodist Hospital (the mecca for cardiovascular bypass surgery) could arrive at a negative study comparing EDTA with a placebo in patients with pure peripheral vascular disease. After all, the most famous cardiovascular surgeon in the world, Dr. Michael Debakey, is the Chancellor of Baylor University Medical Center.

The Baylor study, a feasibility study, will soon be published. According to Dr. Kim Dunn, 23 patients were enrolled in the study. Twelve were in the treatment group and 11 in the placebo group. Of the 23 patients, at least a half dozen were smokers. Initially, the investigators tried to enroll patients who had "pure" peripheral vascular disease (this means that they did not have high blood pressure, coronary artery disease, or evidence of arteriosclerosis in the carotid or cerebral vessels, did not smoke, and did not have diabetes). They eventually concluded that there were no such patients who only had peripheral vascular disease. Nevertheless, they tried to eliminate most of these associated conditions and complicating clinical factors. Both groups received 30 treatments. The carrier solution contained lidocaine, magnesium chloride, and bicarbonate. The patients complained of no pain at the infusion site.

According to Dr. Dunn, when the analyses on these 23 patients were completed five years after the study began, they found no significant differences between the treatment group and the placebo group. The investigators used blood pressure indices, ultrasound and doppler studies, treadmill tests, and arteriographies. Significantly, there were no significant differences immediately after the thirty treatments or three months after the thirtieth treatment. Since this was a pilot study, the investigators decided that it was not worth expanding into a multi-center clinical trial.

Dr. Dunn also noted that, at first, there seemed to be a difference in the blood pressure indices of those receiving EDTA and those receiving the carrier solution by itself. Later on, however, this difference was not there. The entire study took five years. Even if comparisons were made four years after the initial 30 treatments, the treated group would have had ample time to regress, particularly if they had made no substantive changes in their lifestyles.

Also, it is very likely that EDTA as a drug alters a basic mechanism, bringing about benefits in a lot of different, seemingly unrelated areas. It is considered a free-radical scavenger, so many age-related conditions can reverse. This quality, however, actually works against its acceptance by orthodox medicine. If something has too beneficial an aspect to it, the skepticism about it begins to rise.

An interesting study was done by Canadian veterinarian Dr. Lloyd McKibbin, internationally recognized for his treatment of race horses. He evaluated "Racehorse Performance Before and After Magnesium EDTA chelation Therapy." His results were positive and could not have occurred as a result of a placebo effect as the trotters didn't know what was going on. His abstract reads as follows:

Three hundred (300) horses were administered chelation Therapy at Wheatley Hall Farms Limited, over a two year period. From this population a sample of 68 horses (N=68) were randomly selected by computer. This was done after 3 pre- and 3 post-treatment race times had been recorded for all horses.

Pre- and post-treatment race performance were standardized using the Equalator System. This program allows individual horse performance to be mathematically standardized, controlling for 27 individual and track variables.

Significant differences in pre- and post-treatment performances can be calculated as a result. The sample in this study showed a significant (p=0.07) time improvement in three post-treatment races after 1 to 3 chelation treatments.

The U.S. Army Study is now underway; thirty patients have been evaluated to date. Unofficial reports indicate the following data:

Those receiving the usual 3.0 gm dose of EDTA reported maximum improvement.
Those receiving only 0.5 gm EDTA reported intermediate improvement.
Those receiving no EDTA reported no improvement.

On the basis of these preliminary results, the pharmaceutical company Wyeth-Ayerst, in January, 1992, committed $6 million to fund clinical studies in the private sector parallel to the Walter Reed Trial. They will use these funds to complete the necessary studies required by FDA, and, in return, they will have a three-year exclusive patent on di-sodium magnesium EDTA, which the FDA will regard as a new compound because of the addition of magnesium chloride.

At the present time, when chelation therapy is given, magnesium chloride is added to the bottle immediately before its administration. Wyeth-Ayerst will simply put the magnesium in ahead of time and give it some shelf-life. Wyeth-Ayerst, however, may well be in for an interesting turf war. With this unexpected movement into established "bypass territory," a confrontation with Organized Med may be unavoidable.

Rumor has it that the patients in the Walter Reed Hospital study compared notes in the outpatient department and noticed that some of them were getting better and improving, while others were not. So they wrote a letter to President Bush, in which they questioned the ethics of including the low dosage and control groups, when the efficacy of EDTA in the usual and customary dose is so readily apparent. Good for them!

Dr. Raymond Lepicky, Head of the Cardio-renal Division of the FDA, commented to Dr. Ross Gordon of the ACAM (the chelation doctors' organization and the group to whom the IND for EDTA in arteriosclerosis was issued) that Dr. Gotto and, presumably, Dr. Efrain Olszewer and I, were foolish in doing studies on EDTA in Peripheral Vascular Disease independently, without first clearing the studies with the FDA, because the issue is so controversial. Where is it written that doctors must first "clear" our research with the FDA? Dr. Olszewer, Dr. Gotto and I and a host of other physician/scientists are most capable of doing their own research without input from Dr. Lepicky of the FDA, thank you!

This comment on our "foolishness" indicates how a senior FDA official views himself in his role, not only as the gatekeeper who allows only certain safe and effective drugs into the marketplace, but also as "the man" to pre-approve independent research that could count toward a drug's eventual approval for a specific purpose.

Dr. Stuart Nightingale and others at the FDA, together with the former CCHI of the AMA, the Councils Against Health Fraud (the "shadow CCHI"), Dr. David Spence, and the Louisiana State Board of Medical Examiners were all to blame for allowing a safe and effective alternative to expensive coronary bypass surgery to fall through the cracks in the first place. If the American patients and public taxpayers only knew, charges of malfeasance would be in order for the pain and suffering on the part of 600,000 Americans who die annually from cardiovascular disease due to arteriosclerosis and its complications. These groups are to blame for thwarting a viable medical alternative.

CHELATION WORKS—PUBLISHED MEDICAL EVIDENCE

Perhaps the most convincing compendium of research papers and studies showing the efficacy of EDTA chelation therapy can be found in *A Textbook on EDTA Chelation Therapy*, edited by chelation specialist Elmer M. Cranton, M.D. author of the best seller, *Bypassing Bypass*, distributed by Hampton Roads Publishing Company. The chelation textbook was published by Human Sciences Press, Inc. of New York City in 1989, as a special issue of the *Journal of Advancement in Medicine*. The forward was written by Linus Pauling, Ph.D., two-time Nobel Laureate.

The book is divided into five sections:
Section I: Mechanisms of Action
Section II: Clinical Data
Section III: Safety
Section IV: Protocol for Administration
Section V: Laboratory Evaluation

Section I presents articles on free radical pathology and age-associated diseases, on iron and ischemic heart disease, and on the cross-linkage theory of aging. These were written by Elmer Cranton and James Frackelton, Jerome Sullivan, and Johan Bjorksten, respectively.

Section II, on Clinical Data, is impressive, with reports by Cranton and Frackelton on EDTA chelation therapy in occlusive arterial disease and by Casdorph on EDTA chelation therapy in brain disorders. Cerebrovascular and peripheral vascular dynamic studies also showed improvement in blood flow and in blood pressure relationships after EDTA chelation therapy. These were written by Drs. McDonagh, Rudolph, and Cheraskin. There is also a paper on averting the need for amputation by treatment of peripheral arterial occlusion with EDTA by Casdorph and Farr. Lastly, a retrospective study of 2,870 patients with various cardiovascular (coronary artery, cerebrovascular, and peripheral vascular) diseases and senile dementias after EDTA chelation therapy, by Dr. Efrain Olszewer and me, was also included in this section.

Section III deals with Safety and presents articles on the kidney effects of EDTA chelation therapy and several articles, by Dr. Mc-Donagh, Dr. Rudolph, Dr. Cheraskin, and Dr. Keith Senaert, which actually show an improvement in renal function following EDTA chelation therapy.

Section IV gives the details of the protocol for administration and questions the need for supplementation with iron and copper in all but females in the reproductive age group.

Section V, on Laboratory Evaluation, focuses on the monitoring of renal function during EDTA chelation therapy and the excretion of urinary trace and toxic elements and minerals. This section also deals with the interpretation of trace and toxic element levels in human hair and discusses the need for replacement therapy for some of these minerals and trace elements.

After reading this book, I do not understand how anyone could come to the conclusion that there is no evidence supporting the efficacy of EDTA chelation therapy in the treatment of arteriosclerosis and its complications. Unlike some orthodox researchers who have falsified data, the chelation specialists are not lying or exaggerating.

Clinical studies aside, no one, after reviewing cases and patient interviews of those who have received EDTA chelation therapy—often after traditional medicine has failed—and listening to what patients have to say about how they felt then and how they feel now, could conclude that this therapy is of no benefit and that the only reason that these patients feel better is because of the placebo effect. The differences before and after are too dramatic.

THE CYPHER REPORT

Cypher is a group of physicians experienced with EDTA treatment of obstructive vascular disease. These physicians were interested in demonstrating and documenting the value of the EDTA program. Their goal was to gain acceptance of this program as a valid medical approach by physicians not familiar with it and by insurance firms. To this end they collaborated to produce the Cypher Report, a landmark clinical study. The report surpasses all others in establishing the efficacy and therapeutic value of EDTA chelation therapy, beyond a shadow of a doubt. No statistician can argue with the sheer number of the cases. The report is a retrospective statistical analysis of 19,147 case studies of patients with obstructive vascular disease, all of whom were treated with EDTA. The case studies were extracted from the patient profiles of physician participants from across the U.S. They were evaluated before and after treatment by independent experts in high-resolution infra-red thermography.

The treatments were administered in accordance with the American College for the Advancement in Medicine (ACAM) protocol. The treatment program included recommendations for dietary change, nutritional supplementation, and systematic exercise, as well as infusions of intravenous magnesium ethylene diamine tetraacetic acid (MgEDTA). To evaluate changes in the patients' diseases, infra-red thermography was employed. This process displays the temperature profile of the body, illustrating the effective tissue perfusion of blood, and enables an evaluation of peripheral arterial competence. Thermography has the advantage of being non-invasive and passive and is essentially artifact-free under properly controlled conditions. It is recognized by even the AMA's Diagnostic and Therapeutic Technology Assessment Division as an acceptable modality for the evaluation of peripheral and cerebral vascular diseases. It is also listed in the Medicare-Medicaid guide for the evaluation of peripheral vascular disease.

Each case study was thermographically analyzed by examining 37 separate standard reference points. The resulting data was evaluated by computer and analyzed using the sophisticated methodology of independent expert statisticians specializing in high-reliability analysis. Approximately 86% of the MgEDTA-treated patients showed a significant enhancement in the arterial perfusion of the upper and lower extremities. Furthermore, a significant dose-response relationship was established.

The study can best be described as the "expert system" approach to artificial intelligence, applied to clinical research. The report of this study will soon be published with Dr. Phillip Hoekstra, III, Ph.D., as the first author, under the title, "Serial Infusions of Magnesium Ethylene Diamine Tetraacetic Acid Enhance Perfusion in Human Extremities." Dr. Hoekstra's father, Dr. Phillip Hoekstra, Jr., Ph.D. originally started the study but died before its completion. The other authors are H.T. Louis, A.J. Scarchilli, J. Baron, and P. Parente. At the time of this writing, the paper had been accepted with revisions by the editors of a European journal, *Cardiovascular Research*. With the publication of the Cypher Report, the therapeutic value of EDTA should be established to any intelligent person, physician, or scientist. The case against EDTA chelation therapy, on the basis of lack of efficacy and scientific evidence, is closed!

On June 8, 1990, a group of vascular surgeons in Denmark held a press conference at which they announced that they had just completed a study of chelation therapy, and, after twenty consecutive treatments, they had found no differences between the treatment group which received the drug EDTA and the control group which received normal saline solution. Sixty percent of both groups allegedly showed improvement in walking distance before the onset of leg pain.

Our Danish colleagues in chelation, Dr. Mogelvang and Dr. Christensen, had previously expressed to me their concerns about the Danish study. They felt that the investigators were biased and that the purpose of the study was to prove that EDTA chelation therapy did not work. They were also concerned that the study did not include the use of vitamin and mineral supplements, such as magnesium chloride, vitamin C, vitamin B6, and zinc.

I tried to allay their concerns with the fact that some of the original studies done by Dr. Norman Clarke and his colleagues also did not include the addition of vitamins and minerals but still achieved positive results. I assured them that if the Danish investigators were honest the results should be favorable, regardless of whether they added these substances or not.

Naive, I assumed that, under the Danish system of nationalized health services, EDTA would have a reasonable chance of being studied objectively; after all, this was a chance to save a great deal of government money and prevent considerable patient suffering.

I will never again underestimate the arrogance of these cardiovascular surgeons. Their usefulness was on the line, to say nothing of their paycheck. Successful results from a study on chelation would result in competition from a cost-effective treatment. Was it of no concern to them that the real results would surface along with their failure to give it a fair clinical trial and objective appraisal?

The politics of chelation therapy in Denmark are interesting and complex. Its major proponents, Dr. Christensen and Dr. Mogelvang, have been offering it in the private sector. In a completely nationalized health service, or a system of socialized medicine (not merely the provisions of a national health insurance plan such as Canada and New Zealand), such as in Denmark, any attempt to offer health services in the private sector, outside of the system of socialized medicine, is likely to be viewed as an attempt to reintroduce the private practice of medicine. Therefore Drs. Christensen and Mogelvang were opposed by some members of Parliament, as well as the Danish Medical Association, members of which are organized into a union.

The infamous study of EDTA in Denmark was conducted by the vascular surgeons who had everything to lose and nothing to gain.

Their opposition to the therapy was well known, even before the study started. The principal investigator, Dr. Svend Juul Jorgensen, a vascular surgeon from the Central Hospital in Hilleroed, went on Danish National Television at a very critical moment during half-time of the first world championship soccer game, with, of course, millions of television viewers, and announced that EDTA treatment was no better than IV saline solution in the treatment of peripheral vascular disease. Can you imagine the foolishness as well as the impact of such an announcement being made during half-time in the Superbowl?

Dr. Christensen describes the reaction:

> The effect of this TV announcement was moderate in the press, but the medical establishment did not hesitate to use the statements made by Dr. Jorgensen as a weapon against us, and our attempts to open a private chelation clinic in the city of Gram.
>
> They seem to be fighting to close us down, because of a lack of patients. The Danish FDA is totally passive.
>
> The Danish AMA is negative to any private medical practice, that is to say, not publicly financed, as are politicians in the left wing. The conservatives however, are positively interested.
>
> The real opponents are, of course, the vascular surgeons who risk a cut-back in a planned expansion of their services of an enormous dimension.

To understand and analyze the Denmark trial which began in 1989, let us review it step by step. The principal investigators were cardiovascular surgeons, the group most opposed to chelation therapy. The form of EDTA selected was di-sodium EDTA, administered in normal saline; the amount of EDTA given was 3 grams. The control group received only normal saline, without EDTA and without any other vitamin or mineral supplements. Both groups received two to three treatments a week for a total of twenty treatments.

About three-quarters of the way through the trial, some of the investigators announced that they were not seeing any differences between the treatment and control groups. This announcement was surprising in that the study was being conducted in nine different hospitals, and the code (who was receiving EDTA and who was receiving normal saline) had not yet been broken.

Needless to say, it would not have been necessary to break this code, because it is well known that di-sodium EDTA, given in this fashion, hurts. It causes a painful sensation at the site of administration or insertion of the intravenous needle. So in effect, if the objective was to conduct a double-blind study, such a study would have been impossible with the use of di-sodium EDTA.

Generally, magnesium chloride or magnesium sulfate are added to the bottle containing di-sodium EDTA right before its administration. If magnesium chloride were added to the bottle before its administration, sodium magnesium EDTA would have formed after the addition of magnesium and chloride. Hydrochloric acid would also have been formed, and this in turn would lower the pH of the solution. Such a solution containing hydrochloric acid can also be slightly painful or uncomfortable at the site of administration. We are reasonably sure that magnesium chloride was not added to the treatment mixture in the Danish multi-hospital study. A slower rate of administration (+ *4 hrs*), however, might reduce the pain and discomfort—but only slightly.

The study was abruptly terminated after the twentieth treatment. This was not the intent, as announced in the original protocol or design for this investigation. Originally, it was planned to continue to follow these patients after twenty treatments, at an interval of six weeks, three months, and six months after completion of the first twenty treatments. This is important because we know that if di-sodium EDTA is the form of the drug to be administered, it will take longer for the drug to have the desired effect of improvement in circulation. Di-sodium EDTA will remove calcium but will not replace it with magnesium.

The magnesium will have to be replaced, more slowly, through the intake of foods containing magnesium in the daily diet. In addition, the delayed effect (which has always been thought to be due to the growth of collaterals around vessels obstructed with plaque) takes time. Therefore, after the conclusion of twenty treatments, maximum benefit may not be observable in patients receiving the drug for possibly an additional six weeks, or maybe even three months, after the conclusion of the initial series of twenty infusions.

With these parameters in mind, it is important to find out whether the patients in the treatment arm of the study did indeed received di-sodium EDTA. This can be confirmed by asking the patient-volunteers if the infusion hurt at the injection site. None of the patients complained of such pain, in spite of the fact that the final solution was definitely acid (pH 3.2).

If they did receive di-sodium EDTA, and if there were no differences between the treatment and control group after twenty treatments, then it is of the utmost importance to continue to follow these individuals and to obtain additional measurements at six weeks, three months, and six months after conclusion of the treatments. Regrettably, however, this is just one more instance of a poorly-designed study for the sole purpose of disproving the effectiveness of EDTA in the treatment of arteriosclerosis. This was also one conducted by extremely biased investigators, who didn't bother to consult the experts, pro or con, before undertaking their study.

What are we to make of the Danish study? The vascular surgeon Dr. Jorgensen admitted in a statement to the press that magnesium chloride had not been added to the solution, but he stated "of course, we used EDTA; but for the liquid to be used in a double-blind study, we had a liquid developed which in its composition corresponds to the blood stream." The solution was also pasteurized by heating to high temperatures before administration.

The results and details of the Danish study were published in the *American Journal of Surgery* in August, 1991. There was no bibliography to the article, and there was evidence that the sub-sample of thirty patients reported on had been manipulated in order to obscure any differences between the placebo and study groups. It is significant, for example, that, out of a total sample of 153 subjects, only thirty were reported on. What happened to the remaining 123 subjects is not discussed anywhere in the paper. Of interest too is the fact that there were 106 smokers in the group of 153 volunteers; of the thirty patients selected to be reported on, twenty-nine were smokers. If these thirty had been selected randomly, the chances of selecting a group of thirty in which twenty-nine are smokers are less than one in 14,838. This strongly suggests that the sample reported on had been manipulated.

The investigators also said that they haven't finished calculating the effects of EDTA and placebo at three months after termination of the treatments. It is possible that the electrolyte composition of the solutions used both in the case of EDTA and in the case of the placebo were such that the viscosity of the blood and its flow were subsequently improved, resulting in the equivalent of a "thinning effect," and that this might account for the greater-than-expected improvements in both groups. After all, the curves for EDTA and placebo, according to the Danish investigators, were parallel, with 60% effectiveness in both groups. Normally, with just the placebo effect, there is no more than 30-40% effectiveness. This improvement in viscosity and blood flow, however, would be expected to be temporary, at best. The follow-up evaluations at three months after the termination of the study would, therefore, be crucial in determining whether there was a difference between EDTA and placebo groups.

THE PLACEBO OR THE TOMATO

EDTA fell through the cracks because of benign neglect or because of the "tomato effect," which is a medical expression that refers to any good therapy that was originally rejected because it did not make sense. The tomato effect was described by Dr. James S. and Jean M. Goodwin, husband and wife, in the introduction to their classic article published in *JAMA* on May 11, 1984 (Vol. 251, No. 18):

> THE TOMATO (Lycopersicon esculentum) is a New World Plant, originally found in Peru and carried back to Spain from whence it quickly spread to Italy (*pommidoro*) and France, where it was know as the *pomme d'amour* and thought to have aphrodisiac properties (this is the first recorded confusion between the placebo effect and the tomato effect, described herein). By 1560, the tomato was becoming a staple of the continental European diet.
>
> Of interest is that while this exotic fruit from South America (along with other novel products such as potatoes, corn, beans, cocoa, and tobacco) was revolutionizing European eating habits, at the same time it was ignored or actively shunned in North America. During the 18th century, tomatoes were not even cultivated in North America. Not until the 1800s did North Americans accept the tomato as edible; commercial cultivation of tomatoes was rare until the 20th century, although in the past eight decades the tomato has grown to become our largest commercial crop.
>
> The reason tomatoes were not accepted until relatively recently in North America is simple: they were poisonous. Everyone knew they were poisonous, at least everyone in North America. It was obvious. Tomatoes belong to the nightshade (solanaceae) family. The word "nightshade" is usually preceded by the word "deadly," and for good reason. The leaves and fruit of several plants in this family, for example, belladonna and mandrake, can cause death if ingested in sufficient quantity. The fact that the French and Italians were eating tomatoes in increasing quantities without seeming harm did not encourage colonial Americans to try them. It simply did not make sense to eat poisonous food. Not until

1820, when Robert Gibbon Johnson ate a tomato on the steps of the courthouse in Salem, N.J., and survived, did the people of America begin, grudgingly we suspect, to consume tomatoes.

The previous paragraphs are meant to explain the derivation of the term "tomato effect." The tomato effect in medicine occurs when an efficacious treatment for a certain disease is ignored or rejected because it does not "make sense" in the light of accepted theories of disease mechanism and drug action. The tomato was ignored because it was clearly poisonous; it would have been foolish to eat one. In analogous fashion, there have been many therapies in the history of medicine that, while later proved highly efficacious, were at one time rejected because they did not make sense. We contend that the tomato effect is in its own way every bit as influential in shaping modern therapeutics as the placebo effect.

While the placebo effect has contributed to the enthusiastic and widespread acceptance of therapies later shown to be useless or harmful, the tomato effect has stimulated the rejection or nonrecognition of highly efficacious therapies. Recognition of the reality of the tomato effect, while not preventing future errors, may at least help us better understand our mistakes.

According to Dr. Sterling M. Planters, we have at least one informant in the FDA, someone with a conscience who has decided to let the chelation good guys in on some FDA insider information, whom we dubbed Sore Throat—our counterpart to Watergate's Deep Throat.

Dr. Louis Sullivan, current Secretary of Health and Human Services, announced in February, 1990, the appointment of a commission to investigate the FDA. According to Sore Throat, the Justice Department was also represented on this commission. However, news of the appointments and the progress that has been made is very hard to come by. Supposedly, they were to re-examine the purpose and mission of the FDA, to determine whether goals and objectives were being met and if changes are needed. (Surely when the FDA was established, Dr. Harvey Wiley did not intend for it to be used by the AMA and the pharmaceutical industry to further establish monopoly, contributing to financial crisis in the health services.)

The recent Pentagon scandal was widely publicized, but the FDA generic drug scandal was not. In the case of the generic drug scandal, only the tip of the iceberg was scratched. Worse fraud and collusion, with far-reaching consequences, lurk beneath.

EDTA chelation therapy to treat arteriosclerosis in this country can be traced back to the great Dr. Norman Clarke of Ohio, who died a few years ago at the age of 91. A clinician and researcher, he had no influence on the American Heart Association or the FDA and NIH (National Institutes of Health). After all, his observations were anecdotal. They were not strong enough to prevent the FDA from reversing its earlier decision approving EDTA for the treatment of arteriosclerosis.

This disdainful, bad attitude about clinical observations continues today. As recently as March, 1990, the director of the National Cancer Institute refused to allow a researcher to speak on the National Institutes of Health (NIH) Campus, because that person had been identified as someone "sympathetic to macrobiotics and the macrobiotic diet." This is another suppressive behavior for future government hearings to investigate.

Both the FDA and the NIH should provide an office to study these observations of practitioners, physicians, non-physicians and even lay persons. They ignore the fact that all science starts with observation and the recording of data. Sir Isaac Newton watched the apple fall from the tree, and he made certain observations and deductions. Newton could never have obtained a government grant to conduct the research necessary to verify his observations, to prove or disprove his hypothesis. While not required courses in medical school, arrogant ignorance, a bad attitude, and mental inflexibility are commonly observed regarding many members of the medical power structure.

THE FDA—A BIG PART OF THE PROBLEM

Chief of the recently formed Fraud Division of the FDA, Dr. Hollohan (whose job it is to protect the American public from fraudulent medical claims, including untested cancer remedies) revealed his ignorance when he said:

> For the major alternative therapies being offered today, there is virtually no scientific evidence that one can expect any benefit from any of them. The public in general doesn't have the knowledge to be able to make an informed choice.

This represents the problem, not the solution. This government bureaucrat accused you, the public, of not having the intelligence to make a good decision regarding medical treatments. That's an unproven insult. Patient choice of chelation therapy would demonstrate intelligence superior to Dr. Hollohan and the FDA. Chelation therapy could never have survived had it not been for patient improvement, all medically documented. The horrendous sanctions quietly applied to chelation doctors would have forced these alternative practitioners to give up long ago, had the treatment not worked.

The creation of Dr. Hollohan's office, within the FDA, reflects a belief that the public is incapable of judging for itself. Actually, the Washington office and its regional divisions could be considered fraudulent themselves—a fraud which has been perpetrated on the public, namely misuse of the FDA to implement a system of disinformation, to harass physicians using alternative therapies, and to help mete out punishment by the State Boards of Medical Examiners to control and manipulate medical practice to the advantage of physicians and the pharmaceutical industry.

Dr. Hollohan and his staff have demonstrated incompetence and ignorance at best and malfeasance at worst: Haven't billions of dollars been wasted annually for the approximate 90% ratio of unnecessary bypass surgeries, not to mention patient suffering? Chelation patients demonstrate more wisdom in choosing chelation therapy than the FDA demonstrates.

It was at the urging and prodding of the AMA and other organizations representing the private practice of medicine that an office was established to decide which medical therapies are in the public's best interest (and which are also in the best financial interest of Organized Med). In effect, the FDA acts in its regulatory capacity as an AMA surrogate, an obvious conflict of interest.

Our FDA informant, Sore Throat, says that at any time there might be an official leak that NaMg EDTA chelation therapy is going to be approved for the treatment of peripheral vascular disease. While this development is very good news, it unfortunately simultaneously suggests a rapid build-up of resistance to the entry of NaMg EDTA into mainstream medical practice, allowing more time for continued treatment of cardiovascular disease by surgery and thus providing for more profit for professional and surgical special-interest groups before conceding that there is a more cost-effective alternative.

An Agency of Health Care Policy and Research program officer believes that a proposal to study a cost-benefit comparison of NaMg EDTA treatment of cardiovascular disease to conventional medical and surgical therapy may be rejected on the basis of an argument that NaMg EDTA is not yet approved by the FDA for the treatment of arteriosclerotic cardiovascular disease in any form. This argument is presented despite the fact that the drug has been in common usage for this purpose for nearly thirty years and is produced by mixing di-sodium EDTA and magnesium chloride at the time of intravenous administration. This argument is also the basis for giving Wyeth-Ayerst an exclusive license for three years. The FDA rationale is that di-sodium EDTA constitutes one drug, magnesium chloride constitutes a second drug, and the two together constitute a third, new drug, as far as FDA law is concerned.

It is becoming apparent, however, that, because of the likely outcome of the Walter Reed study, forces are already at work to grant approval for NaMg EDTA only in the treatment of peripheral vascular disease and not in the treatment of coronary artery disease or carotid artery disease. The argument will be made that insufficient studies have been done to document its efficacy in the treatment of coronary and carotid artery disease. It will also be argued that the fact that EDTA improves circulation to the lower extremities does not indicate that it will do the same for circulation in other parts of the body, *e.g.*, the heart and the brain. This argument, of course, is patently absurd; clinical scientists, however, are not always known for their common sense, especially in matters which affect their profits.

The decision of American Home Products, which owns Wyeth-Ayerst, to invest $6 to $8 million to pick up the remaining costs of the Walter Reed Study and to expand it into the private sector had purely business, not altruistic, motives. Investment of such a sum for a drug as good as or better than Trental, the drug which currently has the largest market share, should earn them $500 million a year for three years, for a total of $1.5 billion. This profit can be made even if EDTA is approved only for the treatment of peripheral vascular disease.

Wyeth-Ayerst and others were investing in the belief that doctors will rush to use the "new" compound and will rationalize its use by asserting that they had always suspected that there was merit to EDTA chelation therapy and were only awaiting proof. Wyeth-Ayerst's investment would likely not pay off, however. There is tremendous opposition to the therapy, because physicians have been brainwashed during their training to believe that it does not work and that it is dangerous because of its toxicity to the kidneys. In addition, physicians have little incentive to switch from the more lucrative surgical intervention, when a non-surgical one reduces their income by as much as 90%.

Apparently Wyeth-Ayerst is not as naive as their original decision made them appear to be, however. On April 28, 1992, I was informed by Professor Martin Rubin that the company had reversed its decision to support the research on the use of NaMg EDTA in the treatment of peripheral vascular disease—an obvious last-minute turnaround. The reason given for this reversal was that "a new President for Research and Development, Robert Levy, M.D., a cardiologist, has decided that the resources of Wyeth-Ayerst should be utilized for other purposes."

Well, What do you know? In an instant, Wyeth-Ayerst turned from being part of the solution to being part of the problem. Was this change a result of pressure on the company to forego $500 million a year profit for the sake of the much larger bypass surgery and angioplasty industry, which, together, in 1990 made $10 billion and is growing at a rate of $1½ billion per year? Was it based in part on the manipulated, at best, or fraudulent, in the worst case scenario, results of the Danish study published in the *American Journal of Surgery?* Who knows? In any case, it is obvious that the manipulation, "fix," and/or wise-guy tactics that are being used go to the highest levels.

SITTING ON THE DOCTOR—DOWN IN NEW ORLEANS

Every spring semester, at Tulane's School of Public Health, in the course Applied Public Health Nutrition, we give our students some exposure to the regional office of FDA, to its activities and functions. Annually the Compliance Section of the Regional Office takes great pride in "educating" our health science graduate students as to how they handled "the famous case of Dr. Ray Evers." This is one student's account of what the FDA has to say about one of the chelation doctors:

I was at a meeting at the FDA and spoke with one of the compliance officers and he was describing to me his job duties and the job of the FDA, and one of the cases that was mentioned that came up for compliance was that of a doctor in the Greater N.O. area, Dr. Evers, I believe, who was using EDTA chelation therapy for patients with a variety of illnesses, but primarily cardiovascular diseases due to arteriosclerosis.

Evidently, there were several complaints made to the FDA that patients were dying under the care of this doctor who had a small clinic in Belle Chase, La. They took legal action against this doctor and used a physician from U.C. San Francisco as an expert witness to testify that EDTA therapy was ineffective for this purpose and also fatal in some instances, because of kidney damage. The doctor lost his license to practice medicine in the State of Louisiana.

Dr. Evers moved to Alabama, where the FDA was not successful in their legal case against him for using chelation therapy, but his license was eventually revoked after a fifteen-year legal battle for using alternative methods of treating cancer. The Medical Practice Act was specifically amended in order to get Dr. Evers for what the Board considered to be the use of unproven and illegal therapies. The real reason, of course, was chelation therapy; and the conflict goes all the way back to 1975 in Louisiana.

The FDA Regional Office, on occasion, also tells our students:

> Dr. Evers was running a clinic for the treatment of arteriosclerosis in Belle Chase, Louisiana. His medical practice, although grossing $2 million a year, was highly irregular and he was using products contraindicated for arteriosclerosis. After many attempts and confrontations, Dr. Evers was finally ordered to stop. With the help of and at the instigation of the State Board of Medical Examiners, and with the assistance of an expert witness who was a Canadian, they were able to prove that 14 people had died in Dr. Evers facility, and that their deaths were the direct result of the use of EDTA for the treatment of arteriosclerosis.

The Louisiana State Board of Medical Examiners has always opposed chelation therapy. In 1974, they revoked the temporary license of the pioneering chelation doctor Ray Evers and denied his request for a permanent one because he used chelation in his small private hospital in Belle Chase, Louisiana. Having moved from Alabama as a result of persecution in that state, Dr. Evers applied for Medicare certification and it was through this application that a "red flag" popped up, because Dr. Evers had previously been blacklisted by administrators of Medicare and the FDA for his previous use of alternatives such as Laetrile and other remedies.

Reliable sources note that Dr. J. Morgan Lyons, chairman of the state's medical board during the litigation, had interned concurrently with Dr. Evers at Charity Hospitals. During this time they dated a mutual woman friend; bad feelings may have arisen, and this did not help Dr. Ever's situation in 1974.

To stop Dr. Evers from performing chelation, the FDA and the Louisiana State Board of Medical Examiners used a medical resident to serve as an expert witness against Dr. Evers. Dr. David Spence, a Canadian citizen doing his residency in internal medicine at U.C. San Francisco, was asked by his superior to perform a literature search on chelation therapy and its complications. This resident, hardly dry behind his medical ears, searched for three days in the library for the only available medical literature on chelation—all slanted, as we've seen earlier in this book.

For the trial, the FDA called in the resident expert witness. The FDA subpoenaed the records of the last twenty patients who had died in Dr. Ever's small hospital. Dr. Spence and members of a site visit team (of which Spence was the only doctor and was also the chairman) reviewed the hospital records and concluded that fourteen of the twenty deaths were caused by the drug EDTA administered during chelation.

Chelation expert Dr. Bruce Halstead was called as expert witness on behalf of Dr. Evers and testified that EDTA was most likely not the cause of the fourteen deaths. He pointed out the desperate illnesses of the patients upon admission to Ever's hospital. They had already succumbed to the failures of standard medical therapy in treating chronic disease—no one could save them, not even Dr. Evers.

Dr. Halstead also pointed out that this was not a correct way to evaluate EDTA, by singling out only those patients who had died, to determine whether or not EDTA contributed to their death. In spite of Dr. Halstead's sound testimony, the judge ruled against Dr. Evers on the basis of the testimony of Dr. Spence.

We need to acknowledge that some of the fourteen cases did show less than optimal management by the standards of care in the 1970s; also, the present-day ACAM protocols for chelation had not been completed at the time. But subsequent independent analysis of these cases by qualified pathologists did not agree with Dr. Spence's conclusions that the patients died from receiving EDTA chelation, but noted their cause of death as due to their underlying progressive illness. Many of them had cancer with advanced metastases. EDTA did not cause that.

Dr. Evers, a devout Christian, never turned away any patients who came to him for help. As far as we know, and because another doctor had taken over for him during his legal battles, he was not strictly following the chelation protocol developed in the 1970s, which required certain laboratory tests to be performed before chelation could be started. Dr. Evers was aware, however, that if there was any suggestion of impaired or reduced kidney function, the patient was not a good candidate for chelation therapy; if it were administered under those circumstances, the patient should be monitored closely.

Dr. Evers, who until that time had a temporary license, was not issued a permanent one to practice medicine and was forced to leave Louisiana and reopen his facility in the state of Alabama.

In Alabama, however, when he was called before the State Board at the request of the FDA and dragged into court again, the court decided in his favor. That court's decision is the basis for the current precedent that a physician can use an approved drug for a clinical purpose other than the one for which it was originally intended. In this case, the doctor must explain to his patient that the drug is not approved for this particular purpose, but that the doctor believes the drug will be useful in treating the patient's condition. With the patient's informed consent, it is perfectly legal to use the drug for the treatment of the disease condition in question. The FDA appealed this decision, and they lost the appeal.

Nevertheless, when the question of chelation therapy comes up with EDTA used as the drug of choice, "the fourteen cases who died in Louisiana from chelation" is recited. Whatever FDA official dutifully or ignorantly parrots this lie, there is usually no mention of how the FDA lost in court and then lost on appeal in their attempt to ban chelation for treating plaque in patients' arteries. The FDA never appealed to the next highest court, which would have been the U.S. Supreme Court.

At the end of 1984 and in the beginning of 1985, the Louisiana State Board of Medical Examiners included with each license renewal application an anti-chelation editorial written by Dr. Alfred Soffer. The inclusion of this editorial with the 1985 renewal application was a direct threat to chelation doctors or those who might consider its use. The letter stated that the use of chelation would not be meeting the standards of "acceptable medical care," and those using it might be brought before the Board for formal hearings and possible disciplinary action.

Dr. J. Morgan Lyons, Head of the Louisiana State Board of Medical Examiners, was quoted earlier in 1984 at a meeting of the State Medical Society in Lafayette, La., as saying: "Oh yes! chelation therapy has reared its ugly head again, but we know how to take care of it!"

The fact that the mails were used to circulate this editorial and to convey this message is a possible violation of free trade laws. It was, in essence, an effort to restrict free trade. Now that we are convinced of the safety and efficacy of EDTA chelation therapy (the FDA, in approving, the Walter Reed protocol, said that "safety was no longer and an issue, since nearly 500,000 patients have been treated without serious side-effects") it has moral implications as well.

This threatening letter may have been included with other evidence that was compiled for a petition which was submitted to the Federal Trade Commission in 1991, claiming there has been collusion in the insurance industry to deny claims for payment for EDTA chelation therapy, which is safer and more cost-effective than coronary artery bypass surgery. The cost difference of these procedures should be a major incentive to its widespread adoption. Instead, it is just the reverse. Chelation costs on the average one-tenth of what it costs for coronary artery bypass surgery. Yet because of the politicking going on, insurance companies are paying out more than they would have to.

CHAPTER 8
WILL YOU ALL RISE? KANGAROO COURT
IS NOW IN SESSION. . .

DR. VICTOR HERBERT—A "LEGEND IN HIS OWN MIND"

The most effective way to introduce Dr. Victor Herbert to the reader is to allow Nobel Prize winner Linus Pauling to speak. When asked under oath in Dr. Warren Levin's trial to explain Dr. Herbert, Pauling made the following statements:

> (*p. 1419-21*): I have known [Dr. Victor Herbert] for about 21 years now. I don't think he is a scientist. It seems to me he has little understanding of science and little ability in that field.

> (*p. 1424*): Victor Herbert, you know he is not a scientist; he doesn't know how to assess evidence. I don't think he knows much about biostatistics. He just says he refuses to look at the evidence. I have sent him my analysis of 14 controlled trials; he just refuses to look at it. He continues to make false statements about vitamin C and cancer, and vitamins in general.

> (*p. 1425I*): If you can believe what he says, there is no doubt that his beliefs are not based upon facts; that there is some sort of bias; some sort of other activating influence.
> He is not a scientist in the sense of a person who is able to carry out reliable experiments.

> (*p. 1427*): What do I see? I see in magazines and in newspapers that Victor Herbert stated that values greater than the RDA have no value for persons in health or in disease. Perfectly completely false. I can't understand this fellow. Well, I wouldn't go to him to be my physician. I can answer that.

> (*p. 1428-29*): Double-blind controlled studies are not the only meaningful way to determine what is effective in medicine. There are some situations in which it is just not

BOSCOV'S

007439   01/28/2001   REG SALE

5962 100047D SHAVERS
UPC 075020187505
REGULARLY   62.99 T 49.99

SUBTOTAL   49.99
6.000% SALES TAX   3.00
TOTAL   52.99

ACCT # 4190015007520**** S
VISA   52.99
06/03

APPROVAL 01804900
BOYLE/MICHAEL

CUSTOMER   COPY
Transaction Number
STORE 60   REG 2122   TRANS 02927

THANK YOU FOR SHOPPING BOSCOV'S
KEEP RECEIPT FOR RETURNS & EXCHANGES
VISIT OUR WEB SITE www.boscovs.com

possible to carry out double-blind controls by ethical physicians.

(p. 1432): Vitamin C; it is known that it has no toxicity; it doesn't cause kidney stones. This is the standard sort of false statement Victor Herbert makes; that you may get kidney stones. There is no evidence.

(p. 1434): [Referring to chelation therapy] I should think that this would be a misuse of the word "fraudulent." My understanding of the facts is that EDTA chelation therapy is approved by the FDA for detoxification of heavy metal poisoning. It seems to be essentially perfectly safe; no fatalities; no serious consequences of carrying out these chelations. It has not been approved for use in cardiovascular disease. Nobody has applied for FDA approval, which can be a pretty expensive matter. The reading that I have done and the discussions I have had with physicians who use EDTA chelation therapy for cardiovascular problems, have caused me to form the opinion that it has much value in these cases.

(p. 1554): Based on the statement of the charges; based on my understanding of the tests that he carried out, and the treatments that [Levin] prescribed, I formed the opinion that [Dr. Levin] was a good sound orthomolecular physician.

Dr. Linus Pauling is an extraordinarily credible witness. He has the distinction of being the only scientist to have ever received two unshared Nobel Prizes. He also holds no less than forty-eight honorary doctoral degrees. Mr. Harris, Dr. Levin's attorney, reportedly asked Dr. Victor Herbert, facetiously, "How many Nobel Prizes do you have, Dr. Herbert?" He also described Dr. Herbert as a "legend in his own mind."

The ubiquitous Victor Herbert pops up in sundry legal locations to give great quantities of testimony (for a high fee) against leading alternative practitioners. He also hits the lecture circuit and surfaced a few years ago in Toronto, Canada, to address the Ontario Allergy Society, the Ontario Medical Association and the American Academy of Allergy.

Apparently anticipating an assassination, he requested several policemen strategically located throughout the auditorium. His request for personal bodyguards, however, was turned down. Which alternative practitioner did he fear would follow him across the border, haul off and shoot him? Or was this for heightened drama? Under police protection, here are some pointers he presented to his distinguished audience:

> Our food supply is safe. . . It is impossible to draw any conclusions regarding the safety of any food from the presence or absence of a single carcinogen. . Forget the fiber baloney!

He also pronounced that the term "holistic medicine" has been taken over by alternative practitioners for selfish purposes. According to Herbert, the term actually refers to an approach that all health professionals are taught in medical school, but promoters of questionable schemes have confiscated the term. He claimed that aspirin manufacturers are using questionable evidence to promote the taking of aspirin to prevent a heart attack. He declared that food manufacturers who use the word "may" to link their products with health benefits are wrong. To prove his point, he quoted from the back of a box of bran cereal: "The National Cancer Institute believes that eating certain foods may reduce your risk of some kinds of cancer." He analyzed that the quote is true because it says nothing; in his estimate, the word "may" is a "weasel word" because it carries inherently within it the meaning "may not."

In a lively question-and-answer session, Dr. Herbert traded barbs with doctors on topics ranging from 20th-century diseases to acupuncture. He frequently drew the ire of questioners and nervous laughter from the rest of the audience.

Essentially his message, for which he is paid a substantial honorarium by whatever special interest group has hired him, remains unchanged. Depending on the locale, however, he'll go after any form of alternative medicine. Hired as an expert witness in New Zealand because the New Zealand Heart Association and others perceived the public had swallowed a fraudulent therapy from which the patients were actually getting better, he railed against chelation therapy to discourage the grassroots movement there in its favor. Herbert the quackbuster was summoned to bust the chelation "quacks." It is only a matter of time before such misguided quackbusting backfires on Organized Med. Who sets Herbert up to this? While alternative practitioners take the wrath of the American public, I envision the impervious, teflon-coated Victor Herbert basking in the Caribbean, enjoying the fruits of his life's labor—quackbusting.

Despite the evidence to the contrary, orthodox physicians in the medical establishment continue to portray Victor Herbert as a hero. Dr. Bryant Goldman, for example, in the May, 1989, *Canadian Medical Association Journal,* referred to Herbert as an American crusader who brought a message about health care fraud to Canada and heralded him as "the standard bearer for the anti-quackery movement in the United States." He also lauded Herbert as a hematologist, a professor of medicine at Mount Sinai Medical Center in New York City, an internationally recognized expert in nutrition, and a lawyer.

Dr. Zoltan Rona, president of the Canadian Holistic Medical Association of Toronto, Ontario, responded to Dr. Goldman's description of Dr. Herbert in the July, 1989, issue of the *Canadian Medical Association Journal.* Rona agreed with Herbert's criticism of mail-order nutrition-consultant diplomas and the need for accurate nutrition information for the public. He then pointed out some of the false statements delivered by Herbert:

> Herbert's contention, "of course our food supply is safe," flies in the face of hundreds if not thousands of studies that point out the dangers of chemicals in our everyday diet. The Canadian Cancer Society among many other preventive-minded groups recommends that we avoid foods containing chemical additives. Why would they recommend this, if our food is so safe?

Dr. Rona also pointed out Herbert's attacks on fiber and his failure to even acknowledge the proven benefits of oat bran in lowering blood cholesterol or the use of Metamucil in the treatment of irritable bowel syndrome. Rona went on to remind readers that Herbert's "quack attacks" on the benefit of aspirin in preventing heart attacks contradicted the majority of cardiologists and vascular surgeons in Canada who recommend aspirin for most of their patients with angina or a previous myocardial infarction. Rona asked, "Are all of these specialists quacks, too?"

Rona then criticized Herbert's slandering statement that the term "holistic medicine" is used by promoters of questionable schemes. He pointed out that Herbert did not even define holistic medicine properly yet stated that holistic medicine is taught in medical school. Dr. Rona questioned how a scientific journal could print such false information and quoted the Canadian Holistic Medical Association's definition of holistic medicine:

> Holistic medicine is a system of health care which fosters a cooperative relationship among all those involved, leading

towards optimal attainment of the physical, mental, emotional, social and spiritual aspects of health.

It emphasizes the need to look at the whole person, including analysis of physical, nutritional, environmental, emotional, social, spiritual and lifestyle values. It encompasses all stated modalities of diagnosis and treatment including drugs and surgery if no safe alternative exists. holistic medicine focuses on education and responsibility for personal efforts to achieve balance and well being.

Dr. Rona concluded that the Canadian Holistic Medical Association's definition is a far cry from Dr. Herbert's flippant definition. Rona even suggested that the sponsors of Herbert's Canadian visit owe the Canadian Holistic Medical Association an apology for his unprofessional, sham-like presentation in Toronto. He expressed hope that the *CMA Journal* would omit further dogma by Dr. Herbert and provide a balanced coverage of scientific conferences.

In a chilling part of Herbert's Canadian address, he advocated that the medical profession should fight quackery in the courts. He called the use of lawsuits "the most effective method." He then claimed that the previous December he had launched a lawsuit in U.S. District Court against twenty-six leaders of the "self-styled alternative movement." (This lawsuit was dismissed for twenty-two of the defendants for "lack of jurisdiction" and was denounced by the judge as malicious, frivolous and without merit. There are four remaining defendants.)

In addition to "suing the quacks," Herbert advocated "lobbying for anti-quack legislation." In the state of New York, Herbert said, "We're putting them [the distinguished Dr. Warren Levin, for example] out of business." This is a misuse of the legal system to resolve conflicts of science in court. The courts should be used only to stop an unscrupulous individual from harming the public.

The legal debates over the safety and effectiveness of chelation therapy, evening primrose oil and tryptophan are recent examples of misuse of the legal system to supposedly settle scientific disputes. Such court cases have done nothing to eliminate health fraud and quackery. They have only thwarted competition.

If it were not for the serious and apparently illegal racketeering going on behind the scenes, Dr. Herbert could be brushed off as a playground bully with a "praise mom and apple-pie" philosophy. But as the proud standard bearer of the anti-quackery movement, Herbert resembles a brazen little "gestapo guy" deeply committed to eliminating effective, time-honored and continually-evolving alternative methods of healing that are cheaper and usually more effective in treating many chronic conditions. Loosely defined as alternative medicine, such cheaper, safer methods represent competition to traditional allopathic medicine, which has proven that it is not a satisfactory solution to the chronic degenerative diseases, psychosomatic disorders, and stress-related conditions running rampant throughout industrial civilization.

No alternative practitioners deny that modern medicine can be very proud of its life-saving and life-enhancing procedures for treating injury, trauma and infectious diseases. The entire world is permanently indebted to countless surgical and drug advances. The real issue, however, is the fact that drugs and high-tech medicine have their limitations when battling cancer, arthritis, arteriosclerosis, multiple sclerosis and a host of other degenerative diseases. Modern orthodox medicine is not the answer to many of Western society's medical problems.

There is more to learn about Victor Herbert, this eccentric puppet-like character with strings covertly pulled by business forces that have every intention of holding on to their monopoly in the "business of medicine as usual." In a 1977 meeting at the Brooklyn VA Hospital, Dr. Herbert described himself: "I'm a VA doctor who came here from six years at the Bronx Hospital, where I was Chief of Hematology and the Nutrition Laboratory." (It should be noted that the Bronx VA was one of the worst hospitals in the entire VA system. Filthy and with rats sometimes visible on the wards, it was the hospital depicted in the movie *Born on the Fourth of July.*) Dr. Herbert continued:

> I love being a veteran's doctor. My mother was an army lawyer and my father was leader of the First Army Band. I served on active duty for five years in three wars, and retired as a Green Beret lieutenant colonel. On reserve duty, I used to parachute with the Eleventh Special Forces out of Miller Army Air Field on Staten Island. I was mustered out of the army at Ft. Hamilton in Brooklyn.

Dr. Victor Herbert's actual service record states something quite different. This expert witness, paid to wage court battles against the alternative medicine movement, apparently mis-states his professional background and makes outrageously inaccurate statements on non-medical matters as well. Let the reader note the following documentation from the VA obtained from lawsuits against Dr.

Herbert, summarizing his actual military record:

May 14, 1945-December 8, 1946: U.S. Army, parachutist, rank of PFC, 1½ years

June 5, 1952-July 1, 1954: U.S. Army, medical officer, 2 years

Total time served in the military: 3½ years

This far less prestigious record contrasts sharply with his apparent psychological fantasies of what he would like to be, providing proof of his dishonesty. Does he imagine that he was a Green Beret lieutenant colonel?

In actuality Victor Herbert is a medical propagandist who plays hard-ball and uses questionable tactics that are way out of line. His expert witness testimony is either inaccurate, twisted or so overly simplistic as to not represent valid medical fact. I wonder: Are those who pay his fees embarrassed by his medical gaffs and his flippancy when he is caught red-handed? Do they ever feel that he's out of control, just as the German chemical companies who hand-picked Adolf Hitler as a charismatic puppet that would support business advantages for them did not foresee how things would "get out of hand"?

Fortunately, it is unlikely that Herbert will ever be picked to run for office. But this doctor has served as more than a dirty launderer— he is a strong force in the threat to a pluralistic health care system, in both the United States and Canada. He and others involved in the Strike Force collaborated with Dr. David Spence in the province of Ontario. As a result, Dr. Spence was successful in convincing the College of Physicians and Surgeons in Ontario to ban chelation therapy. Legislation subsequently passed in Ontario Province banned all forms of alternative medicine, and it is unclear whether this presumptuous legal act against chelation and other alternatives will be overturned. If the legislation snowballs, it could in effect ban ministers (who counsel their parishioners), naturopaths, herbalists, and acupuncturists. Fortunately for the residents of British Columbia, chelation therapy has been officially legalized there and for the time being is safe from the Strike Force.

So the misuse of the legal system to resolve controversy in science over new discoveries continues. It reflects a larger, philosophical conflict between the forces of new discovery and the traditional standard-bearers of medical might-makes-right attitude. According to Herbert, medicine is ready and willing to take on practitioners of any medical acts considered questionable from a scientific standpoint; a diagnostic test is questionable if its efficacy has not been scientifically proven and approved through the peer-review process. According to Herbert, there are no exceptions to this rule.

Herbert's pronouncements sound like totalitarian political ideology. His message carries an assumption that patients are too ignorant and helpless to take any responsibility for their condition and have no ability to make informed, intelligent choices in their own health care. A wise physician knows, however, that the American public is not stupid. What the public wants (and could have at this moment were it not for the politics in medicine) is a health care system that heals and doesn't cost a bundle.

PRIMROSE OIL THREATENS ASPIRIN AND HEART DRUGS!

Dr. Robert Olson was the government's expert witness in the case of *U.S. v. Efamol, Ltd.*, in which evening primrose oil had been seized by the FDA, as a vegetable oil classified "generally not regarded as safe." It is known that Dr. Olson and Dr. Victor Herbert have both served as food and pharmaceutical spokespersons and as self-appointed "nutrition quackbusters." They obviously collaborated on the Efamol case.

I submitted a paper on gamma linolenic acid which was published in the June 1988 issue of *Food Technology*. In the opinion of the FDA's senior nutrition expert, Dr. Altschul, the paper was technically correct in all respects. Dr. Herbert, however, wrote to the editor asserting that the paper gave too much credibility to the clinical uses of evening primrose oil. He called the article a "deceptive and misleading promotional piece for evening primrose oil," a natural product which he and Dr. Olson, along with the FDA, had fought to keep out of the country. Why? Because it was a "dangerous substance."

The real reason they wanted to ban this natural oil was that the active ingredient, gamma linolenic acid, in conjunction with the active ingredients in fish oil, EPA and DHA, has the potential to significantly cut into the market share of aspirin and other non-steroidal, anti-inflammatory agents as well as cholesterol-lowering drugs such as Questran and Lovastatin.

THE ARKANSAS STATE BOARD VERSUS DR. MELISSA TALLIAFERRO: A DOCTOR'S NIGHTMARE

Dr. Melissa Talliaferro (pronounced Tolliver) is an excellent family practitioner, who, after graduating from the University of Arkansas and completing her internship and residency, elected to go to a rural, under-served community in her home state. Dr. Talliaferro opened an office in the town of Leslie, Arkansas, which is served by only one regional community hospital. For a serious medical emergency, most patients must be evacuated by air to Little Rock or another major medical center in the state. Dr. Talliaferro makes house calls and travels long distances over poor roads to treat her grateful patients.

She was called before the State Board because of the following emergency, a doctor's nightmare: One evening she received a call from a patient who was desperately ill, apparently having a stroke. She went out to this patient's home and found that the patient was indeed having a stroke; she could not speak and had developed a paralysis on one side of her body. Dr. Talliaferro had been using EDTA chelation therapy in her practice and treated this woman on the spot by administering EDTA intravenously. This caring physician, in a professional manner, wanted to keep an eye on the patient overnight. Since it was impossible to get her to a hospital, the good doctor took the patient home and sat with her, nursed her, and monitored her throughout the night. The next day, the patient made a complete recovery without any evidence of residual defect.

Because this respected, competent physician had treated the patient in her own home and—worse—because she had used chelation therapy and was a chelation doctor, she was called before the State Board for a formal hearing about the care and management of this case—a hearing that was expected to be followed by disciplinary action.

In order to have such a hearing, there has to be a complaint. At the instigation of the Arkansas Medical Examining Board, the patient's son was encouraged to file a complaint. This young man did not even live with his mother, who had no complaints whatsoever about the care she received. On the contrary, she was very appreciative of Dr. Talliaferro's prompt attention and intervention and the results of her treatments. Nevertheless, a formal hearing was called.

In Arkansas, the State Board of Medical Examiners was dominated for years by one physician, Dr. Joe Verser, who single-handedly controlled the practice of medicine in that state. He has little understanding of or regard for due process, as evidenced in the videotaped proceedings of the hearing. Dr. Talliaferro's case attracted a great deal of local media attention. Many of her patients, some of whom had been treated with chelation, came to her defense. They attended the hearing to make their positions known regarding the high esteem in which they held Dr. Talliaferro and to demonstrate how much they appreciated her desire to practice in their community.

About this time, the Arkansas State Board had been asking for an extension of their power and authority and, in particular, for immunity from libel and prosecution. However, after viewing only fifteen minutes of the videotaped proceedings against Dr. Talliaferro, a group of state legislators were appalled by what they saw and heard. They were convinced from that moment on that further extension of this abuse of power was unwarranted.

This blatantly-absurd case against the well-respected Dr. Talliaferro clearly reveals an abuse of power. It proves how a fine and dedicated physician who has devoted her professional life to serving a rural, under-served community can be made to look like a criminal.

Dr Talliaferro's case is a crude version of what is happening to many physicians throughout the country who use chelation and other safe, effective alternatives. As the former Chairman of the State Board of Medical Examiners in Arkansas, the backward Dr. Verser had no regard for legal procedure. Dr. Talliaferro's "trial" was a rather colorful event with a rural community rallying in support of their doctor. Usually, however, this abuse of power by State Boards of Medical Examiners goes unnoticed in urban settings throughout the country.

Dr. Talliaferro's hearing was videotaped; the audio portion of the system was accidentally left on, and it recorded private conversations before the hearing and during the board's executive session. The recorded conversations clearly show the flagrant disregard for due process to which alternative medical doctors are subjected. For example, at one point Dr. Ray Jouett commented, "The Board does not have to listen to a parade of people saying how wonderful I am since I had that medicine. . . Now we have to listen to his expert witnesses, but we do not have to listen to testimonies of that sort."

Because these conversations and the hearings themselves are so indicative of the kangaroo courts which are attempting to destroy alternative practitioners, I have included verbatim further detail of the accidentally-recorded conversations as well as the transcript of the hearing in the appendix of this book.

THE LOUISIANA STATE BOARD OF MEDICAL EXAMINERS VERSUS DR. ROY MONTALBANO

Dr. Roy Montalbano is another excellent physician, who practices family medicine in the towns of Mandeville and Covington, in Louisiana. This doctor became interested in EDTA chelation therapy in his fifties because of his own illness. He has coronary artery disease, and, at the time that the diagnosis was first made, an angiogram showed extensive blockage in all three coronary vessels. He had unstable angina and familial hypercholesterolemia; his total serum cholesterol level had been as high as 900 milligrams percent. At the time that he was first diagnosed, cardiovascular surgeons were not attempting triple and quadruple bypasses. In fact, they refused to operate on him because the disease was so extensive.

Dr. Montalbano then discovered EDTA chelation therapy. He was treated by the eminent Dr. Ray Evers in Cottonwood, Alabama. Later, after completing a course in chelation therapy, he worked as a physician in Dr. Ever's clinic. He subsequently returned to the Mandeville/Covington area, due north of New Orleans on the other side of Pontchatrain Lake. He reopened his practice, much to the dismay of his colleagues because, before he had become ill, he had had the largest family practice on that side of the lake. He has continued to be free of chest pain and to function normally, and he has apparently completely recovered from his illness.

Practicing chelation therapy in Louisiana, Dr. Montalbano attracted the attention of Organized Medicine. When, as related in an earlier chapter of this book, Dr. Lyons made the comment "Oh yes, chelation has reared its ugly head again, but we know what to do about it!" he was making an obvious reference to Dr. Montalbano, since he was the only physician in the state at that time using chelation therapy.

Since EDTA is a licensed and approved drug, the Louisiana State Board of Medical Examiners knew that they had little ground for revoking Dr. Montalbano's license for performing chelation therapy. Instead, they searched for another reason to revoke his license.

In an effort to entrap Dr. Montalbano, the Board first sent undercover agents to his office posed as patients, a not-uncommon technique. One suspected agent was addicted to demerol and other narcotics, which he had been receiving from his physician-girlfriend in Hammond, Louisiana. After several chelation treatments, this patient attempted to file a malpractice suit against Dr. Montalbano, claiming that he had become addicted as a result of Dr. Montalbano's therapy.

In another instance, an undercover agent posed as a patient and requested treatment with acupuncture. The acupuncturist was a veterinarian by the name of Dr. Daniel Zehr, with sound training in acupuncture and trans-cutaneous electrical nerve stimulation for pain control, who performed acupuncture for six other physicians' patients as well. He had been verbally assured by Dr. Lyons, then Executive Director of the Board, that if he worked under the supervision of a licensed physician he would be in compliance with Louisiana law and the Medical Practice Act. Dr. Lyons did not put his assurance into writing, however. The Board accused Dr. Montalbano—but not the other physicians for whom Dr. Zehr administered acupuncture—of "aiding and abetting an unlicensed practitioner." They claimed that Dr. Zehr did not meet the requirements for licensure as an acupuncturist in the state of Louisiana. The requirements included, in addition to formal training, many years of practice in this alternative therapy. These requirements are so rigid and complex that only a few highly-trained and experienced Chinese physician-acupuncturists would qualify.

Dr. Montalbano's attorney, Mr. Donahue, took depositions from other physicians who used the same acupuncturist and found that none of them were ever charged with an offense by the Board. Only Dr. Montalbano, the only physician in this group who used EDTA chelation therapy in his practice, was charged with aiding and abetting an unlicensed practitioner.

The Board recommended that his license be temporarily suspended. The case was appealed twice, and the final decision of the state administrative law judges was that Dr. Montalbano should have checked on the credentials of Dr. Zehr before hiring him. Interestingly, the judges asked a number of questions about the other physicians who had used his services, questioning why they were not disciplined by the Board. These judges also did not render an opinion as to the nature or severity of punishment, and it was on this point that the case went to court again. The State Board recommended two months' license suspension, followed by probation, for Dr. Montalbano only. Attorney Donahue noted that the judges, all the way up the line, felt that the case was petty and not really worthy of serious consideration, judgment, or punishment.

In the fall of 1990, an administrative law judge gave short shrift to the case in her review, commenting that Dr. Montalbano "had had enough time for appeals" and that it was time for him to "pay the price." The decision was so abrupt and so final that one wonders if it had been "fixed" (something not unusual in the state of Louisiana with its system of elected judges), especially in view of the over-whelming evidence that Dr. Montalbano had been singled out and treated unfairly.

I first met Dr. Roy Montalbano in 1982. To attribute his recovery to the placebo effect was not just an insult to this fine doctor, but flagrant disregard for careful observation, where all science begins. Nevertheless, whether EDTA is more effective than a placebo is a problem which could be solved through research, using the scientific method. To that end, I wrote a research proposal, entitled "A Retrospective Study of the Effectiveness of the Calcium Chelating Agent, EDTA, in the Treatment of Coronary Artery Disease and Its Impact on Survival After Myocardial Infarction." Among the documents and letters supporting the proposal was a letter from Dr. Philip R. Lee, then Chancellor of the University of California at San Francisco and formerly Assistant Secretary of Health, Education, and Welfare. I had heard that Dr. Lee had referred the vice-president of the Crocker Bank to Dr. Ross Gordon in Albany, California, for chelation treatments, and that this prominent individual had gotten a good response. This led to the funding of the first FDA-sanctioned American Institute for Medical Preventics (later re-named ACAM) double-blind EDTA study with a dose-response curve.

From chelation therapy, I began to look into other alternative therapies which I felt worthy of scientific inquiry. Little did I realize that some of these drug-sparing therapies were off limits to American doctors and that I would incur the wrath and animosity of my supposed colleagues, particularly the "wise guys" who control medical licensure and take their cues from a "medical Mafia," who intend to thwart competition and maximize profit for themselves and the pharmaceutical companies. My experiences have certainly called to mind that anonymous French physician's statement: "Medicine has become a whore, and the pharmaceutical industry its pimp."

The order to target me may have come from the National Council Against Health Fraud (NCAHF). This council, itself fraudulent, seems to have taken over the work of the Coordinating Conference on Health Information (CCHI), the covert arm of the AMA, at least in the area of chiropractic. A lengthy discussion of these secret bureaucracies has been presented in previous chapters of this book, but it is worth reminding the reader that they use the Federation of State Boards of Medical Examiners and their legal authority to issue, suspend, and revoke licensure in order to regulate and control medical practice and to discourage alternative (less remunerative) medical therapies. This goal is a greater priority for them than the apprehension of criminal physicians or the restriction of the licenses of those repeatedly sued for malpractice. They profess to protect the public from quacks, but their behavior seems primarily concerned with "protecting turf." The NCAHF receives money from the AMA, the National Pharmaceutical Council, the Food Industry, and others. We need to remember, for example, that not so long ago Organized Medicine defended smoking, basically saying that it's okay by allowing medical doctors in their white coats to leer happily at the public in cigarette commercials, extolling one brand's merits over another. Tobacco advertising revenue helped support *JAMA*, as did AMA stock in tobacco companies (which has been quietly sold in fairly recent times). Belatedly they began to attack tobacco companies, never revealing their former shameful support of the tobacco industry. Their self-centered priorities affect public health, and now they are attempting to stamp out alternative medicine.

LOUISIANA STATE BOARD OF MEDICAL EXAMINERS VERSUS JAMES P. CARTER, M.D., Dr.P.H.: DR. CARTER GOES TO KANGAROO COURT

In May or June, 1985, I had been warned by telephone by a Council member, Dr. James Kenney, that I would find out how the Council on Health Fraud could really hurt somebody. I had also been given an opportunity, in writing, by him to "work together with him to dissuade Cernitin American, Inc., from continuing its highly questionable marketing practices."

Cernitin America, Inc. marketed Cernitin Extracts T60 and GBX, Dick Gregory's Bahamian Diet, and a type of lactose-fermenting bacteria (ventrux acido). Cernitin America, Inc. had made a grant of $70,000 to Tulane University Medical Center, for research on some of their products and for a fitness program for overweight New Orleans police officers.

In a medical dispute, using the testimony of a Ph.D., who is unqualified to evaluate clinical issues in medicine but nevertheless sounds authoritative, makes it easier "to pull the wool over someone's eyes." This technique is often used by the CCHI (Coordinating Conference on Health Information). There can exist a real incentive on the part of a Ph.D. to "get" a medical doctor by registering a complaint against him or her. Some Ph.D.s resent playing a "second-fiddle" role to medical doctors and will jump at the opportunity to put a physician down.

I do not personally know Dr. James Kenney, Ph.D. We spoke only once, over the telephone. My assessment of him, however, is that he is a lightweight nutritionist based in Los Angeles, California, whom I refused to deal with because of his lack of breadth and depth in knowledge about products he considers to be fraudulent and examples of nutrition quackery. I chose to communicate instead with another member of his committee, Dr. Rosalyn Alfin-Slater, M.D., Head of the Nutrition Program at the UCLA School of Public Health at the time. I wrote to Dr. Alfin-Slater on December 13, 1984, in an effort to communicate with the Council on Health Fraud and to explain to them the differences between ordinary bee pollen and the Cernitin extracts T60 and GBX. Dr. Kenney revealed his ignorance by indicating in an article he wrote that he didn't know the difference between bee pollen and Cernitin flower pollen extracts. As is so often the case, the quackbusters were not dealing with quackery on this issue. Overwhelming evidence shows that flower pollen extract is a "tomato" rather than a "placebo." (The reader will recall that a tomato is a drug which works but which the medical profession doesn't believe works. A placebo is a drug which cannot work, but the patient believes that it does work.)

On September 7, 1985, Dr. John J. Walsh, Chancellor of the Tulane University Medical Center, was visited by Dr. J. Morgan Lyons (the same Dr. Lyons who was involved in Dr. Ever's trial) and Dr. Gerald LaNasa of the Louisiana State Board of Medical Examiners. They stated that their purpose was to apprise him of "numerous serious complaints which had been lodged against Dr. James Carter." Drs. Lyons and LaNasa represented the Louisiana State Board of Medical Examiners and were, therefore, the plaintiffs at the local level. Also, at a national level, it was presumed that I had made a great deal of money from my research and alleged endorsements, based on the results of our findings, of several commercial health food products. This allegation is unequivocally not true. The Strike Force may have also used its influence to bring about IRS almost-yearly audits, from 1983 to 1989, of my wife and me. The reader will recall that sanctions are sometimes put in place by government (by such means as denying MEDICARE reimbursements and sabotaging and/or denying demonstration and research grant requests). They also use techniques of disinformation and entrapment to construct a case against a physician that uses natural, nutritional, or any unconventional remedies, regardless of their legality or effectiveness.

Chancellor Walsh of Tulane Medical Center summarized his meeting with Drs. Lyons and LaNasa in a memorandum dated October 28, 1985. Dr. Walsh appointed an ad hoc committee to address the Board's complaints on November 13, 1985. This committee concluded its deliberations nearly seven months later, in May, 1986. I met with them on at least three occasions. This type of in-house investigation, to my knowledge, has never before been conducted on a tenured faculty member in the absence of formal criminal charges.

Three attorneys assisted me in defending myself against these charges: Ron Wilson in New Orleans, Henry McGee, III, Professor of UCLA Law School, and James Turner of Washington, D.C.

I was summoned to appear at an informal hearing on May 22, 1986, in spite of the fact that the Board had received a report from the Tulane Ad Hoc Committee exonerating me from any wrongdoing. But they questioned my judgment on certain matters. (Would Daniel have walked, voluntarily, into the lion's den? I had no warning ahead of time that a conspiracy existed.)

The letter requesting my appearance was dated May 9, 1986. It stated the following: "Information has been received that you may be involved in chelation therapy and that you are also allegedly involved in the treatment of prostatic disease with bee pollen and research on macrobiotic diets, and the use of evening primrose oil, etc. . . ."

On the advice of attorney Wilson at the informal hearing, I declined to answer hostile questions or cover ground which had already been covered by the Tulane ad hoc committee. Mr. Wilson and I were then excused.

Our inquiries to the Board (to determine the facts and circumstances surrounding their directive to Tulane University Medical Center to investigate my professional and research activities) all remained ignored and unanswered. On July 9, 1986, I was notified that the Board had scheduled a formal evidentiary hearing for Thursday, September 25, 1986. The specific charges were:

(1) Efforts to deceive or defraud the public

(2) Professional or medical incompetency [The nerve of those guys. I could challenge them, individually or collectively, to an examination which measures general medical knowledge, and I know I would win.]

(3) Unprofessional conduct

(4) Continuing or recurring medical practice which fails to satisfy the prevailing and usually accepted standards of medical practice in this state [which are pretty low].

Mr. Wilson requested documents from the Board to support these allegations; the documents were never supplied.

Further communications were mostly with my attorneys and between Mr. Wilson, representing me, and the law firm of Adams and Reese, representing the Board. On October 23, 1986, I received a letter from the Board chastising me but telling me that the charges had been dropped, apparently on the advice of their attorneys. Other problems remained, however. There was still the nuisance of IRS audits. We were not adequately prepared for 1983 and 1984, this being my first experience with an audit. The expensive firm of Peat Marwick did much less to prepare us for those year's audits than H. and R. Block did in 1988 and 1989. It was not until 1990, when the IRS asked for monthly payments of $800 and threatened to seize real estate and sell it for the balance due, that we consulted another CPA, Jay West, who had previously worked for the IRS. In reviewing our audit reports for 1983 and 1984, he recognized a name. He exclaimed: "Denise Blanton! I know her—she was like a rabid dog!" When he said that, I was convinced that I had been set up.

Before long, I began to feel the effects of the Board's campaign against me. A grant from the Kleberg Foundation, which has a reputation for staying with its grantees, to study a vegetarian diet as it relates to cancer survival was not renewed after only one year. Many other subsequent grant requests have been denied, in sharp contrast to my record of successfully obtaining funds prior to 1983.

At this time, our Department of Nutrition was undergoing a review by the Curriculum Committee. We were getting such an unjustified hard time (some of the members seemed determined to disqualify our doctoral program), that one member of the department suspected racial motivations and suggested that I complain to Chancellor Walsh. The Committee's efforts were backed up by the Ad Hoc Committee on Long-Range (5-year) Planning for the school, on the pretext of complying with an alleged recommendation of the Accreditation Site Visit Team Report.

In addition, there suddenly seemed to be no indication that the school intended to replace the two nutrition faculty members whom we had lost, reducing us to a department of two and one-fifth faculty members. Chancellor Walsh had also reportedly mentioned to the university attorney that he might use the occasion of the ad hoc committee investigation of my professional and research activities "to make some organizational and structural changes in the school."

The Curriculum Committee approved the Masters of Public

Health in Nutrition program for three years in 1987, but they did not approve the doctoral program. They put the doctoral program on probation pending reorganization of the departments. After the Department of Nutrition was abolished and the Nutrition program merged into the Department of Applied Health Sciences, a new Curriculum Committee was established. This new committee now began to question the masters program in nutrition, which had been approved only one year before, an unheard-of precedent because programs are approved for three years at a time.

One interesting observation: When I first met with the Tulane ad hoc committee, I was shown a copy of a letter I had written on university stationery to Mrs. Bobbie Graubarth suggesting that she might want to look into the multi-level marketing of some health food products such as Dick Gregory's Bahamian Diet and the Cernitin extracts. I suggested that, in this way, she could generate financial support for her excellent health promotion program for the elderly called Longevity Therapy.

One of my attorneys, Henry McGee, noted that since I had addressed Mrs. Graubarth by her first name, Bobbie, it could be presumed that I knew her; therefore there was nothing to be commercially gained by using Tulane stationery with its letterhead and that I must have used it merely as a matter of routine and convenience. When the letter was presented to me, however, by the Tulane ad hoc committee, the implication was that I was using Tulane University's name for the purpose of solicitation. It was also implied that Mrs. Graubarth had complained about this to the Louisiana State Board of Medical Examiners. But no such complaint was issued by her. As a matter of fact, according to Mrs. Graubarth/Seiler (she has since re-married), she has never complained either orally or in writing about me to the Louisiana State Board of Medical Examiners or to anyone else for that matter. So where did the letter come from? It must have been removed from our departmental files.

ONLY IN AMERICA—MEDICAL MCCARTHYISM

Another interesting observation: In the interim, the U.S.-based company Cernitin America and its parent company in Sweden, A.B. Cernelle, had been taken over by a Swiss corporation in Lugano. If we were to receive continuing support for research, it would now have to come from the Swiss. On September 23, 1986, retired professor Olov Lindahl of Sweden wrote to me the following letter:

I am indeed very grateful to get all of the material that you have sent to me and to acquire some insight into the Medical McCarthyism in the U.S. Some day, I will make a summary of it all, in the Swedish *Journal of Biological Medicine.*

I have been very active in this matter and speaking on your behalf with different representatives. It seems to me that all except A.B. Cernelle do not want to interfere and to help. A Cernitin employee has been to the main corporation in Lugano, Switzerland, and convinced them that it would be unwise to help you in your legal difficulties with the Louisiana State Board.

This employee seems to have spoken badly about you, saying that you have misused chelation therapy and wrongly injected the solution in the peritoneum. This was such a ludicrous idea which seemed quite absurd to me. This was the statement that was made by President Melera of the Swiss company in Lugano over the telephone. There was much more information, and I had some difficulty in trying to understand it all, but I think that what I am stating here is correct.

A.B. Cernelle in Sweden, as you know, are now in the hands of the Swiss company and their subsidiary Cernitin America cannot do anything, even if they wished to do so. The last word is not in, and I am still talking seriously with them. I think not giving you a helping hand gives a bad reputation, for example, to organizations, such as the American Academy of Medical Preventics, and possibly others as well. Of course, I am convinced that you can manage the matter, yourself, but it is a question of principle.

A subsequent letter from Professor Lindahl in Stockholm, dated February 26, 1988, contained the sentence "I suppose by now, that the Conspiracy against you on the part of the Medical Board is now a memory—but it was an evil attack."

An interesting follow-up to the Board's hearings occurred on or about April 26, 1989, when I received a phone call from Dr. Ross Gordon. He was very concerned that he might be able to get enough patients with peripheral vascular disease for the Walter Reed Army Hospital's study. He said, "The cardiovascular surgeons seem to be dragging their feet." He wanted to know if there was anyone at Tulane and/or Charity Hospital with whom they could sub-contract to do thirty or more cases, following an agreed-upon protocol.

I said that I would ask around, and that there were essentially two possibilities:

(1)   Dr. Gil McMahon of the Clinical Research Center, a private drug-testing facility here in New Orleans

(2)   Dr. Morris D. Kerstein, then head of Tulane's Peripheral Vascular Surgery Division, as well as Associate Dean and Director of Graduate and Postgraduate Medical Education

Dr. McMahon, it turned out, had testified against Dr. Ray Evers when he applied for a license to practice medicine in Louisiana. Essentially, Dr. McMahon testified against EDTA chelation therapy, because the result was that Dr. Evers was denied a license on the grounds that he was using EDTA chelation therapy. Dr. Evers had sued him, and Dr. McMahon said that the suit cost him $5,000 and that he doesn't know how much it cost his insurance company. Nevertheless, he said he believed a scientific study should be done and said he would be willing to do it, if someone like Dr. Kerstein could provide him with the patients.

However, I had been warned by medical students not to expect Dr. Kerstein to go out on a limb. The students believed that Dr. Kerstein wanted to be dean of a medical school one day and for that reason probably wouldn't "rock the boat," although he would probably be honest about it. (Kerstein subsequently became the Chairman of the Department of Surgery at Jefferson Medical College in Philadelphia.)

The students were right. When Dr. Kerstein responded, he said that he had checked with some of his colleagues at UCLA and Harvard and that they convinced him that he would be ruining his career if he did such a study, because the political climate was not ready to accept EDTA chelation therapy even if it did work. His UCLA and Harvard colleagues told him that they would testify against him if anything went wrong with any of the patients in the study. Dr. Kerstein also said that he had spoken to Dr. Martin Litwin, who had also advised him not to get involved. This was not surprising, since Dr. Litwin had also told Dr. Emmett Chapital, a cardiologist at Tulane, not to speak to the American College of Medical Preventics (now ACAM) when they met in New Orleans five years before, because they were practitioners of EDTA chelation therapy. He also warned Dr. Chapital that the Louisiana State Board of Medical Examiners was going to "crack down" on doctors using chelation in Louisiana.

Dr. Kerstein was afraid to take a chance because he, understandably, values the approval of his colleagues over scientific inquiry. (Not everyone is a Simon Wiesenthal when it comes to acting on principle, nor should we expect them to be.) Dr. Kerstein did mention, however, that back in 1983 someone from the Louisiana State Board of Medical Examiners had asked him to testify against me, and he had refused.

My saga with the IRS dragged on, and I was forced to borrow money. The IRS put a lien on my house and threatened to seize it and auction it off for the alleged balance owed in taxes, interest, and penalties. I sold some real estate in a depressed market, and the IRS took its money right off the top. Three months later, they contacted me again to say they had "made a mistake" and that, based on "new calculations," I owed them an additional $2,500. My credit rating was damaged, and I was stripped of my assets. The FDA officials' threat to Dr. Rasmussen, quoted earlier in this book, seem appropriate to my situation: "You've got a nice office and a nice home. If you want to keep them, you better stop using and promoting electro-magnetic therapy."

THE NEW YORK BOARD OF QUALITY ASSURANCE VERSUS DR. WARREN LEVIN

This case erupted in 1980, when the New York Office of Professional Medical Conduct subpoenaed the records of three patients treated by Dr. Levin in 1976. The records on four additional patients were sought in 1989. The state went after Dr. Levin for the use of some twenty specific treatments and eighteen diagnostic and monitoring tests regarded by the American Organized Med as unproven or questionable. The great majority of the tests and treatments are widely used in the U.S. and in many countries around the world. The Office of Professional Medical Conduct continually harassed Dr. Levin in and out of court. It was apparent early on in the case that he was to be made an example for other physicians in the Empire State. The Levin case climbed up and down the court ladder until it was scheduled for decision following a series of hearings to begin in September, 1989. Dr. Levin's personal account on audiotape is both chilling and hilarious.

The panel that was established was chaired by an administrative law judge by the name of Larry Storch. This panel heard the list of charges against Dr. Levin and in November, 1989, recommended dismissal of a veritable laundry list of charges against him. The *Hoffman Center News* related in its January, 1990, edition, the following observations:

[Dr. Levin's attorney Robert H. Harris] finally backed Victor Herbert into the position where he refused to answer the question of whether he was in fact the complainant who had reported alleged violations by Dr. Levin to the Office of Professional Medical Conduct in the first place. Herbert refused to answer, despite direction to answer by the presiding administrative law judge.

After the hearing, attorney Harris observed that the State's attorney had taken the remarkable position that there was no other person besides Herbert prepared to provide significant testimony against Dr. Levin, and no other witnesses were called in. Noted that the State of New York had reached a road block after spending a fortune in mindless prosecution of Dr. Levin, a doctor recognized by his colleagues for his preeminent qualifications, competence, and compassion for his patients!

Attorney Robert Harris was also able to convince Judge Larry Storch that Herbert, who had repeatedly cited Levin during a 1984 congressional hearing on quackery, could not possibly testify as an unbiased expert. Attorney Harris referred to Herbert as the "self-anointed quackbuster" and the "man with the loose-leaf notebook resumé." Having thoroughly researched Herbert's background, he brought into evidence repeated examples of material damaging to the credibility of the so-called expert witness. Under examination by Harris, Herbert acknowledged—among other things—falsehood in his application to medical school. (He had lied about his financial status.) Harris also got him to acknowledge that he had been asked to resign from a Veterans' Administration Hospital post in Brooklyn.

All the Storch panel could do, however, was to recommend dismissal of the charges. To be enforced, the recommendation had to be upheld by Dr. David Axelrod, Commissioner of the New York State Department of Health, who subsequently refused to do so. Dr. Axelrod is not a friend of alternative medicine. Nevertheless, we have to assume that he was familiar with the charges against Dr. Levin and that he realized that the most serious charge of all, as far as the Office of Professional Medical Conduct is concerned, was the use of chelation therapy on some of his patients.

If this indeed is the case, then the Commissioner of Health of the state of New York is collaborating and directly taking part in a conspiracy to withhold this effective treatment from clinical use in the state of New York. In doing so, he is endorsing the payment of $35,000-$50,000 for a surgical procedure which does not work as well as the non-surgical series of chelation treatments which cost only $3,500. His position most certainly cannot be justified as a cost-containment effort.

Nearly twenty years ago, I participated in a National Academy of Sciences workshop on the Applications of Science and Technology to Development in Zaire. The occasion was a visit to a research laboratory which had obviously been cleaned up and made to appear operational for our benefit. Writing the report in French, I translated the expression "snow-job" from English into French as *un travail de niege,* and twenty years later this expression came to mind when I read the transcript of Victor Herbert's testimony as expert witness in Warren Levin's hearing before the New York State Office of Professional Medical Conduct. Herbert is a master of the snow-job, in pulling wool over a court's eyes. The court doesn't know and understand medicine, and Herbert succeeds in blatant character assassination of good doctors.

Herbert had no difficulty in making up a diagnosis: "Mega doses of vitamin C can cause deposits of oxalates in the heart, which among other things can produce first-degree heart block." He refers to this condition as metastatic oxalosis. No one else, however, has ever heard of metastatic oxalosis.

Dr. Levin and his attorney, Mr. Harris, went to Dr. Levin's office and did a computer search for metastatic oxalosis. First, they searched Medline, which included all the articles in the peer-reviewed literature from 1983 on. They punched in metastatic oxalosis, and the computer replied "zero documents found." Dr. Levin then surmised that it might be in the older literature, so he looked in the MESZ computer search, which goes back to 1966 and includes the peer-reviewed literature from then to the present. Again, the computer responded, "zero documents found." Dr. Levin turned to the Core Content Medical Library of the BRS Colleague Service. It contains the complete texts of a number of major textbooks in medicine, as well as the complete texts of many of the major medical journals of the western world.Computer response: "zero documents for metastatic oxalosis." Furthermore, it is not listed in the ICD9 *Official Book of Diagnoses.*

Dr.Herbert was challenged with their findings on his last day in the witness chair. When confronted with them, he scoffed at the computer printouts. He attested under oath, "You didn't do it right! I have dozens of articles." On a subsequent day, Herbert produced what he called documentation of metastatic oxalosis. His attorney presented as evidence *Dorland's Medical Dictionary,* in which he pointed to the words "metabolic" and "oxalosis," saying that if you put them together, you get "metabolic oxalosis." He also presented a book in which one chapter made reference to metabolic oxalosis. Who was the author of that chapter? None other than Victor Herbert. Dr. Herbert's description of the condition follows:

> What you do when you find a first degree heart block is a thorough evaluation of what medications the patient may have been taking, what over-the-counter stuff the patient may be taking, what things may be in the patient's environment which can produce cardiac damage. For example, patients taking megadoses of vitamin C can get deposits of oxalate in their heart, which among other things can produce first degree heart block, this condition of metastatic oxalosis.

Dr. Levin also did a Medline search in which he asked for "oxalosis" and "ascorbate," truncated. The computer came up with only eight references having to do with "ascorb" and "oxalosis." Those articles all talked about the problem of oxalosis with excessive doses of vitamin C in patients in chronic renal failure; not in people with normal kidney function. What Herbert is talking about is a theoretical pathway of metabolism from ascorbate to oxalate. But actual studies show that when people are given large doses of ascorbic acid, they don't get any significant change in their oxalic acid status. This is just one example of how Herbert is unable to differentiate (his own) theory from practice. And we need to remember that he is paid to say this pseudo-science.

An interesting twist has developed in the Warren Levin trial. Both the prosecution and defense have called all their witnesses and have rested their cases. The last one for the prosecution, a well-respected cardiologist from one of New York's finest medical schools, turned out to be a good witness for the defense, because even though he was opposed to chelation, he was honest about his lack of experience and showed his ignorance as well. At this writing, it looks good for a decision in favor of Levin.

During the Thanksgiving holidays of 1991, a scandal erupted when a New York City OB/GYN attempted to abort a seven- or eight-month-old fetus. The abortion was unsuccessful; the infant was born and survived, but an arm had to be amputated. The *New York Daily News* picked up and pursued the story. The New York Office of Professional Medical Conduct leaked to the *Daily News* the names of other "dangerous physicians" it was investigating, and Dr. Warren Levin's name was on the list, in the top ten. Needless to say, this was no accident—it was done deliberately to destroy Dr. Levin's practice and career. If opponents of alternative medicine are not successful one way, they will try another.

THE TEXAS STATE BOARD
VERSUS DR. JOHN PARKES TROWBRIDGE

Dr. John Parkes Trowbridge is one of the young bright stars in the field of chelation. He practices just outside of Houston in a town called Humble, Texas. The Texas State Board of Medical Examiners has been trying to get him on charges of false and misleading advertisement. It claims that it is acting on complaints it has received and investigated regarding Dr. Trowbridge's practice.

Dr. Trowbridge had been warned by another doctor that one of the Texas Examining Board members stated, "We're going to get every last one of the doctors who use chelation. We don't care how long it takes, but we will eventually get every single one of them." So it came as no surprise when he was hauled before the Texas State Board of Medical Examiners for alleged false and misleading advertising.

With regard to chelation therapy, the Board claimed that Dr. Trowbridge's advertising was misleading and deceptive on four points:

(1) That chelation can help make stronger bones, partly because toxic metals that are present in the bone structure (in place of the usual calcium) are removed and new bone is made with stronger calcium in place. [The Board claims this is unsupported by medical evidence and is misleading.]

(2) That chelation can reverse or delay aging and disease changes, making chelation therapy seem to be the "Fountain of Youth." [The Board considers the statement misleading and deceptive. Dr. Trowbridge vows that he never made this statement. He also claims that the Board has yet to share the printed sources of these so called quotes attributed to him.]

(3) That chelation shows 75 to 80 out of 100 patients had excellent results. [The Board claims that this statement is unsupported by any medical or statistical evidence. They further claim that there are no objective standards by which to define excellent results, and therefore this statement is deceptive.]

(4) That EDTA is interrupting free radical attacks. [The

Board claims that this is unsupported by any medical evidence and that we do not know if, or how, EDTA causes changes to prevent or preclude arteriosclerosis, arthritis, cancer, inflammation, and allergies; so the Board claims this is also deceptive.]

I testified as an expert witness on Dr. Trowbridge's behalf in Austin, Texas, on July 11, 1990. The expert witness for the Board was the head of Blue Cross and Blue Shield for the State of Texas. Experience around the country, however, indicated that Dr. Trowbridge would have to get out of this kangaroo court and into a real court, on appeal, if he was to win this legal battle. Fortunately, Texas has a secondary level of appeal where an independent arbitrator, usually a lawyer, is called in. Whatever the evidence that Dr. Trowbridge submits to show the efficacy of EDTA chelation therapy, however, the Medical Board can rule that substantial evidence supports their point of view. "Substantial evidence" can mean "any evidence of substance" in their estimation. The phrase "preponderance [over 50%] of the evidence" may not be considered by the Board. The preponderance of the evidence might be in Dr. Trowbridge's behalf, and they could still rule against him. Dr. Trowbridge's case, therefore, would have to go to a higher court on appeal, after the Texas State Board of Medical Examiners ruled against him.

Most of the doctors win their cases once they get into the regular courts on appeal. This, however, is usually only after they have spent $100,000 or more in legal fees, which appears to be a principal objective of these nuisance cases instigated by the Board. The physician pays his fees out of his own pocket; the Board, however, pays its fees with state money. *Illegetimi non carborundum:* from Virgil, this translates into the popular phrase "Don't let the bastards get you down."

The state's arbitrator ruled in favor of Dr. Trowbridge in the Fall of 1990, stating in his decision that he could not do otherwise, because the Board's expert witness, the director of Blue Cross and Blue Shield for the State of Texas, was not an expert on chelation therapy and therefore his testimony in this area was not credible.

THE COLORADO STATE BOARD OF MEDICAL EXAMINERS VERSUS DR. WILLIAM E. DOELL

The Colorado Board of Medical Examiners keeps no written or recorded minutes of their meetings, so there is no way for a maligned doctor to determine whether his civil rights were violated. This in itself creates suspicion of conspiracy at the Board level. Dr. William E. Doell, an osteopath who served on the Board for thirteen years, revealed that the Board consisted of seven medical doctors and two doctors of osteopathy. At every meeting, the enmity between the M.D.'s and D.O.'s was thick enough to cut with a knife. Dr. Doell spent most of his time arguing to protect the licenses of osteopaths that the M.D. members wanted to remove. Dr. Doell, himself an osteopath, describes his own case:

> It has been an exercise, like a trip through wonderland. When you get to the door, the door is too small or the keys don't fit the locks. . . This is pathetic, and it is time that we as an organization, where all alternative physicians (they don't even have to be chelating physicians) raise enough of a stink to get the public behind us to do something about this. We don't have a choice, we have to do something about this; time is short. It is unbelievable; I wouldn't believe it if I had not lived it.

Dr. Doell first practiced traditional family medicine in Grand Junction, Colorado, for eleven years. He moved his family to Denver in 1979 and established a chelation practice in a metropolitan area, where he established himself as a great pioneering osteopathic physician. Patients traveled to Colorado from western Canada, Alaska, Montana, Wyoming, Utah, North Dakota, South Dakota, Nebraska, Kansas and the far reaches of Colorado to receive medical care from this doctor. His practice encompassed a complete array of medical approaches. He very successfully incorporated into his practice EDTA chelation therapy, nutritional medicine, diagnosis and treatment of candidiasis, food allergy diagnosis and therapy, treatment of mercury amalgam incompatibilities, treatment of arthritis with antiamoebics, osteopathic manipulative therapy, treatment of environmental illnesses, and traditional family practice.

Dr. Doell no longer has a medical license. In fact, the Colorado State Board would not even let him "catch on in Alaska" before they took his license. (The reader will note how this scenario is in stark contrast to the story of the anesthesiologist in Massachusetts who was caught sexually copulating with sedated female patients, got his knuckles rapped, and was allowed to transfer his license to New Hampshire and practice there.)

In 1979, Dr. Doell was one of seven doctors providing chelation therapy in Denver. When the Board of Medical Examiners revoked his license in August, 1990, he was the last chelating physician in Denver. They were all "run out of Dodge"!

Dr. Doell's license was revoked without his ever being allowed to face his accusers, i.e. the physician members of the Board of Medical Examiners. The Colorado Medical Practice Act does allow the physician-defendant to be present in person, and to be represented by counsel if he so desires, to offer evidence in his defense, but the Executive Administrator of the Board, who is not trained in any facet of medicine, will not allow this safeguard to be exercised. This entire proceeding is allowed, under administrative law, to be tried and prosecuted by the Attorney General's officers. The proceeding is heard before an administrative law judge, who is another attorney and who, in this case, had never previously heard a medical case. The proceeding is then ratified by a Medical Board that, incredibly, keeps no written minutes. The Bill of Rights to the Constitution of the United States of America guarantees an accused the right to face his accusers. Is administrative law outside of the Constitution? Let the physician beware.

Investigation by a private investigator uncovered a conspiratorial effort to revoke Dr. Doell's license, instigated in the early 1980s and involving charges thought to have been settled eight years previously. Officially, there is statute of limitations as to how long the Board can sandbag complaints against a physician, but one chelation physician whose license was revoked by the Board was hit with a medical malpractice case that had been settled out of court fifteen years before.

In Dr. Doell's case, the senior associate with whom he worked when he moved to Denver was apparently recruited as an instrument to facilitate the revocation of his license. When Dr. Doell expressed a need to renegotiate the terms of their contract because Dr. Doell was now carrying an ever-increasing share of the patient load, the senior doctor made excuses and stalled for three months, in spite of weekly reminders. Finally, in March, 1982, they arranged an after-working-hours meeting, during which another physician, reported to be a specialist in drug and alcohol therapy, proceeded to lecture Dr. Doell about his prescribing habits for eight patients, whose charts had been sequestered unbeknownst to Dr. Doell. At the conclusion of the lecture, the senior associate pulled out a letter terminating the association—obviously a premeditated act. All of the cited cases involved chronic-pain patients, and the prescriptions were written within the scope of his medical practice. Even so, after the senior physician had written a letter to the Board, and the Board had accepted the physician's answers as outlined in answer to their "twenty-day letter," they leveled a charge of "prescribing outside normal practice" as the major cause for revocation eight years later.

Incidentally, two of the patients cited were seen only once by Dr. Doell. One patient was a young man with arteriosclerosis obliterans, having lost both lower extremities and three digits on each hand, who was condemned to sit on a honeydew-sized decubitus ulcer, in a wheelchair, dependent on narcotics for pain control for physical comfort but not addicted to achieve a high. Another, dependent on narcotics for comfort and pain control, had an osteolysis of the epiphyses of his long bones and the vertebral bodies, necessitating recumbency for twenty-two hours per day. Medical boards seem to deliberately obfuscate the difference between addiction to narcotics for a high and narcotic dependency for control of physical pain, whenever it is politically expedient to do so. Dr. C. Stratton Hill of the M.D. Anderson Cancer Hospital, and a pain-control specialist, has been successful in rewriting the Texas laws concerning prescribing adequate amounts of narcotic drugs for pain control, lifting the threat of license revocation and allowing physicians to properly supply comfort to their acute- and chronic-pain patients. Hopefully this will eliminate one type of trumped-up charge made against alternative practitioners.

The Quackery Committee of the Colorado Medical Society had targeted EDTA chelation therapy in 1981. A committee member who served on the staff of the hospital where Dr. Doell had privileges instituted monitoring of his charts, to further accumulate evidence that could be used to incriminate him. After eighteen months of harassment, a hospital-sponsored kangaroo court was convened to continue the inquisition juggernaut. Again, constitutional protections were ignored to satisfy the clandestine aims. When the hospital discovered that Dr. Doell had to attend a sick relative out of state, during the interval between the two hearing sessions, they rescheduled the next meeting while he was out of town and denied Dr. Doell's appeal for compassionate reconsideration. He was forced to resign his staff privileges, just as their strategy had intended. Resignation of staff privileges under duress is, by law, reported to the Board of Medical Examiners. Now the Board had the grounds that they needed to instigate a full-scale investigation and persecution.

The Colorado Medical Practices Act is supposed to be fair, impartial and nondiscriminatory, and Board members are immune from prosecution so long as they carry out their duties in good faith. The Board is comprised of nine physicians—eight specialists and only one general practitioner, even though general/family practitioners make up largest segment of the physician population. As Dr. Doell noted, there were, on his judging board, seven M.D.s and two D.O.s. Is this fair, impartial, and nondiscriminatory?

There were to be two civilian members of the Board, to be "from the public at large." One was an employee of a health maintenance organization. The last member was an attorney who prosecutes physicians for medical malpractice. Fair? Impartial and nondiscriminatory? Certainly not.

In 1985, an MD/GP wrote a letter of complaint to the Board concerning radio advertising that Dr. Doell was using to educate the public about the benefits of chelation therapy. After a cardiologist suggested, "Now we can end this quackery, once and for all," the Board subpoenaed twenty charts.

Dr. Doell's attorneys were incompetent in dealing with the hospital inquiry proceeding. They referred Dr. Doell to a new law firm, and then they hired the opposing attorney who was so clever at "getting" Doell in the first place.

Dr. Doell's new lawyer and the Board attorneys—actually staff members of the State Attorney General's office—traded correspondence for four years. Finally, a hearing before an administrative law judge was scheduled for January, 1989.

In a typical, small court room, the judge, who had never previously heard a medical case—not an unusual situation, according to a previous Board member—sat at her bench. The prosecutor was a deputy attorney general, assisted by an R.N. advisor. Dr. Doell's legal counsel and the court reporter rounded out the actors. The entire proceedings were started and stopped, interrupted and rescheduled over fourteen different sessions. Dr. Doell was popped off and on the stand many times, in an attempt to accommodate the other physicians. Physicians who had absolutely no expertise in areas about which they were to testify were certified as experts. One physician, who participated in the care of two of the OB/GYN cases that the state presented, should have been barred due to conflict of interest.

None of the physicians allowed to testify against Dr. Doell were even remotely familiar with many of the diagnostic modalities that he employed or treatments for many of the diagnosed conditions. Dr. Doell utilized a dark field microscope, long available in this century, with considerable expertise. But none of the physicians who testified against him on the diagnostic efficacy of this microscope (one was a pathologist-hematologist) had ever looked into a dark field microscope at fresh whole blood; yet they "knew" that it was of no diagnostic value.

One charge, involving the use of only one antibiotic pill, was particularly ludicrous. A nineteen-year-old unmarried female, five months pregnant, presented with right renal colic, RBCs and WBCs in the urine, along with a positive test for nitrites, all indicating an acute urinary tract infection. An obstetrics expert criticized Dr. Doell for not having taken a culture of her vagina because she had presented with a temporary abrasion or an excoriation on the labia. As anyone in gynecology knows, you don't culture the vagina for the herpes simplex virus; you culture the *lesion* if it's present—and in this case it had disappeared. The patient was allergic to penicillin, so she was given Macrodantin. The Board took issue with the choice of antibiotic, but when their expert witnesses were given the *Physicians Desk Reference* for 1983, they could not find a better choice. Even more ridiculous, the patient had taken only one pill; as her pain had worsened, she was admitted to the hospital the very next morning.

Of course by now the administrative law judge was completely adrift, lost at sea. The proceedings give every indication that the entire process was a charade and that the outcome had been determined before the onset—all but one charge had taken place six to seven years earlier.

"Due process" in Colorado must mean to lead one through a maze of administrative law proceedings while the carpenters are nailing up the scaffold in the courtyard. Traditional (expensive) medicine and the economic windfall for the legal profession triumphed; Dr. Doell lost over $600,000 in legal fees and lost wages. Two weeks after the hearing before the administrative law judge, and six months before the judge handed down her initial findings, one of the D.O./G.P. expert witnesses bragged to another doctor, "We finally got Doell's license!"

After the administrative law judge hands down the initial findings, the next procedure is for the defendant's legal counsel to review them and find the exceptions, which are errors in procedure and errors in fact in the document. To aid in this, Dr. Doell hired a constitutional attorney whose expertise is reversing or overturning adverse rulings by administrative law judges. The new attorney's fee was an additional $25,000. When these exceptions are submitted, the attorney for the Board is allowed to submit his exceptions to the errors that the defense attorney has found. In Dr. Doell's case, the Board accepted every single exception submitted by the deputy attorney general and denied every single exception filed by the two defense attorneys. Fair, impartial, and nondiscriminatory? In good faith?

The next step was to appeal to the Colorado State Court of Appeals for a stay of the revocation order, so that Dr. Doell could continue to support his wife and two children until his case could be heard before the Court of Appeals, some twelve to eighteen months later, depending on the case load on the docket. This stay was summarily denied. The next step in the so-called due process meanderings was to appeal to the Colorado Supreme Court for a writ of mandamus, demanding that the Court of Appeals tell why the stay was denied. The Supreme Court read the briefs and denied Dr. Doell's petition. No justice was served.

At this point, Dr. Doell was totally disillusioned with the legal process in the state of Colorado. At a lawyer friend's recommendation, Dr. Doell retained more aggressive counsel from Chicago. Immediately, the new counsel and his firm drafted an entirely new appeal to the Colorado Court of Appeals, requesting a stay of the revocation order until Dr. Doell's case could be heard. Whereas the first denial took only two days, this time a 140-page brief required fifteen days to obtain the same result—denial. Another trip to the Colorado Supreme Court resulted in yet another denial in Dr. Doell's appeal for a writ of mandamus.

Dr. Doell's case is awaiting hearing before the Colorado Court of Appeals. He has been unable to practice medicine for eight months. He has found a semi-retired physician to attempt to carry on the practice, but the regular census of forty to sixty patients per day census has dropped to ten to twelve. chelation therapy—the real reason that Dr. Doell was targeted for extermination in the first place—is still available.

When another doctor, also under fire, asked a state board member at a Colorado Medical Society meeting why the defendant-physicians are not allowed to communicate with the Board of Medical Examiners, one physician was told, "Murderers, rapists and pedophiles are all con artists, too, and we don't want personality to interfere with these proceedings!" So we conclude that in Colorado alternative M.D.'s are on a par with murderers, rapists and pedophiles.

This, then, is the regulatory-agency climate of the state of Colorado:

(1) There is no statute of limitations as to how long the Board can hold ancient charges.

(2) The defendant-physicians are not allowed to appear before their accusers in their own defense.

(3) The Board keeps no written minutes, administrative law judges without medical expertise are allowed to hear complicated medical cases, and physicians without specific expertise are paid professional witnesses and allowed to testify in areas where they are not qualified.

(4) The Board of Medical Examiners audaciously and not in good faith dares to accept all of the exceptions of the Attorney General's staff, while denying every single one of the defense's.

Who could dare recite "liberty and justice for all"?

Tragically for his patients, by the fall of 1991, Dr. William Doell had given up the practice of medicine in the United States.

An anonymous physician recently showed up at Dr. Doell's old office, where what's left of his former practice is being run by a contract physician. This man stopped by to let Dr. Doell's staff know that he had been asked by the Colorado Board to be a consultant and review several of Dr. Doell's cases. When he did so, and said "there was no evidence of malpractice," the Board rejected his recommendations and sought someone else. He stopped by because he wanted Dr. Doell to know that what they did was not right, and that he is willing to testify. Dr. Doell is now preparing to sue the Board.

THE COLLEGE OF PHYSICIANS AND SURGEONS OF ONTARIO AND THE R.C.M.P. VERSUS DR. PAUL CUTLER

The case of Dr. Paul Cutler began early in 1988, when the College of Physicians and Surgeons, a medical licensure and regulatory board in Ontario Province, recommended and got approved by the provincial government a new regulation outlawing the use of EDTA chelation therapy in Ontario.

One of the prime movers in this effort was, of course, Dr. David Spence, arch-opponent of chelation ever since he testified as an FDA expert witness against Dr. Ray Evers in Federal District Court in New Orleans, Louisiana.

The reader will recall that Dr. Spence alleged that fourteen people had died because they had been treated by Dr. Ray Evers with EDTA. The judge decided in favor of the FDA and the Louisiana State Board of Medical Examiners, and Dr. Evers was denied a permanent license to practice medicine in Louisiana. At the time, Dr. Spence was only three years out of medical school, and he was a resident in clinical pharmacology at the University of California in San Francisco.

Dr. Spence has since returned to his home in Canada, where he is now the Director of the Hypertension Program in MacMaster University at Hamilton, Ontario. Dr. Spence has also worked and collaborated with our Dr. Herbert. It is fair to say that the effort to outlaw chelation therapy in the province of Ontario was a trial run, as there followed subsequent attempts to outlaw chelation in the U.S. in Arkansas, Missouri, Indiana, and Arizona, all of which were unsuccessful. West Virginia succeeded, however, in August of 1991.

Dr. Spence and others in the Ontario College of Physicians and Surgeons subsequently introduced or recommended legislation to outlaw all forms of alternative medicine, including acupuncture, homeopathic medicine, herbal therapies, and faith healing, in the province of Ontario. This recommendation became law in Ontario the first week of June, 1990.

Since its passage, however, there has been an uproar on the part of ministers and other counselors who, according to how the legislation is presently worded, would be in violation of the law if they counsel a church member who seeks their guidance and advice—because they were suffering from depression, for example. (The Minister of Health has announced that the legislation would be modified so as not to consider this kind of pastoral counseling as the practice of psychiatry; therefore ministerial counseling would not be in conflict with the Medical Practice Act and the newly-approved regulations.) This appears to be yet another test case and an example of the medical profession legally protecting its turf because it feels threatened by the public's acceptance of alternative therapies.

Shortly after EDTA was banned in the province of Ontario, Sue Rideout produced for Canadian television an excellent, objective report on chelation therapy, in which Dr. Cutler and some of his patients, several of whom had responded dramatically to the therapy, were featured. But before the program, Dr. Cutler's office had been raided by the FDA. All of his medicines were confiscated because they did not have a D.I.N. (Drug Identification Number) on them suitable for use in Canada, even though customs had allowed them into the country for use. Because of this, Dr. Cutler was subjected to much harassment by the R.C.M.P. and the Food and Drug Administration, running up over $20,000 of legal bills. He won his case on appeal only, and the issue was dropped.

About a year later, controversy resurfaced when Dr. Cutler was asked to comment on a complaint that a private group called Citizens for Concerned Care had made to the Ombudsman of Ontario. The group wanted chelation therapy re-instated as an accepted method of treatment. Dr. Cutler's response was no doubt what he thought was conciliatory and tactful. He explained that he had made some innocent remarks, that he could understand why the College had taken the action that they did, in that they consider the treatment dangerous, but that he himself did not consider it dangerous, stressing that he had not seen any complications whatsoever. He further acknowledged the safety concerns of the college; he commented that he had no objection to these concerns, knowing that double-blind studies were in progress; since such studies speak for themselves, he did not mind a moratorium on chelation therapy until they were complete. He stated that he had merely appropriately expressed his learned opinion, that he did not think chelation treatment was dangerous, and that he understood the College's point of view.

Dr. Cutler may have felt that his written response to the Ombudsman's query was innocent and perhaps tactful, but others, especially Ron Dugas of the Association of Concerned Citizens for Preventive Medicine, viewed it differently. He saw the letter as a betrayal of the cause for chelation therapy; yet he was confused by the possibility of Dr. Cutler "selling out" in such a way, and felt that discrepancies in the letter actually made it possible that the letter was not authentic. Dugas wrote a letter to Susan Haslam, an investigator in the Ombudsman's office, expressing his concerns. The letter, though lengthy, is presented to the reader as evidence of how difficult it is for this controversy to remain focused and how hard it is for advocates of chelation to stand ground when attacked by Organized Med:

> I believe that you must have shared the astonishment which I experienced on reading Dr. Cutler's remarks. My response falls into two sections, the first being the form of the letter itself, and the second being its content in relation to what we know about Dr. Cutler's expressions on this matter.
>
> The letter appears to have been typed on Dr. Cutler's usual letterhead. However, the typeface is markedly different from that usually used by his office. The layout of the letter is different in that the code letters indicating the writer and the stenographer are missing from the June 6 letter. Finally, I note that the letter has not been signed by Dr. Cutler. What one must make of these discrepancies I do not know. I make no

comment, but ask that these points be noted.

In dealing with the content of the letter, I am making use of information contained in:

1) Dr. Cutler's remarks made during the interview on the W5 program aired January 7, 1988 (a videotape copy of this interview was forwarded to you along with our letter of June 8, 1988);

2) a tape recording of his presentation of April 30, 1988, at the Total Health '88 Seminar in Toronto entitled "Intravenous chelation Therapy for Arteriosclerosis." An audiotape copy of this address is enclosed for your information.

3) a tape recording of his presentation of April 30, 1988 at the Total Health '88 Seminar in Toronto entitled "chelation, Facts, Fallacies and Government Intervention." An audio-tape copy of this presentation is also enclosed.

4) Dr. Cutler's letter of October 31, 1987, to Dr. Zoltan Rona, President of the Canadian Holistic Medical Association; and

5) Dr. Rona's letter to me of June 15, 1988.

In his letter of June 6, 1988, Dr. Cutler states "however my attitude has totally changed since I received correspondence from the College in November, 1987." Strangely, in the W5 interview aired on January 7, 1988, he was still speaking of the good effects of EDTA chelation therapy. Since then, he has repeatedly mentioned his expertise in this field and emphasized in his April 1988 presentations his long experience of chelation therapy, his certification by the American Board of Chelation Therapists, as well as his thorough and repeated study of the literature over a period of many years.

During his opening remarks at the Total Health '88 Seminar on April 30, 1988, Dr. Cutler stated that EDTA therapy for the treatment of arteriosclerosis in this province is no longer available, as of August 15th last year it was announced. He said, "What I say today generally will not be accepted by the medical profession ... The medical profession unfortunately believes that EDTA is dangerous and of no proven value. This decision was made last year despite myself having treated over 1,000 very ill patients with it in at least ten years with no major side effects, as well as other doctors in the United States having treated over 200,000 patients in the last 30 years."

I find it extraordinary to find Dr. Cutler claiming in his letter that he did not know about the 13 fatalities at Dr. Evers' Clinic in the United States until he received a letter from the

College of Physicians and Surgeons in November 1987. At a meeting of the A.C.C.P.M. on August 29, 1987, Dr. Cutler explicitly mentioned that he was aware of these 13 cases in the presence of 20 witnesses. At this time, he expressed his opinion that these deaths were in no way related to the treatment of chelation therapy but were rather the result of terminal cancer. As recently as April 30, 1988, at the Total Health '88 Seminar, Dr. Cutler upheld this position by asserting that the 13 patients were terminal; they died of their illness, and somehow the Establishment was able to get EDTA labelled as the cause of death . . ."

In his letter Dr. Cutler also states, "However, the College has also considered this aspect, by allowing patients and their physicians to apply for a special exemption to continue EDTA. Certainly this shows consideration on the part of the College."

This remark of Dr. Cutler has me totally baffled and confused as he is very much aware that other medical doctors, as well as himself, have applied for this exemption on behalf of patients and have been turned down by the College. In their reply, the College indicated that if a physician was to approach the College seeking an exemption for a proper clinical trial to be conducted, the college would certainly consider granting an exemption. This is a far cry from granting an exemption for a patient. This matter has been discussed with those concerned on a number of occasions.

I would also like to comment on Dr. Cutler's following remark in his letter: "Although there are articles that show EDTA to be effective and safe in arteriosclerosis, I agree that they are not double-blind studies and this is true. You could probably say that for a lot of other medicines that are presently being used, but unfortunately it is being held against EDTA and was one of the criteria used for getting it banned."

In light of all these facts, we are left to question the authenticity of Dr. Cutler's statement that his attitude toward chelation therapy has completely changed since receiving the letter from the College in November 1987.

Dr. Cutler has assured Dr. Zoltan Rona (letter dated June 15, 1988) that he has received no threats from the College, and we must accept his assurance on this. On the other hand, it does appear that Dr. Cutler may have used the writing of a letter to you as an opportunity to make his peace with the College. The tone as well as the content lend credence to such a view. Of course the awesome powers and influence of the College are well known to all those in the health care professions, and it takes a very courageous, not to say reckless, individual to go against them. This is not to intend or infer any criticism of Dr. Cutler who must take such steps as he sees fit to defend his own interests. Dr. Cutler has done a great deal in this matter, and it may well be that he had enough of the fight.

All in all, this is a very sad business, but it seems to me that Dr. Cutler's extraordinary epistle in no way diminishes the case which is being made against the manner in which the amendment of the regulation was carried through.

Subsequent letters to the editor written by both Dr. Cutler and Dr. Spence, and published in the *Townsend Letter for Doctors,* suggest that not only has Dr. Cutler changed sides (most probably under duress), but the position he is taking on restricting EDTA use to the treatment of heavy-metal poisoning until he and Dr. Spence and others can complete their double-blind studies in atherosclerosis can only serve the purpose of providing a parachute for, or a way to save face for, David Spence, who, more than any other single person, was responsible for keeping EDTA treatment of atherosclerosis out of the mainstream of medical practice.

Dr. Cutler eventually switched to using chelation therapy with the drug desferoxamine on his patients in Canada, but for those who insisted on continuing to receive treatment with the drug EDTA, he opened a second office in Buffalo, New York, where he practices two days a week and continues to treat those patients on the U.S. side of the border, where EDTA chelation therapy has not yet been outlawed. In the process of switching over to desferoxamine, Dr. Cutler made an important observation, which is an excellent example of how a single individual family practitioner can make observations and write up case or anecdotal reports, which can have great significance for the practice of medicine as a whole.

What Dr. Cutler observed was that almost 30% of his patients with adult-onset diabetes or type II diabetes have elevated levels of serum ferritin. Serum ferritin is a form of stored iron; it indicates whether or not the amount of iron being stored in the body is excessive. At least one-third of the obese adult-onset type II diabetics had excessive stores of iron. Since the drug desferoxamine is extremely effective in removing iron, Dr. Cutler noticed that the patients' glucose tolerance or their diabetes also improved when the quantity of iron had been reduced. His observations on some fifteen or so patients were considered important enough that the prestigious journal *Diabetes* published them in 1989.

In addition, since desferoxamine not only chelates and removes iron from the body, but also removes aluminum from the body, Dr. Maclachlan and others at the University of Toronto have been giving this drug intramuscularly to patients with Alzheimer's disease. Their findings were published in 1991, and the results show that the removal of iron and aluminum has delayed deterioration in the mental alertness and cognitive abilities of patients with Alzheimer's.

The differences between the treated and untreated groups were so significant that Dr. Maclachlan has received an additional grant of $16 million to treat the relatives of these patients in a preventive fashion by giving them injections of desferoxamine intramuscular periodically, to prevent the development and onset of senile dementia.

So, once again, further uses for chelation therapy, using either EDTA or desferoxamine, have been discovered, this time the treatment of diabetes and senile dementia. Ironically, both of these discoveries, made by a practicing clinician and an academic researcher, respectively, took place in the province of Ontario, where the College of Physicians and Surgeons and the Provincial Government are regressing in the acceptance of chelation and other alternative medical therapies.

MEDICARE VERSUS LEO MODZINSKI, D.O., M.D.

Dr. Leo Modzinski practices in an economically-depressed area in Atlanta, Michigan. Most of his patients are on Medicaid and Medicare. He is politically very savvy. He is also an inspiration to his patients because he lost over 100 pounds and has managed to keep it off, in spite of continuing stress from harassment by Medicare regulators.

His patients love him, as the Medicare cops learned when they approached some of them, suggesting that they may have been harmed or defrauded by the chelation therapy that Dr. Modzinski had administered to them.

The good doctor's recent troubles with Medicare, however, coincide with an announcement from Michigan State's School of Osteopathic Medicine of plans to open a Health Center in the same under-served area where Dr. Modzinski works, in order to provide health care to the poor and at the same time train their medical students. The project will be financed by state funds, of course, and also with reimbursement from Medicaid and Medicare. Neither of these latter sources pay for chelation, by the way; Dr. Modzinski knows this and would not have billed for these services. Nevertheless, he does appear to be in the way of the University's plan for expansion.

Add to this the fact that Medicare, in requesting to review hundreds of his patients' charts, appears to be going on a fishing expedition. To date, they have spent thousands of dollars of the taxpayers' money and have essentially nothing to show for it. All of this could, of course, be merely coincidental. But the use of Medicare regulators to harass chelating physicians is certainly not a new phenomenon.

THE HEIMLICH MANEUVER BECOMES A SCAPEGOAT

"You can't get air into the lungs 'til you get the water out."
—Chief Fire Surgeon, Washington, D.C.

Dr. Henry J. Heimlich is a surgeon and the developer of the Heimlich maneuver. This lifesaving first-aid procedure saves choking and drowning victims. Dr. Heimlich is president of the Heimlich Institute Foundation, Inc. in Cincinnati, Ohio. He is married to Jane Murray Heimlich, author of a best-seller, *Homeopathic Medicine at Home* and more recently the eye-opener entitled *What Your Doctor Won't Tell You,* to which I had the pleasure of writing the forward in 1991.

The Heimlich maneuver as well as its inventor got in trouble with the medical establishment when Dr. James Orlowski, in a *JAMA* article of July 24, 1987, claimed that the Heimlich maneuver caused a poor result following its use in the resuscitation of a drowning ten-year-old boy.

Dr. Orlowski claimed that the maneuver caused vomiting and that the vomitus was aspirated into the lungs where pneumonia developed, and that the child died as a result. (What was strange was the timing of this published case report critical of the Heimlich maneuver for use in drowning—over seven years had elapsed since the incident had occurred.) Clarification came when a former Cleveland Clinic professional staff member advised Dr. Heimlich that the drowning had actually taken place in the Cleveland Clinic's own swimming pool, a significant fact not mentioned in Dr. Orlowski's article. This staff member, on July 29, 1987, wrote the following to Dr. Heimlich:

May I shed some light on this for you? I worked as an R.N. in the Adolescent Psychiatry Unit of the Cleveland Clinic when the incident happened.

The Cleveland Clinic has an indoor pool and several

patients had been taken to swim. It was the first time William (I forget his last name) had been allowed to go to the pool. I worked 11 p.m. to 7 a.m. and was told of the incident when I got to work that night. I do remember that William and his parents had a family conference with his doctors around 4 or 5 p.m. As I recalled, the dinner trays came to the unit approximately 5 p.m. The doctor wrote the order for swimming after that family conference. The patients were usually taken to swim after dinner without regard of the fact that their stomachs were full.

Therefore, it appears that the Cleveland Clinic was somewhat at fault. I do know that the nursing staff is told that the clinic considers all of its staff innocent in any incident. This way no one will point a finger at or accuse another in order to prove their own innocence. That aids the one being blamed and the clinic therefore is blameless also. In this case, I believe the Heimlich maneuver is being made the scapegoat for William's death.

I do not recall anyone saying that he had vomited. Some said there was blood from the pool to the intensive care unit from trauma cause by the intubation. I would like to add that I was part of a code, once, where a patient vomited profusely, and his head was turned to the side and the contents were dug out, and then efforts resumed to resuscitate with an Ambu bag. This happened repeatedly but we successfully revived the patient.

The lifeguard at the Clinic at the time was remiss in his duties as he would stand and talk on the telephone for long periods of time, ignoring the swimmers.

So you see, the reason this is all coming out now is because the family is probably suing the Clinic, and it is just another ploy of theirs in their defense. William's sister worked in nursing at the Clinic at the time, and I understand she quit soon after the drowning incident. I read about you in the Reader's Digest and admire you for the work you are doing. I hate to see someone try to blight your efforts.

From your quotes in the newspapers you "smelled a rat" and you were right!

There were a number of glaring inconsistencies apparent in the Orlowski case report. He claimed that the vomitus was aspirated, but this supposition is contradicted by his own evidence that the child's lungs were filled with swimming pool water and not stomach contents. Orlowski reports that the water removed from the lungs was pH alkaline, 7.5, ideal swimming pool pH, inconsistent with his contention that gastric contents had been aspirated (gastric juice has a pH of 1.5 to 2.5). Dr. Orlowski also indicated that he had evidence that the collapsed lungs resulted from traumatic or injurious intubation by the rescuers. This confirms what the nurse had written to Dr. Heimlich.

Dr. Heimlich's first definitive article describing the scientific basis for using the Heimlich Maneuver for saving drowning victims appeared in *Annals of Emergency Medicine* in September, 1981. At that time, Dr. Orlowski wrote to the editor expressing concern that the Heimlich maneuver might cause vomiting and aspiration. In his letter, however, he said nothing about the Cleveland Clinic drowning incident, which had occurred more than one year earlier; yet he reported it seven years later.

There have also been many published reports of the lives of drowning victims saved by the Heimlich maneuver, without vomiting, usually administered after mouth-to-mouth resuscitation has failed. Dr. Orlowski did concede, however, that the child might have vomited anyway, since approximately 24% of drowning victims have been reported to have aspirated vomitus. He could have added that half of the drowning victims also vomit when they receive cardio-pulmonary resuscitation, and that nearly 70% aspirate mud, bacteria, chemicals, debris, etc. with the inhaled water.

It is generally considered that the Heimlich maneuver has successfully resuscitated drowning victims after mouth-to-mouth breathing had failed. As the Chief Fire Surgeon of Washington, D.C., put it, "You can't get the air into the lungs until you get the water out." In addition, a press release issued by Surgeon General C. Everett Koop on September 30, 1985, concerning the treatment of choking, stated that backslaps and other methods such as chest thrusts are hazardous and in some instance lethal. The Surgeon General endorsed the Heimlich maneuver as the only method that should be used for the treatment of choking.

How then could the Orlowski article have been published in *JAMA* in the first place? The editor's answer would, of course, be the exalted peer review. Dr. Lawrence Altman, a medical writer for the *New York Times*, wrote in July, 1987:

> Although many doctors have an almost blind faith in it, in reality, Peer Review is largely subjective, and sometimes influenced by medical politics to a greater extent than most people recognize. Further, when editors lean toward accepting

or rejecting a manuscript anyway, then they choose reviewers who will predictably respond in a certain way. Reviewers have been known to let their own biases and vested interests govern decisions about papers submitted by scientific competitors.

JAMA editors rendered a disservice to physicians and the public by publishing Dr. Orlowski's faulted article, since it discourages the use of the Heimlich maneuver, and many drowning persons will die. It is only a matter of time before the Heimlich maneuver is officially endorsed as the most effective means of treating drowning. The water must be removed before air can enter the lungs. Furthermore, the fear of contagion because of the AIDS epidemic is discouraging mouth-to-mouth resuscitation. If the Cleveland Clinic nurse is correct, it is unconscionable that Dr. Orlowski's article was published without mention that the drowning occurred in the Cleveland Clinic's own swimming pool, a fact which was relevant to the duration of submersion, complications in follow-up care, and pending litigation. An investigation of the reported drowning incident is warranted by medical, scientific and legal authorities.

In a subsequent paper entitled "The Medical Establishment Can Be Hazardous to Your Health," which Dr. Henry J. Heimlich presented at the International Platform Association Convention in Washington, D.C., on August 5, 1987, he stated the following:

> Non-scientific, political, self-protectionist actions by medical associations endanger the health of all Americans. These medical organizations meet privately, withhold information, report decisions anonymously, and bring arbitrary charges against individual physicians who do not follow the "party line." Dedicated M.D.s are fighting their own Boards of Medical Examiners in court and are winning. If the medical hierarchy continues to engage in subterfuge, solutions will have to be found through the courts, legislatures, and governmental investigations.
>
> The techniques being used by the medical establishment include withholding information, secret meetings, and anonymity.
>
> The AMA and other medical associations have made many contributions to health care, but the protectionist tactics must no longer be permitted. If that practice continues, Congress, the Department of Health and Human Services (HHS), and state legislators will have to determine whether such uniformity of action within a medical organization and between

medical associations represents collusion and racketeering and constitutes a public health menace that urgently requires correction.

Lastly, Dr. Heimlich acknowledged that there is always room, of course, for a lack of understanding, or difference of opinion. He quoted Mr. Morris Maeterlinck: "At every crossing of the road that leads to the future, each progressive spirit is opposed by a thousand men appointed to guard the past."

In the same vein, Machiavelli advised the Prince that the reformer cannot expect support from enemies, but neither will friends encourage him because a man cannot accept that which he has not seen work. Dr. Heimlich notes this in resistance to scientific innovations. It is his belief that "if all your peers understand what you have done, then it isn't creative," and only through controversy can you answer questions and clarify your opinion.

CHAPTER 9
THE ATTACK DOG: THE ROLE OF THE FDA

The thing that bugs me is that the people think the FDA is protecting them. It isn't. What the FDA is doing and what the public thinks it's doing are as different as night and day.

—Dr. Herbert Ley,
Former FDA Commissioner, 1970

The FDA was created at the beginning of the century by government, with input from the AMA, to govern the safety of foods, drugs and cosmetics. It had no legal power to test drugs for safety, however. The following account of the history of the FDA's role has been taken from a talk entitled "The Rise of the Cult of Pseudoscience," given by Dr. Charles Harris, a pathologist, to the American College of Advancement in Medicine a few years ago.

In 1927, the FDA became a separate agency required to test drugs for safety. In 1959, Senator Estes Kefauver (D- Tenn.) launched an investigation into the pharmaceutical industry which had already been accused of gouging the public. In the midst of the investigation, the thalidomide tragedy occurred. Some historians say this tragedy was significant in that it slowed the development of new drugs, because of the additional bureaucracy which resulted. (Actually, thalidomide remains a useful drug in the treatment of leprosy; it also stimulates the immune system. Instead of teaching doctors how to use thalidomide properly, as it did in the case of the new acne drug Acutane, the FDA prohibited the use of thalidomide altogether.) Also during this time, unethical medical research was uncovered in New York City. Cancer cells were being inoculated into nursing-home patients to determine what would happen to them, unbeknownst to the patients or their relatives.

These events caused opposition to human experimentation, which became severely regulated. A stronger FDA emerged, which was required to guarantee not only safety, but effectiveness as well. This meant that human subjects had to be involved in order to accomplish this. Otherwise, proof of efficacy would be impossible. The pharmaceutical companies then began to offer medicines and monies to the universities to conduct the necessary clinical trials to show efficacy. The academics began to worship at the altar of clinical trials. The result, tragically, was that the double-blind crossover study became the "double-cross blindover study". . .the real cult of Pseudo-science was born.

The new rules and regulations pushed by the FDA resulted in these disadvantages:

—Slower development and delivery of new drugs

—An intimidated pharmaceutical industry (until they began to win friends and influence people)

—Medical services that had been offered voluntarily in connection with clinical trials now made mandatory, either executed or enforced by the FDA

—Refusal to look at alternatives

—Sluggish response times; lost new drug applications; bribery; indifference; promotion of generics leading to a generic drug scandal, and a total lack of flexibility

THE AMA: CAUGHT RED-HANDED COLLUDING WITH THE FDA

The government-sponsored chelation studies (covered in an earlier chapter) at Walter Reed and Madigan Army Hospitals did not originate from any burning desire for scientific inquiry on the part of the FDA, academia or pharmaceutical corporations. What, then, motivated them to help design and approve a controlled study to evaluate the safety, effectiveness, and dose-response curve of EDTA in the treatment of peripheral vascular disease?

The answer lies in the comments of Stuart Nightingale, Asst. Commissioner for Health Affairs of the FDA, when he went on record at a meeting of the House of Delegates of the AMA in Honolulu, Hawaii, seven or eight years ago, telling AMA delegates, "We can't put these chelation doctors out of business by ourselves. We have to work closely with you, the AMA, and other groups, to put them out of business."

It happened that a leading chelation doctor, Garry Gordon, was in the audience intending to plead the case for using chelation in the treatment of arteriosclerosis and its complications. Dr. Gordon hoped to convince the AMA to at least allow time for independent scientific inquiry and to not ban the therapy outright. Dr. Gordon recorded Dr. Nightingale's remarks and later shared them with Attorney Greg Seeley, legal counsel for the chelation doctors' professional organization, AAMP, now called ACAM. Mr. Seeley observed that the FDA should not be in the business of putting doctors out of business for using an approved drug for an unapproved purpose, which is common medical practice. The attorney drafted a letter to the FDA protesting Dr. Nightingale's remarks. He also requested an explanation as to why chelation doctors should be "put out of business" for treating heart disease when chelation is already sanctioned as a medical procedure to remove heavy metal, usually lead poisoning. Attorney Seeley had the AMA over a legal barrel.

The FDA reply did not mention the obvious illegality of Nightingale's remarks, but suggested that a delegation from AAMP meet with FDA officials to discuss controlled clinical studies. A working relationship was established between Dr. Ross Gordon, brother of Dr. Garry Gordon, and Dr. Lawrence Lepickey, chief of the cardio-renal division of the FDA. Working together with his designates, Dr. Ross Gordon developed the research protocol now being used to evaluate the efficacy of EDTA in the treatment of peripheral vascular disease and to determine a dose-response curve. The reader will recall the statement by Organized Med's mouthpiece, Victor Herbert, in his Ontario address, "that the most effective method" of getting rid of a therapy like chelation therapy is by taking the practitioner to court and that the second way to fight the problem is "by lobbying for anti-quack legislation." He added, "In New York State we are putting them out of business." This legal strategy has gotten out of hand. The definition of a quack is too vague and generalized for the courts to be involved in resolving questions and conflict in science. The legal system should be used only to stop someone who is causing harm to the public. The debate over the safety and effectiveness of chelation therapy (after nearly 500,000 people have been treated) and the debate over the safety or toxicity of evening primrose oil (after some eighteen countries have generally recognized it as safe, safe enough in fact to be added to infant formula in Japan) should not be argued in court.

The Walter Reed Army study will be much larger in scope than the study that was conducted in Heidelberg, West Germany, by Dr. Gerhard Schettler and the study conducted by Dr. Anthony Gotto and his associates at Baylor University and Methodist Hospital in

Houston, Texas, neither of which has ever been published. The Danish study published in August, 1991, as we have seen, is patently flawed in that there was obvious manipulation of the sample study. Dr. Efrain Olszewer and I published our study in the April, 1990, issue of the *Journal of the National Medical Association.*

Dr. Lepickey has also remarked that Dr. Gotto should not have conducted his independent study without clearing it with him and others in the Cardiorenal Division of the FDA. This is strange. Isn't respected, competent Dr. Gotto, researcher and administrator, capable of doing his own research?

When all of the studies have been completed, most likely a meta-analysis will be performed. This type of analysis determines mathematically what the weight or preponderance of the evidence shows, an unnecessary hassle to determine what should have been obvious at first glance. The investigations and expenditures are unavoidable in a scientific and legal sense, however, as long as "liars can figure" and as long as people like Victor Herbert can be paid by Organized Med to haul practitioners into court on accusations of fraud, pretending to argue valid science before naive and scientifically-illiterate panels and judges.

GOVERNMENT "GOPHERS" SEIZE EPO AND BLACK CURRANT OIL

In March of 1990, I contacted the late Robert Rodale, CEO of Rodale Press, and Mark Bricklin, editor of *Prevention Magazine,* encouraging them to write an editorial about the evening primrose oil scandal and the way it was being mishandled by the FDA and their consultants, Drs. Victor Herbert and Robert Olsen.

The "case of the evening primrose oil" began in March, 1988, when the FDA seized a batch of oil in Maine, on the pretext that it was not generally regarded as safe (GRAS) as a dietary supplement. A second seizure action was initiated in California in February, 1989. This is absurd! evening primrose oil is a vegetable oil that is generally recognized as safe in some eighteen industrialized countries and is also approved as an additive to infant formula in Japan. The FDA seized it. Surely the FDA has more important business in safeguarding the taxpayers' health than to seize evening primrose oil, a natural, non-toxic food substance.

The company producing and importing the oil in this case is Efamol, LTD. Their CEO and research director is Dr. David Horrobin, a scientist in his own right. He had recently edited a comprehensive volume entitled *The Omega-6 Essential Fatty Acids:*

Pathophysiology and Roles in Clinical Medicine, published by Wiley-Liss in 1990. Efamol decided to fight these unfounded seizures.

Dr. Horrobin set up an ad hoc scientific review panel to study the published data relating to the safety of EPO to determine if the data were sufficient to establish that EPO is generally recognized as safe or GRAS. The panel reported that the FDA officials had the previous year affirmed the GRAS status of rapeseed oil, which contains a fatty acid known to be toxic. Evening primrose oil, by contrast, contains no toxic constituents. The panel concluded that evening primrose oil is GRAS.

One of the anecdotal evidences presented by the FDA to refute GRAS status was that, when given to adult patients with schizophrenia, the oil caused convulsions. These patients, however, were also taking potent tranquilizers and other medications. There was no evidence indicating whether the convulsions were related to evening primrose oil, or reduction in dosage of or withdrawal from tranquilizers, or epilepsy of unknown etiology.

The Panel further concluded that there was no evidence that evening primrose oil was toxic to the immune system and no evidence that it caused cancer or birth defects, as had been speculated by FDA officials. Interestingly, the FDA toxicologist who had made those accusations was subsequently given a bad performance rating by her supervisor. (However, she can probably still count on a good post-retirement job with one of the drug companies.)

Despite the expert testimony of the ad hoc scientific committee members, Efamol, Ltd. lost its cases in Maine and California. The Maine court followed the decision of the judge in California, who either failed to read or did not understand the highly technical material or she relied on the "good will" of government's witnesses, whom she naively believed would have the public's interest at heart. This is another example of judges who do not understand technical, medical/scientific material and consequently get duped by government go-fers into mis-informed legal judgments that continue to protect the financial interests of pharmaceutical and related corporations. The Court of Appeals judge in this case issued summary judgment in favor of the FDA. The Ninth Circuit upheld the decision. Efamol plans to petition the Supreme Court to review the case.

Why don't certain elements in the pharmaceutical industry want evening primrose oil classified GRAS? Primrose oil can become a serious threat to the market share of aspirin and all of the other non-steroidal anti-inflammatory drugs, as well as to the market

shares of cholesterol-lowering drugs such as Questran and Lovastatin.

Primrose oil contains gamma linolenic acid (GLA), an activated
form of linoleic acid, which is found in abundance in corn oil,
safflower oil, and other vegetable oils commonly used for cooking.
GLA, however, in various combinations with the so-called Omega 3
fish oils, could safely replace aspirin.

The non-steroidal drugs, incidentally, include drugs such as
Nuprin and Motrin, both of which contain ibuprofen. It is well
known that these latter drugs, when taken on a long-term basis for
pain, can cause side-effects of gastric and duodenal ulcers and oc-
casionally kidney failure.

It is very probable that anything aspirin and other non-steroidals
can do, fish oil and GLA can do better with fewer side-effects. This
is clearly understood by the drug industry, who, working with the
Councils Against Health Fraud, their consultants, and their collaborators within the FDA, are trying to keep evening primrose oil
from being used for therapeutic purposes in the United States; they
are working hard to keep a cheap, unpatentable "farm and fish"
product off the pharmaceutical market.

In 1988, the FDA also seized two drums of imported black
currant oil (goodness!) which had been shipped from England to
Traco Labs in Illinois. The FDA claimed that the seizure was justified because it was an "unsafe food additive" and therefore an
"adulterated food." This kind of "legal reclassification gymnastics"
is engaged in by the FDA to prevent yet another source of GLA from
being used as a cheap, unpatentable, nutritional pharmaceutical. In
this case, and in another black currant oil seizure in Massachusetts,
the courts ruled against the FDA. The Illinois case is currently
pending appeal before the Seventh Circuit Court of Appeals.

Jonathan Collin, M.D., editor of the *Townsend Letter for Doctors,*
a prominent Illinois alternative medical newsletter, summarized this
unfounded seizure in Illinois:

> In January, 1991, the FDA moved for summary judgment
> on its seizure and forfeiture claims. Sid Tracy, president of
> Traco Labs, did not accept the seizure and sought legal redress
> for the FDA demand. His case has been ongoing during the
> past two years and has led to $95,000 in legal expenses. In a
> decision by a federal judge, Harold Baker, the FDA demand
> for summary judgment against Traco Labs was entirely
> quashed.

The court opinion held that food additive regulations do not apply to the fatty oil supplement black currant seed oil. Further, the capsulation of the currant oil in a gel capsule does not change the status of the oil from food to food additive.

The court informed the FDA that the food additive regulations were very specifically legislated. Further, the FDA must carefully limit its definition of food additives to those substances that are specifically added to foods for the purpose of being an additive for flavor, texture, processing and preservation.

A food supplement which acts only as a food must be considered a food and can be regulated only according to regulations applying to foods, not additives.

The case more specifically ruled that black currant seed oil is a food. Therefore, black currant seed oil, a rich source of GLA, gamma-linolenic acid, is deemed a food source of GLA, not a food additive. Other sources of GLA, including primrose oil and borage oil, generally manufactured outside the U.S., may be legal, but were not defined as such during this case.

This case may offer legal support for other food supplement manufacturers faced with similar demands for adherence to food additive regulations. The FDA will have to show that the substance in question is or is not a food, and if it is adulterated as a food or food additive.

In their attack-dog role that they play for the drug companies, the FDA has long tried to prevent nutrients from being used to prevent or treat illness, ostensibly to protect the public from harm and from fraud. In reality this policy (which the Agency tries to justify or on the basis of the Federal Food, Drug and Cosmetic Act (21 U.S.C. §§ 301-394-1972 & Supp. 1991) is and has been implemented to protect the drug manufacturers from cost-effective competition—the end-result even if it was not the original intent.

In a nutshell, here is the bottom-line threat of the clinical use of the humble essential fatty acids to the pharmaceutical industry: Anything aspirin and the non steroidal anti-inflammatory drugs can do, some combination of fish oil and evening primrose or black currant or borage oil can do just as well or better and safer.

ANOTHER VITAMIN IS IGNORED

Over twenty-four years ago, the following was written by the west coast representative of the FDA to the newly-appointed commissioner, as an "internal communication":

July 10, 1968

The Honorable Herbert L. Ley, Jr., M.D.
Commissioner, Food and Drug Administration
Department of Health, Education and Welfare
Washington, D.C.

Dear Doctor Ley:

First, permit me to congratulate you on your elevation to the tremendously important post of Commissioner of the Food and Drug Administration. It is a position requiring both clinical and scientific judgment of unusual character. I wish you knowledge, courage, persistence and personal satisfaction in this new responsibility.

There is a movement initiated by your predecessor, Dr. Goddard, concerning which I wish to direct your attention: The removal of "vitamin P" from medical use. It is not clear to me what procedure Dr. Goddard was to employ in accomplishing his purpose, but I urge you to hold this in abeyance, or preferably to reverse the process, until a more careful study can be made.

As one who pioneered the study of this complex material in the late 1930s and early 1940s, I have a more than casual scientific and clinical interest in its chemical, pharmacological and clinical developments. When I was in private practice for a few years during the mid-1940s I used a locally produced and distributed concentrate of a lemon peel extract with considerable success in controlling vascular fragility, manifested by excessive tendency to bruising.

During the past twelve years or more I have had opportunity to observe the effect of "CVP," a product of the U.S. Vitamin Corporation, on a granddaughter who had frequent "bruises" and even true ecchymoses, often from no recognized trauma, and associated to some extent with the eating of chocolate, orange juice and egg. I persuaded the child's pediatrician to prescribe CVP and, even before the allergies were recognized, the vascular fragility, or at least the subcutaneous bleeding tendency, was controlled to a remarkable extent.

About a year ago, for a number of reasons, the pediatrician sent my granddaughter, age 14, to the Hematology Department at the Los Angeles Children's Hospital for intensive study. The hematologist stopped the administration of CVP during and following the studies, the details of which I have not learned, but which resulted in a diagnosis of "bleeder."

For a year, on the advice of the hematologist, the pediatrician withheld CVP, and during this period not only were there frequent ecchymoses, but there were frequent respiratory infections. About two months ago the child was placed again on CVP and these problems have again disappeared. This is not only my experience but I find that other physicians have made the same observations.

I admit that there have not been extensive controlled studies which would today be considered acceptable to a clinical pharmacologist (and I am one, including Fellowship in the American College of Clinical Pharmacology and Chemotherapy), but the observations should be given sufficient importance to permit continued manufacture and distribution of CVP and similar preparations, and to stimulate much more experimental and clinical investigation.

As the west coast representative of the Food and Drug Administration, I have frequently taken the witness stand to eliminate misbranded drugs and equipment. But in the two instances discussed above, I find I cannot support the position of the Administration.

For your information, since you probably do not know me, I include my biographical sketch, and have marked my publications on "vitamin P," beginning with number 86.

Respectfully yours,

Clinton H. Thiemes, M.D.

This letter demonstrates that the FDA position on the clinical uses of nutrients, bioflavinoids in the above instance, has not changed in at least eleven years, despite medical observations worthy of investigation.

Considering the current financial mess in health care, we can no longer afford as a nation to support the legal drug habits of the upper crust, and we would prefer to forego the harmful side-effects suffered by patients with no treatment options other than registered synthetic pharmaceuticals. How much longer will Organized Med and the legal drug companies, aided by the FDA, get by with this travesty?

THE GENERIC DRUG SCANDAL—THE TIP OF THE ICEBERG

The American Academy of Family Physicians warned in 1989 that generic drugs may at times be inferior, even dangerous, especially for persons with asthma, diabetes, or heart disease. Nevertheless, generic drugs are now an annual $3 billion dollar industry.

The FDA branch chief for generic drugs, Mr. Gerald Chang, accepted thousands of dollars in illegal pay-offs from generic drug companies, whose applications he approved. He facilitated those who paid him off and inhibited the others. Mylan Labs Pharmaceuticals became suspicious because its drugs were not getting approved. The CEO for Mylan, Mr. Roy McNight, hired a private detective who conducted a one-year surveillance, which included going through Chang's garbage, to find evidence of this government scandal. They found plenty! Companies had submitted fake data and cheated, and there were pay-offs. The generic company Vitarin sent in bogus data and submitted the original drug for testing, claiming it was their generic version. The FDA system of approving generic drugs was subverted by the very industry it was supposed to regulate.

This scandal certainly raises questions about the safety and effectiveness of generic drugs and how they are regulated. A generic drug is usually a discount-version of the name-brand drug. The generic supposedly uses the same active ingredient as the name-brand. However, some companies substituted brand-name drugs for their own generic brands, just to get FDA approval; then they proceeded to manufacture poor quality and/or ineffective generic substitutes. One-third of all drugs sold in the U.S. today are generic. The generics industry claims to offer the same quality as brand-name drugs, at substantially lower prices. Certainly there are ethical generic companies now under serious question, but the challenge lies in determining who cheats and who doesn't.

Congressman John Dingle's sub-committee conducted the investigation and broke the story. In June, 1990, Marvin Seife, the former head of the FDA's generic drug division, was the fifth FDA official to be indicted by a federal grand jury on charges of perjury. This indictment resulted from a two-year investigation of improprieties between FDA officials and generic companies. Four of Seife's former employees at FDA have already been convicted on corruption and racketeering charges. Five industry executives, three companies and one consultant have been convicted of similar charges. Some thirty generics were asked to re-submit abbreviated New Drug Applications. Other evidence uncovered refusal of the FDA to hear complaints coming in from generic companies who were playing it straight and not getting their drugs approved.

The Division of Generic Drugs, in this instance, was guilty of criminal misbehavior. Congressman Dingle stated he could not "vouch for the safety of generics." Former FDA Commissioner Frank Young re-organized the Generic Division, prior to leaving office, uncovering more evidence of fraud, bribery, substitution, and false reporting. Where does it end? Not with the Generic Drug Division. Read on, please.

ADVICE FROM THE PRESIDENTIAL ADVISORS PANEL, 1990

In August, 1990, a Presidential Advisory Panel reported to President Bush at the White House that the federal government should speed up approval of experimental AIDS and cancer drugs, by requiring less evidence of effectiveness before they are put on the market. The chairman of the nine-member advisory panel was Dr. Lewis Lasagna, Dean of the School of the Graduate Biomedical Sciences at Tufts University. Dr. Lasagna warned that thousands of lives are lost each year from delays in approvals and marketing of AIDS and cancer drugs.

The report stated, "Desperately ill patients are prepared to accept the greater risk inherent in the use of such medications. Faced with the consequences of a lack of therapy for AIDS and cancer, an expanded mechanism for early access to investigational drugs is morally, ethically and scientifically justified."

Dr. Lasagna and the panel suggested that approval of a new drug could be postponed until after the drug is on the market providing two types of studies are done first. One study measures the effectiveness of new drugs in comparison with those which are already on the market; the second assesses whether or not a given drug prolongs life. The panel recommended that the government should not insist that a drug company demonstrate "prolongation of life, if a drug can improve the quality of a patient's life."

"For cancer and AIDS patients, time is running out, and they are understandably upset with delays in obtaining the pharmacotherapy which represents their only hope," the panel noted. For these life-threatening diseases, it added, the government should approve new drugs at the earliest possible point in their development, and, in any event, earlier than previous time frames.

At a subsequent news conference, Dr. Lasagna pointed out that the FDA often demands more data than is required by either federal law or scientific criteria for judging the value of new drugs.

It now takes twelve years and costs $231 million to research, test, and get approval for a new drug, according to a Tufts University study which was released in the spring of 1990. This report by the Center for the Study of Drug Development noted that, even accounting for inflation, this estimate is twice what the Center had found when it did a similar study in 1979. The Tufts study was based on a random selection of ninety-three drugs developed by twelve pharmaceutical firms and tested on humans between 1970 and 1982. The cost figures were then adjusted for inflation to 1987 dollars.

Both Congressman Waxman of California and Congressman Wyden of Oregon were critical of the FDA in 1990. They described a steadily deteriorating ability of the Agency to carry out its mission and functions. During the previous decade, the Agency was underfunded and understaffed; there was a lack of information and a lack of independence. This set the stage for the generic drug scandal. Congressman Wyden accused the agency of putting politics before science.

These criticisms are only the tip of the iceberg. Further congressional scrutiny into the agency's association with drug companies is certainly warranted from the evidence surfacing. Why do representatives from drug companies make up more than 50% of some FDA drug-advisory boards? This creates a bias in favor of prescription and over-the-counter (OTC) medicines over natural remedies or herbal products.

The new Food and Drug Commissioner, David Kessler, has been given a mandate to (1) develop food labeling guidelines and (2) increase the Agency's scrutiny over medical devices. Although laudable, these objectives have nothing to do with the change in that is needed in the agency's orientation— from working for the industry it is supposed to regulate, to working objectively for medical advances in the best interests of those who pay FDA salaries, the American tax-payer.

In addition, if the proposed new regulations for medical claims for foods are any indication, then the Agency appears to be going backwards in regard to their first mandate. They are proposing that only two foods and/or nutrients be recognized as having a direct effect on the occurrence of disease: (1) calcium (osteoporosis), and (2) dietary fat (cardiovascular disease and cancer).

The first of these is probably not even a direct effect in terms of treatment or prevention. The fact that they consider all of the other relevant research on nutrition and health inadequate for making clinical claims suggests that, as least as far as food labeling is concerned, business is worse than usual. These decisions are obviously not based on science. The pharmaceutical boys just don't want to open the door to this kind of competition, and they are using their FDA lackeys to help keep it shut. Only a public outcry and/or pressure from Congress and the White House can turn this situation around.

The late comedian Lenny Bruce's takeoff on an American politician, "I'm not a crook—elect me!" came to mind when Dr. Kessler took over the FDA in November, 1990, and said, "I am not going to protect crooks." Jack Anderson, in his commentary "High Noon for the New Sheriff at the FDA," noted that this was something most federal agency heads don't have to say when they take the job. Anderson commented, "[when Kessler takes over] it should be something like grabbing the helm of the Exxon *Valdez* after it hit the bottom."

Dr. Kessler's predecessor, Frank Young, had been forced to resign after the generic drug scandal surfaced under his watch in 1989. The agency's credibility was at an all-time low. It was accused of prematurely approving life-support medical devices, and allegations also surfaced that FDA agents were using insider information on drug approvals to play the stock market.

Anderson's congressional sources provided this insider observation: "There is a big concern on Capitol Hill that Kessler doesn't get captured by any of the bad elements that linger on in the FDA." They went on to say that he should let it be known "that there's a new sheriff in town." His tolerance for the old way of doing business at the FDA remains to be seen. No one should hold his breath, however. This is probably bigger than what one man can do, no matter how well-intentioned.

THE EDWARDS COMMITTEE RECOMMENDS CHANGES IN THE FDA, 1991

The Edwards Committee Report of the Advisory Committee to the Food and Drug Administration was released in May, 1991. It is named for Dr. Charles Edwards, a distinguished physician, former Assistant Secretary of Health and a former FDA Commissioner. Committee members testified before Senators Edward Kennedy, Orin Hatch, and David Durenberger in May, 1991.

The committee was to confront the critical problems affecting the FDA and recommend a series of actions designed to improve the Agency. They were to develop wide-ranging recommendations which, if adopted, would transform the Agency into an organization less vulnerable to slander, blunder and corporate pressure and better equipped to promote the health and well-being of the American consumer.

The central question that the panel had been asked to answer was "Can the FDA currently carry out the responsibilities assigned to it?" Speaking for the committee, Dr. Edwards answered in the affirmative but qualified that it was a very close call. He pointed out that the chronic and pervasive shortcomings of the agency have seriously crippled and hampered its effectiveness for over a decade. Dr. Edwards described the agency as having inadequate resources and diminished authority and as an agency which is "living on borrowed time." Charged with a vast, increasingly complex array of vital health protection responsibilities, it lacks the tools to fulfill its mission.

The report highlighted two major problems at the FDA:

1. A continuous leadership vacuum. "Corrected to a certain extent, with the appointment of Dr. Kessler as the new FDA Commissioner, but there is also a lack of leadership from the Agency's managers within the Commissioner's office and in the FDA's operation centers."

2. The post of Commissioner is seen both in and out of government as an unimportant position. This is attributable to the placement and the status of the Agency in the federal bureaucracy. It is buried three layers deep in the Health and Human Services organization. It is a part of the U.S. Public Health Service (USPHS), which has no institutional sympathy for the agency's regulatory and law enforcement functions. In effect, the Commissioner is responsible to a Public Health Service hierarchy which is not fully supportive of the agency's needs.

The Edwards Committee recommended that the FDA be separated from the U.S. Public Health Service:

The FDA should be made a first level agency within the Department of Health and Human Services. The commissioner should report directly to the Secretary of Health and Human Services. The Commissioner should have a full array of authority for independent action, commensurate with his responsibilities. He must have full authority to run the agency's operations, including regulations, facilities, equipment, and personnel. If this regulation turns out to be unacceptable to the department or the administration, then Congress should enact legislation to reconstitute the FDA as a freestanding agency, not unlike the Environmental Protection Agency.

The FDA is first and foremost a regulatory agency. It is both a scientific and a regulatory agency. The American public fully expects safe and effective drugs to treat the most serious health problems. They also insist on a food supply which is not only safe, but also wholesome, and one that comes with complete instructions as to how the right foods can promote longer and healthier lives. Neither one of these objectives are being achieved under the present circumstances at the FDA.

The retraction of a previous approval of EDTA in the treatment of arteriosclerosis and its complications, the lack of a serious approach to the role of biologic-response modifiers in the treatment of viral infections, and the failure to acknowledge the therapeutic value of nutrients and other natural substances in the treatment of disease—these are examples of the Agency's failure to meet the objectives of ensuring safe and effective food or drugs.

The FDA is not keeping pace with the spectacular progress in the various scientific fields whose technologies and end-products the Agency must evaluate and approve or reject. The FDA lacks the technological resources, the personnel, the information, the management systems, and even the regulatory authority it needs to function in today's modern scientific environment. It will not be able to carry out its mission, which Senator Durenberger and others feel has not been very well defined in the first place.

That the 1990 Advisory Panel to the FDA did not address the failures exemplified by the above examples is inconceivable. It appears that the Committee had a predetermined agenda, which was only to reorganize and raise the visibility of the FDA and to give its new commissioner, Dr. Kessler, authority commensurate with his responsibilities, similar to the head of an autonomous agency such as the EPA.

Dr. Charles Edwards, Chairman of the Advisory Committee, acknowledged the FDA as "an agency which is in crisis." Thus, the Committee recognized the problem; but Edwards then qualified his statement by saying, "Fortunately we haven't had a disaster occur." This is erroneous; disasters have occurred and are continuing to occur.

An example of a continuing disaster is the handling of the contaminated tryptophan, from the Japanese company Showa Denko, which entered the country over a year ago. This was badly handled by the FDA, and the mistakes have still not been rectified. On the contrary, it was a catalyst for new regulations which will remove most amino acids from the GRAS list. Many amino acids were listed as GRAS for nutritive or dietary supplement use from 1962 to 1977. They were deleted from the GRAS list because they were transferred in 1977 to the food additives section.

There is a difference of opinion as to whether the recodification process automatically revoked GRAS status. The FDA has commissioned the Federation of Societies for Experimental Biology (FASEB) to evaluate the safety of amino acids, but it is clear that the agency is in favor of tighter regulation and is using the tryptophan disaster as justification for such regulation.

The committee, and especially committee member Dr. Larry Horowitz, focused much attention on the time it takes for new drugs to get into the market place. This is a major and valid concern of the pharmaceutical industry and should be a major concern of the public. But there was too much focus on this aspect of FDA's problems. This singular focus represents an inherent assumption that the purpose of the FDA is to get new drugs on the market—that there are "magic-bullets" or new drugs out there to treat now-incurable conditions such as cancer and AIDS. Dr. Horowitz and the other members of the Committee never seemed to acknowledge that there may not be a traditional pharmaceutical solution to every medical or health problem. They seem unable to make the necessary paradigmatic shift from the allopathic approach of "drug to kill a bug or cancer cell" to the holistic immune-building rebuilding and fasting body- and liver-detoxifying regimens developed now available.

Dr. Horowitz referred to "access to the frontiers of medicine" as access to experimental drugs. He pointed out that the members of Senator Edward Kennedy's committee could at any time go down to the National Institutes of Health and obtain, for personal use, experimental drugs, whereas the general public is unable to do so. He spoke of this as a privilege or an advantage. If this highly intelligent physician only knew the alternatives.

FDA OVERKILLS ON TRYPTOPHAN—
FAILS TO BAN ONE FORM BEFORE IT KILLS A CHILD

L-tryptophan is an amino acid, essential for life, present in protein foods. Under ordinary circumstances, tryptophan is absorbed from digested protein, and there is no need for nutritional supplementation. Not everyone has perfect digestion of food, however, so not everyone has sufficient tryptophan. Tryptophan supplements have also been taken by hundreds of thousands of people worldwide for help with depression and sleep disorders. It has been used for decades in this manner without ill effects.

Apparently the FDA was concerned enough about the safety of L-tryptophan in 1973 to issue a rule that make its sale as a dietary supplement illegal. This rule, however, was never enforced throughout the 1980s.

In 1989 the Japanese manufacturer Showa Denko produced tryptophan by means of a new process which created a toxic impurity that caused a condition known as eosinophilia-myalgia syndrome (EMS). It was not the L-tryptophan itself, however, which caused this syndrome, but the use of a synthetic means as opposed to the traditional natural-food-sources process, which incorporates care to prevent harmful impurities.

The FDA then recalled tryptophan from the U.S. market for the first time in December, 1989. By the end of January, 1990, the Center for Disease Control in Atlanta suspected contamination as the cause of this new and rare disease. The FDA issued a second recall letter in March, 1990, and by the end of April, 1990, the manufacturer Showa Denko had been linked to the disorder. An article appeared in the *Journal of the American Medical Association* on July 11, 1990, entitled "Eosinophilia-Myalgia Syndrome Associated with Exposure to Tryptophan from a Single Manufacturer." A newspaper article subsequently appeared in the *Minneapolis Star-Tribune* on July 23, 1990, entitled "Minnesota Mafia Tracked L-tryptophan Impurity," and a third article appeared in the *Wall Street Journal* on August 17, 1990, entitled "U.S. Suits Cloud Showa Denko's Future."

The syndrome occurred in approximately 2,300 people and resulted in twenty deaths. The Showa Denko tryptophan was produced by a microbiological fermentation process. The particular organism used to manufacture tryptophan by this fermentation process was a genetically-engineered organism. However, the contaminant got into the final product because the filters were not properly cleansed.

There was no evidence that the genetic engineering of the organism had anything to do with the presence of the impurity. It was found by gas-liquid chromatography that the contaminant was a substance identified as "peak E." Investigators have subsequently determined that the "peak E" substance is an ammonal of acetaldehyde and is a by-product of tryptophan. This chemical may be the one responsible for causing the allergic reaction known as eosinophilia-myalgia syndrome.

However, it came to the attention of a concerned group of manufacturers of nutritional products that, in recalling tryptophan from the U.S. market, the FDA used a double standard. It had also issued misleading letters. The three FDA recall letters, when examined in detail, revealed the following:

1. All L-tryptophan was not recalled as was claimed by the FDA in media reports.

2. The product which was not recalled was left available for parenteral use. (This means for intravenous feeding and for the manufacture of infant formulas.) Apparently these products were not analyzed or certified to be free of contamination with tryptophan produced by Showa Denko. The FDA stopped all other sales of tryptophan, including tryptophan coming from safe non-contaminated sources.

At least one three-year-old child contracted eosinophilia-myalgia syndrome from his parenteral formula and died. The FDA had failed to verify the safety of the L-tryptophan in the formula. In a tragically late response, the Agency subsequently recalled all parenteral products containing Showa Denko tryptophan, but this recall was kept quiet, with no media coverage.

The National Council for Improved Health (NCIH), an organization founded by concerned manufacturers of nutritional products, justifiably questioned the FDA's motives. It stated, "The FDA demeaned the American nutritional industry, while at the same time it exposed vulnerable segments of our population, *e.g.*, infants and invalids, to a contaminated product available only through the pharmaceutical industry. How can it be justified to recall *all* of a product (safe or unsafe) only from the nutritional industry, even after numerous published reports established that only one manufacturer caused the problem? How can they (FDA) exempt the drug industry from recalls and scrutiny, at the expense of the health of infants and invalids (those needing parenteral feeding)?"

NCIH claims that the FDA caused their industry millions of dollars and the loss of many jobs and that it caused unbelievable mental anguish, threatening the confidence of many Americans who have consumed tryptophan as a safe nutritional supplement for over twenty years. The Showa Denko L-tryptophan which was used in parenteral nutrition, intravenous solutions, and infant formulas was never under the same regulatory concern as all other L-tryptophan. This, according to NCIH, raises a lot of questions, to say the least. The NCIH commented,

It appears that the FDA has had a hostile agenda against the sale of L-tryptophan as a food supplement since 1972. It took advantage of the unfortunate contamination of L-tryptophan by one single manufacturer to brand all L-tryptophan taken as food supplements as dangerous. This is part of their ongoing strategy to promote over-the-counter and prescription drugs over nutrients which can often be used as safe, reliable, and less expensive treatments for depression, sleep disorders, nervous conditions, pre-menstrual syndromes, etc. One can hardly doubt the existence of a double standard.

The decision of the FDA to withdraw all tryptophan from the health food stores has led to a congressional inquiry and at least one lawsuit. The congressional inquiry is in the form of a House panel which is reviewing whether the FDA's failure to aggressively regulate the dietary supplement L-tryptophan contributed to dozens of deaths and thousands of injuries from the substance in 1989. The panel consists of members of the Human Resources and Intergovernmental Relations Subcommittee, chaired by Rep. Ted Weiss (D-NY). The first of these hearings were held on July 18, 1991. Perhaps subsequent hearings will reveal the reasons for the recall from the health food stores but not from the manufacturers of infant formulas and IV solutions, who received product from the same contaminated source.

The lawsuit, filed against the FDA by holistic leader Dr. Jonathan Wright of Washington state, seeks the return of L-tryptophan. This lawsuit probably provoked the May, 1992, "Vitamin Raid" on Dr. Wright's office in Kent, Washington. Armed federal agents stormed his office, broke down the front door and, with their guns drawn, ordered the staff to raise their hands. The patients and their relatives in the waiting and examining rooms were terrified. The warrant for the search and seizure stated that the purpose of the raid was to seize selected nutritional supplements and an Interro machine which is used to measure electrical fields at various acupuncture points of the body, in order to select appropriate homeopathic remedies.

Some have speculated that the real reason for the raid was to retaliate for Dr. Wright's lawsuit and to discourage others from doing the same, *i.e.*, suing the federal government. In any case, the "Vitamin Raid" has had a chilling effect on other alternative practitioners and has become a cause celebre for the proponents of freedom of choice in health care.

CHINESE HERBS REVERSE LUPUS IN SPITE OF THE FDA

A woman, whom we shall call Dr. M.L. and who is an M.D. and an M.Ph., is a retired health care administrator. This fifty-six year-old doctor was diagnosed in 1983 with mixed connective tissue disease, a rare variant of lupus. She had been hospitalized four times for exacerbations of her disease and once for aspiration pneumonia. She was treated with steroids, methotrexate, leukeran, non-steroid anti-inflammatory drugs, and repeated plasmapheresis with only temporary improvements, followed by more exacerbations and always with side-effects from the medications. Steroid dosage was as high as 40 mg of prednisone daily.

This auto-immune disease exhibits many manifestations of the various immune diseases; in her case, she had manifestations of lupus, scleroderma, rheumatoid arthritis, and a vicious form of polymyositis, which caused most of her symptoms. Along with this, the doctor experienced baldness, Raynaud's phenomenon (sudden constriction of blood vessels in the arms and legs, causing numbness, tingling, and cold hands and feet, a kind of vascular instability), sphincter problems due to muscle destruction, severe weakness, and problems with fingernails and skin.

The presenting manifestation of her illness was a severe case of hives associated with what physicians term severe angioedema (swelling of the tongue, pharynx, etc.). That was the first time she was put on steroids, simply as a life-saving measure. With that illness, she also experienced nodules under the skin. Unfortunately, these were never biopsied by the NIH specialist she saw on five or six visits prior to being diagnosed by another physician. She was hospitalized four times for exacerbations of the disease, each time losing more muscle structure and of course more function. One hospital stay was for severe aspiration pneumonia (results from inhaling vomit) due to the fact that her gastroesophageal sphincter was in the same shape as the rest of her muscles. During this time she lost her wonderful singing voice, due to deterioration of the muscles of her vocal cords.

During the course of this illness, in 1985, following a severe relapse and hospitalization, it became apparent to Dr. M.L. and her physician that she had undergone a severe personality change and moderate-to-marked mental deficits; she could not think straight, she could not remember, her immediate recall was virtually nil and she could not read. Depression accompanied an extremely flat emotional effect. She avoided people, not unusual for her condition. She did not wish to converse and had nothing to say. Following the plot of movies with more than a few characters was impossible—her short-term memory could not retain which character had done what. This physician-patient had studied music for thirty years; now she could not learn a new tune or remember a simple one. The loss of her voice was devastating. The periodic relapses caused extreme misery—the Raynaud's phenomenon and periodic loss of sphincter function (whenever she would relapse), to say nothing of the baldness, etc., persisted until she began a particular brand of herb formula.

The doctor had only two more relapses since she began taking a Chinese herb formula. She is happy to report that by taking only the herbs (and no drugs), and particularly the immune formulas, she has been able to avoid hospitalization and return to a very good functional state.

Dr. M.L. commenced taking a responsibly formulated Chinese herbal product in January 1990 with noticeable feelings of remission. Even though she noticed near-immediate physical improvement, and her mental function was improving, she was reluctant to take the immune formulas. But in June, 1990, she started relapsing. The doctor stated:

> It only takes a day or two for me to know what is going on, because of either the increase in arthritic-like symptoms, the mental confusion, and an inability to recall immediate conversations or conversations in the present time. In addition, the polymyositis unfortunately sets in almost immediately.

At any rate, her options at this point were plasmapheresis and steroids; she could not take the latter because of having suffered the severe complication of osteonecrosis in 1988. (Fortunately, when she began the herbs in 1990, her doctor had been able to rapidly decrease the steroid dosage, a necessary step anyway, because of the severe osteonecrosis.) Faced with a decision, she decided against both any more plasmapheresis treatments and any more steroids or methotrexate. (There was no point in having the plasmapheresis since it required steroids and methotrexate afterwards to hold it, anyway.)

Originally Dr. L. had avoided the immune stimulant herbs because product information stated that the formulas would normalize the immune system. Such a treatment flew in the face of her medical training—she knew that you *suppress* the immune system in these diseases, not do anything to stimulate the immune system. But with her rapid decline, with weak thighs and inability to climb stairs, etc., she overcame that medical mind-set to take a chance by trying the immuno-augmenting herbs. Dr. M.L. ingested thirty to forty immune stimulant capsules daily, in addition to the other formulas she was taking.

In about ten days, the doctor noted that mental confusion had cleared remarkably. This traditionally-trained physician was amazed. On steroids and the other medications, her doctor would always say, "It will take six to eight weeks before you begin to feel better." But by the time muscle improvement would be noted, the side-effects of the medications had made her so sick that she would agonize over whether she should take the toxic prescription. With the improvement that she could see from the herbs, however, she diligently consumed the formula every day, including a dose in the middle of the night.

The results: Within three months, the relapse of June, 1990, was history. When it re-occurred in February, 1991, a particularly vicious attack, the doctor repeated the herbal regimen, including the herbal immune-stimulant herbs. Remission occurred, and her speaking and singing voice returned just fine. On June 1, 1991, she sang like a lark in a regular church service; both her music teacher and her doctor were amazed. Her doctor recommended, "Don't stop taking the herbs." But he does not recommend them to any of his other patients with connective tissue disease—apparently he values his medical license.

When ill, Dr. M.L.'s biggest problem had been the osteonecrosis, but her mind recovered remarkably while taking the immune herbs. The doctor is back to her original mastery of the three R's. She read six novels, one 650 pages long, and could discuss that plot with you today. She also made a presentation, with a friend, before the City Council, following up arguments and offering rebuttals on the spot— a total impossibility two years ago, prior to the herbal therapy. In October, 1990, her friend suggested that she resume swimming despite walking with a cane with a great deal of difficulty. By January, she could walk on her own. Because of fixed shoulders, she can only dog-paddle, but swims twelve or fifteen lengths of the hospital pool in about ten minutes—quite an accomplishment for her degree of disability. Her muscles are firming up and her fingernails are healthy; there are no more bald spots, and her hair is back to its thick, lustrous growth; her skin looks better, but the scleroderma (skin tightening under the eyes and the narrowing of the lips) may be permanent. Many other positive changes are very evident.

One of the strange results to appear following the last dose of steroids was a typical truncal obesity. This has remained despite the fact that she has not taken steroids since February, 1990. She still has a somewhat-Cushingnoid steroid habitus (truncal obesity and fat posteriorly at the base of the neck—a "buffalo hump") which her physician cannot explain.

Dr. M.L. still takes most of the herbs and continues to improve. She comments about her current status:

> I find little physical or mental exercises I could not do before, I can now do. For instance, I used to write poetry so easily. I wrote rhymes and songs for special occasions at people's requests. During my illness and drug treatments, I lost the capacity entirely. I could not think of two words to rhyme, and then after that summer of remarkable recovery, I note that I can rhyme and sing again and now on quite a complex and sustained level. Recently I sang one of my compositions at a friend's birthday party. I am so very thankful for the chance opportunity to take the herbal foods, and the results. I do wish that patients with autoimmune disease, of any significant degree, could all benefit from this therapy!
>
> I like me, I really do—that's why I can like you!

Dr. M.L.'s laboratory work shows that her hemoglobin has always been between 9 and 10 gms. The white count is usually low for one reason or another, most likely from the drug methotrexate. The serum proteins, albumin and globulin, showed a profound reversal—an albumin of 2 and a globulin between 6 and 8—but this is returning to normal. Recently, it was almost 4 and 4, the albumin slightly lower than the globulin. The muscle enzymes during relapses were outrageous. When she entered the hospital in 1983, her CPK was approaching 7,000 and her aldolase was 50. All muscle enzymes have returned to normal for the past 1½ years. Current hemoglobin is 12.6, and has been for the past three lab tests (over a period of nine months). There is reason that the change is genuine.

M.L. concludes her medical history: "Of course, one of my problems is that I am traveling, running around. I went recently to Los Angeles and rented my own car, and I had a good time. You have to realize when you have been an invalid for as long as I have, and you feel better, then it's time to 'make whoopie.'"

The reader should note well: As it is not possible (nor is it the intent) of this author to be the reader's doctor, the specific herbal brand and formulations are omitted. The history of this respectable, intelligent Dr. M.L. is mentioned for exemplary purposes only, and not to be mistaken as medical advice for self-doctoring. Consult the licensed alternative physician of your choice for any such endeavor.

FDA AND NIH REGULATORY ABUSE THWARTS CLINICAL RESEARCH ON NATURAL REMEDIES

What about the host of other patients with lupus and other connective tissue diseases? Very few have the good fortune to learn of the herbal formulas that saved Dr. M. L. A young lady with lupus from New York City learned of the Chinese formulas and contacted Dr. M.L. She also went into remission. But should patients have to depend on fate to lead them to valid alternatives? Where's the FDA?

The FDA serves as the pharmaceutical industry's watchdog which can be called upon to attack and destroy a potential competitor, under the guise of protecting the public. We know what they and select members of Congress did to companies such as Herbal Life, Nutri Systems, Efamol, Ltd., and Allergy Research, among others. As defined in the Food, Drug, and Cosmetic Act, a food cannot be a drug simply because it affects the structure or function of the body. This represents a classic "Catch 22"—a paralysis of inaction. With any alternative or natural remedy that is not "usual and customary," FDA agents interpret the law and inflict their regulatory abuse. Just as with cancer and heart disease, FDA officials and their loved ones stand to suffer from their condemnation of effective alternatives as much as the rest of us.

No rheumatologist will seriously consider such herbal remedies without controlled clinical trials. Yet they are unwilling or fearful to conduct those trials. There should be a head-to-head comparison of steroids and the Chinese herbs in the treatment of lupus. A controlled trial using a placebo in treating such a serious disease would be unethical, in my opinion. Nevertheless, the effect of these herbs, in correcting any immune system abnormalities which occur in lupus, needs to evaluated.

The next step would be to determine which of the herbs in the two immune-enhancing formulas are immunologically active. This can be determined in the laboratory by testing extracts of each one of them against the lymphocyte in tissue culture. In this way, we can determine which of the herbs stimulate the parent cells of the immune system—in other words, which ones are biologic response modifiers, the key to disease reversal.

After conducting controlled clinical trials and identifying the immune system regulators among the herbs, the data acquired should attract the attention of the National Institutes of Health, our lavish tax-supported center for disease research.

When such a proposal is written and submitted, it is eventually reviewed by a group of scientists called a Study Section. Humans all, they lug their heavy suitcases filled with biases and prejudices up to the table with them. These medical science pros have been trained in the corporate-influenced, post-Flexnerian basic science era, namely in the belief that herbal, homeopathic, and manipulative medicine are worthless. These healing arts were thrown out, like the baby with the bath water, when the Flexner report recommendations were implemented throughout all med schools in the early part of the century.

Consequently, any proposal utilizing any of these healing modalities is flatly rejected by the Study Section. A review of the grants and contracts funded by the NIH would reveal that so very few, if any, had anything to do with natural remedies, homeopathy, spinal manipulation, "nutriceuticals," or even what the Europeans call biological medicine.

On October 24, 1990, the United States Senate passed the Hatch-Metzenbaum compromise version of H.R. 3562, and the House agreed to the amendments on October 26, 1990. This bill was signed by the President on November 8, 1990, and became P.L. 101-535. This new law, among other things, establishes specific conditions under which health and diet-related claims may be made; it incorporates an essential right of our citizens to have access to vitamins, minerals, herbs, and other nutritional supplements without fear of such supplements being branded as unlawful drugs; and it protects a dietary supplement from being considered a drug solely because it carries a valid health claim.

Its principal purpose, however, is mandatory nutrition and food labeling, by mandating that all processed packaged foods have uniform nutritional labels and by defining ambiguous terms such as "light" or "free." The law is supposed to take effect no later than May 8, 1992.

However, five recent (1991) FDA enforcement actions against small dietary food supplement companies in California, Oregon, Arizona, Utah, and Illinois demonstrate that the FDA intends to ignore the intent of Congress and continue to regulate "medicinal foods" as if they were drugs, even when valid health claims are made for them. (See Congressional Record 10/24/90, S16611.)

"QUALITY OF LIFE" FROM EXPERIMENTAL DRUGS— BY WHOSE STANDARDS?

Actor Michael Landon was diagnosed in April, 1991, with an inoperable pancreatic cancer which had already spread to his liver. He underwent an experimental chemotherapy treatment using donosomes. Dr. Cary Presant, chairman of the Los Angeles Oncological Institute at St. Vincent Medical Center, was Mr. Landon's oncologist. Donosomes are small microscopic bubbles of fat. These bubbles are loaded with a standard cancer chemotherapeutic drug, in Mr. Landon's case Donarubicin. The theory is that these fat bubbles, which are called liposomes, enable the treatment to be targeted specifically to the cancer cells and not to other normal cells of the body.

Before administering the donosomes, Dr. Presant announced to the press that the treatment would be evaluated by measuring Mr. Landon's "quality of life," as well as using various blood and other diagnostic tests to see if the tumor had shrunk in size.

After several injections, Michael Landon was admitted to St. Vincent hospital with chest pains and multiple blood clots in his circulatory system. From the press accounts, he appears to have developed thrombi, or clots, in his blood vessels which broke loose, spreading to his lungs and to elsewhere in his body.

The following interchange went on between Sonia Friedman and Dr. Cary Presant on the CNN TV program "Sonia Live":

Sonia: Because of the side-effects which in some cases are as damaging, and particularly in terms of lowering the immune system, could you talk to the side effects of this type of chemotherapy?

Dr. Presant: The side-effects of chemotherapy, which were quite considerable 10-20 years ago, when I first got established in this field; these side-effects are more manageable. We have much better medicines first of all, that have fewer side-effects. In addition we have a lot of treatments that minimize any side-effects that the chemotherapy may still have; various anti-nausea medications, various other treatments to maintain the body's blood cell counts, and as we have monitored individuals to see how these treatments really affect the immune system, we have been very surprised to see that most of the types of chemotherapy we use today, whether they are standard or whether they are experimental, most of these types of chemotherapy actually are associated with a preservation of a good immune system. The immune system may be temporarily decreased, but then it rebounds up above where it was to begin with. The immune system, in many cases, may be enhanced by chemotherapy.

Sonia: What about the idea of caffeine enemas? Do you, as a physician, do you just say go ahead and try anything that might work, or are there are certain things that you feel not in the patient's best interest?

Dr. Presant: Well, there are things that are not in the patient's best interest, and when you take care of a patient, regardless of whether it is a well-known patient or a very unknown patient, the patient's quality of life is the most important thing. [How ironic!] We deal with a lot of additional treatments; treatments which are necessary to help the patient feel better, and in fact, I spoke to Mike about many of the other types of treatments that had been prescribed for him which were to help him feel better. Many patients seeking a good quality of life will turn to unorthodox therapies, and I think that each doctor should talk with these patients in terms of what the hazards are of using an unorthodox therapy versus the benefits, and the potential risk of conventional therapy and also investigational therapies.

What we do with our patients is, we urge them very strongly to accept traditional standard therapy or investigational therapy; that particular therapy which we think will help them the most. We then counsel them about their unorthodox therapies, that they may be wishing to, or have already started, and we counsel them about which can be continued and which should not be continued, because they are very potentially harmful.

Sonia: Actually, I wanted to ask a second question which has to do with the spirit of the person; one has to be cautious the individual does not become the disease, and I think certainly he seems in wonderful spirits. We all have something to learn. Thank you again for your time.

Considering what happened to Michael Landon, who is deluding whom? Apparently the donosomes or fat bubbles which were injected intravenously either caused blood clots or escaped to other parts of the body other than the pancreas and the liver, or both, and instead of providing quality of life perhaps cost Mr. Landon his life earlier than necessary. This tendency to form clots or thrombi could have mistakenly been diagnosed as Rousseau's syndrome, which sometimes occurs with hidden or occult cancers, which cancer of the pancreas often is. Mr. Landon subsequently discontinued the chemotherapy as his "quality of his life" deteriorated. In my opinion he would have been better off had he remained with Dr. Gonzales "for a better quality of life."

Committee advisory member Dr. Horowitz had this to say regarding privileged access to experimental cancer drugs:

> All drugs are not alike. Not all diseases are alike, and there are diseases for which there are no drugs at all. All of those factors have to be taken into account. The FDA is, in essence, the gatekeeper between the frontiers of medicine and the application of the fruits of research for all the people. As members of this committee, you can have access to the frontiers of medicine; you can go down to the clinical center at NIH and get an experimental drug, before it is available to the general public. Most people with cancer, most people with AIDS, don't have that privilege. They have to wait until the FDA says, "Now is the time that you can have the benefits of this research, now is the time."

> And the critical question for the FDA is "When is the right time, what is the balance?" To prevent harm by not letting unsafe medicines on the market, you cost lives by taking six months longer to get a needed cancer drug on the market and who makes that decision? Where is the balance and what role should the patient, who is suffering from a terminal illness play in deciding that they want to take that risk with proper informed consent? Make no mistake about it, this is about people's lives, because if it takes six months longer, we will lose lives!

There is no doubt that Dr. Horowitz, a former congressman himself, was sincere. There is no conspiracy here, but delusion. What gives him the idea that Joe or Mary Public, suffering from cancer, is clamoring to try a new experimental chemotherapy? The knowledgeable may want to try a pain-free, non-toxic biological therapy with Dr. Rosenberg at NIH, but a new chemotherapeutic drug with more toxic side-effects? Unlikely. The good doctor's statement is another example of blind faith in a "new drug breakthrough," a technological solution to every medical problem. The future will show that cancer, a chronic systematic condition, cannot be effectively treated with a magic medical bullet, however powerful. The public is now beginning to adopt this perspective.

184 \ Racketeering in Medicine

Why doesn't the Commissioner of the FDA heed this? Instead, he helps the likes of Dr. Herbert, who is in cahoots with the New York Board of Medical Quality Assurance to harass physicians like Dr. Gonzalez who use effective, safe (key words used in FDA evaluation procedures) treatments which have proven benefit in the treatment of certain types of cancer.

Following Dr. Horowitz's comments, Senator Durenberger of Minnesota requested that Secretary Louis Sullivan of Health and Human Services develop a Mission Statement for the FDA. This is unusual. Doesn't such a Mission Statement for an important regulatory agency already exist? Apparently not. This would be a first step toward improving upon the rigidity and inconsistencies in the current FDA approach to the development of new and potentially toxic drugs. The necessary paradigmatic shift cannot come about until these weaknesses are addressed.

Senator Durenberger also pointed out that he had been given the clear-cut impression that the FDA is principally a regulatory agency:

> It is not in the business of adding value judgments of any kind. Its 1970 statutes do point out that it is supposed to push the frontiers of our knowledge; it is supposed to help find that cure or find that better way of doing things.

Durenberger also pointed out that there is a difference of opinion as to whether or not the agency should be concerned with risk versus benefit, as opposed to complete safety and efficacy. The Health Care Financing Administration is one of the few departments in Washington that is trying to find out the relationships between cost and benefit. Durenburger said,

> Those people dying of cancer can't do that. They want everything they can get. Some are going to holistic medical centers and hospitals in Southern California and Mexico. They go there seeking alternatives.

On the other hand, we seem to be throwing money hand-over-fist at finding medical technology for the purpose of cure. The medicalization of cancer, for example, is a marvel. You pound away at my friends with chemotherapy, with this chemical and that chemical, this radiation treatment and that radiation treatment. I just lost a friend who was hopeless, and two and a half months from the discovery of cancer he was dead. But I bet, they put hundreds of thousands of dollars of somebody's resources into that guy.

This goes perhaps beyond the statutory charge to the FDA. But when the chairman says why aren't we doing more on AIDS, why haven't we found a cure for cancer, why aren't we doing more on Alzheimer's, I find that the only place in America where these judgments get made are by politically powerful persons on behalf of people who are less politically powerful. There is no other place in America for us to assess our values and then try to apply those values in specific instances.

Senator Durenberger also quickly retorted that the FDA was not the place to make those value judgments. He appealed to committee member Dr. Edwards to draw the line with regard to the FDA's functions so that he could be a better judge of what its function is and of the resources necessary to be applied to carry out that function. Durenberger argued that because of a lack of visibility of the Agency, buried three layers deep in Health and Human Services, he could not guarantee his medical-device manufacturers or seafood processors that they will not face competition from manufacturers/food processors who have the appearance of quality while actually producing inferior products because they are better able to manipulate the regulatory components of the agency. According to Durenberger, this is a reality, and whether we call it a crisis or not is irrelevant. Given the present arrangement, the system cannot guarantee the kinds of protection against these abuses that the laws that established the FDA are designed to provide. If the FDA ranked with the Securities and Exchange Commission, perhaps business would be conducted in a more open and honest manner.

The FDA Advisory Committee also recommended that alternative approval routes be developed for new drugs. They recommended more flexibility in the development of different regulatory pathways. The nature of these pathways should be determined by the disease circumstances. For example, there are those diseases which are disabling but not life-threatening, for which there is no effective treatment. On the other hand, there are life-threatening diseases which present another set of circumstances. There are segments of the population who use drugs about which research has never been done as to the safety and efficacy of those drugs in that particular group. For example, there are therapeutic orphans: 90% of the drugs used on children were never tested for use on children.

Also, once a drug is approved, it is put out on the market, and each doctor becomes his own scientist and uses it according to his or her best judgment. In this way, patterns of use are developed. All of these issues, according to Horowitz, have been around, but the solutions have not been found or implemented.

Senator Orrin Hatch, in the Edwards hearings, pointed out the need for consolidation within the FDA. He asked Dr. Edwards if he believed that a consolidated facility for the FDA would help their management capabilities. Dr. Edwards replied that the entire committee felt that a consolidated facility would be ideal for the FDA. Edwards was quick to point out, however, that there was an emergency situation at the FDA with regard to a number of its facilities. The committee therefore felt that certain action had to be taken immediately and could not wait for the development of a larger consolidated facility that would take several years to establish.

Dr. Edwards stated that the FDA needs more money now to correct deficiencies that could not be addressed without it. Senator Hatch also supported Dr. Horowitz's recommendations to expedite approval of drugs for life-threatening conditions. Hatch requested that Horowitz work with him to formulate the type of legislation needed to accomplish that. Dr. Horowitz pointed out that the state of California had a very active FDA equivalent. Drugs that should be able to be tested at a national level, under FDA regulations, are not being evaluated at that level because the process is so laborious. Many of these promising drugs are being tested in California instead, after the company has applied for and received an IND or new investigational drug application. Many smaller companies want to get started in California for this reason. The state of Massachusetts is also considering emulating what California has done.

Another agenda was apparently hidden in Senator Orrin Hatch's questions to Mr. Gardner about food additives. In hearings of this type, it is obvious what kinds of legislation the senators tend to favor, or are promoting, by the kinds of questions they ask. For example, Hatch's questions to Mr. Gardner were "What can FDA do to streamline the approval of new petitions for food additives?" and "Are there some specific statutory changes that need to be made in order to bring about improvements in this area?" Gardner had suggested the creation of a Foods Advisory Panel, to make available to the agency experts of the kind that are not on the payroll. These would be experts in biotechnology who would supply not only expert technical information, but outside views as well. The views within the Agency tend to become provincial over time; experts brought in from the outside would serve to offset this tendency. Hatch also pointed out that unscientific methodology was being applied by the Agency, because of pre-existing legislation such as the Delaney clause.

Senator Hatch then stated that the agency needs to move to a "negligible-risk standard." The Delaney clause, according to Hatch, is outmoded and unscientific; it does not give the Agency enough flexibility to do a better job. Senator Hatch also predicted that if we moved to a negligible-risk standard, we would have an even safer food supply. He felt that we would develop a more predictable safety record and that there would be more predictable benefits to the American public.

The Edwards report was so concerned with the big picture of the "forest" that it neglected the blight that was affecting its trees. In many respects, it has been unable to see its own biases. Some recommendations were on the mark. But others were not based in reality, such as the assumption that the public is anxious to continue experimenting with chemotherapy for cancer and AIDS despite the horrific side-effects that diminish the remaining quality of life of the survivors. The Landon fiasco is one publicized case in point. The only other visible person, of whom I am aware, who benefitted from an experimental cancer chemotherapy drug, and in the long-run was cured, was Maurice Abrams, former Ambassador and President of Brandeis University. He had to go to Israel for that chemotherapeutic. The avoidable suffering will continue as long as the "know-it-alls" in and outside of the agency dominate public health policy, with their prejudice, egotistical bias, and economic incentives.

The Church of Scientology was on the "hit-list" of the AMA's Coordinating Committee on Health Information (CCHI). From documents obtained during disclosure in the case of the chiropractors versus the AMA, the CCHI engaged in covert activities designed to eliminate or neutralize the efforts of Scientology and the founder, L. Ron Hubbard, whom the AMA considered to be working against their interests.

In 1969, the Church of Scientology established the Citizens Commission on Human Rights (CCHR), which is dedicated to the eradication of psychiatric violations of human rights. In the late 1960s, CCHR documented and exposed illegal experiments with LSD, which were conducted in some instances without informed consent. This exposé culminated in U.S. Senate hearings and regulations to prevent future recurrences of experiments of this type.

In 1990, the Commission investigated and exposed a treatment at Chelmsford Hospital in Australia which put patients into a deep sleep and, while they were sleeping, administered electric shock therapy. These treatments were also sometimes administered without patient consent or knowledge. Through the Commission's persistent efforts, the medical records of these patients were made public, and the cases of forty-eight men and women who died as a result of this therapy were exposed. The public outrage which followed led to the banning of deep sleep followed by electric shock therapy, the closing of Chelmsford Hospital, and the establishment of a Royal Commission of Inquiry in Australia, which ultimately recommended prosecutions. All over the world, the Citizens Commission on Human Rights has documented psychiatric crimes. Laws have been enacted in many states in the U.S. to prevent psychiatric sexual abuse of their patients, again as a result of the Commission's work.

Hubbard had a long mistrust and dislike for psychiatrists. Hubbard focused on numerous negative areas of psychiatry: "In fact its barbaric practices of electric shock, brain operations, and drugging patients were killing and maiming people on a daily basis." The mental health community quickly rejected his ideas in his book *Dianetics,* a blueprint for successful living. The conflict has more recently included Eli Lilly and other pharmaceutical manufacturers of mood-altering and mind-controlling drugs. The scientologists claim that the nation's number-one selling medicine for severe depression, Prozac, manufactured by Eli Lilly, is a "killer drug" that drives some of its users to murder or suicide. Scientologists have condemned the drug for dangerous side-effects that they believe has led to numerous instances of mass violence and one-on-one violence. In particular, there is one case brought out in the media of a mother put on Prozac who, armed with a kitchen knife, stood behind her daughter who was standing at the kitchen sink. The husband disarmed his wife, who, the next day, had no recollection of this incident.

The scientologists have, through the media and congressional lobbying and by confronting the FDA, attempted to have the drug banned. In the *Wall Street Journal,* in April, 1991, an article reported some success in this campaign: "Although Prozac's sales are huge, its share of the anti-depressant market has slipped from 25% in July 1990, to 21% in April 1991."

Time magazine, in its May 6, 1991, issue, attacked Scientology in a cover story, questioning its religious veracity and accusing it of being a greedy business with some aspects of paramilitary organization. This attack on Scientology evoked a response from its followers somewhat like the emotion that Rushdi's book evoked from the

Islamic fundamentalists. The scientologists went on the offensive and mounted a $3 million counter-attack with ads in *USA Today*. The ads focused on *Time,* Eli Lilly and Prozac ("which is only the latest in a series of drugs brought to market, sometimes unethically, with harmful side effects"). The June 13, 1991, ad boldly criticized the FDA and raised the issue of legal drug peddling in general: "Who controls what foods and drugs the public may consume?" Another ad, on July 1, 1991, focused on psychiatric violations of human rights. On July 5, 1991, an ad revealed how self-interest groups influence governmental policy to everyone's detriment, leading to impending economic collapse of the U.S. health-care system. The corruption and malfeasance at the FDA were also brought out with impressive accuracy and courage.

What kind of a church is this? It states its aims as follows: "A civilization without insanity, without criminals and without war, where the able can prosper and honest beings can have rights, and where man is free to rise to greater heights." Scientologists believe that humans are spiritual beings who, through an examination of their past, can rid themselves of the harmful effects of negative experience and therefore increase personal happiness and spiritual freedom.

Less then a month after founder Hubbard's *Dianetics* was published, the editor of *JAMA* solicited adverse information from so-called authoritative sources for articles on *Dianetics.* Typical of the medical profession, these authorities relied not on analysis or on an objective evaluation of whether or not Hubbard's blueprint for successful living worked, but merely on their arrogant and adverse pronouncements, all of which condemned *Dianetics.* Critical articles appeared in *Time* and other publications, demonstrating that the psychiatric community was upset with this encroachment on their territory. But they were unable to halt the *Dianetics* philosophy on their own, so they enlisted their government connections. This tactic has worked before. We cannot forget what they did to Hoxsey and to Drs. Gerson and Koch, what they're still doing to chelation doctors, and how they removed from the package insert information that said that EDTA was effective in the treatment of arteriosclerosis and its complications; all of these actions required AMA/FDA cooperation, in retrospect amounting to racketeering, in order for their success. Hubbard also exposed the pain-drug hypnosis experiments that were being conducted by the Central Intelligence Agency, fully twenty-five years before the existence of these experiments was made known to the public through documents released under the Freedom of Information Act.

No doubt Hubbard's proposal for living did provide a viable alternative when psychiatry did not help people solve their mental health problems, as have the growing number of self-help groups patterned after Alcoholics Anonymous: Overeaters Anonymous, Gamblers Anonymous, Narcotics Anonymous, etc. (nature, after all, abhors a vacuum).

As psychiatry increasingly resorted to drugs to treat mental illness, psychiatrists and the drug companies became natural allies. The psychiatrist would diagnose a mental illness, and a new drug would be produced to correct the so-called chemical imbalance. Psychiatry, according to Hubbard, had, since its earliest beginnings with Freud, been fascinated with mind-altering drugs; Sigmund Freud himself was a cocaine addict.

The book *Dianetics* continues to be a best seller. Readers attest as to how it provides answers to basic problems and gives them a grasp of how to handle their lives and how to find happiness by following a blueprint which raises their self-esteem. The scientologists regard psychiatrists as enemies and consider them important tools of powerful drug manufacturers. According to scientologists, these manufacturers rely on psychiatrists to prescribe and sell their mood- and mind-altering drugs. Needless to say, Scientology and its Citizens Commission on Human Rights are viewed by major drug companies as mortal enemies.

This was the background for the sustained assault by the CCHI initially, and Eli Lilly and *Time* recently, on the Church of Scientology, which culminated in *Time* magazine's May 6, 1991, cover story. The church, in a rebuttal published in *USA Today* said, in essence, that "the social reform activities of the Church had encroached upon the interest of *Time* magazine and its owners." Scientologists who for decades had opposed mind-bending drugs had committed the unforgivable sin of attacking the drug Prozac, costing Eli Lilly, its manufacturer, dearly.

Time stated in a July, 1991, edition, "There is no need for everyone to be scared away from Prozac, since it has proved safe and effective for many people." But the Church of Scientology and the Citizens Commission on Human Rights, in their educational campaign to inform the public about Prozac, stated:

> More then 14,000 adverse reactions by Prozac users have been reported to the Food and Drug Administration since Prozac's release in 1987. These include delirium, hallucina-

tions, convulsions, violent hostility and aggression, psychosis, and attempted suicide. Major medical journals have reported the emergence of suicidal thoughts in persons taking Prozac.

In the last year, nearly 50 lawsuits have been filed against Eli Lilly seeking almost one billion dollars in damages by families of people who have committed suicide while on Prozac, families of people who have been murdered by patients on Prozac, and people who have been themselves damaged while taking Prozac.

On September 14, 1990, Joseph Wesbecker entered his former work place in Louisville, Kentucky, and opened fire with an AK-47, killing eight people and wounding twelve before killing himself. Results of the coroner's drug scan revealed Wesbecker to have a therapeutic level of Prozac in his blood. There are, increasingly, other similar accounts. The American Trial Lawyers Association has established a special Prozac litigation section to service attorneys, and a recent issue of *Texas Lawyer* reported that Texas personal injury attorneys view Prozac as "the next Dalkon shield."

Ironically, the ads run by the Church of Scientology brought out some of the problems at the FDA that the Edwards Committee did not address. The medico-pharmaceutical industrial complex stirred up a hornet's nest by attacking religious beliefs. Although I am not a follower of Scientology, my observations of Scientology members would have me agree with Marvin Bordelon, President of the American Conference on Religious Movements: "The Scientologists we are privileged to know are sincere, dedicated human beings, who are striving hard for the betterment of all."

I would also agree with the Reverend Dean M. Kelley, Counselor on Religious Liberty for the National Council of Churches, when he said, "I have found them [Scientologists] to be earnest, enterprising, public-spirited and committed people." Bravo to them for taking on legal drug merchants.

In a recent confrontation on *Sixty Minutes*, psychiatry did not accept its own shortcomings, and the Scientologists insisted that the field of psychiatry is no good and neither is their Prozac. Neither, however, acknowledged the role of biochemical individuality in explaining some of these bizarre symptoms and behavior. Prozac, in effect, can help some and create harm in others. A careful monitoring of each patient, something not always done, was acknowledged as essential by the psychiatrists.

CHAPTER 10
CHELATION DOCTORS FIGHT FOR HEART PATIENTS:
A PETITION TO THE FTC

In the spring of 1991, eleven chelation doctors filed a petition with the Federal Trade Commission, requesting the FTC to prosecute their case to retain their legal/economic right to use chelation in their practices without further harassment from the medical power structure. The eleven plaintiffs requested trade opportunity equal to that granted traditional treatments for heart disease: bypass surgery, balloon angioplasty and the heart drugs. The doctors named the following as defendants in the petition:

The American Medical Association (AMA)

The Federation of State Medical Boards

The Health Insurance Association of America (HIAA) including Emprise (attorney Monaco's data bank on alternative practitioners)

The National Council Against Health Fraud (NCAHF)

Chapters of Blue Cross/Blue Shield

The petition alleges that there is a coordinated effort by these powerful institutions to thwart the development and use of various legitimate medical alternatives, in violation of federal anti-trust laws. The petition recognizes that while not all procedures labeled as alternative are necessarily valid, there are established safeguards to protect the public from dangerous drugs and unfit physicians. Deaths directly attributed to alternative treatments are insignificant in contrast to the seventh leading cause of death in hospitals, which is iatrogenic (caused by doctor or staff decisions and procedures as well as acceptable drug treatments and surgery).

The lawyer for the plaintiffs, Attorney Kay Pierson, understood the medical value of chelation from observing the recovery of an elderly friend whose senility was reversed under the care of Drs.

Edward McDonagh and Charles Rudolph of Kansas City, Missouri. Before his chelation treatments, the elderly man was feeble-minded and barely able to walk, but he regained his mental clarity and his former ability to walk. Lawyers who have learned first-hand the value of alternative therapies are a valuable asset in establishing the rights of these doctors to practice.

Attorney Pierson's legal investigation into chelation reveals an unwarranted struggle required by these doctors to conduct proper studies and publish their medical findings. They have been thwarted at every turn. By 1968, bypass surgery was heralded as a godsend in the cardiovascular wards despite the lack of any controlled studies proving effectiveness on mortality. This unproven procedure quickly emerged as a multi-billion dollar hospital industry.

That same year, in contrast, the FDA required chelation doctors to call their use of EDTA experimental. This made it impossible to collect insurance on the treatment and forced the doctors to have patients sign a consent form acknowledging chelation to be an experimental procedure. How ironic. Chelation therapy is a routine, standard medical procedure in the treatment of lead poisoning, digitalis intoxication, and acute hypercalcemia. Because this is an approved drug, it is thus absolutely legal for any licensed M.D. or D.O. to use this drug in any other way as the doctor sees fit, with his patient's informed consent.

BLUE CROSS ENTERS THE PICTURE

By the time bypass surgery arrived on the health care scene, a strong trend was underway for the burgeoning insurance industry to ally with doctors. It was a group of doctors who started Blue Cross. Although laws have tempered some physician involvement in insurance, doctors still play pivotal roles in deciding which types of claims will be covered and which will not, including those procedures which are economic competitors. Conflict of interest? You bet.

Doctors associated with insurance companies have a record of deploring chelation therapy. Without any scientific or legal justification, they have branded chelation doctors pariahs in the medical field and the insurance industry. Chelation specialists get no referrals from other doctors. They constantly battle state medical boards who challenge chelation without any proof of harm. Insurance companies deny payment for inexpensive, reasonable diagnostic tests, usually under $1,000, that chelation doctors must perform to determine kidney function and the location and extent of plaque deposits in heart-diseased patients before proceeding with the IV chelation treatment.

Most chelation doctors cannot advertise for fear of reprisal from narrow-minded colleagues, as well as from an unfounded FDA regulation, because EDTA was originally approved for lead detoxification, not plaque removal. Chelation patients must sign a form stating the treatment is experimental (which it is not) and then the patients have to pay for the treatment out of their own pockets.

Despite the administrative, economic and social obstacles, these medical pioneers have survived, some for more than twenty years. Their patient records are impressive yet are never objectively reviewed through the peer-review process—the only way in which medical progress can enter the medical establishment. Chelation patients swear by their doctors; some have even moved to be within commuting distance for treatment and follow-up.

Attorney Pierson stated the issues in this way:

> The issue and the reason for the petition is not whether the therapy works, but whether the physicians have the right to practice it free from social, economic and political harassment. Furthermore, there are few valid scientific challenges to the therapy, based on research.
>
> Circumstantially, it is apparent that the machinery of the State Medical Boards, the Health Insurance Association of America including Emprise, Inc. and the National Council Against Health Fraud, the American Medical Association and chapters of Blue Cross/Blue Shield is being used to stymie the growth and development of this therapy for reasons related to their economic interests rather than the public interest.
>
> It is also clear that unless affirmative steps are taken to protect the rights of these physicians, their situation will only worsen.

The letter of complaint asked the FTC for relief. It was divided into seven sections to put forth the above contentions and to establish a precedent and need for FTC involvement.

Section I identified the defendants, listed earlier in this chapter. Of particular significance is the inclusion of Blue Cross/Blue Shield and The Health Insurance Association of America.

Chapters of Blue Cross/Blue Shield are state prepaid medical insurance plans providing coverage for office visits, surgery and related hospital costs. They have a well-established local and national structure and many competitive advantages which give them the lion's share of nearly every market in which they operate.

The Health Insurance Association of America is a trade association of major private and non-profit insurance companies. HIAA is responsible for creating and disseminating much of the policy information upon which the industry relies. Pierson identified the consultant for the organization as none other than Grace Monaco of Emprise, insurance lawyer, and a well-paid proponent of the need for insurance companies to regulate and determine what should be acceptable practices in medicine. Through her written and spoken diatribes against some of the finest alternative medical facilities and their doctors, she serves as a convenient mouthpiece for big-bucks insurance/medicine to thwart competition.

Publicly-available information ("Health Insurance Digest News" and the "Blue Cross Network Exchange") shows that as early as in 1987 the insurance industry put together a network containing data on alternative doctors and the types of treatments for which insurance will not pay. Grace Monaco's anti-alternative data base, Emprise, and the NCAHF were both formed in the mid-1980s, with one of their purposes being to create information networks of doctors engaging in fraudulent practices. Both had been based in Washington, D.C., and had boasted of national membership which included major insurance companies. These two organizations have had considerable input/influence in the National Health Care Anti-Fraud Association (NHCAA), which organizes conferences and meetings sponsored by most major insurance companies. NHCAA was formed in 1988 by at least nine insurance companies, each contributing at least $25,000 cash.

MONACO ATTACKS ALTERNATIVE PRACTITIONERS

On November 12-13, 1990, the NHCAA held a conference at which attorney Monaco presented a paper entitled "Foreign Claims for Methods Untested and Unproven in the U.S." If this paper is representative of the quality of the data base that Emprise has assembled for NHCAA, those relying on that data base are being grossly misled. The section "Profiles of Selected Foreign Health Spas and Clinics" is glibly libelous. Her "Abbreviated Critique of Subcategories of Treatments in Foreign Clinics" is amateurish and inaccurate. She slanders Dr. Lawrence Burton's center on immune enhancement, then adds that she hopes he sues her. She falsely claims that Burton's Bahamian Clinic is raking in $10 million a year.

She unashamedly displays abject ignorance about European live-cell therapy developed by the Swiss scientist Paul Niehans, who founded Clinic La Prairie in Neuchatel, Switzerland. This technique is also practiced with good results by the Austrian physician

Wolfram Kuhnau at American Biologics, a full-scale, international-ly-networked hospital outside of Tijuana, Mexico. Her critique on the medical results of live-cell therapy ignores the follow-up research on children with Down's syndrome or Mongoloidism. Those who had received the bovine (fetal calf) live-cell injections performed at higher cognitive levels than their counterparts who had not received the periodic live cell injections. Embryonic cells, for unknown reasons, are not rejected by the adult organism of a different species. Also, no single drug or chemical can match the complex biochemistry of a living cell. Recently retired after twenty years practice at American Biologics, Wolfram Kuhnau, a physician who made invaluable contributions in furthering Niehan's techniques, proudly states in his book *Live-Cell Therapy,* that he comes from a long line of German doctors in the best tradition of medicine.

Attorney Monaco also ignorantly dismisses the German oncologist Dr. Hans Nieper, of the world-renowned Nieper Clinic of Silversee Hospital in Hanover, Germany. She blithely omits Dr. Nieper's prominence in cancer therapy and research, his temporary training at Sloan-Kettering in New York City, his past-presidency of the European Oncological Association, his expert testimony before the U.S. Congress, and his occasional lecture tours in the U.S. She foolishly trivializes his understanding that cancer is a systemic breakdown of the body's immune system through a stressed, abnormal metabolism.

The lady doesn't know when to quit. Next she dismisses Dr. Nieper's research emphasis on the effects of electromagnetic fields, ignoring a recently-released report of the EPA which corroborates his views; then she belittles Nieper's use of DNA-repair substances (the theoretical basis for which has only recently been established with the identification of the RAS and other oncogene-cancer causers).

Monaco quotes an "FDA talk paper dated August 19, 1986," stating, that "the German medical group" [no identification] carried out an extensive review of all facets of the Nieper regimen and concluded that there are no published objective findings for his claimed efficacy of calcium EAP in the treatment of multiple sclerosis. Are, therefore, the many American MS patients who can afford to travel to Germany for Dr. Nieper's treatment wrong also, and their case studies fabricated?

Further "gospel according to Grace": Dr. Nieper's prescribed treatment for MS is dangerous. She claims that it is troublesome to patients since there is no possibility of terminating the injections, the patients must take 20-25 tablets per day and the treatment is expensive. How can she ignore the "troublesomeness" of the expense of traditional MS treatments and subsequent expenses from a deteriorated body, to say nothing of the physical and psychological misery and possibility of an early death? There are thousands of documented cases of remission, not only Nieper's patients but thousands of others who have come under the care of less-famous alternative practitioners who have used calcium EAP throughout the Western Hemisphere. One lady from the east coast has written a small book, edited by her physician-husband, about her travel to Dr. Nieper and her subsequent remission which has lasted to this date.

Obviously, to extract such comments from an "FDA talk paper" and attribute them to an unidentified "German medical group" is to use irresponsible hearsay that has no business being entered in a federally-funded database on untested and unproven methods of treating cancer. I will grant Ms. Monaco one irrelevant grain of truth: There certainly could be a German medical group voicing opposition to Hans Nieper in the traditional allopathic medical community; but, overall, alternative therapy facilities fare better in Europe than in the U.S. We Americans have a superior, stronger heritage of racketeering in medicine.

The question is, will we accept a more pluralistic health-care system before high-tech, allopathic medicine has thoroughly bankrupted our medical care system and severely affected the entire economy? Will we be able to pull ourselves up far enough to economically survive? Remember, 80% of this nation's medical needs are largely chronic, degenerative conditions such as heart disease, cancer, MS, and arthritis, as opposed to acute infectious disease and injury, which make up approximately 20%.

In the petition, attorney Pierson cites the following:

> The Court, in *Wilk v. American Medical Association,* has already found that the AMA has the greatest number of physicians and hospitals which provide a larger percentage of medical services than any other comparable society. Because of their pervasiveness, largesse and uniqueness, the Court found them to be a de facto monopoly in the arena of policy formation, information, and influence.

The State Medical Boards license new or transferring physicians by administering a test to those with medical degrees from accredited schools. They also discipline physicians who violate the codes established by each state's Board of Medical Examiners. In the petition, it is alleged that these boards have also been used as a tool for anti-competitive purposes by those who prosecute doctors practicing chelation therapy, often for no legally sound reason. Although their jurisdiction is thought to be within state boundaries, the Federation of State Boards of Medical Examiners, based in New Mexico, uses its national network to harass doctors who are identified by various medical associations as "unacceptable."

Section 2 of the petition to the FTC, entitled "The FTC's Role in Regulating Health Matters," begins by citing *American Medical Association v. U.S., 317 U.S. 519, (1943)* and *American Medical Association v. Federal Trade Commission, 638 F Supplement 443, Second Circuit (1980)* as the precedents allowing quasi-legislative and judicial review of self-regulating activities of medical associations for anti-competitive abuse. Since some degree of self-regulation is useful, the challenge is to distinguish legitimate self-regulation from unwarranted restraints on professional practice for the purpose of stifling the growth and development of innovative alternative medicine.

The Supreme Court's decision in *Goldfarb v. Virginia State Bar, 421 U.S. 773 (1975)* and *National Society of Professional Engineers v. U.S., 534 U.S. 679 (1978)* affirmed that professional associations and societies are subject to anti-trust scrutiny under federal statutes in case law. Of the three doctrines that are tangentially involved in an anti-trust analysis, the one on interstate commerce is most appropriate for this petition.

It is said that the FTC does not participate in purely intra-state matters unless some degree of interstate commerce is involved. Here the market, although presented in the context of a case-by-case basis, is truly national because the Health Insurance Association of America promulgates policies to local affiliates; the AMA reaches its constituency through a national structure; and even the state medical boards have a national organization which is capable of disseminating information to state boards. It is clear that none of the cases presented in the petition would have occurred without a national superstructure operating to create, disseminate and enforce policies which systematically target doctors using chelation therapy, wherever they practice.

At issue is whether these physicians are illegally eliminated from competing by systematic means (through insurance claims, state medical boards, and unprotected uses of AMA statements and practices of non-referral), which are used to denigrate the treatment without scientific basis and to pressure other traditional physicians and medical institutions against referring cardiac patients, despite the demonstrated benefits of the treatment. Right or wrong, consumers are entitled to know about the treatment, and doctors should be allowed to practice it without economic and political harassment.

In Section 4, entitled "The Federal Antitrust Standard as defined by the FTC and the Court," the petition cites "the policy published by Federal Trade Commission on October 5, 1981, which was meant to affect physician agreement to control prepaid medical plans." The idea was to promote competition among sellers of health plans, along with the providers of health care, by investigating those practices which tend to "injure or threaten such competition," and finding "any resultant concerted activity illegal if they unreasonably restrain trade." The Commission decided to handle such antitrust actions on a case-by-case basis. The steps for reaching such a conclusion include defining and determining the existence of physician control; assessing the plan's market power using traditional economic concepts; and applying the rule of reason to the plan's operation in order to determine its ultimate purpose and effect on competition.

In defining "physician control," the petition states that the FTC's enforcement policy defines the process of determining control as analyzing the relationship between the plan and the physician group, to ascertain whether the group has effective, overall power over the plan's policies and actions. Such control may be either formal or de facto.

"Market power" was defined by the Commission as the ability to affect market prices or exclude competitors from the market. Market power has been traditionally viewed as fundamental to a determination of anti-competitive behavior. The traditional factors the Commission stated it would consider are product and geographic markets, barriers to entry, market share and the size and number of competitors. These standards have all been set by judicial precedent.

Section 5 of the petition is entitled "The Market Analysis of the Insurance Industry." Attorney Pierson states that although Blue Shield Plans vary in size and extent of market penetration, most plans are the most significant underwriters of medical coverage in their respective areas. The network of the Blue Shield plans is coordinated and to some extent controlled by the Blue Shield Association (BSA). BSA licenses the Blue Service Mark, conducts national advertising, public relations, lobbying and liaison programs, controls standards for plan membership in the Association, administers subscribers' transfer and reciprocity programs among the plans, and, perhaps most importantly, coordinates solicitation of national accounts. Blue Shield Association also performs or coordinates solicitation of government business and provides statistical, actuarial, marketing, administrative, technical and research and development services to member plans.

The membership standards generally require that each plan operate on a non-profit basis, conform to certain financial requirements, adhere to quality-assurance performance standards within each program in which it participates, and make available a certain minimum level of benefits that Blue Shield Association has incorporated into a model Blue Shield Comprehensive Contract.

In general, when a request for a quotation is received from a group which has members in more than one plan area, the control plan ascertains what kind of coverage the group desires and obtains information with which to estimate the amount of utilization that can be expected. The control plan then calculates a rate for the proposed coverage and transmits the information to Blue Shield Association and to each of the plans that would administer coverage for a significant number of members of the group.

Favored treatment under state regulatory systems may afford many Blue Shield plans significant cost advantages over competing prepayment plans. Many plans are exempt from state taxes that are assessed against commercial insurers, including premium taxes, income taxes, property taxes and sales taxes. Many plans are also exempt from various state and local insurance laws, including requirements that insurers maintain large reserves.

Insurance claims are sent to a local Blue Cross or Blue Shield by the physician or patient. These claims are reviewed for internal standards for what is reasonable and necessary. Anything which is deemed to be unreasonable or unnecessary is rejected. Blue Cross or Blue Shield then sends out a letter asking for more information to justify the claim as medically necessary. It can send as many letters as it takes to clarify the charge and then still reject claims based upon standards about which they do not know and the setting of which they did not participated.

THE RED-FLAG SYSTEM

There is an apparent pattern in the practice of denying claims. It is effected through a "red-flag" system, which has a legitimate use to identify physicians who have been disciplined or otherwise sanctioned for abuses of insurance claims. Circumstantially, it can be shown that this practice of red-flagging physicians is used to deny the legitimate claims of physicians who have been targeted because they practice an alternative type of medicine, which is seen as unacceptable by their economic competitors, often because it is a less expensive, albeit more effective, method of treatment.

Blue Cross and Blue Shield also administer Medicare on a statewide or regional basis. Medicare, created in 1965 as part of the Social Security Act, consists of two parts: Part A is a mandatory hospital insurance funded by deductions made for employment taxes; Part B is a supplemental program paid for by voluntary contributions by the insured.

Part A of Medicare provides limited medical coverage for those who are either under a statutory disability or are retired recipients of Social Security annuities. Under Part A, inpatient hospital care and a limited amount of post-hospital care are covered. Those who qualify for Part A coverage and have paid for Part B coverage can get up to 80% of such charges as physician's care, x-rays, lab tests, medical supplies and a limited amount of medical equipment. (4242 U.S.C. Sections 1395 [c, i, k, x]) Part of the payment for this program is provided by subsidies from the federal government. Both of these programs fall under the purview of the Secretary of Health and Human Services.

Part A is administered via intermediaries, or insurance companies under contract with the Secretary, which review the beneficiary claims to determine the amounts to be paid for the medical services.

Part B of Medicare is managed by carriers, or insurance companies, which also review the claims and decide which to pay and how much. In many markets, Blue Cross and Blue Shield act as intermediaries and carriers to process the beneficiary claims. Apparently, there are also practices in the Medicare system whereby physicians are identified by the red-flag system. Physicians branded with the red flag by Medicare have been targeted for consistent rejections, regardless of the type of tests being performed, principally because of the type of work they do, *e.g.*, their use of chelation therapy.

Section V of the petition also says that the Health Insurance Association of America (HIAA) is a national Washington, D.C.-based trade association which meets annually with members coming from across the country to discuss issues and policies affecting the health insurance companies nationwide. The HIAA can be said to use its network to influence insurance companies around the country to discount the value of "undesirable" treatments, perhaps as a basis for denying claims of doctors who practice alternative medicine.

An article published by the American Bar Association and written by attorneys Grace Powers Monaco and Rebecca L. Burke features a discussion of how it is the duty of insurance companies to monitor alternative treatments and to control their development by encouraging its members to deny claims made for these treatments. They define an "alternative practitioner" as one "who purveys questionable and often worthless cures as well as false hopes, and creates a health marketplace in which even the well-educated can be duped."

Monaco and Burke state how various consumer groups are emerging to challenge limitation of insurance coverage for alternative practitioners. These consumer groups advocate the patients' right to make their own choices of doctors for a designated service, whether preventive or therapeutic; and for the consumers of health insurance to decide for themselves the competency of their chosen physicians.

It is this desire of the advocates to decide which doctor works best for them that is the basis for Monaco and Burke's premise that "insurers have a responsibility, as part of their quasi-public nature, to separate the legitimate claims from the illegitimate, and in essence, act as a 'gatekeeper.'" Furthermore, assert Monaco and Burke, insurance companies should not agree to payments for subjective results (such as stated feelings of relief or physical well-being by the patient) but objective measures established by published articles and studies through physician peer review. These two hired guns of the insurance/Organized Medicine's business-as-usual forces go on to say, "Should insurers now review each patient's medical records before they reject a claim for an unproven treatment? We believe the answer is no. This may be a proper approach where one is considering the appropriateness of a proven therapy. However, it has no place in the questionable therapy realm." In other words, don't even consider reimbursing a patient treated by alternative methods.

Monaco and Burke proposed that the way for insurance companies to get around ambiguous interpretations of what is effective is to adopt this proposed language in their policies: "Eligible expenses will include only charges for therapies which are recognized as potentially safe and efficacious for the care and treatment of the injury or sickness by the medical community, including the American Medical Association."

How could these methods of determining reasonableness be called objective? Who made the insurance industry the gatekeeper? Just how can an entire group of people with competing commercial interests in medical treatments become the arbiters of what is acceptable medicine? How can they decide the merits of a treatment by ignoring the actual results in favor of their more subjective standard?

One would intelligently assume that insurance companies would have an economic interest in promoting inexpensive and effective treatments. However, the premium charged (to consumers and to third-party payers, such as private employers and the federal government) is determined by a formula which factors in the costs of accepted procedures. Costly procedures equal higher premiums. There is therefore an economic incentive for insurance companies to insure more costly procedures.

As a final request to ensure their ability to compete in their practice without fear of harassment, the chelation doctors' petition requests that the FTC revisit, or reconsider, a rule that the FTC had recommended in 1979. This rule prohibited physician associations from selecting members of the insurance plans' governing boards. It also provided that, for a period of five years, physicians who compete for a plan's funds may comprise no more than 25% of that plan's governing body, regardless of whether such physician members are selected by physician organizations.

They made the request that the FTC revisit the rule by stating, "We would like to see the FTC revisit this former recommendation, after conducting a full investigation of the interrelations, practices and policies of the AMA, HIAA, and Federation of State Boards of Medical Examiners."

For reasons left unknown to the public, the FTC decided against revisiting this rule, choosing instead to use the enforcement policy discussed above. To date, however, no cases have been successfully prosecuted under that policy.

PART 3
A PRACTICAL SOLUTION TO THE HEALTH CARE CRISIS

CHAPTER 11
OUR HEALTH CARE CRISIS: THE HIDDEN CAUSES

Washington's latest answer to the health-care crisis is a new federal agency. It is called the Agency for Health Care Policy and Research and was created by Congress before Christmas, 1990; $500 million was earmarked. One of its functions is the assessment of new technology. Another function is to control the rising costs in health care through research and experimentation. "We don't know what we're doing in medicine," said Dr. David Eddy, Director of the Duke University Center for Health Policy Research, who addressed a health care conference in Atlanta earlier in 1990 and who is one of the leaders in the movement to guide doctors out of the confusion. He added, "The imperative for the 1990s is to fix that problem."

"That problem" refers to the fact that at least 20% of the nation's health bill—or $125 billion as of 1989, a figure big enough to wipe out the federal budget deficit—is wasted on unnecessary, inappropriate or dangerous treatments because of a lack of knowledge and consensus as to what really works.

The new federal agency, in cooperation with private medicine programs, over a period of five years, is to determine what works and to develop "practice guidelines [and] standards. . . to assess and assure quality of care."

The program was the result of several sobering assessments concerning the status of American medicine, including these findings:

Perhaps one-quarter to one-third of medical services may be of little or no benefit to patients. (Institute of Medicine)

The link between the process of care and patient outcomes has been established for relatively few procedures. (Office of Technology Assessment, U.S. Congress)

Uncertainty about the most effective diagnostic and therapeutic approaches is pervasive. (Dr. Dennis S. O'Leary, President, Joint commission on Accreditation of Health Care Organizations)

The embarrassment of our ignorance about the efficacy of health care practices is both hard for us to admit and hard for our clients to accept. It is difficult [for doctors] to face the disillusionment of the patients and the anger of the payers who ask, "But how could this be? I thought you knew what you were doing." (Dr. Donald Berwick, Vice-president of the Harvard Community Health Plan)

Part of the evidence that much of modern medicine is still based on guesswork comes from the recent pioneering work of Dr. John Wennberg, a professor of community and family medicine at Dartmouth Medical School. For almost twenty years, Wennberg and his colleagues have been collecting evidence of contrasting variations in treatment patterns between different cities, hospitals, and even different doctors, without any appreciable difference in outcome for the patient.

For example, hysterectomy—removal of the uterus—is one of the most frequent operations that American women undergo. Most doctors agree that it should be performed for uterine cancer, but surgery is optional for less threatening conditions. Its use varies widely from one community to another, for no clear reason. Wennberg discovered one city in Maine where 70% of the female population would lose their uterus by the age of 75. In a city less than twenty miles away, only 25% the women would have the operation. Wennberg said these variations occurred "because the profession lacks consensus on the correct way to practice medicine. . . We should invest our time and effort into finding out what's going on. We don't know."

Similar unexplained variations occur in many other medical tests and procedures, from simple x-rays to complex heart surgery. In Rutland, Vermont, seven times as many children have their tonsils removed as in Hanover, New Hampshire, only fifty miles away. In one city in Iowa, 15% of the men have had prostate surgery, contrasting sharply with 60% in another Iowan city. Two top teaching hospitals associated with the Harvard Medical School showed great differences in the way they delivered babies. In one hospital, 19% of newborn babies came into the world surgically—by Caesarean section. In the other, only a few blocks away, the knife was used 30% of the time, for no apparent medical reason. Boston has 55% more hospital beds and spends 70% more money on health care per capita than New Haven, Connecticut, even though both are sites of major medical centers. According to Dr. Wennberg, "There is a vast difference in the cost and quantity of care between [Boston and New

Haven], but no difference in mortality."

Such discrepancies are "potentially damning evidence" of inappropriate medical care, according to Dr. Frederick Robbins, Dean of Case Western Reserve School of Medicine in Cleveland and former president of the Institute of Medicine. "You can cover it up all you want, but it looks bad, and it is not an appropriate way for a profession to behave," said Robbins.

Because of this inconsistency, medicine is in an "intellectual crisis," said Wennberg. "For most common illness and medical conditions, the necessary assessments to establish correct theory have not been done."

Dr. Eddy has commented, "We're really flying blind on an awful lot of important problems. The same patient can go to different physicians, be told different things and receive different care."

It is doubtful, however, that the designated agency for Health Care Policy and Research will successfully solve these problems if it ignores the racketeering-for-profit element of medicine. What about the costs? Why are they so much out of line with the Consumer Price Index or with the slower rise of health-care costs in Canada? Several health economists predict that if the present trends in the escalating costs of health care continue, shortly after the year 2000, for many companies, nearly 100% of their profits will be spent paying medical bills. In addition, by the year 2040, 100% of the country's gross national product will have to be spent for health care. We know that these predictions cannot logistically come to pass. But what on earth is causing this trend? What are the reasons for continuously increasing costs of health care? The reasons are many and complex, but they can be divided into six categories:

(1) Control of Congress and the courts
(2) Manipulation of the health charities
(3) The big-bucks role of insurance companies
(4) Uncontrolled release of new technologies
(5) Bloated physician fees and prescription fees
(6) Paper-pushing for a third party

(1) CONTROLLING CONGRESS

Lobbying efforts on the part of the medical profession on members of Congress are well known. The American Medical Association, for example, is the second largest contributor to Political Action Committees (PACs), second only to the NRA.

Organized Med skillfully ramrods members of Congress and state representatives to enact laws, policies, and procedures which institutionalize the goals of establishment medicine and prevent competitive and alternative treatments from entering mainstream medicine. In 1989 and 1990 alone, the forces opposed to holistic, complementary, and alternative medicine made the following advances:

HR4079, sponsored by Newt Gingrich and co-sponsored by fifty-seven other members of the House, provides for the suspension of constitutional rights in cases of "health fraud."

The Federal Register states that the FDA has proposed pulling off the market various nutritional supplements, such as vitamin E, calcium, and lactobacillus acidophilus, effective July, 1991.

In the state of Illinois, legislation was proposed which "creates the Health Care Fraud and Quackery Act, which provides that the misrepresenting of material facts, scientific terms, professional relationships or degrees, or the effect of a diagnosis or treatment constitutes health care fraud and quackery; makes both health care fraud and quackery a class IV felony; makes the condition of Health Care Fraud and Quackery against persons aged 60 years and older Aggravated Health Care Fraud and Quackery; makes Aggravated Health Care Fraud and Quackery a class III felony."

In Colorado, in September, 1990, Dr. William E. Doell, D.O., had his licensed revoked for practicing "nutritional medicine." This followed the continuing litigation in New York by the Office of Professional Medical Conduct against Dr. Warren Levin, in an attempt to revoke his license, also ostensibly for practicing "nutritional medicine." These cases are the first attempts to use the legal system to eliminate doctors who use nutrition to treat disease or who practice alternative—or, as Dr. Linus Pauling has labeled it, orthomolecular—medicine. (Whatever happened to Hippocrates' "Let thy food be thy medicine and thy medicine be thy food"?)

In the state of California, Senate Bill 2172 passed easily through the senate with a vote of 34 to 0. This bill would provide for personal property to be confiscated in the event of anyone supporting and practicing unconventional medicine, other than allopathic medicine, for the treatment or prevention of any disease, including cancer and AIDS. Therefore, a person convicted of "health fraud" would be treated the same as a convicted drug dealer. The bill was eventually dropped by Senator Marian Bergeson, who had introduced it, because of the successful lobbying efforts of advocate groups for Freedom of Choice in Health Care. Similar bills are expected to be introduced in other states and will be re-introduced in California.

The Food, Drug, Cosmetic and Device Enforcement Amendments of 1991 (H.R. 3642), authored by Congressman Henry Waxman (D-Calif.), would grant sweeping new powers to the FDA. These would include:

—Power to conduct warrantless searches

—Power to conduct electronic surveillance

—Right to embargo or recall products without hearing or right of appeal

—Unlimited authority to conduct fishing expeditions through company files

These powers would be backed up by civil penalties of up to $250,000 on individuals and $1 million on companies for each alleged violation.

In short, H.R. 3642 will give FDA new enforcement, recall, embargo, subpoena, inspection, and civil penalty powers. As the National Council For Improved Health points out, "due process includes protection against government abuse of power. The law guarantees criminals charged with rape and murder far more due process than H.R. 3642 will allow citizens who FDA alleges have committed minor civil violations."

A PROXMIRE AWARD FOR JUDICIAL IMPRUDENCE

This goes to the Supreme Court of the State of North Carolina, which on July 28, 1990, decided against Dr. George Guess, M.D., ruling that he did not have a right to practice homeopathic medicine and that homeopathy was not the acceptable and prevailing medical standard in North Carolina.

Dr. Guess was put on trial before the State Board of Medical Examiners in North Carolina for using homeopathic remedies in his family practice—not on a whim, but after several years of study of homeopathy under one of the great European masters, Dr. George Vilthoukas of Athens, Greece. Fortunately, Dr. Guess received substantial contributions for his legal defense, because he was not the only one on trial. The entire healing art/science of homeopathy was on trial—in 1990, mind you! Scientific Enlightenment, where are you hiding? Dr. Guess lost his case at the Board level, but won on appeal to the Superior Court level. The Board then appealed to the State Supreme Court.

The order to Dr. Guess from the North Carolina Board of Medical Examiners was that his license would be revoked unless he desisted from using homeopathic medicines in his practice. This order was issued despite the fact that homeopathic medicine has been practiced in this country for approximately 150 years.

Discussing this case, Dr. Henry Heimlich said:

> Like most physicians, I was induced by the medical establishment to look down on homeopathic treatment. My attitude changed when my wife, Jane, wrote a best-selling book, *Homeopathic Medicine at Home.*
>
> I learned that the royal family of England has been treated by homeopathic physicians since the time of Queen Victoria; that homeopathy is widely practiced throughout much of the world; and, in three states of this country, separate boards of homeopathic medicine have been established by state legislatures.

Homeopathic doctors are qualified M.D.s who have graduated from the same medical colleges as their allopathic counterparts.

The North Carolina Board of Medical Examiners, however, had decided that in utilizing homeopathic medicine Dr. Guess "departed from the standards of acceptable and prevailing medical practice in the State of North Carolina."

The Board offered Dr. Guess the option of retaining his license if he ceased to dispense homeopathic medicines, but Dr. Guess refused to practice in a manner other than according to his skills as a doctor and the dictates of his conscience. Although the Superior Court overthrew the action of the North Carolina Board of Medical Examiners, the Board's decision was upheld on appeal to the State Supreme Court. The Supreme Court further ruled that "there is no right to practice medicine which is not subordinate to the police power of the States." They also stated that there is "no fundamental right of the public to receive unorthodox medical treatment".

Dr. Guess was accused of "unprofessional conduct, including but not limited to any alternative form of therapy which fails to conform to the standards of acceptable and prevailing medical practice or the ethics of the medical profession, irrespective of whether or not the patient is injured thereby."

The only witnesses for the North Carolina State Board of Medical Examiners were two physicians who reported that they "had never been taught such things in medical school," and that Dr. Guess was the only physician in North Carolina who practiced homeopathy. The opposition to holistic, complementary, and alternative medicine successfully uses the legislative process and the courts to implement their policies. This is the same bunch of guys that complain bitterly about malpractice suits and the tort system in general.

What is glaringly apparent is that neither scientific controversy nor the right to practice other internationally recognized types of medicine nor medical ethics can be resolved in the courts. Concerning the latter, Robert Merhige, Jr., U.S. District Judge in Virginia, in responding to a hypothetical case of a pregnant mother dying of cancer, with a viable fetus, on a PBS TV program on ethics in medicine, said the following:

> These are tough decisions. I am sorry it is here, in the courts. Unfortunately, it is left to the courts to decide. The court is the wrong institution to decide a matter like this one. It is the doctors and the family who should be deciding this. But somebody has to speak for the patient, who is dying, and who is unconscious. There is a loss of autonomy when a third or innocent person is involved.
>
> The doctor is not God; the judge is not God but the decision has to be based on the evidence before the Court.

Lawyers and judges who have no background in medicine are making bad decisions in most of these cases. The recent U.S. Supreme Court decision in the case of the Cruzon family in Missouri is a case in point. The Court ruled that the patient had not made her wishes clearly known before she went into a vegetative state and that the state of Missouri had a right and an obligation to preserve life. It was therefore left up to the state of Missouri to decide whether or not her parents had a right to disconnect her feeding. Fortunately, in this case the state of Missouri ruled in their favor, but this might not have been the case in, say, Arizona or North Carolina. This case prompted one physician/observer to remark, "For a while there, I thought it was against the law to die in Missouri!"

If this is how the judicial system resolves conflicts in medical ethics, then none of these issues should be brought before the courts in the first place. But alas, conflicts do arise and there is no place else to turn. Furthermore, in order for a person to protect himself from being kept alive by machines in a vegetative state, he or she would have to prepare a Living Will with such a degree of specificity that it would be practically impossible to allow for alternative plans and contingencies.

If anyone is responsible for this legislative and judicial madness, then it is those who propose laws preventing a pluralistic health care system and those who bring these cases into the courts in the first place. As long as we allow this pervasive influence on our legislators, judges, and quasi-state government officials, such as the members of the State Boards of Medical Examiners, to continue, then we can expect health care costs to continue to escalate. It is a misuse of the legal system to enact laws that favor vested economic interests which are by no means in the public's best interest. The irony is that these laws are being enacted supposedly to protect the public against health care fraud and quackery.

There has been a recent small victory for the proponents of holistic, complementary, and alternative medicine. On June 14, 1990, the Governor of Alaska signed into law House Bill 8146. This bill states:

> In demonstrating professional incompetence, gross negligence, or repeated negative conduct, the Board of Medical Examiners may not base the finding of professional incompetence solely on the basis that a licensee's practice is unconventional or experimental, in the absence of demonstrable physical harm to the patient.

This law is a first step in overturning this legislative nightmare. The governor of Alaska, Walter Hickel, who has personally benefitted from chelation therapy, also recently appointed an alternative practitioner to the State Board of Medical Examiners. In addition, the Insurance Commissioner recently ordered none other than Aetna to pay for chelation, a decision which was based on the administration's interpretation of the Alaska Medical Practice Act.

(2) MANIPULATING THE HEALTH CHARITIES

Unknown to the public are the lobbying efforts of the so-called voluntary agencies, such as the American Cancer Society, the American Heart Association, and others who spend outrageous sums of money (donated by the public) to lobby Congress for the same predominant views of Organized Medicine. These charities have sincere volunteers down in the trenches working the door-to-door campaigns, but could it be that these charities are working on behalf of Organized Med on the higher up, administrative level? Some observers consider the major charities to be thinly-disguised lobbying fronts for Organized Med.

Professor James Bennett of George Mason University published a study of three major health charities. The study, released in July, 1990, suggested that the following three charities may have been misleading the public: the American Cancer Society, the American Heart Association, and the American Lung Association. The report states that all three have been telling the public that they are supporting research and "looking for a cure." The facts are, however, that while 87% of the American Heart Association's income in 1988 came from tax deductible donations, only 30% of their funds were spent on research. The American Cancer Society also depends on public generosity for 90% of its funds, and yet it spends only 25% on research. The American Lung Association gets three-fourths of its money from public donations and spends a mere 4.1%, a pittance, on research. Each of these charities spend about 25% of their budgets on fund raising, administration, and salaries for their executive offices. The ACS president receives a salary of $174,000 a year; its senior vice-president for medical affairs receives a salary of $180,000. The ALA chief executive officer gets $118,000, and the president of the AHA receives a salary of $181,000. Of course, these salaries exclude donor-provided expense accounts and fringe benefits.

In addition, the ACS has assets which include lands valued at $14 million, $42 million in buildings and leasehold improvements and $6 million in buildings under construction. The ALA has assets totaling $42 million, and the AHA's assets total $52 million. These figures do not include assets in the form of stocks and bonds, which each agency also owns.

Professor Bennett observes, "Most people are unaware that some health organizations are thinly disguised political organizations." He points out that the primary function of these organizations is to lobby Congress for legislation. They say they are for research and for finding a cure; their real agenda, however, is political. They also lobby Congress to tax us for more medical research. Bennett goes on to say that health charities should refrain from political advocacy and do what their contributors give them money to do, such as mobilize volunteers, screen for disease, and educate the public.

American Heart Association's stand on chelation was wrong.

Chelation medical experts proved that, first in a retrospective study and then in a pilot double-blind study. Hoekstra and his colleagues also proved it, in their review of over 19,000 cases who had been treated with EDTA, 80% of whom showed improvements in blood flow afterwards.

The American Cancer Society was also wrong about the macrobiotic diet. We proved that in a study of long-term survivors on the diet with cancer of the pancreas and with stage D_2 prostate cancer (which had spread to the bones).

Both organizations' political activities, in the opinion of many seasoned doctors, have included disinformation campaigns and participation in the Strike Force's overt and covert activities.

Critics of Dr. Bennett's report tried to blame the conclusions and the negative publicity surrounding the report's release on the tobacco industry, which has long been a target of these charities, but the figures on the expenditures speak: "Where there is smoke there is fire."

(3) THE BIG BUCKS' ROLE OF HEALTH INSURANCE

The health insurance industry determines which treatments a given company will pay for and which they will not. These decisions are not made by actuarial executives, but by the physicians who work with them. These doctors bring to the bargaining table their own baggage of bias and drug-oriented perspectives on medicine and financial prosperity for physicians.

The decisions these doctors make about which treatments and procedures will be covered are so critical that observers of the health care industry conclude that medical services are reimbursement-driven.

Question: Why would a health insurance company pay up to $50,000 for bypass surgery in preference to $3,000 at the most for chelation therapy? Answer: The doctors performing the surgery and the insurance company have the same financial interests—the higher cost of a bypass is no sweat off these guys' backs; they simply raise the premiums, based on a complex formula. Remember, in order to make more money you have to spend more (of someone else's).

Mr. Harry Day of Ohio, now deceased, sued Aetna Life and Casualty Insurance Company following treatment for heart disease. He was advised to have coronary artery bypass surgery without benefit of a second opinion. Since his insurance policy recommended second opinions for most surgical procedures, Mr. Day sought a second opinion. As a result, he underwent EDTA chelation therapy. He had a good response, once again became functional, and added additional good quality years to his life. Aetna agreed to pay for the very expensive coronary artery bypass graft (which has resulted in about 4,000 deaths in 300,000 cases), but refused to pay for the non-invasive chelation therapy which has caused only twenty deaths in nearly 500,000 cases (and these occurred before an exacting protocol was developed; remember, chelation therapy is a medical procedure and needed to be thoroughly researched and studied). Aetna refused to pay $891.90 for the chelation therapy, which they labeled "experimental." So Harry Day sued.

The lower court ruled in favor of Mr. Day; the appellate court upheld this decision. However, the Supreme Court of the State of Ohio overturned the appellate and lower court decisions and ruled in favor of Aetna. This case was appealed to the U.S. Supreme Court, but that court took the easy way out and decided not to hear it.

Aetna, whose legal consultant is Grace Powers Monaco of Emprise, is also involved in a tumultuous multi-million-dollar legal battle with Dr. Burzynski of the Burzynski Research Institute in Houston, Texas. There are also other instances in which Aetna has refused to pay for cheaper alternative therapies. Bear in mind what motivates an insurance company to pay $35,000 for a surgery which rarely works as well as a non-surgical procedure which costs less than $3,000: The insurance company and the surgeons have a mutual goal, *i.e.*, higher prices, which bring higher profits.

With the development of angioplasty, it was felt that this procedure would reduce the number of CABG's being performed. However, both are growing at alarming rates:

Year	Number of CABG'S	Number of Angioplasties
1983	180,000	30,000
1986	280,000	130,000
1991	350,000	300,000

In 1990, the costs associated with CABG and angioplasty totaled $10 billion, and those costs are growing at a rate of $1½ billion per year. It will take much more than the invention of a "better mousetrap" to turn this around. In addition, recent studies show that angioplasty causes a new and different kind of injury from that which initiates and causes arteriosclerosis; the re-occlusion rate is high, 25 to 40%; and it appears to be of little or no benefit in the treatment of peripheral vascular disease in the lower extremities.

Recently a courageous executive in the insurance industry put forth the premise that there are innovative medical therapies existing today that offer solutions to health problems and, at the same time, offer significant reductions in health-care costs. He prefers to remain anonymous and does want to reveal the name of his company on the advice of legal counsel.

His observation is that there is a role for the insurance industry in advocating evaluation of innovative medical therapies. Actuaries, after all, are focused almost exclusively on statistical results as opposed to theory. The insurance industry should have great economic motivation to see safe, effective and inexpensive therapies extensively evaluated and widely disseminated. The way that the industry behaves in this regard, however, suggests that they are quite satisfied with the status quo. This is the case because the amount of money they collect is far greater than the amount of money they have to pay out, even when they have to pay $50,000 for an unnecessary operation for a patient who could have been treated non-surgically for $3,000-$4,000.

This vice-president and director of research for an $11-million insurance company, who has written editorials making a case for alternative therapies, wrote to me the following:

> I, too, think it is important to let the public know that there are some individuals in the Health Insurance Industry who rely on actuarial analysis and common sense, instead of just taking the doctor's word for which therapies work and which ones are cost-effective. However, to me the presentation and context are as important as the message. If my new company decides to pick up on this research, we will try to effect change from the inside in a non-confrontational manner. My editorials or a variation thereof will no doubt be a part of that approach. I don't want my work caught up in *Racketeering in Medicine—The Suppression of Alternatives,* a tone that promises to be inflammatory and confrontational.

But can we expect this giant of an insurance industry to suddenly awaken to the cost-containment possibilities of alternative therapies and even *slowly* turn itself around and do the right thing? Not when it means a loss of revenue to the health-care providers from whom they take their cues about which treatments to pay for and which ones not pay for. When California enacted malpractice reform by passing the Medical Injury Compensation Reform Act, the rate of growth in malpractice insurance premiums slowed down considerably. But the cost of practicing defensive medicine has not lessened—it has gone up. This is because defensive medicine makes money, an amount estimated to be at least $20 billion nationally every year.

Besides, the points raised by the vice-president are a re-hash of the age-old argument about whether it is better to change the system from within or from without. I believe that when there are economic disincentives for the all-important provider constituency of the health insurance industry, *i.e.*, doctors and hospitals, change which comes from within, with an accompanying loss of revenue, is nearly impossible.

Only three issues matter in selecting a treatment or therapy: Does it help? How toxic is it? How much does it cost? In baseball, when the veteran is hitting .200 and the untested rookie is hitting .350, the rookie gets a chance.

About fifteen years ago, the John Alden Insurance Company targeted for coverage what was then a low-risk group, namely gay, white male professionals. The AIDS epidemic nearly devastated the company, but as they analyzed their situation, it was noted that a cluster of their patients treated by Dr. Joan Priestly of Southern California were improving remarkably and living longer than those treated by other doctors. Of particular interest was the drastically lower costs submitted for payment.

Dr. Priestly uses a regimen which includes the parenteral use of Thiamine, B_{12} and other B vitamins, not unlike the mega-vitamin treatments used by Frederich B. Klenner in the 1970s to treat multiple sclerosis and other neurological disorders. Her program, however, also includes the elimination of all alcohol and tobacco, following a semi-vegetarian diet, and the taking of supplements by mouth. Currently the monthly nutritional supplements cost about $75. They include vitamin C, protein powders, AL721, omega-3 fatty acids, GLA, and some herbs such as quercitin, St. Johns wart, etc.

Instead of cutting this doctor's insurance payments because her therapy did not involve AZT, DDI, and other usual medications, John Alden judiciously investigated her use of nutrients and other biologic-response modifiers to stimulate her AIDS patients' ailing immune systems and to prevent or delay central nervous system involvement.

The company is now investigating a cooperative effort with Dr. Priestly to develop specific protocols for a more natural treatment of AIDS patients. It is also under consideration to recommend that all of the AIDS patients insured by them receive this treatment protocol, a policy which could help save the insurance industry a great deal of money and improve the quality of life of HIV-positive persons and AIDS patients.

(4) UNCONTROLLED RELEASE OF NEW TECHNOLOGIES

The unrestrained introduction of new technologies into the U.S. medical market place should be noted in a contrast to Canadian policy. In 1989, health care expenditures in the U.S. were 11.3% of the gross national product. A comparable figure for Canada would be somewhere between 8% and 9% of GNP.

Observers blame the introduction and use of new technology in the U.S. Actually, Canada and the U.S. have the same new technology, but they use it differently. In the U.S., a new test is simply added on to the list of older tests that an individual must undergo as part of a diagnostic work-up. In Canada, however, a patient might undergo the new tests first, thereby obviating the need to repeat the older ones.

Also, hospitals in the U.S. can purchase any kind of new technology they wish, with no restrictions. In Canada, on the other hand, only certain facilities are allowed to have CAT scanners, nuclear magnetic resonance imaging, PET scanners, etc. Each one of these machines cost $1-3 million. (Canadian doctors and patients do complain, however, of long waiting lists, sometimes as long as six months.)

Furthermore, until recently, new devices were not reviewed by the FDA for safety and efficacy in 98% of the cases. Also, cost is not considered in any way by the FDA. The FDA says it is in no position to decide if a new technology would (1) give a better result, (2) provide a more cost-effective therapy, or (3) replace what is already in current use for a particular purpose.

In addition, when a new technology is used, health professionals are actually paid to use it. (They are not, however, paid to evaluate it.) This drives up health care costs. For example, if a PET scanner is installed in a hospital, the hospital may advertise its PET scan to attract more patients to make more money. However, the value of the PET scan in the diagnosis of coronary-artery and heart disease has not been fully established.

The use of lasers to treat blockage in arteries is another case of unproven technology which is being marketed and hyped in order to bring in the bucks. It has not been proven that laser treatment of blocked arteries is better than currently-available treatments. Nevertheless, hospitals advertise lasers just to bring more patients into the system. Interestingly, despite the fact that the use of lasers in the treatment of coronary artery disease is still experimental, the U.S. Government, through the Health Care Financing Administration and Medicare, is considering paying for PET scans.

Another example of the ways in which new technology drives up costs is found in the use of mammography for detecting breast cancer. A report from the National Cancer Institute, in October, 1990, raises an ironic question in the diagnosis of breast cancer. It suggests there are too many breast x-ray machines, which drive up costs; the costs keep many women from being tested, especially since many insurance plans do not pay for mammograms. Anticipated costs keep people from even inquiring about breast-cancer screening. Researchers at NCI say that anywhere from two to four times as many machines are installed than are needed for current usage. It is estimated that there were 10,000 machines in operation by 1990. With the current number of machines and the current usage, the average clinic does about six to ten mammograms per day. Operating at that level, a clinic cannot deliver the service at a low price, in the range of $50.00.

Some say the problem is one of under-utilization. There are 64 million women in the United States over the age of forty who need mammograms on at least an annual basis. Only a small fraction of that number are actually having it done. The cost of a mammogram varies from a low of $35.00 to a high of $250.00. The NCI estimates that wide-spread screening with mammography at $50 apiece could save $750 million in U.S. health care costs.

It must be remembered, however, that early detection is helpful but is not prevention. Prevention is concerned with curing the disease tendency before the fact, rather than after the fact of obvious disease. We need to detect and "cure" the tendency or propensity to develop disease by intervening and/or making appropriate lifestyle changes.

New technologies are bursting onto the market place according to the free-market principles of Adam Smith. But they are not being paid for according to free market principles. Instead they are reimbursed by compensation regulations set by doctors and insurance companies to maximize their profits and to keep out cheaper, more effective alternative therapies. They are set without regard to public health and health care policy concerns. Many of the new technologies are unproven but are more readily incorporated into mainstream medicine and accepted by practitioners than long-established, cheaper, safer therapies such as chelation. Who pays for these unproven technologies that cost more and may not yield any better results? Those lucky enough to have insurance policies—and, of course, the taxpayer.

Who will pay for the research to evaluate new technologies? Industries refuse because they need to make a profit. Most health care institutions are prohibited from involvement, because of the cost of the purchase of the new technology in the first place. Government has cut back its funding of basic research to evaluate new, especially proprietary, technologies.

If an old test is 40% accurate, and a new test comes along which is 45% accurate, but costs twice as much, who decides which test shall remain in common use? It isn't just the new technologies being introduced which contribute to the escalating costs of health care; it is the inappropriate or unnecessary use of the older, well-established technologies as well.

The Rand Corporation and UCLA proved this point by evaluating three common medical procedures for the elderly. Preliminary results were announced in October, 1990. The procedures evaluated were endoscopy, cardiac catheterization and carotid endarterectomy. The study reviewed cases over the past ten years. Appropriate use of the procedure was defined when there was more health benefit than risk to the patient. The results showed that one-fourth to one-third of these procedures were used inappropriately. They also showed no relationship between inappropriate use of any one of the three procedures and the patient's age, sex, or race, the doctor's age, experience, or board certification, or the size of the hospital. The study did show, however, that there was more appropriate use in teaching hospitals.

Another significant finding was that the more procedures done by a given physician, the more likely was the use of the procedure to be considered inappropriate. This correlation suggests that the physicians who do a large number of these procedures, and presumably have a lot of skill in doing them, are more likely to do them unnecessarily, or when they are not really indicated. In other words, they are doing it more for profit than for patient benefit.

When the use of nuclear magnetic resonance imaging machines in Canada and the U.S. was studied, there was again a contrast between the two countries. The U.S. has thirteen times as many such machines as Canada. Consequently, patients in Canada may sometimes have to wait for as long as a year before they can get the study done. The province of Ontario, for example, has only one NMRI machine. On the other hand, the providence of British Colombia offers free mammograms for all women over the age of forty, with intervention and follow-up when needed. In the U.S., the uninsured and the poor have one-third fewer mammograms then those who have insurance, and the mortality from breast cancer among the uninsured and poor is 15% higher.

Coronary artery bypass grafts in the U.S. in 1989 cost $9 billion dollars, more than the cost of any other medical procedure. This represents twice as many bypass operations than are performed in Canada, and four times as many bypass operations than are performed in Europe. If chelation therapy were openly available as an appropriate alternative to bypass, approximately seven out of ten of heart patients could avoid bypass surgery, with a 90% savings in costs. Think of it—90% of $9 billion dollars equals ....!

Americans have been brainwashed into assuming there is a technological solution to every health problem; that there is a treatment rooted in scientific principles for every disease; that the science of medicine never fails to "cure sometimes, relieve often, and comfort always." We have also been duped into the false belief that there exists no drugless cures or controls for dreaded chronic illnesses. We are overlooking the fact that therapies, sometimes centuries old, have proven themselves to be more effective in treating chronic pain syndromes, neuromuscular disorders, psychosomatic illness, allergies of all kinds, and stress-related disorders than so-called scientific medicine has ever been or ever will be. The incorporation of these time-proven alternatives into the health-care system will help hold down escalating costs. Additionally, most of them can be performed by medical personnel with less specialty training.

If introduced in a laissez-faire and unregulated fashion, new technology can contribute to escalating costs, but it doesn't have to be that way. Canadians have the same technology, but use it differently. The Canadians require that new technology prove itself to be better than currently-available treatments. They then limit the use of that technology to strategically-placed hospitals in their health-care delivery system.

Organized Med is considerably more powerful in the U.S., however. Power brokers in medicine and insurance team up to determine the treatments for which insurance will pay; they encourage the introduction of new technologies for the sole purpose of making money; and they discourage the adoption of alternative traditional and natural therapies. Lastly, they reject the use of established drug therapies for new purposes, such as is the case with EDTA.

(5) BLOATED PHYSICIAN FEES AND PRESCRIPTION FEES

The escalating costs of American doctors' fees cannot be ignored. Physicians in the U.S. charge sometimes more than twice as much as Canadian physicians for the same work. A study published in the *New England Journal of Medicine* found that despite their fatter fees, U.S. doctors earn only about one-third more than Canadians. The reason: Canadian doctors make up for their lower fees by seeing more patients.

Unlike the United States, Canada provides complete, fully-paid health coverage for all its citizens. A study conducted by economist Victor Fuchs of Stanford University found that in the U.S. one in seven people has no health insurance. Those with coverage typically have to pay at least part of the bill. Despite these differences, health care costs 20% more per person in the U.S. than in Canada.

Our health-care system is way out of control. The U.S. has no national health insurance. The U.S. ranks right down there with South Africa as the only industrialized countries which do not guarantee universal access to health care. The U.S. is number one in the world in health care spending, but number twenty in infant mortality. Canada, on the other hand, is number two in health care spending and number five in preventing infant deaths. American babies are 38% more likely to die before reaching their first birthday than Canadian babies.

In the U.S., 75% of eligible women get prenatal care and are promptly attended to early on in their pregnancies. In Canada, on the other hand, 95% of eligible women get prenatal care in the first three months of their pregnancies. If a mother receives no prenatal care, her baby is five times more likely to die and three times more likely to need care in the neonatal intensive care unit. Every day in the United States, 100 babies die and 600 are hooked up to support equipment in neonatal nurseries. All of this is wasteful—for every dollar spent for prenatal care, $3.00 is saved in the first year of life, and $9.00 is saved over a child's lifetime. One day in the neonatal intensive care unit costs as much as the total cost of providing prenatal care to an expectant mother.

Nearly 30 million Americans are without health insurance of any kind. The Pepper Commission report estimated $70 billion for a National Health Insurance plan to cover them. Across the country, individual states are struggling with Medicaid, which is the medical assistance program for the poor administered by the states. When the poor need medical care, they turn to Medicaid, but what happens when Medicaid runs out of money?

What has happened is that the medical assistance program for the poor has become a type of health insurance for the poor, the near-poor, and the working poor. Nationally, Medicaid expenditures have grown to $50-60 billion annually. Currently there are 25 million Medicaid recipients. Overall, Medicaid has doubled in the past decade. But the supply of dollars isn't meeting the demand for services.

Although the Federal government shares the cost of Medicaid with the states by contributing 50-90% of the costs, according to a complex formula, many states are still unable to come up with their share of the matching costs. California, with 3.4 million recipients in the Medicaid program, provides health services to the greatest number of the medically indigent. In one month, however, in 1990, Medicaid came up $100 million short and had to seek emergency relief from the state legislature.

Rationing, combined with a more efficient health care delivery system, may be inevitable. Some feel that Medicaid should be expanded into a form of national health insurance. Given the present growth in health care costs, the entire health care system is precipitating economic disaster.

This is happening at a time of horrendous social health problems:

(1) Babies are born at higher risk of mental retardation than ever before largely because of crack cocaine, AIDS, and the fetal alcohol syndrome.

(2) 300,000 babies are born every year from pregnancies during which there was direct exposure to street drugs, mostly crack cocaine.

(3) 68,000 babies are born in a state of homelessness.

(4) Two million babies are born in circumstances where child abuse and neglect are likely to occur.

If this nation cannot arrive at realistic solutions, how can individual health victims? Those who will live long enough will inevitably lash out at all of us in irrational, desperate and dangerous ways that will cost even more money. Can we afford not to at least clean up our own backyard by bringing our health care systems under control?

Prescription drug prices in the U.S. are the highest in the world, despite the fact that major American drug companies are internationally linked. In the last decade their prices have risen three times faster than everything else we buy.

Senator David Pryor (D), Chairman of the Senate Special Committee on Aging, released this example of the projected growth, if our current trend continues, in the price of a single drug costing $20 in 1980:

1980	$20.00	
1991	$53.76	
1995	$77.06	
2000	$120.00	Overall increase: 604%

Senator Pryor further noted that the profits for the top ten drug manufacturers were up 15½% last year, while they were only up 4.6% for the average Fortune 500 Company. He stated, "The average American spends 62% more for prescription drugs than the average Canadian citizen, and 54% more than the average European citizen."

This data supports accusations of price-gouging on the part of drug manufacturers. The Pharmaceutical Manufacturers' Association, a contributor to the National Council Against Health Fraud, protests that Rx drugs are the best buy in the health care system. Investigation suggests, however, that they are major players in the game of health care profiteering and/or racketeering, contributing to spiraling costs.

The FDA should be an adversary to the pharmaceutical industry, but the drug review and approval process has to a large extent been corrupted by drug companies. Drug companies maintain their pervasive influence on medical education. They are financially intertwined with the AMA, and together they wage joint lobbying efforts and directly and indirectly participate in medical McCarthyism.

Time magazine, in January, 1990, revealed that the price of prescription drugs (at $40 billion annually) had jumped 135% during the past decade. Inflation rose during the same time by only 53%. Profit margins on drugs continued to rise by as much as 15% annually through 1991.

Time also noted that the U.S. drug industry dominates the $130 billion pharmaceutical market and that the U.S. drug industry is the only industry in which American firms are the biggest and fastest growing. Chairman Waxman, a member of the House Sub-committee on Health and the Environment, asserted, "The price is out of control!"

At one time West Germany, another major player in the internationally-linked drug cartel, cut drug revenues by 40% in an effort to control this financial crisis. In December, 1989, Japan also cut prescription prices by about 9%. And the United States. . . ?

American corporate rebuttal to this fiscal wildfire is that research and development costs on new drugs increased from $55 million to $125 million in the last twenty years. Another problem for U.S. drug manufacturers is that the FDA takes up to seven years to approve a new drug application. That shrinks the fourteen-year patent monopoly, the time a company can recoup its investment plus sell at a profit, before its patent on a new drug runs out. It takes seven years and many millions of dollars to produce and research drugs, as well as to prove safety and effectiveness. (So this—not motivation for profit and financial greed—is why U.S. companies cannot lower their 800% mark-up on drugs?)

Ironically, the State Boards of Medical Examiners and the state and local Medical Societies still argue that the relationship between the doctor and patient is sacred, a relationship based on trust. Therefore, physicians argue that they must be granted extra powers to govern themselves in order to maintain high standards of medical care. They have even lobbied the federal government to exempt the practice of medicine from the laws, enforced by the FTC, which govern other interstate commerce. Luckily, Congress rejected this notion. When medical licensing boards are granted added powers and immunity from liability suits, they have misused this added authority to eliminate competition from alternative practitioners and to strengthen their own financial turf.

(6) PUSHING PAPER FOR A THIRD PARTY

An untamable, parasitic bureaucracy has developed around the 1,500 private, independent health insurance companies and their personnel needed to push, shovel, and plow the paper necessary to process routine claims.

Canadian doctors have considerably less paperwork and undergo much less scrutiny in order to collect their fees. In Canada, the doctor simply checks a box on a simple form and mails all bills straight to the government. There was a recent public television documentary entitled "Borderline Medicine," narrated by Walter Cronkite. The documentary revealed the contrasting amounts of insurance paperwork required to process a claim in the U.S. and in Canada. One Canadian hospital, Vancouver General, employs fewer than a dozen billing clerks; their primary work involves billing foreign patients. But in the U.S. (brace yourself) Beaumont Hospital in Detroit has an entire building devoted solely to billing and collection, with 300 employees to push paper. Let us follow one patient's paper trail. A single patient, upon discharge from Beaumont Hospital, created the following enormous paper trial:

Hospital bill to Medicare
Hospital bill to the secondary carrier
Hospital bill to the patient
CRNA bill to Medicare
CRN bill to the patient
Physician's bill to the patient
Physician's secondary bill
Medical-surgical bill
Cardiologist's bill
Physical medicine bill
Anatomic pathologist's bill
Radiologist's bill

Plus 24 other bills from non-hospital-based physicians such as anesthesiologists and two consulting surgeons, for a grand total of 41 original bills going out for a single patient for a 30-day hospital stay.

No wonder pushing paper for a third party costs five times more in the U.S. than in Canada. The insurance companies vow they need this amount of paperwork "because hospitals and doctors have to be watched." That's true, but the insurance companies bear watching, too. They'll drop your policy if you get seriously ill, if they can get by with it, so they'd better be watched as well. When insurance companies are asked to help contain costs, their answer is to cut back on health care benefits.

Three-quarters of all strikes and labor disputes in recent years in the United States have been over health-care benefits. Many companies have raised the insurance premiums for individual employees who have developed chronic illnesses requiring expensive hospital-based care, and in many instances they have raised the premiums for an entire company just because one of its employees happens to be a heavy health-care user.

Most employers cannot, or understandably will not, pay for these exorbitant premiums; $2,000 a month for an employee with cancer is not unusual. If an employee tries to pay his own insurance premiums, he will end up spending $20,000 for six months of insurance, payable in advance.

At the present time, one-third of America's health care costs is paid by employers. Lee Iacocca of the Chrysler Corporation estimates that approximately $700 is added on to the price of every new car produced by his company, in order to pay the employees' health insurance benefits; this alone makes it difficult to compete with the Japanese "with such an albatross around one's neck."

Beyond this frenzied feeding at the health-care trough remains that strange, medical mind-set discussed in earlier chapters. Just like their tenured counterparts in cancer research, the new self-imposed leaders in the AIDS establishment, for example, seem incapable of reasoning or comprehending that there are ways of treating this virus other than with toxic killer drugs or a vaccine. They know that there are many strains of the AIDS virus, just as there are cold viruses. Do they intend to develop a vaccine for each of the strains? This mind-set directed the FDA to refuse approval of the biologic-response modifiers Interleuken II and Granulocyte Colony Stimulating Factor.

When the medical mind-set is joined with medical politics, progress indeed looks bleak. In the recent exposé *Good Intentions,* Bruce Nussbaum details how big business and the medical establishment have played hardball in AIDS research. He describes an "old-boy network" of powerful medical researchers who dominate in every disease field from A to Z, and how these power brokers control the major committees that run the most important clinical trials but are accountable to no one.

Nussbaum discusses how medical scientists have society convinced that only they can police themselves with no supervision. The book follows the money trail from the billions appropriated by Congress, through a network of government-supported laboratories, finally into the profit ledgers of—in the case of AIDS, for example, Burroughs-Wellcome—internationally-linked corporations. Bear in mind that this is only one of the disease-research scandals.

What we are facing is an issue of professional misconduct. Professionals in key positions within government, private industry, universities, even in the private practice of medicine have engaged in apparently illegal business and practices restricting free trade—in other words, racketeering.

These apparently illegal business practices are waged throughout an intricate system with powerful sanctions imposed on doctors who attempt to provide alternatives for their patients. Evidence points to the Councils Against Health Fraud, the State Boards of Medical Examiners, federal officials in the FDA, the U.S. Postal Service, the

Department of Justice, the FTC and other agencies.

Such practices are in apparent violation of the federal RICO (Racketeer Influenced Corrupt Organization) statutes. What are they up to? Collaborating knowingly, sometimes unknowingly, for profit maximization. During another kind of national scandal, G. Gordon Liddy quoted a phrase attributed to Adolf Hitler: "Get them by the balls and their hearts and minds will follow." Sadly, in the moral and financial disaster now facing medicine, that phrase could appropriately be reworded, "Get them by their bank accounts and their hearts and minds will follow."

THE OREGON EXPERIMENT—RATIONING HEALTH CARE

The Oregon state legislature recently passed an insurance rationing law, proposed by Senator Kitzhaber, that could deny payment under Medicaid for procedures that are not deemed cost-effective. As is the case in all states, Oregon had too many uninsured people because their income was above $5,500 per year, making them ineligible for Medicaid but too poor to afford health insurance on their meager incomes. Dr. Senator Kitzhaber, an emergency room physician and now President of the Oregon State Senate, was determined to correct this injustice.

Twenty percent of working people do not have health insurance. Medicaid (which is two-thirds federally- and one-third state-supported) pays for those who earn less than $5500 a year. Rationing is already unintentionally occurring. Patients are denied access to ongoing and definitive health care. Medicaid rations on the basis of money, marital status, gender, and age.

Dr. Kitzhaber launched a series of community meetings at the end of 1988, the purpose of which was to provide less care, but at the same time to insure more people—450,000 more people. Oregonians in these meetings decided what is to be covered and what is not to be covered. These town meetings were held during 1988 and 1989. Their aim was to be to provide care for people who were not covered before. The organizers held forty-seven town meetings and twelve public hearings and conducted a statewide survey.

Seven hundred nine (709) treatment categories were listed and their cost-effectiveness determined. The preventive services were at the top of the list; AIDS and cancer (terminal) cases were at the bottom of the list. Few poor women participated in the town meetings and public hearings. The attendees were mostly white middle class and upper-middle class. Ninety-three percent were white; 69% earned more than $29,000; 67% were college educated.

Oregon can pay for only 80% of the services agreed upon. As health care costs continue to escalate, the proportion of services provided that the state can afford to pay for could drop to only 60% over the next five years; then another set of services or procedures would have to be dropped.

Input from the business community was requested by Senator Kitzhaber. Business would have to provide health insurance to every employee. In Oregon, however, more than 80% of the companies have fewer than twenty-five employees, so small businesses will be hurt the most.

In the new legislation, the medical providers were taken care of. The legislation proposed by Senator Kitzhaber passed in June 1991, with the full support of political and health groups. Medicaid, which formerly paid half the M.D.'s fee, would now pay the full fee. Hospitals would get 450,000 more patients covered.

In order for Oregon to implement the program, however, they need a waiver from the Health Care Financing Administration or an Executive Order from President Bush. They could also do the same with, but are unlikely to win, a vote in Congress. Sen. Packwood and Rep. Ron Wyden, both from Oregon, are leading the fight in Congress. Gail Wilensky, Ph.D., Head of HCFA, is also known to be sympathetic.

Women, infants and children in Oregon will have services cut back. Seventy percent of those eligible for Medicaid are women and children. The elderly and disabled attended the town meetings, however; they spoke up and were included.

The plan will cost the state of Oregon $33 million for the first two years, plus an additional $70 million from the Feds. The actual costs, however, will be around $140 million, and not $103 million. Cost underestimates, such as this one, will be the downfall of the Oregon and similar rationing experiments.

Rationing or cutting back on services to include more people, as in the case of Oregon, or reducing the rate of increase in health care costs will not work in the long run, if nothing is done to correct the profit-maximizing structural defects in the system itself; profit maximizing or patient care and well-being—what will it be?

Choice of treatment is reimbursement driven—driven by what the health insurance will pay for. As long as preventive and non-drug alternative therapies are ignored and only the lucrative, high-tech curative interventions are reimbursed, the spiraling health care costs will never be brought under control.

The Oregon experiment could change the rules for every state.

THE HAWAIIAN EXPERIMENT

Hawaii now has an efficiently-run universal health plan that requires all businesses to provide insurance to employees. This state also provides a state-financed basic health insurance for residents not covered on the job. Hawaii has used its Medicaid program and legislation passed by their House and Senate and signed into law by the governor to create what amounts to a statewide health insurance program. The plan provides for 98% coverage for all of Hawaii's residents. Health promotion and disease prevention are emphasized in expenditure of the Medicaid combined state and federal funds. The program is carried, however, on the backs and shoulders of the employers. If health care costs continue to escalate, many of the smaller companies will be forced out of business.

The latest figures, released October 1, 1991, show that health care costs in 1990 were $666 billion, a 10.2% increase from 1989. They also reached 12.2% of the GNP. By the year 2000, at the current rate of increase, health care will cost $1.6 trillion! The cost per person in 1990 was $2,500, which is twice what it costs in any other Western industrialized nation.

The federal government's principal health-care cost-containment measure has been prospective payments to hospitals, *i.e.*, payments up-front of a fixed amount for pneumonia or heart attack, lung cancer, etc., on the basis of DRG's (diagnosis-related groups). This has not worked.

In January, 1992, Physician Payment Reform was instituted with the implementation of the new relative values scale; the fees for certain procedures such as cataract surgery were reduced, and those paid to pediatricians and internists who spend time thinking about and diagnosing and treating their patients were increased. These measures will also fail to curtail rising health care costs, however. Why? Because the structural defects—the sins of omission and sins of commission—are not being addressed.

The Secretary of Health and Human Services, Louis Sullivan, M.D., speaking on the causes of double-digit inflation in health care costs for the past three years, stated in October, 1991, that Health and Human Services analysts attribute:

A. One-half of the increase in costs to general inflation in the economy

B. One-fourth of the increase to the increasing costs of specific medical services, and

C. One-fourth of the increase to increased complexity and intensity of services (so-called volume of services), which includes the cost of "defensive medicine," the ordering of additional tests for the purpose of defense in possible malpractice suits.

Assuming these estimates are correct, the factors in B and C are the direct result of sins of omission and sins of commission.

Sins of omission are the problems inherent in the system such as the lack of prevention and almost no support in helping individuals to change their destructive health-related behaviors (smoking alone contributed to 434,000 deaths in 1990, and only 30% of adults exercise on a regular basis); they include the insurance industry's failure to pay for services unless required to do so by state and federal laws. Sins of omission also include the rewarding of sickness, the paying of large sums of money for curative medicine.

The sins of commission are a compilation of the monopolistic and racketeering practices of organized medicine and include:

1. Their lobbying activities through political action committees;

2. The price-gouging of the pharmaceutical companies by inflating the costs of recently-released medicines, as compared to the costs of the same medicines in other countries;

3. The unrestrained use of, and media hype associated with, the introduction of new but unproven technologies;

4. The 1,500 generally parasitic, and undependable health insurance companies who contribute to the problem by simply raising premiums every year and dumping patients back on to the public hospital system when they cost too much, etc.

The double-digit inflation in health care costs cannot be solved until these structural defects in the system are addressed and then corrected.

CHAPTER 12
WHAT'S EUROPE DOING ABOUT THIS?

In his address to the Great Lakes Clinical Medicine Association in 1988, Belgian doctor Andreas Maestian revealed a most interesting survey conducted by the European Board of Consumers Association. Studies were conducted on the fifty most frequently prescribed drugs in Belgium, England, France, Germany and Italy. Their findings were perhaps a bit embarrassing.

It is an established fact that these countries have similar rates of disease; the same illnesses occur in these countries at similar rates. These countries also share the same patterns of mortality, but something was "fishy" about their findings: Doctors in these countries prescribe certain drugs at a rate not in accordance with the disease rates that occur in their respective countries.

This inconsistency raised concerns over the effectiveness of the National Health Services, the effectiveness and value of the drugs, and the possible effectiveness of their prescribers. The pattern of the inconsistency is apparent in these examples:

In England, the most prescribed drug is Ventolin, an anti-asthmatic produced by the British drug firm Glaxo.

In Germany, the most prescribed drug is Erglukol, an oral anti-diabetic produced by the German company Boerhinger.

In France, the most prescribed drug is Tanacort, produced by a French company, for poor circulation.

In Belgium, the most prescribed drug is Fibromycin, an antibiotic from the Flemish company Phizer.

In Italy, the most prescribed drug is Tagamet for gastric and duodenal ulcers, and (you guessed it) is manufactured by an Italian drug company.

So, even though the countries have the same disease patterns, they have drugs prescribed that don't correspond to their disease rates. There are no more asthmatics in England than in the other countries, so why is an anti-asthmatic most often prescribed? The French have no more circulatory disease than other countries—why is a circulation drug number one in sales? The explanation, of course, lies in the fact that a British drug company produces Britain's most prescribed drug, a German company produces Germany's most prescribed drug, a French company produces France's most prescribed drug, and so on.

There are other unusual twists in the findings—the drug of choice for ulcers throughout Europe, for example, is the Italian drug Tagamet. It's high in sales in every country except Belgium, where it ranks number eight in sales. Why? Because the Belgian National Health Service does not allow reimbursement of the drug unless the doctor proves there is a gastric or duodenal ulcer. The Health Service is not consistent in the enforcement of their rules, however; although there are controls in Belgium for the ulcer medication, this is not so for the Belgium-produced antibiotic Fibromycin, despite the real danger of developing resistant strains.

These findings came to light several years ago. Following the release of the commission's findings, a complete revision in prescription patterns has come about in Belgium. Another positive change has also taken place. Before the findings were released and acted upon, only 30% of the population used natural means of health care (acupuncture, homeopathy, nutrition, etc.). Now 50% are using one or more natural remedies.

The European countries are to be commended for their fact-finding and honest acknowledgement of the discrepancy in drug prescriptions. This survey by the European Board of Consumers Association raises some uncomfortable issues in modern Western medicine.

We should expect better ethics from those who market drugs for medical conditions than from those who sell, say, toothpaste. The sad truth, however, is that selling is selling—in many cases it doesn't seem to matter what the product is, even though the products manufactured by drug companies involve serious matters of life and death. Drug salesmen hawk their products to doctors with the same sort of hype attributed to used car salesmen or those selling un-requested insurance. This demeanor is also true of many health-care professionals who are more concerned with selling their services and products than with the promotion of health, disease prevention and, sadly, even disease treatment. Their actions speak louder than words.

It was largely in-country marketing and sales programs that

caused the European countries to prescribe certain medicines out of proportion to patient disease rates. It had nothing to do with the spectrum of disease seen in the population, or the most common causes of death in various age groups within the population.

THE SWEDISH COMMISSION ON ALTERNATIVE MEDICINE

A summary of the report prepared by the Swedish Commission on Alternative Medicine was published in English in October, 1989. The Committee's final report is in four volumes:

(1) The main report

(2) A survey of alternative therapies available in Sweden

(3) An evaluation of various therapies

(4) A study of health homes. (A health home, health farm, health ranch, or spa was defined as an institution which, with the aim of preventing disease and promoting good health, uses methods based on vegetarian food, fasting, physical exercise and other activities and provides training and information in matters concerning lifestyle.)

The main report is in two parts. Part I contains the committee's starting points, together with its considerations and proposals. Part II deals with alternative medicine, its historical development, its standing today, etc. Part II also contains a review of the studies concerning the position of alternative medicine made by the committee in collaboration with the Central Bureau of Statistics.

Members of the Committee were experts from the medical profession and the National Swedish Welfare Board. The work was difficult and was carried out with a lot of resistance from the physician representatives. This group defended their territory in various ways, but ultimately they capitulated in regard to several points. The Committee's report and proposals can be considered a major advance for alternative/biological medicine, a model for other post-industrial countries which are grappling with similar problems.

The Committee emphasized that "[e]very person should have the freedom to choose those forms and methods of treatment available, as long as attention is paid to his or her needs and safety." In other words, grown-up people have the right to choose the medical care they want, even if the advocates of conventional medicine do not think it is the best. There was one qualification for the treatment of children. Children cannot decide for themselves and are dependent on their parents' choice. The permissible age for children to be treated by "untrained" persons was raised from eight to fifteen years, justified by the belief that only after the age of fifteen are children able to make up their own minds about matters relating to their health.

The Committee also proposed that certain diseases may not be treated by practitioners of alternative medicine, namely contagious diseases and diseases contracted by women during pregnancy. It was also proposed that acute, life-threatening conditions be exempted from alternative treatment.

Certain serious diseases such as cancer, endocrine diseases such as insulin-dependent diabetes, systemic connective tissue diseases such as SLE (systemic lupus erythematosus) and psychoses may be treated by a practitioner of alternative medicine only on the condition that the patient has first consulted a registered doctor about the disease. Furthermore, vital treatment prescribed by a doctor, with the purpose of maintaining life, may not be discontinued by a practitioner of alternative medicine. The committee was of the opinion, however, that it would be difficult to prosecute successfully in cases relating to a prohibition of this type.

Presently, in regard to Swedish alternative medicine, according to studies made by the committee in collaboration with the Central Bureau of Statistics, every fifth adult has, at one time or another, received alternative treatment. Almost 70% of the Swedish population have a positive attitude toward such treatment. The most widespread form of alternative treatment is chiropractic (utilized by 13% of the population) followed by homeopathy (4%), acupuncture, naturopathy, and herbal medicine. Approximately 50% of those seeking help from alternative practitioners were encouraged by relatives and friends. Just over 40% stated that they had chosen alternative medicine treatment because they had not been helped by the National Health Services. Some 70% considered themselves cured of their complaint or said that their health had improved; only 1% thought that their health had deteriorated. Generally, the attitude of those who had undergone alternative treatment was more positive toward alternative medicine than toward the National Health Services.

The committee also proposed the formation of a new group of therapists who are to have one year of basic medical education and who will thereafter be registered by the National Social Welfare Board. The new therapists will have permission to treat children as young as three years of age, on the condition that the children also have regular medical check-ups from a physician. Only physicians may treat children under the age of three years.

The new category of therapists will be comprised of those practitioners of alternative medicine who have not undergone formal training. They are separate from those alternative practitioners who have had a certain stipulated basic medical training. This measure proposed by the committee is intended to provide the skills and proficiency which a practitioner needs if he or she is to be able to make a general assessment of the state of health of his or her patients and, when necessary, refer them to the health services.

The existing prohibition against the use of anesthesia and radiology by alternative practitioners was upheld and maintained. In addition, the committee proposed that, in the health services, it should be permissible to use alternative forms of treatment if the patient has expressed a desire for such treatment, if the type of treatment is not dangerous, and if it is only given after generally accepted methods have been tried or it is given in conjunction with such methods.

Formally, as is the case in the United States, the National Board of Health and Welfare, the Swedish equivalent of the FDA, made a sharp distinction between items which were considered to be foods and those which were considered to be medicines or pharmaceutical products. In other words, either a substance was considered a food or it was considered a medicine. There was no room for it to fall in between these two distinct categories.

One important recommendation, therefore, of the Swedish Committee on Alternative Medicine was that stricter controls be applied to the advertising of natural remedies. A natural remedy in this sense is defined as a medicine which has been exempted from the regulations concerning pharmaceutical preparations. A natural remedy may be sold freely after it has been submitted to, and has undergone, controls exercised by the National Board of Health and Welfare and a fee has been paid. It must be shown that there is no health risk if the remedy is used properly.

On the other hand, it does not have to be shown that the remedy has any positive effect. Since the existing regulations came into being at the beginning of the 1970s, new remedies have been introduced which are either more advanced preparations of original remedies or which, in certain cases, have no connection with popular tradition. To an increasing extent, the natural remedies are intended to be used over long periods of time to prevent poor health, rather than to be used for temporary complaints, as was the case originally.

The marketing of these remedies is now directed more toward healthy people.

The indications for natural medicines which may be advertised may consist only of symptoms/diseases which are specified at the time of registration and which correspond to self-treatment. However, if the indications for natural medicines are quoted in the advertisement, the positive effects of the natural remedy must be substantiated. Both historical proof of efficacy and controlled clinical trials are acceptable for appropriate advertising claims. Predictable results based on many similar case histories can also constitute sufficient proof for a natural remedy. A double-blind study is not required.

The Swedish Commission, as well as the Netherlands Commission and the U.K. Committee on Complimentary Medicine, concluded that the majority of alternative therapies have not been the subject of scientific study. The committees or commissions considered it important that the value of different alternative therapies be tested scientifically. They also concluded, however, that the right of people to choose between available therapies must be respected, regardless of the scientific value a therapy is considered to have. In this context, the committees/commissions particularly recommended that further research be undertaken, that the practice of alternative medicine be studied on a multi-disciplinary basis, and that projects be carried out cooperatively between representatives of alternative medicine and the health services.

This research should be undertaken by an institution with wide experience in similar multi-disciplinary research tasks. The Swedish Committee, therefore, proposed that the Swedish Council for the Planning and Coordination of Research, which has substantial experience with multi-disciplinary research, be given the responsibility for initiating and financing research into alternative medicine.

The Committee determined that spinal manipulation treatment can provide desirable effects for certain thoracic and lumbar complaints, and that treatment comprising vegetarian food, fasting, and exercise, such as that rendered in health homes, can be recommended in certain diseases. It was also recommended that well-trained doctors of chiropractic, who have received their education in the United States, should be licensed and possibly receive a contract with the County Council and should be allowed to practice in Sweden. The Committee also determined that certain studies indicate that acupuncture, meditation, and magnetic therapy can have desirable effects in the case of certain diseases and/or have a preventive effect.

Also, health homes were classified as either unlicensed health homes, where health care but no medical care can be practiced, and licensed health care homes, where medical care has to be given. Medical personnel are essential for the licensed health care homes and some collaboration, therefore, should exist with physicians.

The committee concluded that the best way to improve the safety and security of patients in the field of alternative medicine is to guarantee that those who practice alternative medicine have undergone a certain amount of basic medical training. The National Board of Health and Welfare, which maintains a register of authorized personnel working in the health services, should, therefore, also maintain a register of practitioners of alternative medicine.

This Board will also have the responsibility to ensure that new laws on all alternative medicine are followed. This responsibility means that the Board will deal with any complaints, for example, relating to the treatment by a practitioner of alternative medicine of a child under three years of age or the treatment of diseases which according to the law shall not be undertaken by a practitioner of alternative medicine. On the other hand, the regional offices of the Board will not make any checks of individual practitioners of alternative medicine, or their methods, unless it is suspected that they have harmed patients.

It was the intent of this sagacious committee that the increased freedom of the individual patients and the reduction in the physician monopoly which would result from the recognition of alternative practitioners would be good for both patients and future scientific development. The post-industrial culture and heritage that we in the U.S. share with Sweden necessitate our giving serious consideration to this balanced, far-sighted report.

THE NETHERLANDS' COMMISSION FOR ALTERNATIVE SYSTEMS OF MEDICINE

Because of a decree issued on May 13, 1977, the State Secretary for Health and Environmental Protection in the Netherlands set up a Commission for Alternative Systems of Medicine to investigate the significance of alternative forms of treatment for health care in the Netherlands. The Commission was instituted for various reasons, including the growing public interest in alternative health care systems and plans to amend the Medical Practice Act.

The Commission decided to examine acupuncture, homeopathy, naturopathy, and anthroposophical, paranormal, and manipulative medicine. These six alternative medical systems were investigated by five different working parties.

The Commission's report, published in 1981, begins with a short account of the philosophical and historical background of modern orthodox medicine and alternative systems of medicine. Orthodox medicine, it says, like other systems of medicine, is based on certain pre-scientific assumptions or principles on which a scientific model, which elucidates and interprets reliability in a specific way, has been constructed. In view of this fact, the commission considered it wrong that one particular scientific model should be regarded as the only correct one and all others rejected.

According to their report, in 1865 the government of the Netherlands enacted legislation which permitted only one group of professional persons to practice every branch of medicine. Subsequent changes in society and in medicine have made a such monopoly of one particular approach to health care no longer acceptable. Large numbers of patients are turning to persons other than doctors, especially if registered practitioners have failed in their efforts to help them. Alternative forms of treatment have gradually come to satisfy a need—a fact that must be realized in establishing policy that regulates health care. The unifying principal of all alternative systems of medicine is that they represent activities that are related to human health but are not officially recognized.

The Commission defined the terms "holistic" and "reductionist." Their report acknowledged that, because of their theoretical backgrounds, alternative systems of medicine often provide wider possibilities for a holistic approach than is usually the case with orthodox medicine, which is still dominated by "scientific" thought.

The commission listed several criteria for determining what a "charlatan" is. These criteria were both subjective and objective. The subjective criteria included the therapist's personal approach, integrity, and readiness to work with others working in the health services. The objective criteria included: the openness of the social system of which the therapists and his patients are a part; the training he has received for his work; his willingness to keep abreast of developments in orthodox medicine; his readiness to explain his work and to allow it to be assessed; and his desire to make a constructive contribution to the overall system of health care in the Netherlands.

The commission also considered the terms "suggestion" and "placebo" in the context of alternative therapies. It concluded that because of modern developments in orthodox medicine (specifically the development of the new discipline of psycho-neuro immunology), these terms have acquired different and more positive meaning than in the past, although they are often used disparagingly. It goes on to say, however, that accepting the fact that the mind affects the body did not imply that every alternative system of medicine is based on suggestion or that we are moving toward a placebo culture.

The commission also observed that some people are under the impression that orthodox medicine is the only true form of medical science. The commission concluded that not everything that registered practitioners do is based on conclusively demonstrated scientific facts and that the practice of doctors assessing one another's work is also still in its infancy. It further concluded that the Netherlands seems to have a social system in which alternative forms of medicine are used with discrimination, although therapies that can only be described as marginal or provisional were sometimes used and recommended.

Lastly, it concluded that the opinions which conventional and alternative practitioners hold of one another are still frequently colored by prejudice. The differences in their terminology, their concepts, and the meanings they ascribe to those concepts are not conducive to greater mutual understanding. Undoubtedly the supremacy of orthodox medicine intensifies this mutual negative image and contributes to the effective rejection mechanisms. The Commission considers the present distinction between alternative and orthodox medicine to be based more on social and historical background than on purely scientific grounds. U.S. doctors should take serious note of these conclusions.

On the basis of the literature, the working parties' reports and several recent investigations, the commission concluded:

> The proportion of the Dutch population that at one time or another has consulted a practitioner of alternative medicine is about 20%. In 1979, 7-8% of Dutch men and women of 18 years and older consulted an alternative practitioner: that is to say, a total of 700,000 patients or 5-6 million consultations.
>
> The alternative fields consulted by the public were homeopathy, acupuncture, naturopathy, manipulative and paranormal medicine. The improvement effected by such treatment, as perceived by the patient, is often substantial. The number of qualified medical practitioners practicing alternative medicine has also increased considerably.

The reason most frequently given by patients for seeking alternative treatment was that orthodox methods have no effect on their chronic disorders. After talking to friends and acquaintances who had benefitted from an alternative therapy, they decided to follow their example. Only a small proportion (14%) chose an alternative treatment primarily on principle. The chronic disorders afflicting most patients who go to an alternative practitioner are largely neuro-muscular-skeletal disorders; psychological factors are also frequently a factor.

The Commission concluded that, in all probability, more use, evidenced in the number of consultations per year, is indeed being made of alternative therapies. There was also, however, a general consensus that alternative forms of treatment should be regarded as a warning sign with regard to developments in conventional medicine.

With regard to the role of drugs in alternative systems of medicine, the Commission concluded:

> For centuries, medicinal herbs have featured prominently in the pharmacopoeia, but, as pharmacy developed, pharmacologists set out first to isolate in as pure a form as possible the properties responsible for the effectiveness of the herbs and then proceeded to manufacture new synthetic drugs analogous to the substances obtained from nature. This shift from natural products to chemical synthetic drugs which occurred in the world of orthodox medicine did not take place in the alternative systems.
>
> Perusal of the official French or German homeopathic pharmacopoeias, for instance, shows that they are based mainly on medicinal herbs. The use of herbs in the alternative systems should not be regarded as a passive attachment to obsolete remedies, but rather as a deliberate choice, which may be influenced by philosophical considerations, particularly the conviction that the living plant contains special properties.
>
> Practitioners also justify the use of herbs by pointing to the side-effects of synthetic drugs and the fact that a synergistic result can be achieved by the natural combination of various components. It is not always known, however, exactly which components of the herbs are efficacious or how they combine to produce a synergism. In such cases, the experience of centuries may provide some guidance when herbs have been found to contain beneficial substances.

The Netherlands report also documented, in so far as was possible, the situation in other countries. In some, as in the Netherlands, doctors enjoy a medical monopoly by law. Other countries have a system of protecting titles, whereby unqualified persons are forbidden to practice in certain areas of health care and/or to treat certain diseases.

In the Federal Republic of Germany, the *heilpraktiker* is as familiar a figure as the doctor. He is an officially-recognized practitioner of naturopathy who receives a license to practice after taking an examination.

Some countries' private health-insurance schemes anticipate future change. For example, in Italy, they have started refunding the cost of acupuncture treatment. In Norway and Denmark, there is an agreement between the National Health Services and chiropractors, who are not regarded by law in the Scandinavian countries as independent practitioners, as they are in the U.S.A., Canada, and New Zealand.

In the English-speaking and Scandinavian countries, the most important alternative therapies tend to be chiropractic and osteopathy. In Germany, naturopathy is followed in popularity by homeopathy and anthroposophical medicine. The latter is also well represented in Switzerland, while the same is true in France of homeopathy, manipulative medicine, and radio-anesthesia.

The commission's report concludes with a discussion of the legal, economic and financial aspects of alternative forms of treatment. With regard to the legal aspects, the commission believes that the individual's right to choose an alternative medicine should be respected, provided he or she behaves responsibly (which could perhaps be achieved by means of reliable information promoted by the government). The government, on the other hand, should assess the results of alternative systems of medicine and set certain conditions for and supervision of alternative medical practice.

Official recognition of an alternative form of treatment invariably means the statutory regulation of its practitioners' activities. Personal recognition of the practitioner precedes inclusion of the treatment he provides in health insurance schemes. Alternative systems of medicine may be said to have gained official recognition if the government and the medical world no longer regard them as undesirable.

Some government officials who determine health policy urged inclusion of alternative medicine in the various insurance schemes. This is because they are convinced that alternative medicine saves money. Others say it cannot be included because that would increase medical costs. In a time of retrenchment in public spending and rising costs in health care, it is especially important to ascertain the extent to which alternative medicine renders health care more effective or less so.

An important consideration in determining the eligibility of a particular alternative medicine for inclusion in the health-insurance scheme is whether research findings could show whether it would raise or lower medical costs. Calculating the debit and credit aspects of a therapy would entail establishing (1) the direct cost of treatment, (2) the indirect cost (production losses), and (3) the gain in health. Significantly, the commission did not consider randomized controlled trials to be practicable in the case of alternative systems of medicine.

In summary, the commission believes that the division between alternative and orthodox medicine is not—or is not principally—of a scientific nature, but owes its origins and its continued existence to both political-social and scientific factors. This implies that the gap cannot be closed simply by making scientific recommendations. The demand that alternative practitioners must demonstrate the effectiveness of their treatments before they can be granted any form of recognition thus seems to the commission to be indefensible. If attention is focused on the scientific conditions for recognition, the commission feels that the presentation of new facts and ideas should conform to the following requirements:

(1) A consistent theory; accurate records and reports; accessible publication and willingness to supply further information for research purposes.

(2) The Medical Forum should be prepared to examine, properly evaluate, and promote research into what alternative medicine has to offer, so that the Forum principle can operate at the right level and lead to decisions concerning the acceptability of ideas, facts, and the treatments based upon them.

(3) The Commission considers the present state of research into alternative therapies in the Netherlands and elsewhere to be at a more or less embryonic stage, which is attributed in part to the fact that alternative medicine, through a variety of factors, has been largely excluded from institutional research activities.

The report ended with eleven specific recommendations.

COMPLEMENTARY MEDICINE IN THE UNITED KINGDOM

The British prefer the term "complementary medicine" to "alternative medicine." They consider previous qualifying adjectives such as "fringe" and "alternative" damaging in and of themselves. "Complementary medicine" is defined as "a body of natural medical skills, incorporating tested techniques—in some cases many centuries old—which are not in opposition to orthodox medicine but work hand in hand with it as its partner."

The British Research Council on Complementary Medicine was formed in 1982, in response to the public's increased use of complementary medicine and the government's concern over its effectiveness. The Council noted that allopathic medicine is responsible for the remarkable technological advances which are inevitably followed by financial pressure to pay for them from the existing resources of the National Health Service. The Council emphasized the expense of new techniques, which require a great deal of funding, and the success of diagnostic and preventive programs, allowing the population to live to a greater age. They noted that orthodox medicine must accept the major role that complementary medicine can play to relieve the financially-intolerable burden—by preventing what is preventable and using natural, biological cures for what may be curable, as opposed to expensive orthodox therapies.

Five years after the formation of the council, the list of achievements is impressive: twelve research projects in hospitals and universities; the holding of seminars and conferences; a computerized information service to aid researchers; the production of various publications; and the establishment of a Fellowship in Research Methodology at Glasgow University. The committee is instigating the consolidation of the disciplines of acupuncture, osteopathy, homeopathy, chiropractic, and naturopathy into one self-regulating body. The major goal is to establish an all-embracing, compassionate and cost-effective National Health Service, while at the same time preserving freedom of choice for its users.

The first report of the Council encompassed the years 1983-1988. It stated their universal agreement that the National Health Service is in crisis, that existing demand is far outstripping the capacity for supply, and that a radical review of the mode of provision of services was long overdue. The encroaching crisis stemmed from a failure to recognize that technology would not eventually provide a cure for every ill. Exclusive dependence on technology had progressively displaced the time-honored reliance on the unique innate recovery mechanisms of the body. In short, costly "science" had ousted the far more economical "art" in medical care.

The commission acknowledged that the country is now reaping the false fruits of the utopian dream that science is all, while ignoring the cheaper, simpler, safer methods of catalyzing the inborn self-healing capability. An intensive educational campaign in self-help care, combined with wider access to validated complementary therapies, could substantially reduce the need—in the majority of instances—for costly high-technology resources, freeing those services for the relative minority of patients who actually need them.

The council held its first conference on conventional/complementary medicine in 1981. At that time the council acknowledged the paucity of research in complementary medicine and the challenge of persuading allopathic medicine to recognize the need for changes in medicine. Research was considered the key to attaining these objectives.

While it is not necessary for the actual research to take place in a university department, a relationship with such a department is essential. The council saw its role as one of fostering and enabling such relationships, with the end result being a productive and mutually beneficial association between the council and an increasing number of university centers and medical schools throughout the United Kingdom.

HRH Prince Charles, in his capacity as President of the British Medical Association, suggested in a speech that doctors consider alternative methods. In October, 1987, Dr. Ronald Dabey, a homeopathic physician, and Physician to H.M. The Queen was appointed "Consultant to the Council." He was charged with contacting the main complementary therapy organizations and training colleges nationwide, introducing research into the curricula, and giving personal guidance to potential researchers.

The year before, Dr. David Taylor Reilly was appointed as the first Research Council on Complementary Medicine Research Methodology Fellow. Dr. Reilly has both medical and homeopathic qualifications. He is based at Glasgow University and is working under the aegis of Professor Kennedy, Head of the Department of Medicine and currently President of the Royal College of Physicians in Glasgow. Dr. Reilly published this year what will undoubtedly be considered the classic paper on the comparison of homeopathic remedies versus placebo, using hay fever as the model. This research fellowship can be seen as a major event in the history of complementary medicine. It was also the council's rebuff to the 1986 British Medical Association Report on Alternative Therapies, which declared, "we know it cannot work so why bother with research?"

In 1987, with the financial assistance of the Evian Water Company, the council won an Honorable Evian Health Award. The Award, presented to President Dr. Richard Tonkin at a ceremony in London, specifically cited the council "for helping to protect the public by raising the medical profession's confidence in complementary medicine through sound, scientific research, thus encouraging the incorporation of complementary medicine into mainstream medical practice."

In his acceptance speech, Dr. Tonkin said that the council "had reason to believe it was in the vanguard of an essential advance in the provision of health care, in that attention is increasingly being centered on the patient as an individual, rather than solely on the analysis of his disease, and in harnessing the individual's own self-healing capability."

In summary, the British Research Council on Complementary Medicine carefully planned and rigorously executed research to prove the efficacy of alternative medicine. They answered the challenge highlighted by HRH Prince Charles in his speech, when he suggested doctors consider alternative methods of treatment. The Council defined the word "complementary" as those long-standing and well-structured therapies such as acupuncture, chiropractic, homeopathy, medical herbalism, naturopathy, osteopathy, and some of the newer treatments of relaxation techniques, biofeedback, dietary programs, etc.

They further stated their objective: To encourage the incorporation of what is best in these therapies and techniques into the mainstream of modern medical practice. They also noted the somewhat interesting terminology changes over the last few decades. In the 1950s and 1960s, "fringe medicine" was the term used for anything unorthodox; in the 1970s, such therapies were called alternative medicine. In the 1980s, those with a vision see them as complementary to conventional treatments.

ALTERNATIVE MEDICINE IN THE
GERMAN DEMOCRATIC REPUBLIC

Shortly after the recent overthrow of the communist German Democratic Republic, the offices of the Stasi secret police were sacked by the public. A rumor then circulated that documents were found linking the Stasi to multi-national pharmaceutical companies in a joint campaign to discredit alternative medicine. I wrote to Professor Erwin K. Scheuch, Director of the Institute of Applied

Social Research of the University of Köln, in Germany, who is an authority on the Stasi, for his opinion. His reply is interesting and informative and reveals the status of alternative medicine in what was formerly communist East Germany.

Dear colleague:

I can imagine the Stasi being involved in nearly every institution, including chemical companies selling material for poison gas to Libya and Iraq. But it is beyond my imagination to see the Stasi conspiring with chemical companies to hurt alternative medicine. Thus, I cannot give you any helpful hints on this matter.

Many of the alternative medical practices are, by the way, acceptable for refunding by the health insurance institutions. There is one company, quite successful financially, that produces nothing but medicine based on herbs: Madaus in Cologne. We even have a medical faculty specializing in anthroposophic medicine: Privat-University Witten-Herdecke, claiming to be an elite institution. Maybe they could be helpful in furthering your work.

Sincerely yours,
Erwin K. Scheuch

This correspondence indicates fewer government obstacles to alternative medicine in the European countries, especially those with National Health Services and extensive Social Welfare programs, no doubt because alternative, biological therapies work and are cost-effective.

Ironically, in the European countries where the private practice of medicine is strongest and its practitioners are organized, or in those countries where the medical profession looks to organized medicine in the U.S. for leadership, alternative medicine is relegated to the status of quackery. In effect, the status of alternative medicine is basically dependent on political—not scientific—considerations. That should sound familiar to Americans.

CHAPTER 13
THE REJECTION AND LEGAL QUARANTINE
OF MEDICAL HYPOTHESES

Certain inconsistencies are evident in nutrition information available to the public. We are told, for example, that there is no need to take nutritional supplements because we get all the vitamins, minerals, trace elements, fiber, and fatty acids we need in the regular foods we eat. We are also told that if we do take supplements we are wasting our money and that most of the excess nutrients are excreted, giving us "expensive urine." Yet the same physician who tells us this might also perform coronary artery bypass surgery on his patient and not be concerned at all about what the patient's spouse buys at the supermarket, what kinds of foods he eats on a daily basis, or how they are prepared. There are no limits to the amount of alcohol and cigarettes you can buy legally or, as a practical matter, to the amounts and kinds of drugs you can buy illegally, but there are restrictions on how much of certain vitamins can be sold in over-the-counter preparations.

Advertising is, in general, misleading and designed to sell products, whether it be calcium to prevent osteoporosis, ibuprofin for pain, or Monoxadil to treat baldness. Only recently do we have warning labels on some alcoholic beverages about use in pregnancy. There is either confusing labeling on most foods high in fat, salt, and sugar or none at all. It's a crazy, mixed-up world, in which we have to make decisions based on available information. Add to that the deliberate attempts to mislead the public for economic gain, and you can easily appreciate some of the reasons for inappropriate health-related behaviors, despite interest in leading healthy lives.

Most of us wouldn't presume to claim expertise in technical areas; however, where human behavior is concerned, we all believe we are experts. We believe that our personal experiences make us competent to judge others, when actually our range of experience may be quite narrow and hardly the product of detached, dispassionate, controlled scientific observation. Our assumed expertise can be misleading.

In lectures, an epidemiologist at the University of California at Berkeley often presents material from the U.S. War Department's

World War II research into the life of American soldiers, noting that more than 300 studies, including more than 600,000 interviews with soldiers, were analyzed for four years and then published with a grant from the Carnegie Corporation in four massive volumes, entitled *The American Soldier*. As he begins his presentation, the lecturer lists the following data, which he attributes to *The American Soldier:*

1. Better educated men showed more psychoneurotic symptoms than less educated men.

2. Men from rural backgrounds were usually in better spirits during their army life than soldiers from city backgrounds.

3. Southern soldiers were better able to stand the climate in the hot South Sea islands than Northern soldiers.

4. White privates were more eager to become non-commissioned officers than Blacks.

5. Southern Blacks preferred Southern to Northern white officers.

6. As long as the fighting continued, the men were more eager to be returned to the U.S. than they were after the Germans surrendered.

This list usually provokes snickers and laughter from members of the audience who think that a lot of money and effort was spent in gathering obvious information. These same people are surprised when he tells them that the facts in the study were actually exactly the opposite of those listed and that the true findings don't sound as obvious. The true facts are:

1. Men with less education had more psychoneurotic symptoms than men with more education.

2. Men from city backgrounds were usually in better spirits than soldiers from rural backgrounds.

3. Black privates were more eager to become non-commissioned officers than whites.

4. Southern Blacks preferred Northern white officers to Southern white officers.

And so on.

The point is that we have a marvelous capacity for making sense out of anything we hear. We can develop instant hypotheses at the drop of a hat (or statement). Many things may seem obvious, but only some actually can be supported by the evidence. Our common-sense approach to things is not always accurate, and sometimes we need to select from all the things that seem obvious and correct only those that really are. All of this brings us to the way the scientific community in the United States determines what is "obviously" true and what is "obviously" not factual.

In the United States, too frequently, the scientific community and some doctors employ a double standard which prevents useful remedies from being added to the arsenal of disease-fighting therapies. The following are a few of the many scientifically supported biological or natural remedies that are still not accepted by some doctors and other scientists, who have accepted other drugs with much less scientific data in their favor: Padma 28, cernitin extracts T6O-GBX, ventrux acido, garlic, feverfew, fish oil, evening primrose oil, Gerovital H-3, phosphatidylserine, exsativa, and acemannan (a complex carbohydrate from the juice of the aloe vera plant). Some of these products are ignored because they cannot be patented or because they are potential competitors of registered pharmaceuticals. Some are ignored just because of the prevailing ignorance and prejudice against natural products still found in American medicine.

PADMA 28

Padma 28 has one of the widest ranges of indications of all herbal remedies. Generally, it improves circulation, aids healing, and normalizes immunological responses. It heals by correcting the balance of the body's own production of prostaglandins and by altering the interaction of thrombocytes (blood platelets). It is used as both a preventive agent and a remedy.

It is suggested for treatment and prevention of bronchial asthma, chronic infections, coronary disorders, poor circulation, peripheral arterial occlusion and disabilities of old age caused by deficient circulation, such as senility, poor memory and depressed energy levels.

Padma 28 tablets contain a combination of twenty-two herbs prepared in accordance with principles of Tibetan herbology. Padma 28 is made entirely from wild-picked and organically-grown herbs. Pharmacological studies show presence of flavones, coumarins, and silicon compounds and other active ingredients. Toxicity tests have established its complete non-toxicity. Long-term extensive use of this formula has demonstrated minimal side-effects and no drug interactions.

Double-blind clinical evaluations and other investigations on Padma 28 have been conducted in Switzerland and Poland. In Poland, Dr. J. Wojcicki studied inpatients suffering from stable, frequent angina pectoris. Patients received a placebo for two weeks, then Padma 28 for two weeks, and finally the placebo for two more weeks. During Padma 28 treatment, compared to the previous two weeks of placebo, patients' angina attacks were reduced in frequency by 63%, and use of nitroglycerine tablets was reduced by 69%; the amount of work needed to induce an angina attack was doubled, and the platelet aggregation threshold increased by 65%.

In Switzerland, in 1978, Dr. F. Huerlimann divided twenty-four patients with severely limited walking distance into two groups; one took Padma 28 and the other took a placebo. Pain at night was reduced within two weeks in 70% of the group taking Padma 28, compared to 30% of the placebo group. Pain-free walking distance was increased by 54% in the Padma 28 group compared to 6% of the control group. Five years after the original study, Dr. Huerlimann reported similar findings in more than 220 patients treated with Padma 28 over the five-year period.

Another Swiss researcher, Dr. R. Waelti, treated severe cases of peripheral arterial occlusion, including diabetic patients with peripheral gangrene which normally requires amputation; over a two-year period he saved at least six diabetic patients from amputation when vascular bypass surgery could not be performed.

In 1982, Polish researcher Dr. W. Brzosko reported that clinical applications and laboratory studies of the action mechanism of Padma 28 revealed its effects on the immune system as the most likely explanation for its benefits to patients with allergic diseases and chronic inflammatory pathology of the respiratory, digestive, and vascular systems. Blood samples from patients who had been treated with Padma 28 for at least one month showed changes in immunological tests.

In his report, "Padma 28, The Tibetan Remedy in Relation to Immunology," Dr. Vladimir Badmajew, of the New York Downstate

Medical Center, wrote that because of increasing evidence from several European physicians that this drug alleviates such immunological disorders as bronchial asthma, allergic dermatitis and ulcerative colitis and that, because two of its components are described in the literature as having broad immunological actions, detailed research of the immunological properties of Padma 28 is important.

In the laboratory, Padma 28 improved the performance of a specific population of lymphocytes, known technically as T-lymphocytes. T-cells play a sophisticated regulatory role in the immune system. The preliminary results imply that Padma 28 may normalize to some extent the function of impaired T-suppressor lymphocytes, possibly creating conditions for recovery from some immunological disorders.

Advances in immunology have revealed that the cardiovascular and immunological systems share many common mechanisms; therefore malfunction of blood flow decreases the immune system's efficiency, and disorders of the immune system often affect circulation. Also, arteriosclerosis seems to be regarded as a disease of both systems; therefore, Dr. Badmajew suggests that Padma 28 and other Tibetan remedies may hold important clues to health problems and deserve continued research.

Because of FDA objections to one Padma 28 ingredient, an herb called monk's hood (aconite), and because the Swiss refused to change the formula to market it in the U.S., Padma 28 is no longer available in this country. With the coming of a united Europe in 1992 and a potential market of 300 million people, the Swiss manufacturers can afford to tell the FDA to go to hell and refuse to alter a centuries-old formula.

CERNITIN EXTRACTS T60 AND GBX

In Europe, Sthenorex (cernitin extracts T60 and GBX, traded as No. 2 Cernilton) is used to stimulate appetite in people of various ages and with various reasons for appetite loss. Studies have shown that this product is reliable in treating anorexia, weight loss, and physical and psychological weakness in states of undernutrition or actual or potential malnutrition, in a very wide range of patients from infants to very old people, in hospital practice, in nursing/convalescent homes, and in general medicine and surgery practices, as well as pediatrics, psychiatry, and ear, nose and throat practices. Also, it can be given without ill effects to patients suffering from asthma-like breathing difficulties or spasmodic bronchitis and pollen allergies.

Europeans use the extract in the treatment of anorexia nervosa in adolescent girls. Also, Europeans have studied pollen extract's effects on the common cold, lipid levels, and chronic prostate diseases.

Sthenorex is made from flower pollen and consists of water and fat-soluble extracts containing nutrients and plant sterols. It is composed of cernitin T6O (aqueous) and cernitin GBX (lipid) extracts of pollens, which include pine and alder tree pollen, rye, maize, hay-grasses, timothy, and cocksfoot grass pollens. The pollen extracts in the product are first de-allergised by destroying the polypeptides in the capsule and then fermenting the endosperm until its components are converted into smaller constituents which are easily absorbed by the body into the blood stream. The product is a nutrient or food, not an anabolic hormone or drug, and therefore there are no contra-indications for its use or side-effects which are typical of traditional appetite stimulants. Taken orally and well-tolerated, the earliest effects are felt at the end of the first week's treatment.

A major field study of the effect of pollen extracts on the common cold and its roborant (strengthening) effects in 775 Swedish military recruits did not give unequivocal results in relation to the prophylactic effect of the preparation used against the common cold. It was shown, however, that under certain conditions the product was effective against symptoms such as sore throat and coughing. Also, there was a lower frequency of tired feelings among cernitin-treated persons. The investigators noted the difficulties in assessing effects on military persons in training due to the conditions that prevail under such special circumstances, but concluded that although generalizations cannot be made, it can be said that the preparation under certain conditions combats the symptoms associated with infection of the upper air passage and, for this reason, might be a useful prophylactic. In addition, the preparation showed a roborant effect.

Polish investigators from the Institute for Hygiene and Epidemiology in Warszawa administered various nutritional substances in a study of weight-lifters' working capacities. They found that during a six-week training period, working capacity and the formation of lactate were significantly affected in different ways and that the greatest effect was achieved by the administration of a multivitamin preparation and the combination of amino acids and pollen extracts.

Another Polish investigator, Dr. Ignacy Dabrowski, also studied the effects of pollen on physical and mental capacity. He divided ninety Polish soldiers into three groups during their stay in a subtropical climate, where it was possible to see deterioration in physical and mental capacity during the period of adaptation. He found that addition of preparations containing pollen extractions and amino acids significantly improved such achievements as long distance running, the long jump, concentration and subjective well-being; additionally, there was a decrease in the formation of lactate after exercise on an ergometer cycle. His report said that no explanation can be offered for the observed effects.

A group of Polish investigators of the Medical Academy of Szcecin studied cernitin extracts as a lipid-lowering agent. They noted that the product was useful in treating prostatitis; it removes edema of the urethral mucosal surface from the bladder neck to the external sphincter, improving urination, and it has anti-inflammatory properties as well. Because cernitin is useful in treating patients with prostatitis and in treating geriatric patients, they studied its significance in treating hyperlipidemia. Patients who had not responded to diet therapy were divided into two groups: Group 1 included fifteen subjects whose hyperlipidemia was not previously controlled pharmacologically; Group 2 included thirteen persons whose hyperlipidemia was resistant to clofibrate, a widely used basic drug given for the condition. After one month's treatment of three tablets of Cernilton daily, twenty-two of twenty-eight persons receiving the drug had positive results, a triglycerides decrease of 49%. The investigators reported no complaints, adverse effects or refusals to take the tablets, important because lipid-lowering drugs may need to be taken for the patients' lifetimes. They concluded that Cernilton should be considered for prevention and treatment of atherosclerosis.

Per Ockerman's Swedish study on Cernilton and Cernitromb has shown that the two pollen preparations induced significant decreases in plasma cholesterol and that the decreases were explained by a lowered LDL or "bad" cholesterol with no change or even slight increase in HDL or "good" cholesterol. Noting that flower-pollen is non-toxic and non-allergenic with "interesting effects on the prostate, immune defense and possibly, on blood lipid levels," this study concluded that it may be used "as a much-needed supplement to dietary change in order to decrease cholesterol levels."

Benign prostatic hyperplasia (BPH), one of the aging-process diseases, sooner or later develops in almost all males. Some authors assume that after age 40 almost 80% and after age 70 almost 100 percent of all men show more or less pronounced nodular hypertrophy (enlargement) of the prostate. Because of the prevalence of this condition and because of the increasing life expectancy, finding a conservative treatment of BPH is significant.

A German controlled comparative study of the use of Cernilton versus B-sitosterol in the treatment of BPH, using fifty subjects from a nursing home, demonstrated "marked improvement of symptoms and signs" and pronounced "regression of complaints" under Cernilton. The investigator concluded that cernitin extracts reduced the symptomatology of prostatic hyperplasia and that its anti-inflammatory and urination-improving effects were also confirmed. Also, the preparation was extremely well-tolerated.

Another German field study by 170 urologists of the pollen extract's therapeutic results in 2,289 patients with chronic prostatitis, or BPH accompanied by chronic prostatitis, confirmed the anti-inflammatory and decongestive properties of Cernilton. Effectiveness was judged by decrease of residual urine volume, increase of peak urine flow rate, improvement of symptoms and improved pathological laboratory and palpation findings. Investigators reported that the results suggested a "rationality for application of the pollen-extract in patients with non-pathogen dependent chronic prostatitis, prostate pain, prostatic congestion, BPH with and without accompanying prostatitis, and post-surgical prostatitis." The positive tolerance of the pollen extract leads to patient compliance in chronic and benign prostatic diseases and therefore is indicated for long-term treatment.

A pharmacological report by Professor Kimura and his colleagues of Toyama University in Japan on Cernilton and cernitin pollen extract T6O and GBX was published in *Planta Medica (No. 2, April 1986)*. Professor Kimura studied the influence of Cernilton and cernitin extracts on strips of bladder and urethra from pigs and mice and noted that Cernilton had contractile effects on the bladder and that this effect was related mostly to the cernitin T6O in Cernilton. He also found that Cernilton had a relaxing effect on the urethral smooth muscle and that this was related mainly to the component cernitin GBX in Cernilton. Both effects were dose-related and significant.

Professor Kimura concluded that Cernilton may inhibit the urethral contraction and reduce the intraurethral pressure and thus may facilitate urine discharge, although the pollen extract may possibly act on the prostatic smooth muscle while having a contractile effect on the bladder. Cernitin T6O and cernitin GBX affected the urethra via different modes. Cernilton may directly or indirectly facilitate the discharge of urine in vivo.

This product, in summary, may have many uses: as an appetite stimulant; for prophylaxis against colds and sore throats; to help lower the levels of fat and cholesterol in blood; for a strengthening effect in power athletes; and to treat and possibly prevent prostate inflammation and enlargement.

VENTRUX ACIDO

Since the first bacteria of the lactobacillus group were identified more than a century ago, lactobacillus preparations have been used by physicians and non-physicians to treat a range of complaints from constipation and diarrhea to skin problems and vaginal candida albicans. Researchers have observed that antibiotics can allow candida to take over in the intestine and that immunological alterations may occur because of endocrine dysfunction and auto-antibody formation. A diet of friendly bacteria, including lactobacillus acidophilus and streptococcus faecium—"good guys"—may help conquer candida and help prevent the "bad guys" from taking over in the intestines with the resulting immune-system and hormone problems.

No side-effects and no toxic effects have been observed and no contraindications have been established for ventrux acido, which suppresses or inhibits the growth of bacteria capable of causing diarrhea and restores intestinal flora to normal biological balance. Unlike synthetic chemotherapeutic products used against intestinal disturbances, ventrux acido doesn't cause an unnatural interference in the intestinal processes or unwanted side effects. In severe cases, however, use of synthetic products may be unavoidable.

Lactic acid bacteria occur in milk and in the intestine and are crucial to formation of yoghurt and cheese making. As permanent enteric organisms in man, they contribute to digestion and are involved in vitamin production. In addition to being a digestive aid, lactic acid bacteria have been thought to be health-promoting. With other beneficial bacteria, they form the intestinal flora which protects the intestine against invasion by pathogens. The biological balance of the intestinal flora can be upset by changes in routine such as travel, drug ingestion, or diet changes. When the intestine is unprotected, it can be invaded by pathogenic bacteria; the result is diarrhea and other intestinal disturbances.

Nearly every civilization has consumed fermented milks or cheeses, and foods fermented with lactobacilli are extremely important in the nutrition of people throughout the world. In the past fifteen years, the production and per capita consumption of cultured dairy products and cheeses has increased in the United States and Europe. Oriental foods and fermented vegetable products are eaten in the Far East, Europe and the United States.

Researchers from the Department of Food Science and Technology of the University of Nebraska listed the nutritional and therapeutic benefits of lactobacilli: predigestion of protein and improved protein quality, predigestion of lactose, synthesis of vitamins, destruction of anti-nutritional compounds, and production of anticholesteremic factors. The therapeutic benefits include production of antibiotics, possible protection against disease, and inhibition of carcinogenesis.

The Nebraska research team noted that, when preparing lactobacilli for dietary use, it is important to consider the following:

Benefits from one strain of lactobacillus may not apply to all strains of the same organism, and since the activities of the lactobacilli are strain specific, beneficial properties of each strain must be evaluated properly in the laboratory.

Commercial preparations of cultures which are effective in the laboratory may not provide adequate numbers of viable organisms to be of benefit. Certain strains may be more amenable to the processes of concentration, freezing, freeze-drying or drying needed to make them shelf-stable.

Because lactobacilli are markedly affected by alcohol, antibiotics and other dietary components, it's important that ingestion of these dietary supplements should not be before, after or with ingestion of incompatible food ingredients.

As a prevention for travelers' diarrhea, three to four capsules of ventrux acido should be taken daily for one week prior to travel and three capsules should be taken daily during the trip. Normal adult dose is two to four capsules daily; children's daily dose is two capsules daily.

Swiss and Italian investigators noted that streptococcus faecium, a non-pathogenic type of lactobacillus, is characterized by a very short generation time, high stability, and strong inhibitory effects against some pathogenic microorganisms. They concluded that such properties suggest the clinical use of streptococcus faecium for the treatment of different diarrheal disturbances. Preliminary observations carried out in fourteen patients were said to be very promising and were confirmed by other controlled clinical observations in children as well as in veterinary medicine.

A Swedish team conducted in 1985-86 a double-blind study in three popular tourist areas, Gran Canaria, Tenerife and Lanzarote in the Canary Islands, in which 100 tourists who became sick were contacted through travel agencies and hotels so that they could be given ventrux acido. Contacts were made during the Christmas and New Year holidays, when tourists would be eating a wide variety of foods. Some of the tourists who had acute diarrhea, usually with fever and vomiting, were members of the same family and had been infected from the same sources, including ice cubes in drinks, drinking water or foods with mayonnaise or whipped cream affected by warm weather. The tourists were randomly separated into two groups; one received ventrux acido and the other a placebo. Those who received ventrux acido averaged 1.7 sick days; the placebo group averaged 4.2 sick days. Variable fever appeared to a lesser degree in the treatment group. Some of the sick persons also relied on other preparations which they had either brought from home or bought locally, but use of such remedies was significantly lower in the Ventrux group, indirect evidence that they got better faster.

Italian researchers gave eight normal subjects streptococcus faecium daily for thirty days to study the effects of the bacteria on cholesterol saturation in bile and on serum lipids. Streptococcus faecium has a short generation time, and it produces substances against clostridia and other microorganisms. It also has an effect on fecal and biliary bile acid secretion patterns. They found that during streptococcus faecium administration, the anaerobic bacteria (which live in the absence of oxygen) in feces decrease, whereas aerobic bacteria (which live in the presence of oxygen) increase, and they concluded that changes in fecal flora may reduce the degradation of primary bile acids influencing the bile acid composition in both the bile and the intestine. This means that the organism prevents the breakdown of bile acids into toxic and cancer-promoting chemical compounds.

The underlying elements in acute diarrheal management are reestablishment of fluid and electrolytes and restoration of normal microflora. Early and adequate replacement of sodium, potassium, bicarbonate, and water by oral rehydration therapy circumvents many complications and death from diarrhea. But oral rehydration therapy treats the response to the causative agent; it doesn't dislodge the pathogen itself. Also, administration of antibiotics alters the gastrointestinal micro environment and allows proliferation of antibiotic-resistant microbes, which is a far worse situation. Conversely, recovery from diarrhea may be greatly expedited if normal intestinal flora can be reinstated. Streptococcus faecium therapy has been successful in reversing diarrheal states in both animals and man, relieving diarrhea and abdominal pain in one to three days. Studies have shown that E. coli has never been detected in feces cultures after two days of treatment, nor were any abnormalities detected in blood chemistries.

But of more serious significance than tourist diarrhea is the approximately one-half million episodes of diarrhea which occur annually in infants and children under five years of age and the ten diarrheal deaths which occur every minute, as reported by the U.S. Agency for International Development and the World Health Organization.

Gastroenteritis continues to be a major cause of morbidity and mortality among infants and preschool children in developing and underdeveloped nations. It is caused by rotavirus, enteropathogenic E. coli, salmonella, and vibrio cholera. Rotavirus and E. coli account for approximately 75% of the cases in children between six months and two years of age, and as the above information shows, streptococcus faecium, which is contained in ventrux acido, can be effective in treating at least part of this major health problem. ventrux acido comes in capsules, each of which contains at least 75 million live lactic-acid-fermenting organisms of the streptococcus faecium (C68) strain.

Vital-Plex is a high-potency, hypoallergenic microorganism combination containing lactobacillus acidophilus KL-l, lactobacillus bifidus, and streptococcus faecium. To re-establish intestinal flora, supplementation of 1/4 teaspoon, two to three times daily, for five to seven days (or as recommended by a physician) is recommended. Maintenance dose is 1/4 teaspoon daily. This product can be put right onto the tongue and swallowed or may be mixed with other foods such as applesauce, mashed potatoes, etc. A similar mixture of lactose-fermenting bacteria is called Kyodophilus. As a general rule, microorganisms should be taken with food, because the food environment in the stomach protects the friendly microbacteria from the stomach acid and allows the activated organisms to be nourished as they pass into the intestinal tract where they function.

In summary, the benefits of taking lactobacilli are that it keeps yeast and other harmful bacteria out of the large intestinal tract; it prevents the breakdown of the acids in bile to cancer-inducing compounds, and it works in concert with certain insoluble fiber components in the diet, such as bran, in alleviating constipation.

Nearly all of the research work on the lactose-fermenting organisms has been done on streptococcus faecium. There have been no comparable studies on lactobacillus acidophilus or bifidus strains of the lactose-fermenting organisms. We assume that they also have the same properties as streptococcus fecium. The preparation Vital-

Plex is a combination of all three organisms. However, the strep-tococcus fecium organism in this preparation is not necessarily the same one used in the Swedish studies using ventrux acido.

FEVERFEW

Feverfew is an example of a natural product which is a biologic response modifier. It has somewhat different physiological effects than cernitin extract, which also is a biologic response modifier. feverfew (tanacetum parthenium) has been used since ancient times as a herbal remedy for fever, arthritis, and migraine. As such, it has been used as if it were a natural "aspirin." Recently, Dr. S. Hep-tinstall and his colleagues of Nottingham, England, prepared extracts of feverfew and tested them in the laboratory. The Nottingham researchers found that the extracts inhibited secretions from blood platelets and polymorphonuclear leukocytes (PMNs). They also determined their effects on platelet aggregation and thromboxane synthesis. In summary, they found that feverfew inhibited the release of leukotrienes, substances which cause fever and inflammation, and that it also thinned the blood, making it less prone to clotting and coagulation. This latter effect is similar to that of aspirin and the other non-steroidal anti-inflammatory agents, which inhibit pros-taglandins and are conventional remedies for arthritis.

In their study to determine feverfew extract's effects on platelet aggregation, granule constituents' secretions from blood platelets, polymorphonuclear leukocytes, and thromboxane synthesis, the re-searchers from the Department of Medicine at University Hospital and the Department of Haematology at City Hospital, in Notting-gham, England, found that the pattern of the effects of feverfew extracts on platelets is different from that obtained with other in-hibitors of platelet aggregation and the effect on polymorphonuclear leukocytes (PMNs) is more pronounced than has been obtained with very high concentrations of non-steroidal anti-inflammatory agents. In another laboratory study of feverfew extract, researcher Allen Goldstein found that it prevents a release of leukotriene B4, a sub-stance which causes inflammation and fever at the cellular level.

FISH OILS

Body membranes are composed of lipids, which determine the each membrane's function, fluidity, and porosity. Many degenera-tive diseases can be traced to membrane defects. Therefore, the conclusion of some experts is that, when doing basic therapy at the cellular level, it's better to use nutrients than drugs. One of these nutrients is fish oil.

Fish eat phytoplankton and algae, the microscopic plants found in fresh and salt water which manufacture omega-3 fatty acids. All types of fish and shellfish contain fatty acids, but cold-water ocean fish such as salmon, tuna, mackerel, herring and sardines contain more abundant amounts. Shellfish have a high omega-3 fatty acid concentration and are no longer thought to be unhealthy because of their cholesterol content.

Here's how fish oil works in the body:

Fish oils are omega-3 fatty acids which are converted into regular body chemicals called eicosanoids. Eicosanoids, such as prostaglandins and leukotrienes, help the body's cells communicate. They react to inflammation and infection, telling the white blood cells to attack germs and telling other cells to make interferon for defense against germs. Some eicosanoids tell the body to start the clotting process so that wounds will stop bleeding and begin healing. When the eicosanoids are too active, they can cause hyper-reactions and may eventually produce the diseases research has linked to incorrect immune or inflammatory responses in the body. For example, if an eicosanoid response stays in a coronary artery too long, it may help fatty deposits to build up and produce heart disease. Thromboxane A2, an eicosanoid, promotes clot formation; if a clot in a narrowed coronary artery blocks the flow of blood, a heart attack can be the result. Fish oils slow down some eicosanoid activities, sometimes by altering the eicosanoid's chemical makeup. For example, fish oil helps the body produce thromboxane A3, which lowers the risk of clot formation.

Dr. William Lands, Chief of Biological Chemistry at the University of Illinois in Chicago, said in a *Chicago Tribune* story by Ronald Kotulak that by eating a balanced diet which includes enough fish oil, you may be able to control the tendency of eicosanoids to over-react, and that the potential for major health improvement from a preventive medicine point of view is tremendous.

Interviewed on Physicians Radio Network, both Dr. Warren Levin of New York City and Dr. Michael Davidson of Chicago said that omega-3 fatty acids should be taken as dietary supplements. Dr. Davidson believes that the lack of seafood and excess of pork and beef in American diets results in the prevalence of such degenerative diseases as atherosclerosis (hardening of the arteries), cancer, and arthritis. Dr. Levin contends that omega-3 essential fatty-acid deficiency is the single most prevalent nutrient deficiency in the United States today. Americans eat only fourteen pounds of fish per year per person, whereas Eskimos eat an average of three hundred pounds and Japanese fishing villagers eat an average of five hundred pounds. Both Dr. Levin and Dr. Davidson recommend supplemental fish oil, because they don't believe the typical American will ever eat even half as much fish as Eskimos or the Japanese. They studied deaths from heart disease and found that males who ate no fish were at substantially greater risk of developing coronary heart disease in the Netherlands than those who ate it on a regular basis. Although the study had not shown that overall mortality is affected by eating fish, or that eating fish reduced risk of death from other causes, it was presumed that it was a benefit to health.

At the University of Oregon Health Science Center, Dr. Beverly Phillipson used a fish diet for four weeks with patients who had high triglyceride levels and found that eating fish had a normalizing effect. High-fat fish, such as salmon and tuna, are as effective as low-fat fish, such as cod and flounder. Patients were put on three diets differing primarily in fatty acid composition and fat content. The control diet contained a fatty acid mixture which was typical in a low-fat therapeutic diet (with a ratio of polyunsaturated to saturated fat of 1:4), the fish oil diet contained omega-3 fatty acids and the vegetable-oil diet was rich in omega-6 fatty acid, linoleic acid.

The Oregon researchers found that total plasma cholesterol and triglyceride levels fell in every patient, without exception. Body weights stayed constant, and the diets were well tolerated. In the hypertriglyceridemic patients, fish oil in the diet led to an even more profound hypolipidemic effect than has previously been found in normal subjects. They concluded that fish oils and fish may be useful components of diets for the treatment of hypertriglyceridemia.

Studies at the University of Washington showed that consumption of fish oils favorably affected platelet aggregation or clumping. In a Boston study, administering active fatty acids in fish oils for six weeks inhibited the production of leukotriene B4, and researchers suggested that fish oils may protect against inflammation of rheumatoid arthritis and asthma.

Dr. Joel M. Kremer and his colleagues conducted a non-randomized, double-blind, placebo-controlled, crossover study on fish-oil fatty-acid supplementation for patients with active rheumatoid arthritis at the Division of Rheumatology of the Department of Medicine and Department of Biochemistry of Albany Medical College, the Medical Service of Veterans Administration Medical Center, and the State University of New York in Albany.

This research team set out to determine the efficacy of fish oil dietary supplements in active rheumatoid arthritis and their effect on neutrophil leukotriene levels. Forty volunteer patients with active, definite or classical rheumatoid arthritis participated in fourteen-week treatment periods and four-week washout periods. Treatment with nonsteroidal anti-inflammatory drugs, slow-acting anti-rheumatic drugs, and prednisone was continued. Background diets were not changed. Twenty-one patients were given a daily dose of 2.7 grams of eicosapentaenoic acid and 1.8 grams of docahaexenoic acid in 15 MAX-EPA capsules; nineteen patients were given identical-appearing placebos. (Seven patients left the study.)

The results showed that fish oil, after fourteen weeks, improved the mean time to onset of fatigue by 156 minutes, and the number of tender joints decreased by 3.5. Neutrophil leukotriene B4 production was correlated with decreased tender joints. There were no statistically significant differences in hemoglobin levels, sedimentation rates, or presence of rheumatoid factor, nor was there a significant difference in patient-reported adverse effects. Furthermore, the effects of the fish oil on intervals to first onset of fatigue and number of tender joints persisted beyond the four-week washout period.

Researchers concluded that dietary fish-oil supplementation was generally well-tolerated and resulted in measurable, statistically significant changes in disease activity. Although improvements were noted, patients did continue to have disease activity; however, the researchers suggest that increasing the dose or duration of fish-oil supplementation might result in further clinical benefits. They concluded that, although attributing improvements to the decrease in neutrophil leukotriene B4 production was tempting, the precise mechanism of action of fish oil supplementation in patients with rheumatoid arthritis remains to be determined.

While many researchers say it is too early to make sweeping recommendations about therapy with fish oils, most recommend more research to learn its effects on cancer and other diseases. In my opinion, getting funding for more research is difficult because of the FDA's attitude toward fish oil. Corporate officials who determine which products will receive research funding are reluctant to make commitments when they can't be assured of getting patents on the results and when they can't be certain whether the FDA will continue to consider fish oil a food or will ultimately considered it a drug.

EVENING PRIMROSE OIL (EPO), BORAGE OIL AND BLACK CURRANT OIL

Gamma linolenic acid is a fatty acid constituent of evening primrose oil, which historically was used by American Indians to treat asthma and wounds. Adopted by the English colonists and sent back to Britain, where it became the "King Cure-All," it has been shown in present day studies to provide significant relief for skin problems such as eczema, to relieve the pain and discomfort of fibrocystic breasts, to decrease the irritability, depression and emotional outbursts of premenstrual syndrome (PMS), and to treat hyperactivity in children. It has also been used for a variety of other diseases, including heart disease.

Despite documented results, evening primrose oil is ignored by the pharmaceutical companies and researchers who choose to focus on synthetic rather than natural medicines and remedies. Sir James Black, founder of Efamol Research Institute in Nova Scotia, has been described as one gifted researcher who has made a "leap from the classic pharmaceutical research method of screening thousands of compounds for some therapeutic effect, to the more directly innovative approach of putting two and two together and finding out why they make four."

Research has shown that the naturally-found gamma linolenic acid (GLA) in primrose seed oil is apparently free from side effects, while the synthetic analogues of the prostaglandin-E1 to which GLA is converted in the body, and to which it's assumed to owe its therapeutic effect, does cause adverse reactions. Prostaglandin-E1, to which primrose oil converts in the body, has been found to be deficient in persons who suffer from diseases as diverse as eczema and heart disease.

EPO is effective because the GLA will be converted to a "good" prostaglandin, E1, rather than a "bad" one, E2. E1 is associated with the relaxation of smooth muscle in the blood vessels and the lowering of blood pressure. E2 is associated with high blood pressure and blood vessel constriction and often subsequent thrombosis. If GLA is not directly consumed, it can be manufactured from linoleic acid, found in corn and other vegetable oils, but you cannot count on this reaction occurring because it is easily inhibited or even eliminated by common substances or conditions, such as cigarette smoking, alcohol, diabetes, and obesity.

Dr. David Horrobin studied the pituitary hormone prolactin and found that excess prolactin or allergy-like prolactin sensitivity can cause fluid retention, irritability, and depression, the three main PMS symptoms. He also found that some PMS sufferers had abnormal prolactin levels but found no convincing prolactin-PMS link. As his research led him to the essential fatty acids, key ingredients of all body membranes and building blocks of prostaglandins, the chemicals which affect many biochemical processed in the body in addition to PMS, he learned that women with PMS had abnormally low levels of gamma linolenic acid. To prove his theory that gamma linolenic acid deficiency caused prostaglandin deficiency and triggered the prolactin sensitivity in PMS sufferers, he gave two 500-milligram capsules of evening primrose oil a day to sixty-eight chronic PMS sufferers for two weeks prior to the onset of their menstrual periods. In this group, 61% had substantial remission of PMS symptoms.

Horrobin's findings were corroborated by a placebo-controlled Finnish study of thirty women who had suffered from severe PMS for an average of nine years and who reported significantly fewer PMS symptoms during treatment with evening primrose oil. Also, in Massachusetts, a physician and a psychologist treated about 300 PMS sufferers with evening primrose oil. Dr. Donald Lombard and Dr. Ann Nazzaro claimed significant relief in 60-80% of those treated.

Although evening primrose oil appears to be safe and nontoxic, Efamol researchers have noted such side effects as slight stool softening, nausea if taken on an empty stomach, and headache in migraine sufferers.

PHOSPHATIDYLSERINE

Several double-blind randomized controlled studies have shown phosphatidylserine to be useful in relatively early cases of senile dementia. It is taken by mouth in a dosage of 100 milligrams three times a day, and it takes at least six weeks to achieve an effect. Behavioral improvement has been shown in the subjects taking this substance in the following ten areas: Toilet, dressing, feeding, bowel control, bladder control, interpersonal relationships, relationships with the environment, behavioral problems in their living unit, and verbal expression.

ACEMANNAN

Dr. Bill McAnally, a pharmacologist with Carrington Laboratories in Dallas, Texas, succeeded where others had failed. He isolated and characterized a complex carbohydrate, called acemannan, from the juice of the aloe vera plant; this complex carbohydrate is thought to be the active ingredient responsible for aloe vera's healing effect in burns.

Subsequent clinical studies performed by Dr. H. Reg McDaniel, a pathologist with the Dallas-Fort Worth Medical Center, and others have shown this carbohydrate to be useful in the treatment of some AIDS patients. It stimulates the immune system to proliferate and make more monocytes, T4 cells, and eventually gamma interferon.

There were three separate pilot clinical trials. The first was done in 1985 on fourteen patients with AIDS. They drank the juice and got a 71% improvement in clinical symptoms and laboratory work. The second pilot consisted of fifteen patients, evaluated by a modified Walter Reed Clinical Scoring System for HIV symptoms and objective findings. The patients' symptoms were fatigue, lymphadenopathy, recurrent infections, diarrhea, night sweats, fever, and weight loss. Using the Walter Reed Scoring System, the researchers used P24 antigen, did serial absolute T4 counts, and did culturing of the virus. Those patients taking acemannan improved about 70% in these areas.

The protocol was submitted to the FDA, and an exemption number was obtained for a Physicians Sponsored I.N.D. The approximate dosage of acemannan is 250 mg four times a day.

It will be some time before acemannan is approved as a drug by the Food and Drug Administration. However, Dr. McDaniel's original observations were made on AIDS patients who were taking aloe vera juice. Acemannan makes up 1% of the juice, so a concentrated juice preparation would appear to be a suitable substitute.

EXSATIVA

Exsativa or Swiss Formula A111 (one eleven) is a mixture of extracts of oats (the plant and not just the grain) and extracts of the root of the stinging nettle plant. Dr. Loretta Haroian of San Francisco and others have conducted placebo-controlled double-blind crossover studies, and the results strongly suggest that exsativa stimulates sexual desire and that it is both an erectant and an aphrodisiac. This work has to be corroborated by other investigators, however.

The following are entire systems of thought, analysis, and interpretation which have been rejected out-of-hand, whose proponents have been hauled into court, and the science of which has been argued through mouth-piece lawyers before scientifically-illiterate judges. It is their ultimate decisions which result in the isolation and quarantine of alternative therapies and the exclusion of ideas and concepts which might advance the state of our knowledge and understanding. A "better mousetrap" is not necessarily guaranteed immediate access to the marketplace.

Other examples of this behavior can be found in other chapters in this book. Five are presented here.

SYSTEM 1: THE RIFE MICROSCOPE

The Rife microscope was invented in the 1930s by the doctor whose name it bears, Dr. Royal R. Rife. It can magnify 60×10^3 times, and Rife used it to examine living blood. He described various microorganisms or particles in blood which are able to change form or shape and go from one form to another; they are therefore pleomorphic. They were sometimes shaped like bacteria in the form of rods, and at other times they were in the form of budding yeast cells.

Rife also used ultra-violent light to illuminate these forms. In addition, he used a frequency instrument which produced waves or frequency waves to match the frequency at which an organism vibrates. He thereby induced resonance and subsequently destroyed the organism, in much the same way that sound pitch and vibration can shatter a crystal glass. He used these innovative techniques to treat pneumonia and even cancer.

Barry Lynes, an investigative reporter, wrote a book about Dr. Rife, his microscope, and his techniques. It is called *The Cancer Cure that Worked*, and it is published by Marcus Books in Canada.

Johanna Budwig, a quantum physicist and lipid biochemist, picked up where Rife left off. She began treating cancer in 1951. Budwig believes that:

(1) Sunlight is indispensable for human life.

(2) Living tissue absorbs electrons from sunlight. (This is the source of energy or electrons from the Rife machine.) The absorption of these electrons is called resonance absorption.

(3) Certain seed oils, notably flax with linolenic (omega-6) and alpha-linolenic (omega-3) acids are necessary for this reception and absorption.

(4) These oils form a lipo-protein with sulphydryl-containing proteins which are in synchrony with the incoming oscillations from the sunlight, and they store and later release these resonating electrons. (The Rife machine can also emit sound waves and/or electrical energy with the potential of destroying invading organisms, including viruses.)

(5) These electrons restore both dipolarity and aerobic

metabolism to the cancer cell.

(6) This physical energy takes precedence over biochemical energy it regulates, and it has a higher potential than the Krebs cycle. It accounts for about 30% of our energy outside the Krebs cycle.

Gaston Naessens of Montreal, Canada, in 1991 became the apparent heir to live blood analysis, using a microscope he designed with the help of German opticians. It is called a somatoscope, because it is used to visualize a living particle in human blood which is called a somatid. The microscope can be thought of as a further development of the original Rife microscope, which was never recognized allegedly because Morris Fishbein of the AMA made Rife an offer which he refused: "Turn your invention over to us in return for our recognition and a royalty, and if you don't, we will make sure that it never sees the light of day."

Naessens described the various stages of development of the somatid, and the arrestation of that development in various disease states, cancer in particular. He then went on to develop a treatment for some types of cancer with a nitrogen derivative which is volatile and stabilizes the body's natural defenses. It is non-toxic and can be given by injection into the lymph glands, by drops under the tongue, and by inhalation. It is called 714X and has apparently induced remission in some far-advanced cases of lung and breast cancer, among other types of cancer.

While it is difficult for me to understand all of the physics behind the Rife and Naessens microscopes, it is easy to see how the prototyped concept and live blood analysis were put aside with the development of the electron microscope with its high magnification and focus on the examination of dead tissue. However, both the now-deceased Dr. Virginia Livingston and Dr. Naessens have demonstrated that there is merit in pursuing this line of investigation for cancer treatment, with the intent of determining if all of these clinicians and scientists were not like the story about the blind men, groping and feeling, trying to describe the elephant.

SYSTEM 2: XENOGENIC PEPTIDES
Xenogenic peptides are small proteins, peptides, or amino acids in chains which on the one hand have the ability to convert cancer cells back toward normal and, on the other, can augment the immune response by stimulating the production of and increasing the activity

of natural killer cells. There are six xenogenic peptides in all, and some are on the market in Germany under the trade names of Ney-Tumorin and Neopterin. The latter activates the immune system parent cells known as macrophages. These xenogenic peptides are obtained from human fetal organs. They are used in the treatment of cancer, usually as an adjunct and not as the primary treatment.

Dr. Jesse M. Jaynes, of the Department of Biochemistry of Louisiana State University in Baton Rouge, and Dr. Ron Bernard, an anesthesiologist in New Orleans, have also been working with peptides and attempting to develop and promote the therapeutic use of them in this country in the management and treatment of human disease.

Jaynes discovered some small proteins or peptides which were not only active against bacteria, but were also capable of seeking out and destroying fungi and protozoa, which are larger microbes. In addition, diseased, infected, and cancerous cells were also destroyed by these peptides. These proteins are capable of disrupting cells and causing their dissolution and death.

The type Jaynes worked with are called cecropins. He has since synthesized other peptides which are capable of destroying leukemia and melanoma cells, according to Dr. Ron Bernard; however, this promising avenue of research is being ignored and is not leading anywhere in this country. Also, the thought of harvesting xenogenix peptides from fetal organs in the present pro-life climate is unthinkable, if not impossible.

SYSTEM 3: HEALTH PROMOTION IN THE ELDERLY WITH GEROVITAL H-3

Dr. Anna Aslan is the distinguished Director of the Bucharest Institute of Geriatrics. She is a recognized leader in her field, best known for her research and development of Gerovital H-3 treatments. She has been administering Gerovital treatments through he various clinics in Romania for more than twenty years, and severaɪ hundred thousand people have received these treatments.

Gerovital H-3 is procaine hydrochloride, and it is given by intramuscular injection in a dosage of 100 milligrams. A similar product called KH-3 is manufactured in West Germany and approved for use in the state of Nevada in the U.S. The only difference between GH-3 and KH-3 is one of dosage; KH-3 is given by IM injection as 50 milligrams of procaine hydrochloride. Both treatment programs were first introduced into the U.S. by Dr. Alfred Sapse of Miami, Florida, who worked for many years with Dr. Aslan.

We know that procaine breaks down in the body and becomes an anti-depressant because one of the breakdown products is a monoamine oxidase inhibitor; many drugs which inhibit the enzyme monoamine oxidase are effective anti-depressants. Dr. Aslan, however, also believes that procaine hydrochloride retards the aging process and extends the mental and physical vigor of earlier years. She recommends that these treatments begin ideally around the age of forty. As a result of her treatments, individuals have experienced marked improvement in their physical and mental well-being. Mental awareness and memory have also improved, and periods of mental depression have been greatly reduced.

Most scientists believe that the treatments are useful, but that there is insufficient evidence that they retard the aging process. There is some evidence, however, that in addition to breaking down to an anti-depressant, it also lowers serum cortisol levels and probably thereby mitigates the effects of stress.

SYSTEM 4: McDANIEL'S TREATMENT AND PREVENTION OF KIDNEY STONES

Dr. T.C. McDaniel, an osteopathic physician from Cincinnati, Ohio, developed what is called anionic surfactant therapy to control colloidal aggregation within the ureter (the tube which collects urine from the kidney and drains into the bladder).

This therapy is based on the fact that, normally, blood contains more anions than cations in a ratio of 5 parts to 3 parts. This is known as the anion gap and is a reflection of a negative voltage potential that causes the red cells, for example, to repel one another and prevents them from clumping together. It also keeps other particulate matter in blood and urine from clumping together. This negative electrical charge, called the zeta potential, approaches 19 millivolts. McDaniel proposes that through the use of anions such as K-citrate and Na-citrate, one can develop a safety factor sufficient to interrupt stone formation by restoring the balance of 5:3 anions to cations. This practice should be accompanied and/or followed by a reduction in cation ingestion. Following ingestion of excessive cations, the normal anion gap (5:3) begins to close; therefore zeta potential drops in the direction of intravascular coagulation.

McDaniel also recommends following a certain regimen of therapy to dissolve kidney stones that have already formed. Other physicians have reported that he can successfully dissolve most common stones in six to eight hours. His regimen consists of:

(1) Intravenous infusion of a suitable anionic surfactant, i.e. 1.5 grams of EDTA in glucose 5% made up 250 ml daily X 30.

(2) Consumption of only mineral-free H_2O (distilled or from a competent reverse-osmosis module unit).

(3) Consumption of mineral-free water in a quantity determined by dividing body weight by 2 and converting resulting figure to ounces (for example, if body weight is 180 lbs., drink 90 ounces mineral-free water per day). Mineral-free water raises the zeta potential to a safe degree of dispersion, to 30 millivolts to 60 millivolts Zeta potential.

(4) One-half of this mineral-free water per day will be anionically charged using McDaniel's negative water (to which potassium and sodium citrate have been added), as directed. This negative water mixture is consumed on an empty stomach, i.e. 15 minutes before eating. Time from stomach to plasma is 8 minutes.

(5) Use smooth muscle relaxants (such as Papaverine HCl) to relax the ureters.

(6) Most patients flush out the stone in 4-6 hours with anionic surfactants by intravenous infusion and by mouth.

(7) Analgesics strong enough for complete relief of pain, such as Demerol, Percodan, etc., are mandatory.

(8) Post-incidence: Train patient to avoid cations of food, drink, and medication; iatrogenicity is altogether too common.

This regimen will reduce, if not completely eliminate, episodes of renal calculi.

Prophylactically, a supplemental source of anions can be used, such as McDaniel's negative water added to regular distilled water. This mixture should be consumed daily. About 8-10 ounces of the mixture should be consumed before each meal, three times daily. Alternatively, a source of anions such as SP54, which is a sodium salt of the sugar pentose combined with multiple sulfate anions, can be used as a food supplement.

SYSTEM 5: DR. REVICI'S SYSTEM OF MEDICINE— SUCCESSFUL MANAGEMENT OF CANCER

Another alternative system of treatment which can be used for a variety of pathological conditions was developed by Dr. Emmanuel Revici, M.D., of New York, a favorite target of Organized Med. Best known for his contribution to pathology, he was one of the initial researchers to explore the properties of lipids and the role that they play in disease. This system relies on two opposing processes in physiology: anabolic (constructing) activity and catabolic (breaking down) activity. His examination of lipids demonstrated that they can also be classified as either catabolic (i.e. fatty acids) or anabolic (i.e. sterols).

Through sixty years of research, Dr. Revici has developed and refined his own system of therapeutic alternatives to conventional medical treatment. He has administered his treatments to people inflicted with cancer, radiation, trauma, and infection. His system is based on a combination of theories from Newtonian and nuclear physics, which he has applied to medicine. According to Revici, in order for the body to satisfactorily remain in homeostasis (good health), it fluctuates from anabolic to catabolic activity in response to the demands exerted from the environment and the needs of the body. When a person becomes ill, particularly with a chronic degenerative disease such as cancer, one of these processes is always predominant. Through further investigation into these mechanisms, Revici discovered that they could be applied to therapeutic agents.

The premise of his medical treatment is that during illness an imbalance has occurred between anabolic and catabolic activity and that in order for it to be corrected, a therapy which counteracts the dominating process should be utilized. For example, if a disease has been induced by a predominance of anabolic activity, a therapy with catabolic activity would be used. Revici categorized all of the known elements as either a participant in anabolic or catabolic processes, according to a complex classification scheme which he devised.

Dr. Revici developed a series of analyses which indicate the presence of and changes in these imbalances. This system's approach to treatment is very individualistic. Each person is treated according to his specific needs, and dosages are altered when analysis indicates that the body's daily needs have changed. Revici has termed his strategy of treatment "individually guided non-toxic chemotherapy." This technique is innovative in medical treatment. All of his therapeutic agents are rigorously tested for toxicity before they are used clinically.

GARLIC

In 1988, Dr. Tariq Abdullah, a black American Muslim friend of mine and a garlic researcher, asked for my assistance in his paper published in the *Journal of the National Medical Association (Vol. 80, No. 430),* entitled "Garlic Revisited: Therapeutic for the Major Diseases of our Time?" Alternative doctors have used garlic and onions for decades. They contain a number of curious sulfur-containing compounds responsible for the odor of garlic and the tearing effect of sliced onion. These compounds most likely account for the medical properties long ascribed to garlic and onions throughout man's history.

This initial collaboration led to subsequent investigations of a special garlic preparation called kyolic, which is produced by the Japanese company Wakunaga. Kyolic is an extract from garlic which is aged for at least 1½ years. Garlic is like wine and cognac in that it improves with aging. The vitamin B_1 or thiamine in the garlic, upon aging, is converted to a sulfur-containing thiamine called TTFD. A synthetic analogue of this compound is one of the reagents we are proposing to use in the treatment of AIDS infection and in the treatment of CMV viral infection following kidney, heart and liver transplantation.

In an 1989 issue of the *European Journal,* Dr. Abdullah, Dr. Kirkpatrick and I published an article entitled "Enhancement of Natural Killer Cell Activity in AIDS with Garlic." This preliminary study showed that AIDS patients, when treated with an oral preparation of aged garlic, got a boost to their natural killer cell activity. In two or three patients, there was a reversal of their T-helper and T-suppressor ratios. Some also got increases in their T-helper or T_4 cell counts. Six out of seven of these AIDS patients showed significant enhancement of their natural killer cell response.

We postulated that the aged garlic extract acted in one of two ways: (1) it stimulated natural killer cell activity, or (2) it had a direct anti-viral effect. We now lean more toward the first possibility: it apparently stimulates the body's own natural defense cells to rid itself of the organism. This is most likely done through oxidative mechanisms. In science there has been a single-minded focus only on the anti-viral effects of a drug or reagent, excluding any possibility that the reagent could be acting by stimulating the cells to defend themselves.

There are two garlic preparations that we are interested in testing in patients with viral infections. They are allithiamine, (a synthetic version of TTFD) and allitride, which has been produced by Dr. Lu

Dao Pei in Beijing, China, from a more crude garlic extract and which contains three sulfur atoms in its molecular structure, not just two, as TTFD does.

Dr. Lu has been using garlic therapeutically for over twenty years. He has been using an infusate of garlic ingredients which have been given intravenously for nearly ten years. One problem has been to determine if there is one principal active ingredient in garlic. The ingredient which appears to be a main, if not the major anti-viral principal, is allitride. This compound is chemically known as di-allyl-trisulphide. It represents the largest peak when garlic oils are analyzed by gas liquid chromatography.

There are different species of garlic found in the U.S., Japan, and China. Garlic is used in China mainly as a medicine taken by mouth in pill form. It has also been given by mouth, as we have done, to treat immuno-compromised patients. Sometimes, however, garlic oil is also used. In addition, in the central provinces of China, epidemiologic data suggests a difference in the incidence of stomach cancer, which is lower in the areas where garlic is regularly consumed than in those areas where it is not consumed.

Dr. Lu has used crude whole garlic extract intravenously in many of his patients who have had bone marrow transplantation. Interstitial pneumonia due to the cyto-megalo-virus (CMV) virus is a major obstacle or complication following bone marrow transplantation. This virus is very prevalent in China and antibodies to CMV can be found in 96% of the Chinese population surveyed in urban areas. Infection with this virus is usually sub-clinical. However, in the immuno-compromised patient, such as the patient with AIDS, CMV virus can cause disease and, in the case of interstitial pneumonia, can even cause death. Dr. Lu has been able to treat, but mostly to prevent, interstitial pneumonia following bone marrow transplantation in nearly all of his patients since he has used the intravenous garlic extract. He has had the same success with using allitride, which can be described as a preparation obtained on further purification of the garlic extract. It is allitride, a tri-sulphide, and allithiamine, a di-sulphide, that we are proposing to test against the HIV virus associated with AIDS.

Garlic may therefore have a therapeutic role to play in AIDS because of its potential as an anti-microbial and immune modulator. Additional studies in the test tube in the laboratory and in experimental animals have shown garlic's effectiveness against many of the opportunistic microbes seen in AIDS. The studies in animals and humans suggest that garlic has the capacity to stimulate immunity; that it is a biologic response modifier; that in aged garlic, its thiamine content is converted to a more potent form, TTFD, which is better absorbed, penetrates the cell, and enhances host defense mechanisms.

In the test tube and in human trials in China at Beijing Medical University, bone-marrow transplantation cases have shown the efficacy of a purified garlic extract in preventing and curing CMV virus, as well as fungal infections. These infections are common in this group of patients. CMV and fungal infections are also frequently seen in AIDS patients, and they contribute significantly to morbidity and mortality. The effectiveness of this garlic extract has not been studied in AIDS patients. Studies in animals and humans using oral and parenteral IM or IV preparations of garlic and its derivatives have not been associated with toxicities. Minor local irritations at injection sites and flatulence from oral preparations are the most common side-effects noted. We believe that well-organized and well-monitored clinical trials are indicated to determine if garlic and its derivatives may have clinical applications in the treatment of infections associated with AIDS.

Why then have these reagents or derivatives not been clinically tested in the U.S. or, for that matter, elsewhere outside of China? Have Dr. Anthony Fauci and his colleagues in charge of AIDS research at the federal level been looking for drugs in all the wrong places because they're still in hot pursuit of "magic bullets" designed to kill the AIDS virus? There are no, and will be no, magic bullets—such would almost certainly kill a patient's normal cells as well. Years of conditioning and thought-process programming by the drug companies have caused medicine to seek the paradigm of the allopathic (disease-treating) drug model and ignore the possibilities of the immuno-stimulant (health-building) model.

Sabotage by biological competitors of recently approved antiviral drugs may also be taking place. Recently our compound allitride was compared in-vitro with the anti-viral drugs gancyclovir. Both the first set of results from the University of Alabama (which had been commissioned by the National Institutes of Health) and the results from China showed that 3.8 mg/ml of allitride could reduce CMV infection by 50%. It took 3.2 mg/ml of the synthetic gancyclovir to do the same. Then suddenly these reports were "corrected" by the University of Alabama: The decimal point had been moved one digit to the left for gancyclovir (0.32 mg/ml). Instead of about 3 mg., it now only took 1/3 of a mg. This movement of the decimal point would make gancyclovir ten times more potent than the natural, inexpensive garlic extract, allitride.

Such a "mistake" is excusable in high-school science—but from the NIH? Could the NIH be just another purveyor of pharmaceutical interests? Don't they want the natural, biological therapy to rank on a par with a synthetic registered pharmaceutical? I guess not and it's clear why not.

Garlic has many other therapeutic properties which are beyond the scope of this lay book. The interested reader is referred to the proceedings of the First World Congress on the Health Significance of Garlic and Garlic Constituents, held in Washington, D.C., on August 28-30, 1990. This conference was sponsored by the public relations firm of Nutrition International of California, Pennsylvania State University, and the U.S. Department of Agriculture. The conference was summarized by science writer Jane Brody, on September 4, 1990, in the *New York Times* article entitled "After 4,000 Years Medical Science Considers Garlic: Preliminary Studies Suggest Ancient Herbalists May Have Been on to Something."

Chronic fatigue syndrome (CFS) or, as it is now called, chronic immune dysfunction syndrome (CIDS) is a condition which is also known by the Japanese as low natural killer cell syndrome. There is suggestive evidence that this syndrome, like AIDS, is associated with infection from a retrovirus. It may also respond to garlic extract, allitride, or allithiamine. Other substances such as lentinan, a glucan extracted from the Japanese shitake mushroom, stimulates natural killer cells and their activity, and this substance has been used successfully in the treatment of CIDS.

Even if the Western medical virologists are incapable of making a paradigmatic shift, Western transplant surgeons should certainly take note. Infection with CMV virus is a major cause of failure of organ transplant surgery. This is true regardless of the type of transplant surgery, e.g. bone marrow, kidney, heart, liver, etc. The CMV virus often becomes invasive and causes an interstitial pneumonia with a high death rate.

THE HYPOIONIC PROTEIN PROFILE

There is also a new test, based on blood proteins, which is being evaluated by Drs. Andreas Maestian and Peter van der Schaar in Belgium and Holland and, to a more limited extent, by Dr. Conrad Maulfair in Pennsylvania. The test is called the Hypoionic Protein Profile, and it measures what can best be described as disease tendencies, e.g. the tendency to develop cancer, the tendency to develop gastrointestinal disease, the tendency to develop liver disease or immune system dysfunction, etc. The combination of this test, the

Hypoionic Protein Profile, with the above-mentioned screening maneuvers would appear to be the way of the future for the annual or periodic examination of the future. I am proud to know personally many of the investigators involved in the pioneering work on the development of the Hypoionic Protein Profile, or "HIP," as it has come to be affectionately called.

CHAPTER 14
THE U.N. ENDORSES PRIMARY HEALTH CARE AND TAKES A WORLD VIEW

1989 INTERNATIONAL CONFERENCE ON HOLISTIC HEALTH IN MEDICINE

The first International Conference on Holistic Health in Medicine met in November, 1989, in India. Its major objective was the creation of an international network, one body to promote and represent holistic health in medicine throughout the world. The conference assembled for the first time spiritual leaders, eminent doctors and other practitioners from many backgrounds and disciplines, both modern and traditional.

On the podium were the Honorable Dalai Lama and His Grace Paulose Gregarios, President of the World Council of Churches. Also on the podium were members of the India organizing committee, the state governor and presidents of the British and American Holistic Medical Associations and the World Health Foundation.

The Dalai Lama reminded doctors that in addition to their holistic therapies, they "should not overlook the power of compassion alone, conferred effectively through the warmth of a smile."

Dr. Gregarios stressed five major points that the holistic movement should carefully resolve:

1. Iatrogenic (doctor-induced) disease
2. Secondary effects (side effects) of therapies
3. Long-term effects of antibiotics
4. Technology treatments beyond the patients' financial means to pay
5. The dumping of harmful substances on third-world countries, *e.g.*, toxic wastes, unhealthy food products, outdated medicines, etc.

Dr. Gregarios also cautioned about certain fringe ideas surrounding the valid holistic methods but advised an open mind in their investigation for the possibility of undiscovered scientific truths.

Two other presenters at the conference, Foon and Myrin Boysenko, reminded the group that "it was not scientific to say that prayer is a potent source of healing and is dose-related. Loneliness is a dose-related antagonist to human viability."

In discussing the stresses of modern urban life, Foon found it helpful to imagine herself as a sacred white cow of India when she found herself mired in the urban India traffic (a metaphor which the other participants by this time all understood). As the cow blissfully ignores its surroundings, so should we strive not to stress ourselves. Foon counseled for all to try to release ourselves from the myriad of petty distractions, as no one will make room for us as they do the sacred Indian cow.

Another speaker, Dr. Steven Fulder, informed the group that up to 80% of the population in Europe attended alternative practitioners; three-fourths of the family doctors in England and New Zealand referred to alternative practitioners; and 50% of the family doctors practice some forms of alternative approaches although they are sometimes not well-trained in those methods.

DR. ROBERT MULLER SPEAKS ON HOLISM

Dr. Robert Muller, former Assistant Secretary of the United Nations, spoke on holism at a gathering in Seattle. He announced that the U.N. and the World Health Organization were developing an international holistic medical association. According to Muller, this is the only way in which holistic medicine could become implemented around the world. With UN sponsorship, local antagonistic medical authorities and government officials could be passed over and actually become subservient to a world order holistic medical association.

The impending effects of overpopulation, the depletion of the ozone layer, the destruction of the Amazon rain forest, and legal and illegal drug addiction, supported by governments and drug companies, were some of the imperative reasons to create an international holistic health care system.

Acknowledging the foresight of the famous German philosopher Wilhelm Leibniz, Muller then relayed how Leibniz foresaw the scientific rational revolution in which we are currently engulfed. He predicted that for hundreds of years the human species would be fascinated by and occupied with analyzing the surrounding reality. Scientists would become ever more diversified and specialized. People would have an endless, trusting fascination with science's specializations and forget the totality. He accurately predicted that there would be several hundred years without any universal thinking. That is exactly what happened. He foresaw that the complexity and specialization of our discoveries would create the need for a total, global or, if you will, a holistic view; and this time has now arrived. This holistic revolution, with its wisdom to see the total picture, now appears in all fields throughout the world, making room for a unified interrelationship for all life on earth.

A current major problem for the United Nations: When the U.S. or a like-minded European country bans harmful chemicals or drugs, the internationally linked drug cartels immediately apply for an export license to sell these banned products to Third World countries. These impoverished, struggling nations fall victim to the banned drugs and chemicals. When they learn too late of their deathly effects, they are powerless to effectively rid themselves of the dangers and stand up to the internationally interlocked drug corporations that even the advanced countries cannot control.

For the first time in human history, it is being asked, "Is what we're doing good for the planet, for all humanity—or not?" A crisis from which there can be no turning back is brewing because few nations ponder this question. They ask only, "Is it good for my nation? For my territory? And the rest of the world be damned!" A "my nation, me first" approach is the biggest challenge facing the U.N.: What is good for my firm is bad for our community; what is good for my nation can be bad for our world; what's bad for our planet is good for my firm.

We need to have faith in our future. There exists little interest, little faith in the future. We are bound to the here and now, the physical, the measurable, the statistical. We must develop a perception of the incredible mystery of the Universe.

Dr. Muller spoke of the honor of working with former U.N. Secretary-General U Thant, a Buddhist. This great man deplored verbal violence as Westerners deplore physical violence. Buddhist and Hindu philosophers decry verbal violence—talk is a cosmic process, and violence can enter language.

Taking the concept a step further, violence should not even enter thought. Non-violent thought and language lead to a non-violent world. Physical violence could be reduced if we stopped verbal violence, as verbal violence begets physical violence. Hitler's speeches of violent thought turned into violent action. To this day people applaud language that appeals to the aggressive nature of mankind.

The Hindu culture in India celebrates dance, music, and art to lead into union with the divine. The union is the universe, the eternal stream of time.

On the island of Bali, the highest art is the way people live each day. One's daily life is the greatest contribution that people can make for the peace, love and happiness for all mankind. Let us make our lives a work of art, a masterpiece of kindness, love and peace—multiplied times 4¼ billion of us.

This could change the world—and bring forth the kind of leadership so desperately needed but now thwarted by the trappings of political power, science, and military weapons. We must all demand a holistic, caring approach for the human family. Every single one of us can and must inspire all others. There are no great people any more, for every individual is a great person.

"Make each and every one of your lives a work of art."

For the reader's edification, I have included the text of Dr. Muller's thought-provoking talk on the concept of holism in its entirety in the appendix of this book.

AIDS: AN EXAMPLE OF A LACK OF A HOLISTIC APPROACH

The entire U.S. approach to AIDS is an example of a lack of a Holistic Approach to the study of the AIDS virus and the AIDS epidemic. In a recent issue of the Brazilian equivalent of *Time* magazine, called *Veja,* journalist Cristina Lopes de Medeiros interviewed French researcher Dr. Luc Montagnier in an article entitled "We Are Going To Conquer AIDS."

Ms. Lopes reported that, in 1983, the team of the French professor Luc Montagnier of the Pasteur Institute of Paris dedicated itself to the study of the virus which causes of AIDS. In this same year, ahead of the other scientists in the world, the team isolated for the first time in the laboratory the virus which has come to be known as HIV. Two years later, they were able to repeat the process with the isolation of the strain of virus HIV-II, which is responsible for the illness in the countries of east Africa. The work of Montagnier and his team opened the doors to the development of blood and molecular tests, to anti-viral therapy, and more recently to a vaccine. The discovery of the virus, nevertheless, has always been more associated with the name of the American professor Robert Gallo of the National Cancer Institute, in Bethesda, Maryland. The Institute announced the discovery of the virus in Dr. Gallo's laboratory nearly one year after its discovery in Dr. Montagnier's laboratory. From this moment on, the two investigative teams were locked in a dispute regarding who was the father of the virus and only resolved this question in an agreement which was signed between France and the U.S. in 1987. More recently, however, the *Chicago Tribune* announced the existence of documents which prove that there was evidence of fraud in the work of Robert Gallo.

The *Chicago Tribune* revealed that the respected doctor and researcher, Dr. Robert Gallo, had manipulated certain information in order to identify himself with the discovery of the virus of AIDS, when in reality this discovery belonged to the team of the Pasteur Institute in Paris, with whom he had collaborated. Ms. Lopes posed to Dr. Montagnier the question "Who is the real discoverer of this virus?" Professor Montagnier replied:

> The Administration of the Pasteur Institute in Paris has never recognized Professor Gallo as the discoverer or even the co-discoverer of the virus of AIDS. Our team concluded, in May of 1983, investigations initiated four months before, with the isolation of the virus of a new type and distinctly different from the virus thatGallo had described in his works, which had been labelled HTLV-II.
>
> After this, we proceeded to establish that this virus was the real cause of AIDS, and we arrived at this conclusion after conducting various tests in patients suffering from the illness. We developed for the first time a test of this type of virus which is called ELISA. All of these data were presented in September of 1983 at the respected American Congress of Cold Spring Harbour which earned us the violent scientific criticism of Gallo and his colleagues.
>
> In the same period, we sent various samples of the virus to our American colleagues. Some months afterwards,Gallo announced the discovery of the virus which he baptized as HTLV-III. Comparing his virus with ours, we concluded that the truth was, that they were one and the same.

Ms. Lopez then asked, "Does this mean that Gallo committed a fraud announcing the discovery of a virus which had already been discovered six months before by your team?"

Montagnier replied:

> I cannot prove this. I believe, however, that there could have been a "contamination in his laboratory." This means that it is possible that the virus that we sent to him had contaminated other cultures in his laboratory, giving an edge to Dr. Gallo that resulted in his identifying a "new virus." In any

case, the question was resolved bureaucratically, and the issue was closed with an agreement signed between the countries in 1987. This agreement established a French patent with co-authorship on the part of the Americans. It does not refer to who is the father of the virus, but only to the "applications of the discovery."

Ms. Lopes continued, "What does this mean from a financial point of view? Who receives today the royalties from the discovery of the virus?"

Montagnier replied, "I do not know the exact numbers, but I believe that the Pasteur Institute receives about 8,000,000 francs ($1.2 million) a year in royalties divided among 12 members of the team. What seems to me injust, and even immoral, is that because of the rights of patent authorship in the U.S., the U.S. investigators at NIH also each receive $100,000 per year."

A more holistic approach on the part of Luc Montagnier can also be seen in some of his other responses to Ms. Lopes' questions. For example, Dr. Montagnier believes that AIDS is not the pest of the century, but that it is a serious illness, about which we already know a great deal, and one which can be controlled. He postulates the existence of co-factors of an infectious nature which can accelerate the multiplication and the action of the virus. His experiments indicate that certain bacteria are capable of aiding the virus in its destruction of the cells of the immune system, and, in the absence of these bacteria, the virus is much less devastating and not always fatal. He qualifies, however, that naturally these results which were obtained in the laboratory have to be prudently extrapolated to the human organism. Nevertheless, he believes that if we can eliminate these bacteria, that we will be able to attenuate the effects of the virus of AIDS.

With regard to the development of a vaccine, Professor Montagnier says that it is possible to immunize a person against one type of AIDS virus, but we don't know for exactly how long. Also, the vaccine may guarantee immunity against one type of virus which was used in its manufacture, but the virus of AIDS is very variable, and there are many types of the AIDS virus. One solution would be to produce a vaccine combining the most important types of AIDS viruses. However, in the case of Africa, not all of the different types have been identified. We cannot consider a vaccination campaign against AIDS before we determine the period of efficacy of the vaccine and before we have determined the various types of the virus which have to be included in the vaccine.

Montagnier also believes that the AIDS virus is very old. The factors which propitiate its toxic action, however, are recent. For example, commerce in the sale of blood for transfusions, as well as the use of hypodermic syringes, are only decades old. In addition, the expansion of drug abuse is a relatively recent phenomenon. Homosexuality, on the other hand, is as old as humanity itself, but it has only become massively widespread in the last twenty years, facilitating the spread of contagion.

Actually, comparisons of the percentages of diagnosed cases between 1988 and 1989 revealed that the homosexual and bisexual group represent declines, with the lowest estimated increase in the incidence of the disease. Two important factors have slowed the growth in the incidence of this disease in this group, in the countries of the northern hemisphere. First, in these countries certain types of infectious bacteria which reinforce the action of the virus are very difficult to acquire, due to climate and other conditions of hygiene. Secondly, in these countries the major part of the population is capable of developing a good immune system, thanks to good nutrition.

"Does the doctor mean to say that it is possible to escape AIDS, if you are well nourished?" asked Ms. Lopes.

Dr. Montagnier responded:

Good, balanced, nutrition helps in the development of a resistant immune system to any type of virus, including the virus of AIDS. A person in good health who is well-nourished and consequently develops a good immune system is capable of preventing the virus from establishing itself in the organism. On the other hand, when we examine the various high risk groups, we see that they are more susceptible to the virus because they have pre-existing immune deficiencies.

"This is understandable in the case of drug addicts, for example, those who are addicted to heroin and who have a depressed immune system, but how does this apply to the homosexuals?" asked Ms. Lopes.

Dr. Montagnier responded:

I have proved that male homosexuals also suffer from depression of the immune system. Did you know that sperm contains immuno-depressing substances which are filtered out by the vaginal mucosa, making this mucosa relatively more impermeable to the proper virus of AIDS; but not so in the case of the anal mucosa. For this reason, anal sexual relations is a risk factor, even for women.

I personally believe that Gallo legitimately isolated the AIDS virus one year after Luc Montagnier had done so. In addition, the difficulties arose between France and the U.S. largely because of the arrogance with which Dr. Gallo's announcement was presented in the press and on television. This was not a case of arrogant ignorance, but simply one of arrogance. At the June, 1990, International AIDS Conference in San Francisco, it was announced that an NIH ad Hoc investigative committee had exonerated Dr. Gallo of any fraud or wrongdoing in the isolation of the AIDS virus. This announcement apparently was premature, because, as was subsequently reported in the *New York Times,* only a preliminary report had been completed, which was being submitted for review by higher authorities. The final report recommended that Dr. Gallo be censured, but that recommendation was not accepted by the NIH central administration. Instead, they had the Director of the Office of Scientific Integrity, which had prepared the report, and her staff transferred elsewhere in the bureaucracy and investigated by the F.B.I. for "leaks to the press." "Prime Time Live" put the final nails in the coffin when they did a piece entitled "The Rise and Fall of Dr. Robert Gallo" on April 2, 1992. The whole affair is mentioned here because it is representative of the corruption in the system and the self-delusion and denial which is reminiscent of "The Emperor's New Clothes."

In the interim, Dr. Gallo's assistant in the laboratory, Mr. Syed Zaki Salahuddin, was suspended without pay pending criminal investigation of his ties to a Maryland company, Pan-Data Systems, Inc. Salahuddin and his wife, Firoza, "owned a controlling interest in Pan-Data during a time when Gallo's laboratory was spending hundreds of thousands of dollars with the company." Gallo, according to GAO investigators, is extremely unhappy about the Salahuddin investigation and expressed concern "that damage to his image might cost him [Gallo] a Nobel prize." Meanwhile, Gallo also had to contend with the separate NIH inquiry of himself, which attempted to resolve a "number of apparent anomalies and discrepancies in his research on the AIDS virus." In its entirety, the U.S. approach to AIDS, like its approach to cancer and other chronic diseases, has been fragmented and lacks synthesis; it lacks a holistic perspective.

THE WORLD HEALTH ORGANIZATION'S OBJECTIVE OF HEALTH FOR ALL AND ITS POSITION ON ALTERNATIVES

According to Dr. Maureen Law, former Deputy Minister of Health for Canada and former chairperson of WHO's Executive Board, the World Health Organization's objective since 1978 has been "Health For All by the Year 2000." While this objective now seems unrealistic, the original intent was to provide an opportunity for every individual to achieve optimum health by the year 2000. It was not meant to provide access to comprehensive health care for everyone on the planet by that year. Primary health care, however, is thought to be the principal vehicle by which health for all could be promoted.

Also according to Dr. Law, the historical background of this objective, which was adopted by WHO in 1978, is as follows:

It was at the 30th World Health Assembly in 1977 that the accepted goal of health for all by the year 2000 was adopted. They were not expecting that disease and disabilities were going to disappear by the year 2000, but rather that resources for health would be equitably distributed and that essential health care with a minimum of essential services would be accessible to everyone. And they said that their goal was that all citizens of the world should attain a level of health that would permit them to lead socially and economically productive lives. The following year, in Alma Ata in the USSR, the International Conference on Primary Health Care declared in the Declaration of Alma Ata that primary health care would be the key to attaining that goal of health for all. The Declaration of Alma Ata defined the essential elements of primary health care:

(1) Education concerning prevailing health problems and the measures of preventing and controlling them.

(2) Promotion of food supply and proper nutrition.

(3) An adequate supply of safe water and basic sanitation services.

(4) Maternal and child health care, including family planning.

(5) Immunization against the major infectious diseases.

(6) Prevention and control of locally endemic diseases.

(7) Appropriate treatment of common diseases and injury.

(8) Provision of essential drugs.

The declaration called on all governments to formulate national policy strategies and plans of action to launch and sustain primary health care as part of a comprehensive national health system and coordination with other health sectors. They also called upon governments and all the array of international organizations, multilateral agencies, nongovernmental agencies, funding agencies, all health workers and the world community to support national and international commitment to primary health care and to channel increased technical and financial support to it, particularly in developing countries.

In 1979, the World Health Assembly endorsed the Declaration of Alma Ata. They began to work then on strategies and policies to implement primary health care. In 1981 the Assembly adopted a global strategy for health for all by the year 2000. The main thrust of the strategy was the development of health systems' infrastructure, starting country-wide programs of primary health care that would reach the whole population. Programs would include the eight essential elements of primary health care mentioned above, that essentially cover the bases of health promotion, and disease prevention, diagnosis, therapy, and rehabilitation. That strategy specified measures that should be taken by individuals and family, as well as by communities and by the health services at all levels. It emphasized the need for technology appropriate for the country concerned. It also emphasized the importance of social control of the health infrastructure and technology, through a high degree of community involvement, and, finally, it spelled out the international action needed to support such national action and provided some monitoring for progress.

At the same time that the Assembly adopted the strategy, it requested the Executive Board to prepare a final document for its implementation. As a result, the plan of action for implementing global strategy was presented and approved at the Assembly in 1982. That plan really expanded on the strategy that had been adopted earlier, but provided more detail about the actions to be taken at national and international levels, and it spelled out some time-tables for their completion. Although all this started back in 1977, it took until 1982 to get the details of the plan of action, and in 1989—more than a decade after the adoption of the goal of health for all and about half-way between 1977 and the year 2000—the Assembly considered the second progress report on the implementation of the strategy. That report was drawn primarily from six regional reports, which in turn had been based upon the progress reports submitted from 143 countries using a common framework for monitoring progress. The report focused mainly on the measures taken and the progress made by member states in the development of health policies and health systems based on primary health care. It also discussed something of the main difficulties and obstacles which had been encountered in achieving further progress.

The report stated that there had been uneven progress in integrating, developing, monitoring, and evaluating the processes of health for all within national health systems and that health information systems were urgently in need of improvement. Despite the adverse socio-political and economic trends affecting many countries during the period, there were some glimpses of hope in the actions taken by some member-states. Nevertheless, there was some indication that the situation of the poorest of the poor might have worsened. For example, food production had fallen drastically in Africa, parts of the eastern Mediterranean region, and Latin America. Although countries in the latter region had made up for this by food importation, hunger had substantially increased in Africa. Moreover, the world's population was growing at an average annual rate of 1.73%, but in thirty-one countries, mostly in the African and Eastern Mediterranean regions, the average annual rate of growth is over 3%.

Many countries throughout the world have had to reduce the rate of growth in government expenditures for social services including education, health, and subsidies for staple foods.

The overall response to the 1989 report from countries seems to reflect a continuing commitment to health for all principles. But there seems to be a better understanding of the strategic changes required, especially by the political and executive leadership, than there is of the processes that are necessary to bring about these changes. Nevertheless, many developing countries have managed to expand community health facilities, especially in the rural areas. A growing challenge is the rapid expansion of poor urban populations. Although the rationale and potential value of intersectional action in health has been generally well accepted, there are many practical difficulties in putting the concept into operation. Few countries have been able to pursue, successfully, a true intersectional policy in a comprehensive framework for health and social development.

It is apparent that countries are moving to increase community involvement in health and related matters. Most commonly in developing countries, communities are involved in local health activities such as selecting and being responsible for village health workers, participating in health campaigns, and collaborating in sanitation activities.

In the developed countries, the emphasis has been on involving the public in promoting healthy lifestyles. Perhaps the most dramatic example has been the campaign against tobacco in many parts of the world. But very few countries have evolved or developed truly innovative or creative approaches to building real partnerships with a view to self-reliance. In most situations, communities are viewed as complementary resources for health activities rather than as the principal actors. The need to increase the knowledge of communities in health matters, to improve literacy among women, and to re-orient health workers is particularly urgent. An appropriate balance of human resources has not been achieved in most countries, nor have they achieved an equitable distribution of resources, particularly between urban and rural areas. That can be said of both developed and developing countries. All too often in developing countries, 80% of the trained health workers are in urban areas and 80% of the population are in the rural areas. Changes in the educational content have been slow. But the Latin American and U.S. Associations of Schools of Public Health, in collaboration with PAHO, did launch a progressive approach to curriculum review for public health professionals in education.

Information on the proportion of GNP spent on health was available for 131 countries. About half spent over 5%, the average being 4.6%. In the least developed countries, the average was 2.3%. In countries facing extreme scarcity of resources, there are few options for mobilizing new resources. The World Bank is working with many countries on "structural adjustments." It appears that if an adjustment takes place those measures further jeopardize the poorest and most vulnerable.

As far as safe water and sanitation are concerned, availability has been improving, but there is a long way to go. It is estimated that in rural areas, availability of safe water supply increased from 31% to 41%, and of sanitation from 14% to 20%.

Immunization coverage is also continuing to improve. In the developing world, immunization services, which were reaching less than 5% of children in 1974, were reaching 60% by 1988. By the end of 1992, they should reach about 75%.

Virtually no progress has been made in the protection of pregnant women against tetanus. Coverage remains at around 20%.

There was poor reporting by countries on local health care coverage and provision of care by trained personnel during pregnancy and childbirth. About one-third of the countries reporting failed to report on these items. For those that did report on them, the coverage for local care ranged from 50% to 100% in some developed countries. The coverage for mothers and infants averaged just over 50%.

Environmental health issues are clearly linked to population growth and technological development. For the past decade, life-threatening environmental hazards have come to light in both the developing and developed worlds. In many parts of the world, the population is growing at rates which cannot be sustained by available environmental resources. In the face of expanding industrialization, energy use, and growing urbanization, the maintenance of a healthy and safe environment will require a lot of attention between now and the year 2000.

When we view, therefore, the activities of Organized Medicine (which includes the pharmaceutical industries and such groups as the NCAHF) and their collaborators in federal agencies in the context of WHO's objective of Health for All by the Year 2000, we come to the conclusion that the focus of these groups in the U.S. is a narrow one. There is as great a need for primary health care in this country as there is in developing countries. Although lip service is paid to general practitioners and family practitioners, in reality we have a medical profession of specialists. These specialists control the practice of medicine, and their vested interests are the driving force for the ever-increasing emphasis on new and better technologies, the fragmentation and compartmentalization of patient care, and the exorbitant fees charged for invasive procedures of all kinds. Their needs become dominant, and a holistic approach to the patient, in the context of primary health care, becomes subservient or, more accurately, falls through the cracks.

The groups mentioned above concentrate on the provision of medical care to those who can afford to pay, using the most sophisticated technology and prescribing only surgery, radiation, and so-called "ethical pharmaceuticals" for the treatment of various diseases. They have organized themselves in such a way as to monopolize the provision of care in order to maximize profits for the medico-pharmaceutical-industrial complex. The concept of an "opportunity to achieve optimum health in order to be socially and economically productive" does not exist. Also, the concept that there should be a partnership with the community does not exist. Lastly, the concept that there should be other health practitioners, non-physicians, who could facilitate and aid in the processes of health promotion and disease prevention, does not exist.

This, therefore, is the picture in the U.S. The intent of our medical system is to make money for health-care providers and for the manufacturers of sophisticated technology and drugs used to diagnose and treat various diseases. It makes a mockery of the concept of Health for All by the Year 2000, which was intended for all nation-states and not just for the developing countries.

Another aspect of Health for All by the Year 2000 which is relevant in this context is the incorporation of traditional medicine, as it is called in the developing countries, or "natural medicine" as it is called in some industrialized countries. The latter also includes the incorporation of Eastern pain-control, healing techniques such as acupuncture and stress-management techniques, such as yoga and Zen meditational practices and other alternative or complementary therapies discussed in this book. If they are safe and effective and have been proven by the test of time, or in other words "generally regarded as safe," then these treatment modalities are to be, and should be, included in the array of therapeutic and health promoting procedures/maneuvers which can be provided within the context of primary health care.

In 1978, WHO published, as part of their Technical Report Series (Number 622), a report of their meeting on the promotion and development of traditional medicine. In the recommendations of this report, the meeting took into consideration the fact that traditional systems of medicine remain the major source of health care for more than two-thirds of the world's population and that impressive progress has been made in certain developing countries, such as China and India, in the integration of traditional with Western systems. Progress has also been made in the application of modern science and technology to the promotion and development of traditional medicine.

The meeting also recommended that the organizers of the 1978 International Conference on Primary Health Care at Alma Ata, USSR, should consider the importance and necessity of fully utilizing and developing the vast manpower that exists in the form of traditional medicine practitioners. This should be done in order to make effective health care available to under-served populations.

The Report also recommended educational programs to change the unfavorable attitudes of members of the health and allied professions toward traditional medicine. In the area of the application of traditional medicine to primary health care, the meeting recommended the selection of lists of essential plans, drugs, or techniques employed in traditional medicine for use in public health services and particularly in primary health care. In addition, they approved of the methods and techniques such as acupuncture and yoga for use in public health services.

As far as manpower development is concerned, they recommended encouraging traditional medicine practitioners to organize themselves into societies, as a means of checking harmful practices and eliminating quacks and charlatans, and to promote continuous informal education as well as the conservation of a high level of professional ethics and practice. They also recommended the organizing of educational activities in traditional medicine, by establishing training centers or by revising existing curricula to include subjects related to traditional medicine.

Lastly, they recommended that a planned multidisciplinary research program should be formulated and implemented and that this program should include operational research on traditional medicine in health care systems, as well as including various aspects of medicinal plant research. Studies in psychosocial and cultural aspects and behavioral patterns should also be included. Manpower development and health team training, including the development of effective training methods, should be emphasized.

In general, therefore, the recommendations of the expert Committee on the Promotion and Development of Traditional Medicine called for the acceptance and integration of what is useful in traditional medicine into western medicine. The combination of the two is a better product than either one alone.

More recently, the World Health Organization (WHO) pointed out that 80% of the world's population still gets most of its medications directly from plants, as herbal teas and herbal or plant remedies, in spite of the fact that the pharmaceutical industry becomes more multi-national by the hour.

ACUPUNCTURE FOR DRUG DETOXIFICATION
In the early 1980s, a group of politically active recovering drug addicts in New York City started a drug detoxification program using acupuncture, which they had learned from the Chinese. These advocates considered the methadone clinics to be institutions that only substituted one addiction for another, thus perpetuating the "slavery of addiction."

They treated addicts on their own, without the supervision or cooperation of the medical community. The group's criticism of New York City's drug abuse programs put them in conflict with Mayor Koch and with his Commissioner of Health. The result of this political battle: the activists were forced out of the very detoxification program they had started in the South Bronx. Dr. Michael Smith from the Department of Psychiatry at Lincoln Hospital was called in to take it over. But the acupuncture detoxification treatment was not abandoned, because everyone had observed that it worked.

Dr. Michael Smith continues to offer this alternative treatment to drug addicts and has added other adjunctive treatments, such as Chinese herbal teas. His success rate has been very good. He testified before the Senate Mental Hygiene-Addiction Control Committee in Congress in 1985.

It was not until the criminal-justice people became involved in Dade County in Miami, Florida, however, that acupuncture detoxification was seriously put to the test, with statistical evaluation of the results of two-year follow-up. The criminal-justice people were seriously looking at alternatives to residential or in-patient thirty-day treatment programs at a cost in the range of $7,000-$15,000. Besides, there was simply no way to provide this kind of in-house treatment, especially in correctional facilities.

After they heard Dr. Smith's presentation to the National Association of Criminal Justice Planners, they invited him to Miami to help them start their first detoxification clinic, as part of a statewide strategy to combat drug abuse. An associate chief judge of the 11th Judicial Circuit had been appointed by the Supreme Court of Florida to develop and coordinate the public sector's anti-drug abuse efforts in the Dade County community. A strategic plan entitled "Strategies for Action" was developed, and implementation of this action plan commenced.

One aspect of the action plan, a Diversion and Treatment Program, was started in June, 1989. The purpose of the program is to divert first-time drug-related felons from the criminal-justice system into treatment. The philosophy of this program centers around treating the offender as an addict instead of as a criminal unless proven otherwise. A new Drug Court was established, with the judge, prosecutor and public defender all specially trained in drug addiction. Participants are routinely tracked with urinalyses, ensuring the consistent and tough oversight that is needed to make the diversion program a viable alternative to incarceration.

What has been most impressive about the diversion program,

however, is the success of the acupuncture detoxification component. As of May 20, 1990, approximately a year after its beginning, 1,613 people had opted for the program; 75% have continued in the program; and only 16 program participants have been re-arrested. The state attorney and public defender both urged the expansion of the diversion program from 2,000 to 4,000 defendants per year.

Implemented nationally, it may be possible to treat the increasing numbers of cocaine addicts in urban areas as out-patients with acupuncture detoxification. The 45-minute acupuncture treatment consists of the application of disposable needles to the outer ear on a daily basis. The treatment has a calming effect on the individual and relieves the compulsive desire and craving for the drug. Seventy-five percent of the people come on a voluntary basis every day because it helps reduce the drug craving during the time of withdrawal.

This program succeeded in Dade County, Florida, because the criminal justice people were behind it. But health professionals in the business of treating chemical dependency are involved in expensive 30-day in-hospital stays or 30+ day programs in free-standing residential facilities. The cost of these programs varies from $7,000 to $15,000 a month. Most are for-profit and cannot afford to operate at a loss. Understandably, they are not interested in an inexpensive treatment alternative, such as acupuncture, which can be administered on an outpatient basis.

Another hindrance to widespread acceptance of acupuncture is that the Louisiana and Texas State Boards of Medical Examiners have modified medical practice acts so that only licensed physicians with additional training can do acupuncture. These laws were passed to keep acupuncture specialists out of these states. Acupuncturists are competition, especially in the burgeoning field of pain management. These laws were passed before acupuncture was deemed useful in the treatment of cocaine addiction.

Dr. Smith asserts that a woman skilled in ear piercing can be trained in fifteen minutes to insert the needles into the acupuncture points and to administer a treatment to a cocaine addict. The restrictive laws should be revoked to allow acupuncture treatment for cocaine detoxification. The doctors will not change the law, but hopefully the criminal justice people will. Of course, research and evaluation should proceed to carefully follow and document this alternative method. The Dade County figures are sufficiently impressive to warrant the method's inclusion in any comprehensive chemical dependency treatment program.

Participants in these programs must abstain from the use of drugs, monitored by daily urine examinations for the presence of toxic drugs and their metabolites. The numbers in the alternative detoxification program who remain drug-free can then be compared to the numbers of first-time offenders who are sent to jail or prison or alternative sentencing programs, who do not have the benefit of the alternative treatment which is being evaluated, and who also have their urine checked on a daily basis.

Only with this kind of research and evaluation can we be sure that we are helping people get off drugs, and only then can we begin to put some of them in more long-term programs that deal with rehabilitation, which are based on the twelve steps of Narcotics Anonymous and which will hopefully result in vocational and social rehabilitation.

CHAPTER 15
THE NINTH AMENDMENT—
LET MEDICAL FREEDOM RING!

A private citizen from Wisconsin, Conrad LeBeau, has initiated a movement to end fifty years of government-controlled medical monopoly by unleashing the power of the Ninth Amendment to the U.S. Constitution. This little-known amendment reads:

> The enumeration in the Constitution of certain rights shall not be construed to deny or disparage others retained by the people.

LeBeau has developed a "Ninth Amendment Legal Defense Kit," which outlines practical steps to win freedom of choice in medicine and health care, one of the rights retained by the people under the amendment.

LeBeau has also reprinted an interesting book, *The Forgotten Ninth Amendment: A Call for Legislative and Judicial Recognition of Rights Under Social Conditions of Today,* by Bennett B. Patterson of the Texas Bar (Indianapolis, Indiana: Bobbs-Merrill, 1955). Mr. Patterson writes in his conclusion:"The Ninth Amendment to our Constitution is a guarantee of our individual personality .... May all of us be humbly grateful to a Creator who has endowed us with a soul, and a constitutional government which guarantees to us the right to own it."

The Ninth Amendment has been used as a successful defense in at least one case where the right to freedom of choice in health care was being challenged in California. "Other rights retained by the people" can be interpreted to mean almost anything as long as it doesn't infringe on the rights of others: the right to freedom of choice in health care, the right to smoke cigarettes, the right to view pornography in the privacy of one's own home, the right to die in a hospital without having to undergo heroic life-sustaining invasive procedures, etc.

The amendment essentially guarantees that natural, unenumerated rights are reserved to the people under the U.S. Constitution. The founding fathers who wrote the Bill of Rights, the first ten amendments to our Constitution, enumerated a variety of rights: Freedom of speech and press, the right to bear arms, freedom of religion, counsel of choice, and trial by jury. Fearful of the empirical power of a central government, the founders sought to limit its powers by adding the Ninth and Tenth Amendments to the U.S. Constitution. LeBeau describes the addition of the Ninth Amendment as a "constitutional wild card." (In a card game, the wild card is whatever you claim it to be.) Under the Ninth Amendment, you may claim whatever rights you want to, subject to the approval of a jury.

The question of whether "freedom of choice in medicine" is an unenumerated right reserved to the people under the Ninth Amendment may have to be decided by the Courts with opinions from experts in Constitutional Law. The prevailing viewpoint is that the Ninth Amendment is open to legal interpretation by Constitutional law scholars. Southern University legal scholar Charles Donegan believes that the current conservative Rehnquist court is not likely to find new rights under the constitution. So it may be some time before it can be used as a legitimate legal defense for alternative health care consumers or practitioners.

We do know, however, how one physician signatory to the U.S. Constitution, felt about freedom of choice in medicine. Dr. Benjamin Rush gave this opinion:

> The Constitution of the Republic should make special provisions for medical freedom as well as religious freedom. To restrict the art of healing to one class of men and deny equal privileges to others will constitute the Bastille of medical science. All such laws are un-American and despotic.

If we recognize this doctor's statement of 200 years ago and the fact that he participated in the creation of the U.S. Constitution, freedom of choice in medicine would definitely appear to be reserved to the people under the Ninth Amendment.

In his book, Patterson observes that the Ninth Amendment to the U.S. Constitution, when given its proper meaning and construction, could be the most significant and forcible clause in the entire Constitution. Until now it has been the "stone which the builder refused, but it could in fact be the cornerstone of the Constitution. Individual freedom and the recognition of the spiritual nature of mankind are the essence of democracy; indeed they are the essence of life itself. There is no clause in the Constitution except the Ninth Amendment which makes a declaration of the sovereignty and dignity of the individual."

Mr. Michael Biddinger, Esq., is a music professor and a lawyer. He presented an overview of the Ninth Amendment to the Great Lakes Clinical Medicine Association in September, 1991, in Cleveland, Ohio. He asserted that the Ninth Amendment to the U.S. Constitution can operate as a rule of construction to guarantee people the right to choose, including, for example, the right of a patient to choose, with informed consent, any method of treatment—including alternative approaches—that he or she desires. This choice provides the individual the right to control what is done to his or her body. Biddinger argued that this choice, as a preferred right, should not be denied or disparaged by state actions, as a compelling state interest. Unfortunately, the validity of this argument does not mean that it will prevail in court.

It is generally accepted that the Ninth Amendment was proposed by James Madison. He feared that a specific listing of rights in a bill of rights might someday be misinterpreted to withhold any rights not already listed. Those rights which are not listed could fall into the wrong hands, *e.g.*, the government could confiscate them. Considering our government's record in other matters of rights, this concern of Madison's was well-founded.

Norman Resnick, a constitutional law scholar at New York University, revealed that Madison had an inherent distrust of words. Madison felt that ideas should be expressed by words distinct and exclusive to their definition. But no language can supply words and phrases exclusive for any particular abstract idea. Ideas cannot be exclusively defined; terms that define an idea cannot be exclusive. Resnick concludes that the Ninth Amendment arose from Madison's two concerns: (1) a fear that certain rights by their omission will forever be lost or unattained, and (2) a fear that the vagaries and inadequacies of language might affect other rights which were intended to be included. The adoption of the Fourteenth Amendment in 1868 provided the legal mechanism to apply restrictions to states as well as to the federal government. The Rehnquist court, however, is removing restrictions from state power.

In 1965, the famous right-to-use-contraception case (*Griswold v. Connecticut*) was decided by the Supreme Court hearing arguments that the right to privacy was not explicitly stated in the Bill of Rights and therefore was beyond the reach of official protection. The court decided that there are certain fundamental rights, including the right to privacy, essential to orderly existence. Once it was decided that a fundamental right to privacy existed, then this right, because of the Fourteenth Amendment, is also applied to the states. Consequently, the Connecticut State Law forbidding the use of contraception was held to violate the notion of privacy surrounding the marriage relationship.

In 1973, the significant Ninth Amendment case *Roe v. Wade* was decided, resulting in a fundamental right to privacy of a woman's decision with regard to procreation. The zone of privacy surrounding a woman's decision about whether or not to terminate a pregnancy was considered fundamental. The moralistic issues of whether abortion was right or wrong were not addressed. The Court held that it was a private decision protected by the Constitution. This decision may well have been a watershed with regard to privacy rights. The court, however, has been retreating from this position ever since.

The noted constitutional law scholar Lawrence Tribe has stated that if the Bill of Rights were beyond the reach of federal judicial protection, the implications would be quite radical, indeed. One might then hope to trust local majorities to exercise self-restraint in wielding the power ceded to them. But majorities are not trustworthy when it comes to enforceable judicial protection.

A more recent case in Georgia, *Bowers v. Harper,* was decided in 1986. The court decided that a Georgia statute prohibiting sodomy was constitutional. The court therefore refused to extend the privacy issue addressed in *Roe v. Wade* to encompass homosexual relationships. Arguably, the court took a moralistic approach to homosexual relationships, which in many states has always been illegal. The Court, therefore, rejected moralistic overtones in *Roe v. Wade,* but it accepted them in the Bowers case.

Lawrence Tribe noted that the traditional definition of the word "disparage" in the Ninth Amendment means "to marry out of one's peerage or beneath one's social class." He suggested that the unenumerated rights should not be decided by social consensus. A patient's choice about medical treatment, therefore, which lacks moralistic overtones, ought to be much less controversial than right-to-privacy issues such as abortion and homosexuality.

What kind of message do these "mixed signal" decisions send to State Medical Boards? The members of State Medical Boards are conventional medical practitioners and are thus biased toward conventional standards of the community. Medical review boards can therefore effectively shut the doors to alternative treatments such as chiropractic, naturopathy, yoga, meditation, therapeutic massage, and acupuncture.

Patients, however, are becoming increasingly dissatisfied with conventional medical practice. Just as they want more control over death and dying, they desire control over their lives by taking initiatives for building health and seeking second opinions, whether orthodox or alternative. This change in patient expectation should support physicians who practice non-conventional medicine. Such support was shown in Alaska, on June 15, 1990, when the state legislature passed a law stating that a physician could not be disciplined by the medical board simply because his practice was unconventional or differed from the norm, in the absence of any demonstrable harm to his patient. The state of Washington has recently followed suit with similar legislation. Hopefully other states will do likewise.

Another barrier to practitioners of unconventional medicine is traditional tort (civil law) theory, which forms the basis for conventional malpractice suits citing negligence. Scholars have therefore suggested a new legal approach which is called the contractual method. Under tort theory, in order to recover, the plaintiff must prove that the traditional doctor breached the standard of care. This standard of care is defined by the skill and knowledge normally possessed by the members of that professional trade in good standing in similar communities. Generally the courts apply this same standard to alternative practitioners. The expert witness who is called to testify on the standard must be of the same "school" as the defendant alternative practitioner. When an alternative practitioner is not already licensed by the state, the courts may refuse to recognize, or simply be unable to find, an expert witness of the same school as the defendant. Consequently, conventional practitioners are called in, and they testify that the alternative practitioner is a charlatan. Some of these problems may be solved through the contractual approach. Instead of having a traditionally-imposed standard of care, the practitioner and patient can establish the practitioner's duties by contractual agreement. Because both the patient's responsibilities and the doctor's duties are agreed upon contractually, there should be no need for expert witnesses. This approach also promotes individual responsibility.

Another problem which exists for alternative practitioners under tort law is the requirement that non-medical practitioners refer their patients to medical practitioners when it becomes evident that a particular alternative treatment will not work. A Washington, D.C., appeals court, for example, held that the non-medical alternative practitioner has the duty to refrain from treating problems that are purely medical; he should refer patients to medical practitioners when the need for medical treatment becomes apparent. The problem with this approach is that the healing process may be long-term, and therefore the time "when the need for medical treatment becomes apparent" is not easily determined.

Tort-based rules are inappropriate for the alternative health care setting. In a contractual agreement, the parties can estimate the approximate time for referral if the patient does not respond to a particular alternative treatment. First, any such contract should state the purpose of the agreement; secondly, the contract should explicitly discuss the responsibilities of the practitioner and the patient; third, the agreement should define the working relationship between the parties. In addition, the parties should agree to mediation should a dispute be unable to be resolved.

Should this approach fail to be sanctioned by the courts, the legislative process, exemplified by the Alaskan law protecting alternative practitioners, may be a viable alternative.

Some states require a general-practitioner license for those who desire to practice alternative medicine. Most commonly, these statutes make exemptions for chiropractors and osteopathic physicians. These states impose criminal penalties on alternative practitioners who do not have licenses to practice medicine.

Mr. LeBeau, also a writer for *Health Freedom News,* was led to develop his kit to assist people in asserting their Ninth Amendment rights from his experience from 1981 to 1987 helping farmers successfully defend themselves against foreclosure. The kit directs that in order to logically exercise Ninth Amendment rights, one should declare those rights in a written statement, as our country's founders did when they wrote the Constitution. Mr. LeBeau created a document entitled "A Declaration of Ninth Amendment Rights." This document can be filed by an individual as part of any ongoing court proceeding. A person simply lists those rights he or she desires reserved under the Ninth Amendment.

The document could, for example, read as follows:

> The undersigned thereby notifies the Court that the following rights are reserved under the Ninth Amendment to the U.S. Constitution:
>
> 1. The right to a trial by jury.
>
> 2. The legal right of counsel of choice.

3. The right to present arguments of law as well as facts before a jury. The right of the jury to rule on motions of either the plaintiff or the defendant.

4. The right of the jury to ask any questions they want of me or any witness I call and our right to answer their questions.

5. The right of the jury to hear arguments on the constitutionality of any laws used in this case and the right of the jury to rule on the constitutionality of these laws. The right of the jury to rule on which Ninth Amendment right they will recognize as just and necessary in the interest of justice.

The individual then signs, dates and notarizes the document; the document is filed in a court case, and the individual actively asserts those rights immediately. Copies are given to government officials and are posted in the individual's office or place of business. These rights are declared and exercised openly.

What are not considered to be Ninth Amendment rights? LeBeau's response:

You do *not* have the right to deceive anyone; to deliberately harm anyone; to impersonate government officials or professional persons; and you do not have the right to rip off customers with excessive charges and unneeded services. These are selfish aspirations and not amendment rights.

The exercise of the Ninth Amendment may be a way to restore certain reasonable rights to the people. It could be utilized to return certain powers of government, which never should have been taken by the government in the first place, back to the individual. The Ninth Amendment could restore the proper relationship between the government and the people.

LeBeau, to illustrate the use of the Ninth Amendment to declare the right of freedom of choice in medicine, gives an example of how a patient might ask a naturopath for an evaluation using his Ninth Amendment rights:

I, (name of client) request of (name of naturopath) an evaluation of my current state of health. I further request advice on diet and supplements to help improve my condition of health. I agree not to act on this advice until I have had an exam by a licensed medical doctor and receive his evaluation and advice. I reserve the right to choose a medical doctor, chiropractor, naturopath, or even an Indian medicine man or someone from the general citizenry to conduct this evaluation.

I shall exercise this right as a natural inherent right and one reserved to the people under the U.S. Constitution, Article IX.

The health care practitioner, in this sample case the naturopath, then creates his own "Declaration of Ninth Amendment rights." He declares his right to provide health counseling and advice as requested by his clientele. Thus at any future trial, if the naturopath is accused of "practicing medicine," the constitutionality of the law upon which this accusation is based could be challenged as a violation of the Ninth Amendment rights of his client. He would then have the signed statements to back up his testimony.

Conrad LeBeau rightly concludes that the integral relationship between the FDA and the multi-billion dollar drug companies constitutes a monopoly on the approval and sale of new drugs, to the exclusion of drugless remedies. He notes that this monopoly is clearly a violation of freedom of choice in medicine. Freedom of choice in medicine involves more than just the right to an evaluation of your choice; it also involves the right to obtain safe medication of your choice and information on how to use it.

LeBeau says that there should be only three major requirements for any health product to be marketed as a right under the Ninth Amendment. They are:

(1) All claims for the product and its intended use must be true.

(2) The product cannot be harmful when used as intended, and/or the product label and accompanying literature must list all known contraindications and side-effects.

(3) There must be adequate instructions on how to use the product for its intended purpose.

LeBeau notes that even though the FDA does not recognize testimonials, the right to use these testimonials, if they are true, could be claimed as a Ninth Amendment right simply by filing a declaration of Ninth Amendment rights with an affidavit and support. The claims and the three conditions mentioned above would also be listed as these conditions are reasonable in the public interest.

LeBeau concludes: "It is time that we the people challenge this unjust medical monopoly and assert our natural inherent rights as they exist, which are protected under the Ninth Amendment to the U.S. Constitution."

EPILOGUE
THE WAY OUT OF THE FOREST

The *Wall Street Journal* recently ran the following ad:

> Once, three Executives were lost in the woods. The first pointed to a tree he recognized. "There's a deciduous shagbark hickory." The second said that it looked like a common chokeberry, but he had to consult his tree people. But the third climbed to the top of the tree and got something the others didn't. A view of the forest and a pathway out. You know which of them reads the *Wall Street Journal* and why.
>
> The *Journal* gives you perspectives, to see beyond your own experience, finding patterns, instead of just facts, to make informed decisions instead of educated guesses. The *Wall Street Journal* gives you a magnificent view of the forest, while others are still focusing on chokeberries!

Like the executives in this story, too many in the medical profession today are still focusing on the cost of malpractice insurance and defensive medicine. The way out of the health-care crisis lies in taking an overview of the forest of factors that are contributing to it. Some of these factors are:

(1) Detrimental lifestyles
(2) Lack of emphasis on preventive medicine
(3) Suppression of alternative therapies
(4) Failure to incorporate alternative therapies into our existing health-care system
(5) Lack of appreciation for the role of nutrition in disease causation and disease modulation
(6) Us-and-them mentality regarding allopathic versus the other healing arts and sciences.

We need to focus on some of the solutions. In a paper entitled "The Evolution and Culture of Mass Cardiovascular Disease," presented to the American College of Chest Physicians in 1984 in New Orleans, Dr. Henry Blackburn of the University of Minnesota said, "Americans still have a hunting and gathering metabolism, yet have sedentary lifestyles."

In selecting diet and lifestyle, Americans tend to ignore their evolutionary and cultural legacy—our metabolic adaptations and social behaviors. We forget that Australopithicus was largely vegetarian. The result, Dr. Blackburn pointed out, is that:

> We spend most of our time digesting all the excess calories we ate yesterday; burning 10 times more triglyceride than we need for essential fatty acids and vitamins, with which they are associated; converting the excess glucose that we ate to various stores of one sort or another in various organs; excreting 20 times more sodium than we need for homeostasis, etc. This is our homeostatic legacy of evolution and mass cultural change. The legacy is not modifiable, but our eating and exercise habits are.

Dr. Denis Burkitt, a British surgeon, missionary, and clinical researcher, agrees with those who emphasize the importance of preventing disease:

> Not only does prevention add to the quality of life, but ultimately, it is the best way to cut health care costs. We in the West spend far too much of our time and money on curing, when we ought to be preventing diseases, most of which are preventable. We're spending our time and money trying to pick up the pieces instead of trying to prevent the casualties.
>
> Just as we have, in the past 100 years of nutrition development, been taking away the outside of the wheat grain, which contains the fiber and which could be called the "carton," and emphasizing the contents, which is the starch or the nutrition, we've made the opposite mistake in medicine. A person's spirit is in a biological carton. We have gotten so good scientifically at tinkering with the biological components of humans, that we lose sight of people as patients when they go into the hospital. Humans are spiritual creations, temporarily resident in a carton, but we are more than a "carton," because our cartons change about every seven years.
>
> It's important for physicians to look after the biological carton, but physicians must remember that it's much more important to consider the destiny of people's contents than it is to focus on the repair of their cartons.
>
> We have to pay more attention to what's on the inside than the outside. Major problems of life are never academic or technical, they are always in personal relationships, honesty,

reliability, trustworthiness, persistence and so on. Children need to be reared as people who care and who have compassion and honesty, rather than to be only academic geniuses or athletic prodigies. Perhaps it's wrong to select people for medical school by having their chemistry and physics grades put into a computer. People are more than molecules and chemistry.

If physicians are to make contributions to their communities or professions, it takes more than academic attainment or cleverness. Making a contribution depends on attitudes and motives, outlook and values. Attitudes are more important than abilities; motives are more important than methods; character is more important than cleverness.

There is a need for alternative health therapies and services, many of which are preventive as well as therapeutic for the "walking wounded" with chronic conditions. Alternatives are generally not available from most Western-trained medical practitioners, who know very little about them; what information they do have is usually based on false and negative propaganda which they have learned from former teachers and colleagues—false information which usually stems from arrogance, incredulity, and frustration at being unable to fit certain phenomena into a fixed model often mislabeled as "scientific." Unless government officials and state legislators wise up to the fact that they and the public are being "had," sometimes in the name of improving standards and excellence and sometimes in the name of eliminating fraud, present policies can be expected to continue until there is public outcry, demonstrations, and even revolution in the streets. It's been estimated that at least 70% of patients treated by primary care physicians are neither sick nor well, don't need drugs to cure their ailments, and really need rest or relief from stress and changes in their lifestyles. Also, very recently, the value of the annual or periodic physical examination in asymptomatic adults has been called into question. Dr. Sylvia Oboler, of the VA Hospital of Denver, Colorado, and Dr. Marc La Force, of Genesee Hospital and Rochester School of Medicine, evaluated the different components of the annual physical check-up. They found that for the asymptomatic, nonpregnant adult of any age, no evidence supports the need for a complete physical examination as traditionally defined. What is important, however, are the so-called screening procedures or maneuvers. They made the following recommendations:

The efficacy for three screening procedures has been established: Blood pressure should be measured at least every two years; women more than 40 years of age should have a breast examination done by a physician annually; and sexually active women should have a pelvic examination and a Papanicolaou test at least every three years after two initial negative tests have been obtained one year apart. Because of the prevalence and morbidity of specific diseases, and the sensitivity and specificity of screening tests, several other maneuvers are recommended for screening asymptomatic adults, although the optimal frequency has not been determined experimentally. Weight should be measured every four years. Visual acuity should be tested annually in adults older than 60 years of age. To identify patients at high risk for melanoma, a complete skin examination should be done once. Hearing should be tested by audioscope annually in adults older than 60 years of age. Physicians should encourage patients to have annual dental visits. To identify valvular abnormalities requiring antibiotic prophylaxis, cardiac auscultation should be done at least twice in an adult. Men older than 60 years of age should have a yearly examination of the abdomen for the presence of aortic aneurysm. Although the other components of the complete physical examination may be important in establishing and maintaining the physician-patient relationship, they have not been shown to be effective screening maneuvers for asymptomatic disease.

What does this mean, however, in a practical sense? It means that our present health care system and, more importantly, our system of reimbursement will not facilitate patients being seen and screened in this manner. It would require a complete turnaround in Medicare and insurance company payment practices, which this industry is either unwilling or incapable of doing. It may also require Congress to pass new legislation specifically including provisions for screening procedures, such as the 1991 bill which specifically states that Medicare will pay for breast-cancer screening by the mini-x-ray procedure called mammography.

Preventive medicine can be categorized into two areas:

(1) Services which are delivered to individuals by health care providers to promote optimal health and wellness and to prevent illness, and

(2) Information (health education) provided to the public, but where the basic responsibility for implementation or put-

ting it into practice rests with the individual or recipient of that information and newly acquired knowledge.

In health care, people are more willing to pay for the former than for the latter; the latter is not unlike a payment of tuition, similar to what one would pay to go to college, generally made by the better-educated and middle- and upper- socio-economic classes, who are activist and motivated to attain optimum health and functioning and who have a long-range point of view. Newer technologies will also facilitate personalized information packages, through the use of interactive computer software programs, increasing the efficiency and range of dissemination of information.

Also, as health care consumers in New Zealand, Europe, and the U.S. have discovered, health services can be greatly improved by combining Eastern and Western medicine. Many European physicians and researchers are beginning to see the differences between the two as complementary factors in treating patients. Acceptance of herbal remedies seems to be difficult for most Western practitioners, however. Western medicine is more physically oriented, relying upon drugs and surgery for therapy. It is reductionistic, in that it tends to see the body decomposed into smaller units, and the belief is that if we understand what happens to the smallest unit of the body, we can put the pieces together and determine what the problem is. Western medicine is also more emergency-oriented, waiting until a disease is evident before treatment begins. There is a greater fascination with technology and the use of the latest techniques in Western medicine, and the tendency is to standardize medications for all patients by diagnosing and then prescribing the ideal drug.

Eastern medicine, on the other hand, acknowledges the tripod of body, mind and spirit, and the merits of each, when looking at the past and total pattern of symptoms. It is more prevention-oriented. Practitioners try to catch the early warning signs, before a disease is evident. Slight changes are not written off as hypochondriasis, as often happens in Western medicine, but such changes are seen as part of a global pattern, then analyzed according to a set of classifications which describe imbalances in the body, such as yin and yang, hot and cold. Such terms don't make much sense to most Western practitioners who don't understand their meanings. In Eastern medicine, disease is seen as an imbalance in the body; therapy involves seeking the underlying cause rather than immediate treatment of symptoms. Herbal remedies are given in the context of aiding the individual patient's problem and treatment of the whole body. While relief is generally slower than with most Western drugs, when it does come it is not just relief of pain but relief of the underlying cause of the pain.

A good example of integration of Eastern and Western medicine can be found in China, where, after the revolution, the government tried to build Western health systems. However, the traditional Chinese system using acupuncture and herbs was so entrenched that it survived, and both systems became interwoven. Traditional and Western hospitals, schools, research institutes, and pharmaceutical firms flourish separately and are used by the Chinese people in different ways. The people tend to use Western medical facilities and practitioners for quick symptomatic relief, and traditional Chinese medicine for long-term treatment. Some hospitals integrate Western surgery with use of traditional Chinese acupuncture and herbal remedies, and the result is more rapid recovery than treatment solely with Western methods. We can learn from this example.

We can also learn from other medical systems such as the Ayurveda, Siddha and Unani traditional medical systems which provide health care for most of India's population. Ayurveda comes from *ayu* (life) and *veda* (knowledge), and its instructions have been written in Sanskrit, the language of ancient India. It is a system for prevention and cure of diseases which offers a philosophy for achieving and maintaining health. Holistic, it emphasizes health as soundness of body, organs and mind; thus the "tripod of life"—body, mind and soul—get equal attention, recognizing the psychic influences on the body's health. Apart from genetic influences, a person's constitution is also affected by age, environment and diet. An imbalance between any of the body's fundamental units determines an individual's susceptibility to certain diseases. Diet is considered to have a direct effect on one's physiological and psychological state, which brings this ancient system into our century, where brain functions and mental diseases have been shown to be altered by diet. Like the Tibetan and Chinese therapies, many herbal remedies are used to treat psychiatric disorders, asthma, hypertension, and other problems. When and with what foods drugs should be taken has always been considered, which shows how this remarkable, centuries-old medical system compares with recent developments in modern therapeutics and chronopharmacology emphasizing the importance of drug administration times on drug actions.

In an article in *Whole Foods Magazine*, in March, 1983, by Anita Fieldman, entitled, "'Us' and 'Them,'" I was quoted as expressing my concern regarding the emergence in this country of two exclusive spheres of influence in regard to food and nutrition: the established medical practice and medical centers on one hand, and the health food stores and the National Nutritional Foods Association (NNFA) on the other. There is very little communication or dialogue between the two. When I heard some of the speakers at a NNFA convention remark about staying one foot ahead of the law and the AMA, it was not hard to make a diagnosis of mass paranoia. Nonetheless, when a senior faculty member in my department refused to go to the Rivergate Convention Center because she didn't want to "have anything to do with those quacks," then I too was forced to call it what it is—discrimination and bigotry.

Perhaps it is too late for this generation of practitioners from our separate spheres of nutritional influence to break down long-standing barriers to understanding. We could work together, however, to ensure that the next generation is exposed—objectively—to the best each viewpoint can offer.

In the years since that article was published in 1983, because of the activities of the Strike Force through the National and Regional Councils Against Health Fraud, both overt and covert; because of the sometimes successful lobbying efforts of the dietitians for State Boards of Dietetics; because of the legal activities of FDA in seizing products such as tryptophan and evening primrose oil; and because of the control Emprise and other groups have over what treatments the insurance industry will pay for, my concern back then has been justified. Much more than what I feared would happen has happened. It is much bigger than two opposing spheres of influence in theories of nutrition.

Heart patient Mitch Newell of Kansas is one of many sufferers of heart disease who underwent CABG surgery, took many medications with equally poor results, then recovered substantially with chelation therapy.

Mr. Newell underwent four separate bypass operations (coronary artery bypass graft) and eight separate balloon angioplasty procedures. In the process, he endured fifteen separate angiograms and took twenty-nine different medications every day. The poor man was so sick that he could not totter from bed to bathroom without shortness of breath or chest pain. His heart specialists told him that his only chance to live was to have two more operations: first, implantation of a temporary artificial heart-assist device, followed by a transplant when a donor heart became available.

Fate intervened; unwilling to suffer through more surgery, Mr.

Newell learned about chelation and gave it a try. He reasoned that he could always have two more operations if the chelation failed. But fail it did not; after twenty-five IV chelation treatments, Mr. Newell could once again walk for as long and as far as he wanted. He returned to part-time employment and resumed management of his own business. Free of chest pain now, he rarely gets short of breath on exertion. His pill intake has reduced from twenty-five a day to only two.

Despite success stories such as Mr. Newell's, the harassment of chelation doctors continues. Don't forget that as recently as March, 1990, the FDA listed chelation #7 on their "ten most common health frauds" list. However, in October, 1991, after Wyeth-Ayerst committed $6-8 million to complete the Walter Reed Study and fund parallel studies in the private sector, one phone call from them to the FDA put a stop to their congressional and public information offices sending out derogatory material on EDTA chelation therapy; the attack had continued since the inception of the Walter Reed Study, despite a moratorium on such negative campaigning called for by FDA's own Cardio-Renal Division, while the study was in progress.

Can you believe it? And, incredibly, the state medical examining boards pressure state legislators to grant them more power and immunity from lawsuits. They claim a need for immunity to better prosecute doctors repeatedly sued for malpractice, who are presumed to be a major cause for rising malpractice insurance rates.

The reality is this: Repeat malpractice doctors are rarely brought before the board. Recall that 60% of a state board's efforts deal with chemically-dependent and otherwise impaired doctors, and 40% of their effort is directed in ferreting out alternative practitioners.

Despite their strong legal expertise, our elected representatives have no real knowledge of clinical medicine. They tend to leave regulatory agencies such as the State Boards of Medical Examiners to regulate themselves. Legislatures tend to rubber-stamp decisions created by state medical boards. Because of this, most physicians falsely accused and brought before the board have no chance of winning their cases, that is, clearing their names, regaining their licenses to practice at the board level.

The powerful lobbying of the health-care industry manages to keep the wool pulled over legislators' eyes. In some cases the legislators really do not care. They enjoy the perks and attention, not to mention the PAC contributions, proffered by the medical lobbyists. It's just plain hard to outdo Organized Medicine, and there needs to be overall reform in the lobbying system.

But none of this need concern Mr. Newell, of our earlier success story. It was sheer luck that he found about chelation therapy in time. It was "better mousetrap," free-market forces at work that has enabled chelation to survive in the first place, and to be available for him when he needed it, in spite of every conceivable effort on the part of Organized Medicine to kill it. Thank God for that—and for whatever else we can pull out of the cracks!

This crisis of attitude and outlook in medicine is continuing, and furthermore is occurring during a time period when we have had escalating costs in health care and a financial crisis in the delivery of curative and also, consequently, preventive health services. Health care in the U.S. cost $462 billion in 1986. In 1989, the total estimated health care expenditures were $600 billion, or $19,000 per second. Health care expenditures are rising at two to two-and-a-half times the inflation rate. In 1989, they were 11.9% of the gross national product. By 1995, they will be 15% of the gross national product; and by the year 2040, were this trend to continue, they would be 100% of the gross national product.

Nearly thirty-seven million people are without health insurance, and the state Medicaid programs are nearly all on the verge of bankruptcy. Therefore, all of this rush of protectionist activity on the part of drug companies, physicians, and dietitians is understandable, but by no means excusable, especially when the entire "house of cards" is about to all fall down. But perhaps this has to happen before we can replace the existing system with something else, a little bit more efficient (if we are lucky) than the Canadian system with its method of payment. Of course, we should avoid the legalistic attempts to outlaw alternative health care that we have seen in recent months and years in the province of Ontario, and we should promote a conversion to a more pluralistic system of health care, which should include, of course, safe and effective treatments, including alternatives, in a free-market, competitive environment.

There are three things that the government can do, immediately, to help lead us out of the forest of the health-care crisis:

(1) Enact national and universal health insurance, based on the Canadian model. The 1,500 private insurers will always raise premiums on high-cost users or eliminate them from their insured. They are in business for profit. Also, as long as there are many different companies, there will be excessive paperwork, which presently costs as much as 40 cents on the dollar.

(2) Facilitate, through tax incentives and other legislation,

the changes and transformations that we have seen are necessary.

(3) Put an end to the racketeering and profiteering, by enacting new legislation if necessary.

We must act now, if the crisis is to be alleviated.

APPENDIX I

Excerpts from Taped Conversation Before the Hearing of The Arkansas State Board v. Dr. Melissa Talliaferro and Excerpts of the Transcripts of That Hearing

Board Members Present:

Dr. Vernon Carter, Mr. Dewey Lantrip, Mr. John Curri , Dr. Jim Lytle, Dr. Warren Douglas, Dr. Bascom Raney, Dr. James Gardner, Dr. Joe Verse, Dr. John Guenther (then chairman of the Arkansas State Board of Medical Examiners), Dr. Ray Jouett, Dr. Alonzo Williams, Dr. George Wynne

Arkansas State Medical Board Hearing
Pre-hearing comments
December 3, 1987

Dr. Jouett: Yeah, I got the other — So now I've got more information on this matter than I really care to know about.

Mr. Curry: So I don't know how they can keep chelation out of this, John (to Guenther). I was hoping they could but exhibit A has it mentioned in there and since it does, that opens the door as far as I'm concerned. But that's all right. I tell you one thing—

Dr. Jouett: I tell you one thing that the Board does not have to do. The Board does not have to listen to a parade of people saying how wonderful I am since I had that medicine. Now we don't have to do that. Now we have to listen to his expert witnesses, but we do not have to listen to testimonies of that sort.

Mr. Curry: Now I would like the letter written by the guy from Oschner Clinic—Call that kind of testimony or that kind of research or something.

Mr. Curry: Well, I tell you the straight truth. I'm feeling bad about the idea that here we are trying to pick at folks. We ain't got no business picking at them. And if they want a bigger room and we could get it, I thought we ought to have it.

But he said no and I guess I'm—I can't understand what they're doing with all this television in here. Why—

Mr. Mitchell (Board attorney):
I don't either.

Mr. Curry: It's on now. They're getting your picture and mine right now and they're getting what we've got to say.

Dr. Jouett: (to Mitchell) Now if I'm going to chair this I need to know what the guidelines are and if you are going to chair it then it won't make any difference, you can—

Mr. Mitchell: No, you need to chair it. Now let's just talk about it a minute, Paul. Now we've got some additional evidence, do we not, since last time?

Mr. Curry: Let me tell y'all, y'all are being recorded right next door right now and if you—ah—if there's anything you got to say that you—ah—

Dr. Jouett: Okay.

Mr. Mitchell: Thank you. I think the procedure should be; Paul may want to just summarize where we are and then allow us to rule on the additional evidence—and allow them to present their defense. Don't you think that's the way to do this, Paul—and then I think we've got to give them a reasonable opportunity to present their case but when they start being cumulative, we need to address the lawyer here.

Mr. Curry: You're not recording this are you? Cause we're entitled to some privacy somewhere.

Dr. Jouett: He agrees that we do not have to listen to a parade of people. We listen to their experts and that's it. Because that's all we are going to use.

Mr. Curry: Did you read that in there about their complaining about our experts wanting to testify by letter where they couldn't be cross-examined? Then I saw where we had subpoenaed our experts.

Dr. Jouett: We have. We have some coming from the University.

Mr. Curry: Hopefully, hopefully. I'm trying to find the original complaint on her and there ain't no telling where it is.

Mr. Clampett (Board secretary):
Do you have the complaint and notice of hearing?

Dr. Jouett: Yeah, that's what I'm looking for. I don't know where it is. I've got it somewhere but I don't know where it is.

Mr. Curry: You say we're supposed to have a letter from Dr. Bates and Dr. Ackerman in lieu of this subpoena?

Dr. Jouett: Yes.

Mr. Clampett: Yes, sir. (to Curry) Here is the letter from Dr. Ackerman

	and Dr. Joseph Bates. Now I can show you a copy of the letter that was written when you get to that spot.
Mr. Curry:	No, I don't need you to show me anything right now. I feel like that's a bad thing when we subpoena somebody and they don't answer and we just think that's a good idea.
Mr. Curry:	We want to get a statement from them that they have not recorded anything that was said in this room prior to the meeting.
Dr. Jouett:	We will.

Verser and Mitchell:

We're going to try to stay with the charges against the physician as opposed to any—all of this extra stuff. We've got a citizen that's charged the physician. It's the complaint against the physician. Not all these off the wall complaints— not all this other stuff involved with chelation— but whether what she did for that patient was appropriate. If we can keep it within those bounds —we're interested in the charges against the doctor that's our question—Dr. Joe—there's other things too—. Didn't she give some rates in the chart Paul?

Mr. Ward (Board attorney):
We established that.

Mitchell:	She denies the question, Dr. Verser.
Dr. Verser:	Mr. Chairman, could we go into executive session for 10 to 15 minutes:
Dr. Jouett:	Sure.
Dr. Verser:	Does anybody have any objection? The secretary would like to talk to the board in executive session.
Mr. Ward:	Dr. Joe, you need to declare before doing that, the purpose for the executive session.
Dr. Verser:	Well—uh, uh—my purpose would be actions that we might take in the future. Actions that we took yesterday and actions in the future. How are we going to handle situations.
	Ward: I think that would not be allowed under the Freedom of Information Act. The only main exception that would allow the board to go into executive session would be to consider the disciplining or hiring or firing of an employee of the agency. Discussing the general business of the Board, policy-making of the Board—you can't do that in a closed session. If the Board did that I think they would violate the Freedom of Information Act.
Dr. Verser:	Well, I lost another one now.
Dr. Jouett:	(to Court Reporter): Are you ready?

Mr. Bowers:	I'm ready.
Dr. Verser:	Well, can I take the floor?
Dr. Jouett:	Yes - we'll give you the floor before we start. Dr. Verser has the floor before we begin.
Dr. Verser:	What I really wanted to say is, in all the years that I have been secretary, I've certainly abided by the majority of the decisions of this board. Many times when I've voted in the minority and after I got to thinking, I thought the majority was right. But I get the feeling that this Board now are using the word "reprimand" too much, too often. We're not taking the action that we should take against the physicians for violations. What does a reprimand do to a physician? He puts it in his file and that's the end of it. It may get in the paper and it may not. Sure he had to come down here and all this publicity. But I think this Board in the past has had a reputation of being a fair and, like the attorneys said, tough, but fair and honest with everybody.

Paul Johnson (Dr. Talliaferro's Arkansas attorney):	
	Excuse me—
Dr. Verser:	And I think that we're going to have to just—
Mr. Seeley:	Excuse me, this should be on the record. [Greg Seeley is Dr. Talliaferro's attorney.]
Mr. Ward:	No, it's not necessary.
Dr. Jouett:	We're not—we do not record everything that goes on in the Board on the record. You make a record of it if you want to. But she doesn't make a record of it.
Johnson:	Is this not to be a part of Dr. Talliaferro's hearing?
	(Many No's)
Dr. Verser:	This is over all. This is over all.
Dr. Jouett:	This has nothing to do with her.
Mr. Curry:	This is about something that happened here yesterday I think
Mr. Johnson:	Well the timing appears to be—right before—You know her sitting here and him making this speech.
Dr. Jouett:	Well I think this has got nothing to do with her.
Dr. Verser:	It has nothing to do with this case. I sincerely assure you it doesn't. The Board on a physician last meeting who overcharged—persistent and flagrant overcharging twenty one hundred dollars—13 skin lesions. He got a reprimand. You name back the physicians and what they've done. Are we being stuck on just "reprimand"? Now years ago we suspended licenses and we had a reputation at being one of the best states for the least use of drugs and the least over-prescribing of drugs of any state in the union.

And I'm questioning if whether we're getting a reprimand for this.

I think it—the one fear that a physician has in this state is having if he's done wrong to come before this Board. My wife's nephew asked a man the other day: Do you know Dr. Joe Verser? He said, Yes, but I don't ever want to have to come before that Medical Board. I don't want to do anything wrong. I don't want to come before that Medical Board. He knew that he would get what probably he would deserve and action would be taken for his wrongdoing, but if when we get the idea and everybody adopt it. We have 7,000 people licensed by this Board now and you know the story.

I say that everybody has a little larceny in their heart, and the longer I live the more assured I am that everybody has a little larceny in their heart but when people get out and say, that Board's not going to do anything but reprimand me. Are we saying, look, don't worry about doing wrong. I think we need a deterrent in order that the physicians of this state will practice good medicine and won't be tempted—won't be tempted by a patient that comes in and says I have chronic back pain, like the physician we had yesterday, writing Percodan by the hundreds all up through Missouri, coming to Arkansas to get the Percodan. What did he finally get? What? Two months suspension of his DEA.

Now this man was a well-educated family practice trained physician. We brought it out. He was not trained to do this. He just got in the habit of writing. And this thing has a habit if you get a drug addict, or a person who's a drug abuser, once he finds out that he can go to Dr. Brown over here, Jones over here, they're going, and they're going to keep going till you say No. And I get the feeling we need to get a little bit tough and take some action rather than just saying a reprimand. Thank you.

Dr. Jouett: The first item on the agenda is Dr. Sharon Talliaferro.

Dr. Talliaferro is here. Before we uh—and represented by counsel. Before we begin, the attorney for the Board will summarize the position that we are in at the present time, referable to material that was presented on the last occasion and also any new evidence that he might wish to introduce.

Proceedings

For our first witness we'll call George M. Stafford, who is the patient's son.

(The witnesses were sworn.)

DIRECT EXAMINATION OF THE PATIENT'S SON

By Mr Ward (Q.): [Attorney for the prosecution against the accused doctor]

Q.   Could you tell us your name and where you live, please?

A.   My name is George M. Stafford. I live in Leslie.

Q.   You wrote a letter to Dr. Verser in June of this year regarding the treatment rendered to your mother by Dr. Talliaferro?

A.   Yes, I did.

Q.   I'd like to ask you some of the specifics in that letter, which I think the Board has already read. As I understand it, your mother had a stroke and was then later treated and seen by Dr. Talliaferro?

A.   Yes.

Q.   Tell us what happened when she was first seen by Dr. Talliaferro, and describe in your own words what you observed?

A.   Well, from the beginning, my mother had a stroke late one evening, and about 11 o'clock, my nephew came down to my house and told me that she had a stroke and was being treated by some doctor that he didn't know, at her home. So, I went up there, and Dr. Talliaferro was there, and she was giving her an IV injection of some sort. And mother didn't much know what was going on. My father was there, and he had agreed to let the doctor treat her. I asked my father to make them take my mother to the conventional hospital in Harrison. She had a doctor there, a personal doctor, Dr. Bell, that had operated on her just previously for cancer. And he said, "No, let Dr. Talliaferro have her chance."

Well, Dr. Talliaferro wanted to take my mother to town to her home, to her mother-in-law's home. Which she did. And I went with them, along with the rest of my family. In the course of the night, I asked the doctor—I had seen the doctor before, and she didn't have her license at that time, and I asked the doctor if she had her license now, and she said, "Of course she had her license." I asked her to see it, and she wouldn't show it to me. So I asked her what was in the injections that she was giving my mother. She wouldn't tell me what were in the injections. She said that it was a new thing that they had come out with, and that it was top secret; that the doctors and the government and other high officials didn't want it known around the country that they cure cancer and stroke and one thing and another with these injections. And that was why she wanted to take her to town there. I told her I was going to call my mother's doctor in the morning, Dr. Bell. And she asked me not to tell Dr. Bell that she was doing anything for my mother except giving her aspirin.

In the morning, when I called Dr. Bell, Dr. Talliaferro had already called him and told him that was all that she was doing. And Dr. Bell told me to try to get my mother up there to the hospital as soon as possible. Well, it took me about a week to get her to go. She had examinations up there. The doctor recommended that she be put in the hospital up there for further tests. But she refused to go because while she was with Dr. Talliaferro, Dr. Talliaferro told her if she went up there and let them operate on her again they would kill her. My mother is very gullible, I guess is the word for it.

Dr. Verser:	How old is your mother?
A.	She's in her seventies, early seventies.
Q.	I understand you saw your mother's chart with some of the injections written on it?
A.	Yes, I did. Before she went up to have the tests and stuff, the chart was there. I am not a medical student or anything, but I can read the chart, you know, enough to know that everything was on there or a lot of the things that were on there that she was giving to my mother. She was giving her injections and things. The day after I called Dr. Bell, her chart didn't show any of that. All it showed was aspirins.
Q.	You mentioned that Dr. Talliaferro didn't tell you what kind of drugs were in the injection?
A.	No, she wouldn't tell me what sort they were, because she said, like I said, it was a secret affair there and the government didn't want it publicized. The doctors of the country didn't want it publicized, because they were able to cure cancer and stuff, and it would cost them millions of dollars.
Q.	Did she tell your mother what chemicals were in the injection?
A.	No. I asked my mother, at a later date, if she knew what they were giving her. My mother continued to take these injections for quite sometime after she had recovered from the stroke, and she said, No, she didn't know what they were in them, and she didn't care. She was going to take them regardless. She had that much faith in the doctor's treatments.
Q.	Did Dr. Talliaferro explain any possible side effects from these treatments?
A.	No, she didn't. She said there were no side effects, when I asked her. Which I later found out to be untrue, because I

took the—I got a list of the drugs that she was giving my mother. I wrote them all down. She had them all on a tray there in my mother's room, and I wrote them all down and I went home and looked in one of my wife's medical books and looked them all up. There were a couple I couldn't even find.

But, a couple of them did list serious side effects.

Q.   I understand Dr. Talliaferro told you and your mother that none of these drugs were harmful?

A.   Yes.

Q.   Did Dr. Talliaferro say anything about curing brain cancer?

A.   Yes, she did. She said that she had cured her own father of brain cancer. He later died from something else.

Q.   Go ahead and continue?

A.   She also told us, my mother included, that she had cured numerous people with massive stroke. My mother was only having a mild stroke. It didn't affect her seriously. But, she said she had cured numerous people of massive stroke. And naturally, my mother decided that was the thing for her. She told my father that, I believe it was the first ten injections that she was giving my mother would cost a lot of money. At a later date, my father told me they were $150 apiece.

Dr. Verser: An injection?

A.   She said then, the following 20 injections that she was recommending would be $75 apiece. And my father corroborated that. At the end of 30 injections, I believe it was 30 injections, then she told my mother that she was going to need to continue to take some of these injections every month for the rest of her life. She hasn't. My father took my mother to Mexico, and I don't think she has taken any since. For a while, she did buy vitamin pills from Dr. Talliaferro at a cost of $45 a bottle. Until my father found out that he could get the same pills in Marshall Medicare Medical Center up there for about $10 a bottle. And he told my mother she could buy no more pills from Dr. Talliaferro.

Q.   How is your mother doing since she left?

A.   She's had several of the same type strokes. They were here just a few months ago, and she had a couple of these mild strokes at home while they were here. At the present, they're in Harrington, Texas, and I don't know how they're doing down there.

Mr. Lantrip: Your mother is on medicare? Is she on Medicare?

A.	She's retired. I guess it's medicare or Medicaid, whichever.
Mr. Lantrip:	Well, if she's seventy, and normally—
A.	They wouldn't pay for any of these treatments.
Mr. Lantrip:	That was my next question.
A.	They wouldn't pay for any of them. My father had to pay for them all.
Dr. Gardner:	Could you describe what kind of symptoms that your mother has when has one of these strokes?
A.	She was unable to talk. Her eyes was rolled up in her head and her face got kind of pulled out of shape. And she didn't know who she was or where she was.
Dr. Gardner:	Would she lose control of her bladder or bowels when this occurred?
A.	I believe she did lose control of her bladder. I am not sure.
Dr. Gardner:	How long would these generally last?
A.	Well, this first one lasted most of that night, and for a couple of days after that, she wasn't real alert, you know, she was still—
Dr. Gardner:	She would gradually wake up the next day?
A.	Yeah. She did eventually go see her physician in Harrison for some tests, but that was as far as she would go. And the doctor in Harrison said that she had a blocked vein, I believe is what he called it, serving the brain. He said the blood going to the brain was unable to get there and it was causing strokes and he wanted to do some such. He said it was a minor surgery on it, to relieve this problem.
Dr. Gardner:	Did she lose the use of either her upper limbs or her lower limbs?
A.	No, she had tingling and kind of like cramps and things like she complained of, you know.
Dr. Gardner:	After she would go through one of these strokes, would she be able to walk and talk and do everything a normal person does?
A.	Yeah. She could do about everything. Her talk sometimes was a little blurry, or slurry, you know. But, yeah, eventually she was just as good as she ever was, you know.
Dr. Gardner:	Thank you.
Mr. Ward:	Mr. Chairman, I have no further questions.

CROSS EXAMINATION

By Mr. Seeley (Q.):

Q.   If I may. Mr. Stafford, my name is Greg Seeley and I represent the doctor.

A.   Okay.

Q.   Now, you indicated that you wrote a letter to the Board that is attached to the complaint, correct?

A.   Yes, sir.

Q.   I'm just going to have you identify this letter. In fact, it's a copy and it has an Exhibit A on it, and it's dated June 1, 1987. Now, it's directed to Dr. Verser. Do you know who Dr. Verser is here?

A.   No, I don't. I had communication with Dr. Verser on the telephone, before this letter.

Q.   Did you write this letter?

A.   My wife wrote that letter.

Q.   Okay.

A.   At my dictation.

Q.   And then you signed it?

A.   I believe I signed it, yes.

Q.   That's your signature?
A.   Yeah.

Q.   Did you write any other letters?

A.   Yeah, that other one you got there. I wrote it myself.

Q.   Okay.

A.   You can see why I had her write the first one.

Q.   And you sent that to the Board's lawyer?

A.   Yes, I did.

Q.   When the doctor was there initially to see your mother, were you in the room?

A.   I wasn't there when she arrived. No one was going to tell me that she had even had a stroke. My nephew came down and told me, because he said he didn't know this doctor and he didn't like the things that she was doing.

Q.   Do you know that your mother and father disagree with you?

A.   No, I don't.

Q.   Are you aware that they have written the Board?

A.	Yeah, I just heard him say they had written the Board.
Q.	Are you aware that your father submitted—has submitted to us an affidavit where she—where he swears that, "I do not have a complaint about medical services of my wife, Hope Stafford, received from Dr. Talliaferro in Leslie, Arkansas?"
A.	I never said he had a complaint. I'm the one that's complaining.
Q.	But, he didn't?
A.	No, he didn't complain.
Q.	He didn't complain?
A.	No.
Q.	In fact, it's his opinion, isn't it, that he was adequate—that your mother was adequately informed about the treatment?
A.	I don't know. I haven't seen the letter.
Q.	Let me show you that affidavit.
	(Off-the-record.)
A.	All right.
Q.	Is there anything in here that you disagree with?
A.	I disagree with all of it, but that's his opinion. You know, it's his opinion. He's entitled to his opinion.
Q.	Do you get along with your father?
A.	Probably as much as any son does with his father. We have our disagreements. I am not a yes man, if that's what you want to know.
Q.	Do you respect your father?
A.	Most certainly.
Q.	It says, "That to my knowledge, I do not feel qualified to appraise the treatments, but I do feel qualified to appraise the results. The results were great."
A.	Maybe that is his opinion. It's not mine.
Q.	"By her own freewill, without coercion or the employment of scare tactics by anybody, she chose to undergo chelation therapy."
A.	That's what he says.
Q.	"I believe my wife is of sound mind and capable of making such decisions." Do you disagree with him?
A.	I would have to say, yes, I would disagree with that. My mother is not, what I would call, of basically sound mind. She's a little senile. And, at the time that she started these

treatments, I didn't agree with her decision to take them then, and I still don't.

Q. Do you think she has the right, though, to make that choice?

A. I gave her that right. She made that choice and she did it. I also have the right to complain about it, which I did.

Q. Have you seen your mother's affidavit?

A. No, I haven't.

(Witness viewing document.)

Q. Mr. Stafford, do you think your mother disagrees with you, too?

A. It appears that way, yes, it does.

Q. Okay.

A. I am not surprised.

Q. You don't really get along with your mother either?

A. I get along great with my mother. She has her opinions, I have my opinions. She belongs to the same religious group that the doctor belongs to and all the big majority of the people that are here belong to. So, I am not surprised that she disagrees with me. Whatever they say goes with her.

Q. Okay.

A. I don't belong to that particular religion group.

Dr. Verser: What religion group is it?

A. It's a non-denominational religion there in Leslie.

Mr. Lantrip: Non-denominational?

A. Yeah. I am not even sure if they even have an official name, you know. They do have a church.

Dr. Verser: Just an independent religious—I don't know why I'm interested, but—

A. Yeah, it's independent, I would say.

Q. Do you respect your mother's opinion?

A. Yeah, I would say I respect her opinion.

Q. Okay.

A. I don't necessarily have to agree with her opinion, but I respect her opinion.

Q. Mr. Stafford, do you have any medical training?

A. No, I don't have.

Q. Are you qualified to diagnose your mother?

A. No, I've never tried to diagnose her.

Q. Are you capable of determining the value of benefits or side effects of any of the drugs that you—

A. No, I'm not. I can read, which I did.

Q. You got all of this information by going through the doctor's bag?

A. No, I didn't go through the doctor's bag. The doctor had her stuff sitting on a little table right there beside my mother's bed.

Q. Okay.

A. Yes, that's where I got it.

Q. Did you stay with your mother the whole time?

A. I did.

Q. You never left the house?

A. Yes, I left the house the next morning. I went home and was gone for a couple of hours. I took my father home, and came back at the same time my father did. That I totally disagree with. I was at her friend's house where she was being treated at there the biggest majority of the time that she was there. When I wasn't there, one of my sisters were there. I notice she didn't mention any of those in that letter there, but they were there. Unfortunately, I couldn't get them to come down and testify.

Q. Do they agree with you or disagree with you?

A. They agreed with me, but they weren't coming down there to face this crowd.

Q. Are you presently employed?

A. No, I am not. Does that have anything to do with this?

Q. What I'm asking is whether or not you have any special training to be able to write these letters and to compose the allegations here. You indicated that your wife—you went through your wife's medical books?

A. Yeah.

Q. Is she employed?

A. Yes, she is.

Q. As what?

A. She works in a sewing factory in Marshall.

Q. But, she had medical books in her house?

A. Yes, she does.

Q.   Does she prescribe any treatment to people?

A.   I wouldn't imagine she would want to do that without a license. She has some medical training. But, no, she doesn't pursue a medical career.

Q.   Did you see all sorts of syringes around?

A.   No, they weren't syringes, they were IV things, hanging up on —

Q.   So, they weren't injections; were they?

A.   I call them injections. They were sticking them in her veins. To me, that's an injection.

Q.   Do you know what a syringe is?

A.   Yeah, I know what a syringe is.

Q.   Okay. Was it a syringe?

A.   No, it was an IV bottle or bag, whatever.

Mr. Lantrip: You do know what an IV bottle is, attorney?

Mr. Seeley: Yes, I do.

Mr. Lantrip: Thank you.

Mr. Seeley: I think it's a little bit different than the syringe, right?

Mr. Lantrip: Uh-huh.

A.   I may be guilty of the misuse of the word injection in my letter.

Dr. Douglas: No, I don't think you are guilty. I think that's appropriate.

Mr. Seeley: You made a comment about the chart; what chart are you talking about?

A.   The chart that was on my mother's bed that the doctor was keeping up there, until I informed her that I was going to call Dr. Bell. When she asked me to tell Dr. Bell that she was doing nothing but giving my mother aspirin, which she said was the normal procedure that doctors went through when people had these mild strokes or whatever it was. The next day the chart was gone. The only thing that was on the chart was giving mother aspirin every four hours by mouth. When I did call Dr. Bell to talk to him, he knew nothing about the chelation injections. As far as he knew, the only thing that had been done for my mother was aspirin by mouth.

Q.   Do you know whether or not, or do you know anything about chelation therapy?

A.   Just the little bit that I've read and heard.

Q.   Where did you read it?

A.	In books. I believe my father had some literature on it that I read.
Q.	Okay.
A.	I also don't know anything about the Laetril treatments, but I believe they found that to be a waste of time and money.
Q.	Do you think that's an issue here?
A.	No.
Q.	Okay. You made some comment in one of the letters to I believe the Board's counsel about a patient Rochester?
A.	Uh-huh.
Q.	Do you know anything about that particular circumstance or situation? Were you there when—if Rochester had gone to see the doctor?
A.	No, I'm sorry to say I wasn't. The only thing I know about that particular incident was that Mr. Lewis told me himself. I went to see Mr. Lewis for a visit a couple of times before he died, and he told me that he had gone to the doctor to have her treat him, and she would not treat him.
Q.	She wouldn't?
A.	She told him the only thing she could do was recommend coffee enemas.
Q.	But, she didn't take him as a patient, did she?
A.	Not to my knowledge, no.
Q.	Okay.
A.	He said she recommended him not to take the chemotherapy treatments.
Q.	But, she didn't recommend that she treat him, did she? She did not take him as a patient, did she?
A.	That's what he told me, no.
Mr. Seeley:	I don't have any other questions of this witness.
Dr. Gardner:	These are the affidavits the counselor gave us. That's supposed to be your mother's words. Does your mother talk like that?
A.	No, my mother doesn't
Dr. Gardner:	I don't even talk like that.
A.	Somewhere back here it said that she had somebody do her— "Request of counsel with friend to assist me in the language of medical terms used in this affidavit." No, my

mother doesn't talk like that.

Dr. Gardner: So, this is really not your mother's true words, but just what somebody interpreted them to be; is that right?

A. I would say, yes.

Mr. Seeley: Do you think your mother would swear to something that if it wasn't true?

A. Not intentionally probably, no, but my mother could very easily have words put in her mouth. I know that.

Mr. Seeley: Are you saying that's what said in the affidavit is something your mother would not have said?

A. I am. I'm saying there is quite a bit in the affidavit that my mother would not have said.

Q. What in particular would you say does not?

A. Well, one instance in particular was that I never came to see her while she was down at Olla's house there. I spent the biggest majority of my time down at that house, which I can produce a witness to testify to that. I would disagree with that. I wouldn't disagree with the fact that she thought that the treatment did her just worlds of good and stuff. I'm sure she did. If she fell down dead tomorrow, I'm sure that, in her mind, it wouldn't be from a stroke. She could die from anything else, but—I'm sure she thinks she got just great treatments there. Like I said, to me, what's at issue here is not what she thinks, it's what— I'm the one that's complaining. I brought the complaint, not my mother, not my father. They may very well be satisfied.

Mr. Seeley: You do think your mother would be able to understand that if she signed an affidavit, she would understand that she was swearing to the truth of what was said in the affidavit?

A. In her mind it may have been what she thought was the truth, or what she had been told was the truth. As I told you a while ago, my mother has gotten continuously more senile ever since she had this first stroke. Sometimes I don't think maybe my mother doesn't know herself what's the truth anymore. Take it from there. As far as getting up here in front of this Board and intentionally lying deliberately, I don't think she would do that, no. But, there are other ways to get things across, especially when you have somebody doing your interpreting for you and writing.

Dr. Verser: Mr. Chairman, could I put the counselor under oath? Would you take an oath, counselor?

Mr. Seeley: I'm here—if you're calling me or subpoenaing me as a witness—

Dr. Verser:	I'm asking if you'll take an oath, so I can ask you a question?
Mr. Seeley:	No. I will, however, answer the question—
Dr. Verser:	I'm asking you if you will under oath answer a question?
Mr. Seeley:	No, but in my role as a party to the Court, I will tell you what your question is; and that is, did I prepare the affidavit for her to sign; is that what the question is?
Dr. Verser:	I am not going to answer you. I'm going to ask you if you'll take an oath?
Mr. Seeley:	I won't take an oath, because as a lawyer, we are duty bound to tell the truth; number one, and number two, I am not here as a witness. I am here as counsel for the doctor. If the Board wishes to subpoena me, that would then, at this point, I think we would have to continue this hearing, so that the doctor would be provided counsel. Because I can't play both roles. I'll be more than happy, if you would like me to proceed as a witness under oath, but I would then request, prior to that, that the meeting and the hearing be continued.
Dr. Gardner:	Can you answer Dr. Verser's question?
Mr. Seeley:	I don't know that, because Dr. Verser indicated he wouldn't ask the question.
Dr. Gardner:	All he said was would you answer a question under oath. That didn't require any elaboration. It required a yes or no.
Mr. Seeley:	Well, doctor, I am not trying to be cute.
Dr. Wynne:	We're not going to require him to be under oath.
Dr. Verser:	It may not be required, but I want the record to show that he refused to. I know our lawyers wouldn't be working for us long if they didn't—if we wanted them to take an oath, and they refused. How long do you think they would be attorneys for us?
Mr. Seeley:	Well, I would like to make a statement then on behalf of the record, to indicate that lawyers from Ohio—
Dr. Verser:	I want you under oath, and you've refused, and the records shows that.
Mr. Seeley:	The record will also show that I have been interrupted repeatedly by Dr. Verser, and that I am also trying to respond to an accusation made by Dr. Verser. That the particular charge that you're attempting to charge me with, is an innuendo. And that I resent—
Dr. Verser:	You don't know what I'm charging. I haven't charged you with anything. I asked you if you would make a state-

ment under oath, and you say no. Yes or no?

Mr. Seeley: Did you understand that the particular role that I am present here today is as counsel to the doctor who is presently the subject matter of this hearing. Ethically I am, as I am in that particular role, I cannot become a witness at the hearing, and represent her.

Dr. Verser: Let me ask my attorney. I don't want to hear you for a minute.

Mr. Mitchell: Maybe I can clarify it.

Dr. Verser: I want to clarify it. I have seen attorneys take the oath under witnesses in certain cases.

Mr. Mitchell: If this gentleman as attorney here appears as a witness in this case, he is disqualified to be the attorney for Dr. Talliaferro. That is in a judicial case. I don't think we have had such a ruling in an administrating hearing. But, that is the law in Arkansas in a court hearing, that an attorney cannot also be a witness. I think if you want to ask him a question, I think it should be asked, and let's forget about the oath, and ask him the question. Because he would be making himself a witness, and he would be disqualified to be the attorney. So, there we are. This is not a court, but its a quasi-judicial function. This administrative agency is a quasi-judicial body. I don't know whether that rule would apply to the administrative hearing that we have here, but it does apply to the court in Arkansas. So, I think we'd be running the risk, if we made this gentleman a witness, of disqualifying him as the attorney for Dr. Talliaferro. I think if there's questions of counsel, we should just ask him. I think we're hung up on the oath issue. I think if the Board has questions of counsel, I think they should just be asked.

Dr. Gardner: Our questions are obviously to address this affidavit. This little lady has got a signature here that looks like it's illegible. Now, you can come back and say, well, a lot of the doctors' signatures are illegible, too. You're right. But, I just have a hard time believing that this lady had much input into this, particularly when it differs so greatly from what her son says. In the language that's used, it just looks like it was lifted from an English textbook. I'm disturbed that we got an affidavit that looks like it was just kind of dictated out, and then say, here, sign this. I am not sure this really expresses just exactly what went on.

Mr. Seeley: Is that a question to me?

Dr. Gardner: I didn't ask a question. I'm saying what I think we're concerned about.

Dr. Wynne: Is there any other questions of the witness? (The witness

Dr. Wynne:	was excused.) Do you wish to call another witness.
Mr. Ward:	That concludes our presentation.
Mr. Seeley:	Prior to beginning our particular case, I would like to be able to have one moment to make a statement.
Dr. Verser:	May I ask you one question?
Mr. Seeley:	Certainly
Dr. Verser:	Did you have anything to do with this affidavit whatsoever?
Mr. Seeley:	Did I participate in the preparation of that affidavit at all—
Dr. Verser:	I said did you have anything to do with this affidavit whatsoever?
Mr. Seeley:	Considering the fact that I just handed it to George Stafford, then obviously I must have had something to do with it. But, the point is, in the preparation of the affidavit, I had nothing to do with it. However, I'd like to point out, I think your counsel would point out, that the preparation of affidavits by attorneys for people is a common practice throughout the entire United States. It is not uncommon for an attorney to, in fact, prepare an affidavit for signature, by taking the information from a particular person. But, in this instance, in fact, I will volunteer to point out that on neither instance of either affidavit did I or my office participate in the preparation of the affidavit.
Dr. Wynne:	You may make your statement now.
Mr. Seeley:	First of all, I'd like to go ahead and excuse and apologize for my particular outburst, because today ironically, because its Constitution Day, I suppose I'm a little bit more aware of the rights of people. Today, obviously, this is an important day not only for Dr. Talliaferro, but obviously for the entire United States because we're honoring a piece of paper that's held up for a couple of hundred years. And by the mere fact that I'm permitted to say certain things at a hearing like this, or any of these people, is obviously guaranteed by that. Today is not only for her protection, but it's for every doctor's protection, and obviously for the citizenry of Arkansas. I'd like to say, though, I am not sure I understand why we're here today for this particular instance. Because if we are talking about the practice of medicine by Melissa Talliaferro, I would say that once you see the evidence you will find out that this woman is an innovative, progressive physician who really cares to practice medicine. And I've been practicing law around this country with a

number of different types of doctors, and I hope you understand how sincerely I mean that. The law profession as well as the medical profession needs more people who are sincerely devoted to the practice of medicine for the benefit of people, not for economic issues, as I heard earlier.

I don't know why we're here based upon the medicine that I have seen done as a result of the charts and the medical records.

I have been able to talk to her patients, who have also recited the same types of things. And we all have certain patients that are more happy with us than others, obviously. But, I would say that this woman, who was practicing medicine in Leslie, Arkansas, miles and miles away from any hospital, on dirt roads, is doing a marvelous job. I would hope that you'll see that the evidence shows that. That the particular activity involved with George's complaint was under emergency conditions. And I would also point out, that the son is not an expert in the practice of medicine. I would suggest to you that a license was granted to Dr. Talliaferro that shows that she has a competence in the practice. I would also point out that the very issues circling chelation therapy, which is the issue in this particular case, has been decided by the courts, has been decided in Florida, Michigan, it's been discussed in Ohio, it's been discussed throughout the United States in various states, and they have already made the decision. People are practicing and utilizing chelation therapy. And the reason for it is partially the fact that the medical and scientific proof does exist, and we will show that to you.

I would hope that after you have an opportunity to listen to the testimony and be able to look at the information, that the doctor won't be subject to any disciplinary action, but would be commended for the type of practice she has in Leslie, Arkansas, and encouraged to continue in a community where she is the only doctor available.

At this time, I'd like to be able to call Dr. James Frackelton to the witness stand.

DIRECT EXAMINATION OF DR. FRACKLETON:

By Mr. Seeley (Q.):

Q.   As you recall, you have been previously sworn in?

A.   Yes, sir.

Q.   Dr. Frackleton, would you go ahead and state your full name and address?

A.   James P. Frackelton, M.D., 24700 Center Ridge Road, Cleveland, Ohio.

Q.   What types of practice do you have, Doctor?

A.   I have a general preventive medicine practice, and also subspecializing in cardiology.

[Excerpt from relevant testimony of Dr. Frackleton]

A.   Yes, sir. As a matter of fact, since the rest of the world is non-surgically oriented for vascular disease, chelation therapy is a very exciting modality developing in many countries, in particular the Communist countries. In countries where the cardiovascular surgery is not an entity, is not promoted, not really a therapy of any kind, chelation is a very exiting modality. And I just came back from an international meeting on chelation in Czechoslovakia, and I gave a speech there, and over a hundred researchers from the world on chelation were there. And my impression was that chelation is a very exciting therapy in countries where cardiovascular surgery is not an interesting subject, in the Communist countries particularly. That is true of China, it's true of Russia, and it's true of Czechoslovakia, Poland, Hungary, and so forth.

Dr. Verser: Exciting therapy for what?

A.   Exciting in the sense that the research is coming more and more available to show that in fact chelation works.

Dr. Verser: How does it work? That's what we want to know, how does it work?

A.   I can certainly give you short—

Mr. Seeley: May we set up a projector, so that we may—

Dr. Verser: No, I want to ask him a question. You can tell me by the mechanism. All I want to know is why do you say it's exciting therapy in these countries?

A.   It's a very valid question, and I'll be glad to answer it.

Dr. Verser: Where is this research?

A.   The research I'm just about to mention comes from the—

Dr. Verser: From what university?

A.   The research I'm about to mention, it comes from Cleveland Clinic on the Eastside of Cleveland.

Dr. Verser: The Cleveland Clinic?

A.   Yes. And I believe—

Dr. Verser: And they are using chelation therapy?

A.   No, sir. They're a research division, which is independent of the foundation. Does their own research on anything

	they want to do.
Dr. Verser:	I'm asking you, do they use chelation therapy?
A.	Yes, sir, they do. But for standard therapies, such as lead poisoning.
Dr. Gardner:	Could I ask a question. You're in active practice; is that right?
A.	Yes, sir.
Dr. Gardner:	Hypothesize for a minute that you're in Leslie, Arkansas, and a family brought to you an unconscious, 72-year-old with her eyes rolled back, and then they possibly have lost control of the bowels and bladder. Would you put that lady to bed in your home and give her chelation therapy?
A.	I'm in Cleveland, and I can't say what I would do.
Dr. Gardner:	No, I'm asking you this question. Is that what you'd do, if you were in Leslie, Arkansas, out in the woods of Arkansas, with a patient who is unconscious, the eyes rolled back, unable to speak, unable to respond, possibly having lost control of her bowels and bladder, or with a history of having just done that, would you put her to bed in your house and give her chelation therapy?
A.	Yes, sir.
Dr. Gardner:	You would?
A.	Yes, and I would because of several things. In the intravenous solution, you have magnesium, you have potassium, you have heparin—
Dr. Gardner:	Even though you don't know what's wrong with this lady, you know, haven't done any other tests. You just automatically know there's got to be a blockage problem?
Mr. Seeley:	Doctor, rather than hypothesize, do you want to go right to the medical record?
Dr. Gardner:	I just want to know if you would do chelation therapy in Leslie, Arkansas, on a patient that appeared to have—
Dr. Verser:	Are you Board Certified in Cardiologist?
A.	No, sir, I am not.
Dr. Verser:	Have you failed any examinations?
A.	No, I didn't.
Dr. Verser:	Did you ever take it?
A.	I said I subspecialized in cardiology.
Dr. Verser:	I know. But, did you take the Board—the Cardiology Board?
A.	I'm in family practice in—

Dr. Verser:	You're not a cardiologist?
A.	I'm a member of the American College of Cardiology.
Dr. Verser:	I thought you testified that you were a cardiologist?
A.	No, sir. I'm a member of—
Dr. Verser:	You're just a general practitioner, right?
A.	I'm a family physician, and I have a lot of advanced training in cardiology.
Mr. Seeley:	Would you mind letting the witness proceed?
Dr. Verser:	I'm talking now.
Mr. Seeley:	No, the point is, he was talking and you keep interrupting him.
Dr. Verser:	Well, I'm going to interrupt him because I'm asking him a question.
Mr. Seeley:	Well, let him finish responding to the question.
Dr. Verser:	I asked him if he was Board Certified.
Mr. Seeley:	And he already answered that question. Do you have another question?
Dr. Verser:	Yeah, what church do you belong to?
Mr. Seeley:	Objection.
Dr. Verser:	Well, I think that I have a right to know. Is this the same group that's promoting this, or does he belong to a different church.
Mr. Seeley:	Is the Arkansas Medical Board concerned about religion? Is that what the issue is here today?
Dr. Verser:	It's a group that is practicing something that—
Mr. Seeley:	Excuse me, but what is the charge? Could we go back to what the charge is. I didn't realize religion was part of the reason for charging—
Dr. Verser:	I asked you what church. Now, he can refuse to answer it or he can answer it. What church do you belong to?
Mr. Seeley:	Number one, let the record show that I object to this particular line of questioning. Point out that it's arbitrary, it's been argumentative to this particular witness. That Dr. Verser has interrupted this particular witness on repeated occasions.
A.	I'm a Presbyterian.

DIRECT EXAMINATION OF
DR. TALLIAFERRO, THE DEFENDANT

By Mr. Seeley (Q.):

Q.   What I've handed the doctor is a copy of her medical records as it relates to Hope Stafford. Maybe what I would request is that she refer to her notes and go through the process of exactly how she would describe the patient when she first got the call to go to her house. What happened? In other words, you get a call from whom?

A.   On the night of 6/22/86, I got a call to see this patient at home. She was having stroke-like episodes.

Q.   Who called you?

A.   The patient's husband called me.

Q.   What did you do?

A.   Well, I drove out to the patient's house. I got there at 11 o'clock, p.m.

Q.   What did you—and describe the condition of the patient when you saw her?

A.   When I saw the patient, she was awake, alert, and she talked to me, and I got a history from her at that time.

Q.   Was there anybody else in the room at the time?

A.   Her husband was the only other person in the room at that time.

Q.   All right. And what type of history did you get?

A.   I got a fairly good history. I found—just to go back to my notes, the patient was coherent. She had been having episodes lasting about one to two minutes of involuntary fixed movement of her head to the right, with involuntary movement of the eyelids bilaterally. She had a constant tremor of hands, arms and facial muscles. At the time that the patient had the episode, she was unresponsive verbally. She was sitting up. She had a vague recollection of events immediately after the episode. The eye blinking was most prominent on the right side. She stated to me that she had multiple episodes like this since 4: 30 p.m. that day. Since 10: 30 that night, they were beginning to last—they were occurring ten to fifteen minutes apart. There was some concern that she had a history of cancer, which she poorly described to me. But, she said there was no history, to her knowledge, of metastasis to the brain of cancer, and she had no history of prior spells like this. The patient was sitting up in bed when I was talking with her.

Do you want me to continue with the record?
Q.   Who else was there, by the way, that night?

A.   Accompanying me was my husband, who drove me there, and then my mother-in-law, who is a very good friend of this patient's, and also she works—

Q.   Personal friend?

A.   Yes, she's a personal friend.

Q.   And she is also your LPN?

A.   Yes.

Q.   And that's your husband's mother?

A.   Yes. So, I immediately did a physical exam. I found her blood pressure to be 170 over 150. I did a neurological exam. The patient was able to stand by herself. Her gait was slow. The finger to nose exam showed right side slow movement with loss of intention. She was alert. She was awake. She was oriented times three, she was lucid. HENT, her pupils were equal round reactive to light and accommodation. She had occasional nostagmus [sic], brief. Heart regulate rate and rhythm, tachycardia. Abdomen, ileostomy was present. Neck questionable carotid bruese [sic], but not real discernable. I wasn't certain of that. My assessment at that time, I suspected that she was having TIA's; and number 2 was, she has a prior malignancy with an unknown current status.

          I had driven out to this patient's house. I live in a county where there is no hospital in my county, and there is a two lane road that goes to Harrison, and that's fifty miles away, and that can sometimes take an hour, hour and a half, usually an hour and a half to get there. And this is in the middle of the night on a weekend.

Q.   What did you do then?

A.   I started an IV immediately on the patient. In that IV I had not only the standard dose of EDTA, but I also had heparin. And never at any time did I say that patient would not go to the hospital. I was extremely concerned.

Dr. Gardner: How much heparin?

A.   How much heparin. I have to refer back to my notes. 10,000 units. That's not a full heparinization of the patient. That's a very low dose. All I had with me was my doctor's bag, and whatever I had in the bag, that's all that I had to work with. And at this time I had not even started my practice, and the patient was aware of that. I had—I was just in town. My clinic was not even open, and the family was aware of this. So, whatever I had with me was all I had to work with.

Q.   How did the patient proceed after that?

A.   So, I began the IV, and I was of course observing very closely. The IV was running at 60 drops per minute. And my notation here is that at 1: 45 a.m. her blood pressure was 158 over 100. Over approximately the following two

hours, she had no further episodes of involuntary movement. That completely stopped. I stayed up with this
patient all night long. And the IV was completed about
3:30 in the morning.

At that time, I had a discussion with the patient about the
situation. I did not feel that at that point she needed to go
to the hospital. And it was at that time that I said that I
thought, at 4 o'clock in the morning, that since she had
not had any further episodes for the last two hours, that
we would be safe in waiting until the next day or later on
that month, and re-evaluate at that time and see what
needed to be done then. It was at that time arrangements
were made between Olla Braden and her, they are friends,
and there was some problems there that she was having
with some family members. And there were some dis-
agreements, and she wanted to leave. And that was her
business, I felt. So, she made arrangements to go to Olla
Braden's home. And it was up to her to contact me the
next morning.

Dr. Gardner: Did you start a bag of IV fluid solution on her was it a
1000 cc's, or—

A. 500 cc's.

Dr. Gardner: And you put the 10,000 units in the bag?

A. Correct.

Dr. Gardner: And you ran it at 60 drops a minute?

A. Uh-huh.

Dr. Gardner: And you saw the lady about 11 o'clock in the evening and
the bag was in by 3:30 in the morning?

A. Yeah, correct.

Dr. Gardner: Thank you.

A. The next morning I went to Olla Braden's house where
this lady was now staying. She had no further complaint
of any further spells. She slept very well through the
night. She said she felt greatly improved. As a matter of
fact, she said she felt better than she had felt in quite some
time. I made a notation in my notes. Her son Mike states
that he disagrees with decision to continue treatments as
we were doing it at a home. Hope, the patient, and her husband and daughters, Teri and Mary, all agree in decision
to continue therapy by myself and at home. The patient in-
sists that I not be concerned about his opinion, because it
is her decision what to do. And she wishes to continue current therapy at home. And she did not want to go to the
hospital at that time that day.

My exam show that vital signs, blood pressure now of a

170 over 70. A temp of 99.2, respirations 14, pulse of 80. My HENT was normal, heart as before, abdomen obese stomach, extremities within normal limits, the neuro exam was awake, alert, oriented times three. She has a persistent constant tremor of the extremities, which is chronic, that was not acute, so, sensation was intact, facial muscles showed good strength, gate and station within normal limit. My assessment at that time was transient [sic] aschemica attacks with good response to current therapy and candiniasis [sic] of the groins. My plan at that time was to give her another intravenous treatment that day, where I added heparin and again in low dose and primarily was standard dose chelation therapy. And I made note to consider referral to Harrison Hospital for a possible CT scan and further workup.

That day I called her physician, Dr. Bell, a consultation by phone. The patient's doctor and surgeon. I gave him the history. I asked for his recommendation. He said that colon cancer very rarely metastasizes to the brain and suspected carotid obstruction, and he suggested a CT scan of the head and ultrasound carotid imagery. This was related to the patient, and he told me specifically, he says, "It's not urgent for her to come here today as long as she is in the hospital sometime this week for testing." Exactly what he told me. And this was all related to the patient. I left it up to her to make the decision. Then I just have more notes about soaks applied to her rash on her groin that day.

Q.   Did you refuse to explain what you were doing to anybody that day?

A.   No.

Q.   Did you explain it to the patient and to her husband?

A.   I explained at length everything to the patient and her husband.

Mr. Stafford: You didn't explain it to me.

A.   You were not even present most of the time.

Q.   Did you refuse to talk to Mike or George, Jr.?

A.   No.

Q.   Did you make some comment about how you cured your father of brain cancer?

A.   No, I did not. My father died of brain cancer.

Q.   Something about, did you scare Hope about the fact that going to the hospital would kill her or leave her paralyzed?

A.   I never said any such thing.

Q.   You've had a chance to read the letters that were the subject matter of the complaint. Is there any truth to the allegations made by Mike in that?

A. They're absolute lies.

Mr. Seeley: Would the Board be interested in the doctor's past training?

Dr. Gardner: Sure.

Q. Doctor, would you give them your C.V.?

A. I graduated from the University of Texas Medical Branch in Galveston, Texas. I went ahead and did a rotating internship with a family practice—

Dr. Williams: What year was that?

A. That I graduated, would have been 1981. Then I did a rotating internship at Corpus Christi Memorial Medical Center. I served as a delegate to the American Medical Association at the time that I was resident in the resident physician section in 1981 to 1982, I believe. I've also received training in chelation therapy. I'm a member of the American Academy of the Advancement of Medicine. I'm a Diplomat Candidate of the American Board of chelation Therapy.

Q. Where did you practice before coming to Arkansas?

A. I practiced with a physician in Texas, who is a Board member also of the American Board of chelation Therapy.

Q. And how long have you been in Leslie, Arkansas?

A. I've been there approximately one year.

Q. Are there any other physicians in Leslie, Arkansas?

A. No, sir.

Dr. Curry: What county is Leslie in?

A. It's in Searcy County.

Dr. Williams: Were you concerned at that particular time of metastatic bleeds to the brain or anything of that nature?

A. I was in my initial assessment, yes.

Dr. Williams: What risks were associated as relates to the therapy that you gave her that particular night?

A. None.

Dr. Williams: No risk whatsoever of giving intravenous heparin?

A. That was a very low dose of heparin. That's not fully heparinized. And I always put down in my assessment the complete differential diagnosis. If I was to quantitate what value I put on everything in my notes, I would say that was very low down on the list, that would be a typical presentation for malignancy of the brain. That would be very atypical, but I do put down a complete differential. I didn't really think that she had that.

Dr. Williams: So, at no point did you think the hospitalization should have been done?

A. No, I never said that. I was extremely concerned about that this patient was going to die right in front of me, and I was concerned also that I was so far from a hospital.

Dr. Williams: So, once she kind of stabilized, the next day did you offer to send the patient to the hospital.

A. That was her decision. Definitely, that was her decision. And she was fully informed about chelation therapy. And she chose at that point to go ahead, and she wanted those treatments right then. She did not want to go to the hospital right then, and the patient was fully informed of all of her choices.

Dr. Williams: What are your customary fees as it relates to chelation therapy?

A. My fee is $75 per treatment, and this is the standard price that the doctors charge on the lower side that belong to the academy.

Dr. Williams: Her son mentioned that you were dispensing her some drugs, some pills, vitamin pills or something of that nature?

A. Yes, I always give mineral supplements along with chelation therapy, because it does remove some minerals that must be replaced orally.

Dr. Williams: He said something about some vitamin or something.

A. Yes, it's a combination of vitamins and minerals that must always be given with chelation therapy.

Dr. Williams: Did you have permissions to dispense any drugs or anything?

A. That is not a drug.

Dr. Verser: It's not a drug. It's vitamins and mineral and, it's just like something over the counter.

Dr. Douglas: What were your diagnosis?

A. On this lady initially, I thought that she was having transient aschemic [sic] attacks. That was my assessment.

Dr. Douglas: I thought you had a list of different—

A. I read that off, and then there was a possibility of—and of course her doctor confirmed that colon cancer very rarely metastasizes to the brain. I don't think there was any real concern at that time that her malignancy was active. So that was on my list. But, I did not feel that that was the cause of her problems. I felt it was more than likely a carotid obstruction which.

PRE-EXECUTIVE SESSION—ACCIDENTALLY TAPED

Dr. Warren Douglas: Wait just a second, just a second. (mike off)

Mr. Curry: That's a recorder back in that next room! I'm totally embarrassed and upset about the way this case has been handled from the beginning by our attorneys. Now its utterly ridiculous to me for them to mail me a complaint and I've got it here and it hadn't ever been tampered with or anything else.

?—— : —It's off now.

Mr. Curry: And there's nothing about those last items that our attorneys have tried to add to it. That's embarrassing to me.

Dr. Vernon Carter: Hold it! (hand in front of camera and turned camera off)

Mr. Curry: And I'm going to move for a dismissal of this as soon as they get back into this room.

? —We don't discuss that.

Mr. Curry: Well that's all right. And I'm going to also announce that I would like for our firm to contact some other attorneys to handle our business in the future. Now I would like to have a vote on that—but if you don't want to vote on it and just let it pass—

Dr. Verser: You are not going to dismiss it; just postpone it.

Mr. Curry: No, I'm going to dismiss it, Joe.

Dr. Verser: Forever?

Mr. Curry: Well, yeah for these charges.

Dr. Bascom Raney:
We are not going to discuss that in here.

Dr. Douglas: There's a solution that we've got to this and that's to do the regulation thing that we were talking about yesterday. Dismiss this and in two meetings from now we'll have it all solved.

Dr. Raney: Well how do you mean—dismiss this motion—now—about dismissing. We are in here in executive session. Let's take a vote on the attorneys. Now, Joe, that's nonsense!

Dr. Douglas: If they are not still on trial we can move forward with this regulation that we were—

Dr. Verser:	That won't come up till—talking about yesterday. That will stop this chelation completely in Arkansas.
Mr. Curry:	I want us to hire some new attorneys, Joe. This is a disgrace the way this very thing—the very idea of all these letters that can't be considered as evidence and I don't think they can be either. This idea they can subpoena people and they just don't pay any attention to it. They can get out of any subpoena we send them.
Dr. Jouett:	Well the subpoena is not the problem, but the fact that information didn't arrive to these people on time and the fact that these things that's been added to the complaint that the rest of us know nothing about.
Dr. Douglas:	We should have—unscheduled this then.
Dr. Raney:	The thing is man—
Mr. Curry:	This is not the only example. At our last meeting—
Dr. Jouett:	I agree.
Mr. Curry:	Our last meeting was a complete fiasco because our attorneys were so gutless that they just laid back and—
Dr. Verser:	They tried me all day rather than to try the client. And they sat there and let them too.
Mr. Curry:	It's time for us to do something about our attorneys and I ain't playing about it.
Dr. Raney:	All right, make a motion.
Mr. Curry:	I move that we empower the chairman and secretary to employ new attorneys for us and—
Dr. Verser:	But I want a committee. I don't want—
Mr. Curry:	All right, we'll get a committee.
Dr. Verser:	The chairman and secretary—
Mr. Curry:	And Warren Douglas. He lives in Little Rock too.
Dr. Douglas:	You are ready to dismiss them. Why not talk to them and say, hey, we got to shape up here and give them a chance.
Dr. Jouett:	This was done. This was done. I talked to them personally and told them I was very displeased with the way things were going and that they really need to get their act together. Both of them I told this.
Dr. Verser:	I told both of them. I said we were out-attorneyed. We have absolutely been out-attorneyed in this meeting. When they permitted this woman to try—Kitty Dye—to try me rather than the other person. This is an old lawyer's trick. Try everybody but—And every damn meeting we've had recently I've been tried. Every time we get somebody else, they try me. I'm tired of being tried.

Mr. Curry:	Let's let the chairman appoint the committee that will look into the hiring of new attorneys. Do we have to announce here in public meeting that that's what we are going to do or can we—
Dr. Verser:	We're going to have to tell the paper that we're going to have new attorneys.
Mr. Curry:	No, no. Can't we just to do this—that we—discussed our client-attorney relationship. Isn't that personnel?
Dr. Verser:	I think you have to tell them any action that you take.
Dr. Jouett:	We haven't taken any action yet.
Dr. Raney:	We haven't taken any action.
Dr. Jouett:	And we'll take none.
Dr. Raney:	Now then we are not going to talk about this case.
	(Several No's)
Dr. Raney:	Now let's get them to come back and get it over with.
Dr. John Guenther:	What are we going to do about this case?
Dr. Raney:	Hey—hey—hey you've got to do this in a public session now. Just stick with your guns.
Dr. Verser:	Wait just a minute, Bascom. Are we going ahead and hear this case? Or just postpone it?
Dr. Raney:	No. No I don't want to hear it.
Dr. Raney:	We don't know what we're going to do about this case until we let the people come in here and see what we're going to do, Joe. I don't know how I'm going to vote. You don't either until you hear what's going to be proposed. Now John is telling you something, on down the line, he may be going to do, but—
Mr. Curry:	No, sir. (many voices) You can hear, you can hear it but I'm going to interrupt it
Dr. Verser:	What are you going to say John?
Mr. Curry:	I'm going to say we dismiss it.
Dr. Verser:	And just forget about it?
Mr. Curry:	Damn right. It's a disgrace. It's a disgrace to this Board.
Dr. Verser:	You don't think that this girl we could get her—for an emergency—
Dr. Raney:	No, don't discuss that in here, Joe.
	(Multiple voices): We don't discuss that, Joe.
Dr. Raney:	You are gonna have an executive session or you are not and that's all there is to it now.

Dr. Verser: But what I'm trying to say—

Dr. Raney: I'm going to start telling them what you are saying. Tell them to come on in here.

Dr. Verser: What I'm trying to say is can we officially take any action against this girl today?

Dr. Williams: Any client—

Mr. Lantrip: You can't discuss that in here, Joe.

Dr. Guenther:
That's what we're told.

Dr. Jouett: Think we might proceed for the benefit of the people and the press that's here. The purpose of our meeting was to discuss relationship of the Board with our counsel which was done. No action was taken. And we are in a position to proceed.

Mr. Curry: Mr. Chairman, I move this case to be dismissed.

APPENDIX II
ADDRESS GIVEN BY ROBERT MULLER ON HOLISM

Where are the limitations? The human species struggle for its fulfillment on this particular planet, the limitations on which we have to work. The first one is a lack of holism. This is expressed by the whole holistic movement. Here, I have the impression that the prediction of Liebnitz is becoming true. Liebnitz said he foresaw the scientific rational revolution, and he predicted that for hundreds of years the human species would be fascinated and occupied in analyzing the surrounding reality and that scientists would become ever more diversified and specialized, and that people would look at their specializations with endless fascination and that they would forget the totality. He predicted that it would be several hundred years without any universal thinking and that is exactly what has happened. But, he predicted that the complexity of our discoveries would be such that at a moment of history the need for a total view for a global view would reoccur, and this time has come. And, you can see this revolution in all fields. The global modeling is a very good example of it. It is not to think in economics, in terms of a nation or of the economics of agriculture, or the economics of energy, as if agriculture was not an energy transfer, things which people have totally forgotten.

And now, suddenly, you have a movement, a request in the universities, in the United Nations, all over the world, for a holistic approach. In other words, you want to see the totality. You would like to have a language that expresses a total view of the inter-relationship of this tremendously complex system, from the infinitely large to the infinite small, from the infinite past to the infinite future, with the incredible richness of life, of matter, and energy on this planet. There is a great avenue and challenge for the holistic movement; the holistic movement has to develop a language and concepts which reflect this totality.

When you come up with the ethics of pharmaceutical, for example, we have now a major problem in the United Nations where when within a country like the United States or Europe you have concluded that a particular chemical or pharmaceutical product is bad and is being prohibited. Automatically, you have the firms asking for an export license the following day, for the developing countries. And then, the stuff goes into the developing countries, because they are not aware of it.

Now, the question is of ethics. The principle problem of ethics which is coming to the floor now, and which is a reason for the many shocks we have. It is that now, constantly, you have to ask yourself for the first time in human history, is this good for the planet? Is this good for humanity or not? This is the crisis which we have, because most nations do not ask this question. They ask only, is it good for my nation? Is it good for my territory, and the hell with the rest of the world. This is why we have all these problems in the United Nations.

We have to think out this ultimate question of what is good and what is bad for our planet. This is the basis for whole environmental issue. It is good for my firm, but it is bad for my community. It is good for my nation, but it is bad for the world.

It is almost as if people, as a result of the physical and scientific development, have been asked not to go beyond the physical, beyond matter, and beyond thinking. Anything that goes beyond that, is foolish, is irrelevant, is fantasy.

For example, you might look at a woman or a human person as a scientist, and how would you look at it. Trillions of cells, fifty miles of vessels, blood streams, all kinds of stuff. Well, it's very interesting—fascinating—you can use this endlessly. But after having analyzed this, there is also another notion, that you see the total human person; and you might fall in love with that person. You might find that this person is beautiful. Now, where is beauty examined by the scientist? Where is love examined by the scientist? All these great notions which are fantastic, a synthesis of all the little components of life, these notions have been neglected in our century.

The word "happiness"; the word "faith"; the word "hope"; the word "beauty"; the word "spirituality"—all this is totally neglected. Now, the poet, the artist, is the one who does the contraction, who gives to our knowledge the vitality and the impulse to go ahead.

We need to have faith in our future. Now, this faith could be shown by the fact that we have achieved so much. But, when you look around today, there is been little faith in the future. We are bound towards the physical, towards the measurable, towards the statistical. And, we do not have the perceptions of the incredible mystery of the universe.

I have worked with a man like U Thant, who was a Buddhist. Now, this man attached almost as much importance to verbal violence as we Westerners do to physical violence. We have learned, now, to be against physical violence. This is accepted. But, here we have a Buddhist, or a good Hindu philosopher, who would also deny what is called verbal violence, because to talk is a cosmic process. So, you can even introduce violence into language.

And then, they go a step further, again, the example of U Thant, I cannot even let violence enter my thought. Non-violent thought, non-violent action, non-violent language. Now, this is a great lesson of the world. We could reduce violence, physical violence, immensely if we stopped verbal violence. But, verbal violence is even applauded. Hitler was applauded. That was violent language, and you still have people today applauding to language that appeals to the aggressive nature of man.

If you have the chance of living for a few months in India, you will note that dance, music, and art, have only one objective. It is to lead you to the Union with the Divine. The Union which is the Universe, the Union which is the eternal stream of time.

As it is said on the island of Bali, our highest art is the way we live each day. And, I would like to say that the highest art and the greatest contribution, every one of the 4 1/2 billion people can do to the peace, love, and happiness of this planet is to make each of our lives a work of art, a masterpiece of kindness, of love, of peace, multiplied by 4-1/2 billion. This is going to change the world. This is going to give us again the ethical, philosophical, and intelligent leaders, which we need in this world. They are so hampered by the notions of power, of science, of arms, and so on, because they, themselves, have not been given different values. So, it is the responsibility of all of us to ask for a holistic view, to ask for an ethical view for the planet and for this human family.

Every single one of us on this planet must be inspiring to others. There are no great people anymore. Every individual is a great person.

Make each and every one of your lives a work of art.

APPENDIX III
ORGANIZATIONS, NEWSLETTERS, AND ADDITIONAL RESOURCES

The following are some of the organizations whose members provide alternative therapies:

The American College of Advancement in Medicine
23121 Verdugo Drive, Suite 204
Laguna Hills, CA 92653
(714) 583-7666 or (800) 523-3688
FAX: (714) 455-9679

The Great Lakes Clinical Medicine Association
Jack Hank, Executive Director
70 W. Haron
Chicago, IL 60610
(312) 266-7246

Canadian Holistic Medical Association (CHMA/OMC)
491 Eglinton Avenue West, #407
Toronto, Ontario M5N 1A8
(416) 485-3071
FAX: (416) 485-3076

American Holistic Medical Association
2727 Fairview East
Seattle, WA 98102
(206) 322-6842

American Academy of Environmental Medicine
P.O. Box 16106
Denver, CO 80216
(303) 622-9755

Foundation of Homeopathic Education and Research
Dana Ullmann, M.P.H., Director
5916 Chabot Crest
Oakland, CA 94618
(415) 649-8930

The following are among the informal newsletters available:

The Townsend Letter for Doctors
911 Tyler St.
Port Townsend, WA 98368-6541

The Choice, Committee for Freedom of Choice in Medicine, Inc.
1180 Walnut Avenue
Chula Vista, CA 92011

The National Council for Improved Health Newsletter
1555 W. Seminole Street
San Marcos, CA 92069

The New Dimension in Scientific Research
P.O. Box 1508
Mount Vernon, WA 98273

International Academy of Holistic Health & Medicine
218 Avenue B
Redondo Beach, CA 90277

Hologram (The Canadian Journal of Health & Well-Being)
491 Eglinton Ave West, #407
Toronto, Ontario M5n 1a8

ADDITIONAL RESOURCES:

Cancer Control Society
2043 N. Berendo Street
Los Angeles, CA 90027
213-663-7801

People Against Cancer
P.O. Box 10
Otho, Iowa 50569-0010

People's Medical Society
462 Walnut Street
Allentown, PA 18102

Sandra Denton, MD
Huggins Diagnostic, Inc.
P.O. Box 2589
Colorado Springs, CO 80901
800-331-2303

What Your Doctor Won't Tell You
by Jane Heimlich
Harper/Collins Publishers
ISBN 0-06-096539-8

Bypassing Bypass
By Elmer Cranton, M.D.
Hampton Roads Publishing Company
ISBN 0-9624375-1-4

Special issue of *Journal of Advancement in Medicine*
A Textbook on EDTA Therapy
Edited by Elmer M. Cranton, M.D.
Foreword by Linus Pauling, Ph.D.
Spring/Summer 1989 (Vol. 2, Nos. 1-2)
Human Sciences Press, Inc.
233 Spring Street
New York, NY 10013-1578
ISBN 0-89885-480-6

Are You a Target for Elimination?
by P.J. Lisa
International Institute of Natural Health Sciences, Inc.,
Publishers
P.O. Box 5550
Huntington Beach, CA 92646

Health Consciousness Magazine
Roy B. Kupsinel, M.D., Publisher
1325 Shangri La Lane
Oviedo, FL 32765

Index

A

acemannan, 249, 264-265
acupuncture, xvii, 40, 44, 56, 114, 123, 145, 174, 232, 234, 236-237, 239, 241, 243, 245, 290-293, 298, 309
Aetna, 48-50, 211, 213-214
Agency for Health Care Policy and Research, 204
AIDS, xvii, 34, 45-46, 81, 84-87, 154, 166, 171, 183, 185, 187, 207, 216-217, 222, 226-227, 265, 271, 273-276, 280-284
Alfin-Slater, Rosalyn, 126
American Academy of Allergy and Immunology, 65, 71, 79-81
American Cancer Society, 3, 34-35, 42, 46, 211-213
American College for the Advancement of Medicine, 8, 61, 97, 109
American Dental Association, 60
American Heart Association, 57, 104, 211-212
American Hospital Association, xvii
American Journal of Surgery, 101, 107
American Medical Association, 5, xvi-xvii, xxvi, 34, 65, 172, 192, 194, 197-198, 202, 206, 342
American Medical Association (AMA), 103, 105, 125
American Pharmaceutical Association, 42
anionic, 269-270
antineoplastons, 49
Association of American Medical Colleges, xxvi

B

Baltimore, David, 25-26
Barrett, Stephen, 45
Berger, Joel, 61
Bio-Tox Reduction Program, 69-70
black currant oil, 159, 161, 262
Blackburn, Henry, 304
Bloyd-Peshkin, Sharon, 43
borage oil, 162, 262
Burkitt, Denis, 305
Burroughs-Wellcome, 85, 226
Burzynski, 49, 214

C

California Council Against Health Fraud, 39, 42-43
Cameron, E., 27
cancer, xvii-xviii, xx-xxiii, xxiv, 3, 8-10, 27-32, 34-35, 40, 46, 49, 51-54, 57, 67, 69, 82-84, 104, 108-109, 112, 114, 117, 128, 137, 140, 148, 156, 160, 166-167, 171, 179, 181, 183-185, 187, 196-197, 205, 207, 210, 213, 218, 220, 225-227, 229, 234, 257-258, 260, 262, 266-268, 271-272, 274, 276, 284, 307, 320-322, 338, 341, 343, 352
candidiasis, 78-81, 138
Carnegie, xxiv-xxvi, 248
CCHI, 14-15, 35, 40, 42-43, 94, 124-125, 187, 190
Cernitin, 125, 251-254, 259

About the author:

Dr. James Puckette Carter was born in Chicago and studied Chemistry at the College of Liberal Arts, Northwestern University, Evanston, Illinois. He received his M.D. from Northwestern in 1957 and an M.S. in Parasitology from Columbia University. He studied Nutrition at Columbia University School of Public Health and Administrative Medicine, completing his doctoral work in 1966.

Coming to Tulane University School of Public Health and Tropical Medicine in 1976, Dr. Carter took the position of Professor and is presently the Head of the Nutrition Section. He also serves as a Clinical Professor of Pediatrics at Tulane University School of Medicine.

Dr. Carter was awarded a five-year Faculty Fellowship by the Milbank Memorial Fund in 1968 to obtain additional training in order to further his professional career as a medical educator in Nutrition and the Social and Preventive Aspects of Medicine; his was one of 44 awards made to preventive medicine specialists and teachers in the Western Hemisphere.

He has written about malnutrition, especially among the underprivileged. Among his nearly 50 papers and books, there is one entitled "Keeping Your Family Healthy Overseas." He is presently completing a book, *Race, Health, and Survival,* to be published in late 1992 or 1993, which deals with the cultural characteristics, lifestyles, health-related behaviors, and inherited disease tendencies of different ethnic groups in the United States. It is a self-help book designed to help individuals to help themselves avoid alcoholism and other addictions, the chronic degenerative diseases which occur in mid-life and later life, and premature death from preventable causes.

Dr. Carter has served as the Chairman of the National Advisory Committee of Meharry Medical College's Kraft-General Foods Nutrition Center, Nashville, Tennessee, and was one of the first Editorial Advisors to *Prevention* magazine. He has served as a consultant in International Nutrition to the U.S. Agency for International Development and as a WHO consultant in Nutrition to the Sudan. He was a consultant in Health Promotion and Disease Prevention to the American Association of Retired Persons, as part of their Minority Initiative. He consults regularly on lifestyle restructuring, clinical preventive medicine, alternative medicine, and holistic health.

BOOKS OF RELATED INTEREST
IN COMPLEMENTARY MEDICINE

BYPASSING BYPASS:
The New Technique of Chelation Therapy
Elmer Cranton, M.D.

Preventive medicine at its best, EDTA chelation therapy is simple, safe, and relatively inexpensive. Harvard Medical School graduate Elmer Cranton, M.D., spells out what's at stake for you if you have atherosclerosis. Includes a chapter written specifically for you to bring to your physician.

5½ x 8½ trade paper, 272 pages, ISBN 0-9624375-1-4, $12.95

QUESTIONS FROM THE HEART
Answers to 100 Questions About Chelation Therapy,
A Safe Alternative to Bypass Surgery
Terry Chappell, M.D.

EDTA chelation clears blocked arteries and improves general circulation. It's safe, legal, has an efficacy rate of about 85%, and has been used by more than 500,000 heart patients in the past thirty years. And it costs 10% of what coronary bypass surgery costs! *Questions from the Heart* explains the benefits and drawbacks of both therapies in a concise, easy-to-read format.

5½ x 8½ trade paper, 136 pages, ISBN 1-57174-026-0, $10.95

ACQUIRING OPTIMAL HEALTH
Gary Price Todd, M.D.

Eating energy-depleted and nutritionally poor foods is the root cause of many degenerative and age-related diseases. This book shows how to heal yourself and achieve optimal health by replacing poor eating habits with Todd's comprehensive dietary and nutritional regimen. "*Acquiring Optimal Health* presents information that could save your life." — *Baton Rouge Advocate*

5½ x 8½ trade paper, 128 pages, ISBN 1-878901-92-3, $8.95

WHY I LEFT ORTHODOX MEDICINE
Healing for the 21st Century
Derrick Lonsdale, M.D.

Dr. Lonsdale, after working in British, Canadian, and U.S. health systems, came to realize that symptom-treating medicine is not as effective as treating causes of disease. He shows medically that nutrition, exercise, and vitamin/mineral therapy can be used as preventive measures. "A testament to nutritional medicine as a paradigm shift in the evolution of our medical understanding." — *NAPRA ReVIEW*

5½ x 8½ trade paper, 256 pages, ISBN 1-878901-98-2, $10.95

HYDROGEN PEROXIDE: MEDICAL MIRACLE
William Campbell Douglass, M.d.

Hydrogen peroxide (H2O2) is the body's first natural line of defense against every type of invading organism. This book reveals how this miraculous healer works, and why the medical establishment wants to suppress it. Over 100,000 copies in print.

5½ x 8½ trade paper, 160 pages, ISBN 1-885236-07-7, $12.95

A SEARCH FOR WELLNESS
F. Kansas Mattson

At age 60, Frank Mattson was diagnosed with 23 health problems, including bursitis, ulcers, and hardening of the arteries. He sought out alternative therapies and practitioners, and within five years had reduced the number to four—learning along the way how ordinary people can preserve (or regain) their health.

5¾ x 8¾ hardcover, 216 pages, ISBN 0-9625584-7-8, $12.95

Hampton Roads Publishing Company
publishes and distributes books on a variety of subjects,
including metaphysics, health, complementary medicine,
visionary fiction, and other related topics.

To order or receive a copy of our latest catalog, call toll-free,
(800) 766-8009, or send your name and address to:

Hampton Roads Publishing Company, Inc.
134 Burgess Lane
Charlottesville, VA 22902

Internet: www.hrpub.com
e-mail: hrpc@hrpub.com